CAMBRIDGE TEXTS IN THE
HISTORY OF PHILOSOPHY

———

FRIEDRICH NIETZSCHE
Human, All Too Human

CAMBRIDGE TEXTS IN THE HISTORY OF PHILOSOPHY

Series editors

KARL AMERIKS
Professor of Philosophy at the University of Notre Dame

DESMOND M. CLARKE
Professor of Philosophy at University College Cork

The main objective of Cambridge Texts in the History of Philosophy is to expand the range, variety and quality of texts in the history of philosophy which are available in English. The series includes texts by familiar names (such as Descartes and Kant) and also by less well-known authors. Wherever possible, texts are published in complete and unabridged form, and translations are specially commissioned for the series. Each volume contains a critical introduction together with a guide to further reading and any necessary glossaries and textual apparatus. The volumes are designed for student use at undergraduate and postgraduate level and will be of interest not only to students of philosophy, but also to a wider audience of readers in the history of science, the history of theology and the history of ideas.

For a list of titles published in the series, please see end of book.

FRIEDRICH NIETZSCHE

Human, All Too Human

TRANSLATED BY
R. J. HOLLINGDALE

WITH AN INTRODUCTION BY
RICHARD SCHACHT
University of Illinois at Urbana-Champaign

CAMBRIDGE
UNIVERSITY PRESS

PUBLISHED BY THE PRESS SYNDICATE OF THE UNIVERSITY OF CAMBRIDGE
The Pitt Building, Trumpington Street, Cambridge, United Kingdom

CAMBRIDGE UNIVERSITY PRESS
The Edinburgh Building, Cambridge CB2 2RU, UK
40 West 20th Street, New York, NY 10011–4211, USA
10 Stamford Road, Oakleigh, VIC 3166, Australia
Ruiz de Alarcón 13, 28014 Madrid, Spain
Dock House, The Waterfront, Cape Town 8001, South Africa

http://www.cambridge.org

First published with introduction by Erich Heller 1986
This edition published with introduction by Richard Schacht 1996
Reprinted 1998, 1999, 2000

Printed in the United Kingdom at the University Press, Cambridge

A catalogue record for this book is available from the British Library

Library of Congress Cataloguing in Publication data
Nietzsche, Friedrich Wilhelm, 1844–1900.
[Menschliches, Allzumenschliches.   English]
Human, all too human / Friedrich Nietzsche; translated
by R. J. Hollingdale; with an introduction by Richard Schacht.
p.   cm. – (Cambridge texts in the history of philosophy)
Includes bibliographical references (p. xxvi).
1. Man.   I. Hollingdale, R. J.   II. Title.   III. Series.
B3313.M52E5   1996b
128–dc20   96–10969 CIP

ISBN 0 521 562007 hardback
ISBN 0 521 567041 paperback

CONTENTS

INTRODUCTION

'*Human, All Too Human* is the monument of a crisis.' With these apt words Nietzsche began his own reflection, in his autobiographical *Ecce Homo* (1888),[1] on this remarkable collection of almost 1,400 aphorisms published in three instalments, the first of which had appeared in 1878, ten years earlier. The crisis to which he refers was first and foremost a crisis of multiple dimensions in his own life. *Human, All Too Human* was the extended product of a period of devastating health problems that necessitated Nietzsche's resignation in 1879 from his professorship in classical philology at Basel University. These problems were to plague him for the remaining decade of his brief productive life (which ended with his complete physical and mental collapse in January 1889, at the age of 44, from which he never recovered in the eleven years of marginal existence that remained to him before his death in 1900). *Human, All Too Human* also marked Nietzsche's transition from the philologist and cultural critic he had been into the kind of philosopher and writer he came to be.

But the crisis was above all a crisis in Nietzsche's intellectual development; and although it was very much his own, it presaged the larger crisis toward which he came to see our entire culture and civilization moving, and subsequently came to call 'the death of God'.[2] In his own case, this crisis was precipitated not only by his deepening appreciation of the profound and extensive consequences of the collapse of traditional ways of thinking, but also – and more immediately – by his growing recognition of the insufficiency of the resources of both the Enlightenment and the Romanticism to which he had been so strongly attracted to fill the void. The three instalments of *Human, All Too Human* are no less important for the insight they yield into the kind of struggle in which Nietzsche was engaged than they are for the many sparks that fly in the course of his efforts to find new ways to go on.

The world around Nietzsche did not appear to be a world headed for crisis. The ordeals, horrors and dramatic changes of the century to come were largely unimagined, and indeed unimaginable, even to Nietzsche, who was far more prescient than most – even to the point of deeming the advent of air travel to be inevitable (1:267). In 1876, when he began working on the material that was published two years later in what is now the first volume of *Human, All Too Human*, Europe was again at (relative) peace. It had been ten years since the Austro-Prussian War that had left Prussia dominant in Central Europe; and it had been five years since the brief Franco-Prussian

War (in which Nietzsche had briefly served as a volunteer medical orderly, with disastrous consequences for his health), which further enhanced and extended Prussia's sway, this time at France's expense. German unification under Prussian leadership had been achieved in 1871, and the new *Reich* appeared to be thriving, with Wilhelm on the throne and (more importantly) Otto von Bismarck at the helm.

Everything seemed to be coming along very nicely for Western civilization in general, Europe in particular and Germany more specifically. It was the heyday of European imperialism, with India recently incorporated into the British Empire, and much of the rest of the non-Western world coming under European sway. The industrial revolution was sweeping all before it, and capitalism was triumphant. New technologies and modes of transportation and communication were transforming Western societies. (Nietzsche himself must have been one of the very first philosophers to own one of the newly invented typewriters, although it proved to be of little use to him.) Despite the success of conservative elements of European societies in retaining their social position and political power, forces preparing the way for their eventual replacement by more popular forms of social, cultural, economic and political organization – for better or for worse – were gathering.

The physical sciences were advancing spectacularly; and while the influence of Karl Marx and Sigmund Freud had yet to be felt, the social and historical disciplines were maturing, and the biological sciences were coming on strong. Charles Darwin already loomed large. His *Origin of Species* had been published in 1859, and his *Descent of Man* in 1871. Germany, making up for lost time, was emerging as an economic, political and technological powerhouse, as well as the world's new leader in many of the sciences. It also continued its century-long dominance in philosophy, with ever-mutating forms of idealism, neo-Kantianism, naturalism and materialism competing in the aftermath of Hegel. Religion, enjoying official state status in many countries and the unquestioning allegiance of the vast majority of their populations, seemed immune from serious challenge. The arts, literature and music were flourishing as well, in Germany as elsewhere in Europe; and in 1876 the frenzy surrounding Richard Wagner – to which Nietzsche was no stranger – rose to new heights, with the opening of Bayreuth, and the performance of the first complete four-opera cycles of Wagner's monumental *Ring of the Nibulungs*.

Yet Nietzsche was convinced that all was far from well. He was repelled by the popular culture and brave new social, economic and political world burgeoning around him, and could no longer take seriously the intellectual and religious tradition associated with it. By 1876 he also found himself increasingly estranged from the newly fashionable alternatives to the tradition that its critics and rivals had been touting, including his erstwhile idols and mentors Arthur Schopenhauer and Wagner. Everywhere he looked, even at those things and thinkers supposedly representing the pride of our culture and the zenith of humanity, what he saw was not only far from divine but all-too-human.

Nietzsche had long yearned – and continued to yearn throughout his productive life – for a higher humanity with a worth great enough to warrant the affirmation of life even in the absence of any transcendently supplied meaning. He now had come to the hard realization that the only possible way to that higher humanity required an uncompromising examination of everything human and all-too-human that at once stands in our way and is our point of departure, and a sober stocktaking of what there is to work with in undertaking what he was later to call the enhancement of human life. The idea and ideal he seized upon at this juncture to guide and accompany him was that of the 'free spirit', older and wiser heir of the Enlightenment. Nietzsche paid explicit tribute to the ethos of this newly adopted lineage in his dedication of the first edition of *Human, All Too Human* to Voltaire, Enlightenment thinker *par excellence*, who had died exactly a century earlier, and whose spirit he now embraced.

Human, All Too Human was Nietzsche's second book; and it was as far removed from the kind of book professors of classical languages and literatures were supposed to write as anything could be. His first book, *The Birth of Tragedy* (1872), had been a scandal in the eyes of his scholarly colleagues owing to its disregard of prevailing norms of scholarship and its blatant advocacy of Wagner as the reincarnation of the spirit of the tragic culture of the Greeks – but it at least had a recognizably classical literary topic. *Human, All Too Human*, as initially published, was a volume of 638 aphorisms – that is, short observations and reflections ranging from one or two sentences to a long paragraph, of a relatively self-contained nature. This style was a radically new one for Nietzsche, reminiscent of the writings of such observers of the human scene as Montaigne and La Rochefoucauld. Nietzsche had long greatly admired their manner of thought and expression, and found himself drawn to emulate them in his search for a voice that lent itself both to his own changing temperament and circumstances and to the decidedly unphilological tasks towards which he was turning.

The publication of *Human, All Too Human* completed Nietzsche's estrangement from his erstwhile scholarly profession, from which he officially retired shortly thereafter. It also completed his much more painful estrangement from Wagner, whose devoted admirer, champion and intimate younger friend Nietzsche had been. Nietzsche himself claimed to have begun writing the book in reaction to the first Bayreuth production of Wagner's *Ring* cycle, the entire social spectacle of which appalled him; and although he in fact would appear to have begun work on it some months earlier, in the spring of 1876, it certainly was written during a period in which his formerly close relationship to Wagner had become severely strained. Nietzsche knew that Wagner would loathe the book; and its dedication to Voltaire was undoubtedly a very deliberate gesture of defiance and independence in Wagner's direction. Eight years after its first publication, when Nietzsche republished it, he dropped the dedication – perhaps because he no longer wanted Voltaire to be taken as paradigmatic of his evolving conception of the 'free spirit', but perhaps also because Wagner by then had died, and such gestures were no longer either needed or fitting.

In his discussion in *Ecce Homo* of the 'crisis' of which *Human, All Too Human* was the 'monument', Nietzsche goes on to say of it: 'Here I liberated myself from what in my nature did not belong to me.' He had given *Human, All Too Human* the subtitle 'A Book for Free Spirits'; and he went on to characterize the 'free spirit' in similar language, as 'a spirit that has *become free*, that has again taken possession of itself'.³ Among the things he clearly had in mind were his attachments to Schopenhauer and Wagner, who had been at the centre of his intellectual life for the previous decade. They had been the subjects of his last two major publications prior to *Human, All Too Human*, in which he had lavished praise upon them even while privately beginning to distance himself from them: *Schopenhauer as Educator* (1874) and *Richard Wagner in Bayreuth* (1876), the final two essays of his four-part *Untimely Meditations*.

A student of classical languages and literatures rather than of philosophy, it had been Nietzsche's accidental discovery of Schopenhauer's magnum opus *The World as Will and Representation* in 1865 that had introduced – and seduced – him to philosophy. His spiritual seduction by Wagner three years later (in 1868) influenced him even more profoundly. The spell cast upon him by the two of them together is very apparent both in his thinking and enthusiasms in *The Birth of Tragedy* and in the fact that he ventured to write and publish such a book. Nietzsche's father had died when he was a young child; and he in effect adopted Schopenhauer as his intellectual godfather and Wagner as his emotional and spiritual father figure. It was for good reason that it occurred to him to write in aphorism 381 of the first volume of *Human, All Too Human*: '*Correcting nature.* – If one does not have a good father one should furnish oneself with one.' Yet by the time he wrote these words he was well beyond this point, attempting to liberate himself from the fathers with whom he had furnished himself.

It is well worth bearing in mind who the Nietzsche was who published this book of aphorisms in 1878. Neither he nor anyone else had the slightest idea of what he would go on to do and become. He was a 33-year-old philology professor whose health and academic career were both failing badly. His youthful vigour and promise were now but sadly faded memories to his professional colleagues. His only book, published six years earlier, was the scandalous *Birth of Tragedy*; and his only subsequent publications of any significance were the two essays just mentioned and two previous 'untimely meditations', *David Strauss, the Confessor and the Writer* (1873) and *On the Uses and Disadvantages of History for Life* (1874). His enthusiasm for and association with Wagner had earned him a certain notoriety, but it had done him no good academically; and he otherwise had little reputation at all, except perhaps as a gamble that had appeared not to be working out. He was not thought of as a philosopher, having had no philosophical training and having published nothing resembling a conventional philosophical treatise. He had written a short, ambitious but sketchy essay, 'On Truth and Lies in a Nonmoral Sense', several years earlier; but it remained unfinished, and he never did publish it. His thoughts had indeed begun to turn toward philosophy, and he had even gone so far as to apply for the Chair in Philosophy at Basel when it became vacant; but he was unsuccessful in this attempt to switch professions, for reasons that are easy enough to understand.

Even if *Human, All Too Human* had been published by a professional philosopher, it very probably would not have been regarded as a contribution to the philosophical literature by academic philosophers either in Nietzsche's own time or subsequently. Nor is it clear that it should be; for there is much in it that does not seem to have much to do with philosophical matters. Even the ideas on philosophical topics it addresses are seldom presented in recognizably philosophical ways. More of it can be seen as having philosophical relevance in retrospect, particularly if one looks back upon it with Nietzsche's later writings in mind, and if one's idea of philosophical relevance has been influenced by the impact of his thinking with respect to the philosophical enterprise. Even so, however, all three instalments of the work are very much the product of a mind in transition, moving in many different directions and in many different ways, heedless of disciplinary boundaries and norms, with only Nietzsche's interests and intellectual conscience as his map and compass.

The aphoristic form Nietzsche adopted (and adapted to his purposes) in *Human, All Too Human* had long been a favoured literary form of observers of the human scene who preferred to comment incisively on many things, rather than writing essays about a selected few. But this form may also have been virtually necessitated by Nietzsche's increasingly severe and disabling health problems, which frequently rendered him incapable of writing or even thinking for extended periods of time. He had to make maximum use of the short periods of respite that came to him between frequent and extended bouts of misery. He struggled to surmount his wretched condition, and did so to much greater effect than most people in his situation could; but it was a hard and tortured struggle, giving poignant significance to his subsequent emphasis upon 'hardness', self-mastery, self-discipline, and to his refusal to become preoccupied and deterred by suffering. The flair he discovered in himself for aphoristic writing at this time thus accorded well with necessity. It would be unwarranted, however, to assume that Nietzsche's recourse to it is indicative of the absence of any underlying unity and coherence of thought and intention here and subsequently. So he himself observes in aphorism 128 of the second instalment, very much to this point: '*Against the shortsighted.* – Do you think this work must be fragmentary because I give it to you (and have to give it to you) in fragments?'

Nietzsche had long been plagued by poor eyesight and eye pain that would afflict him when he either read or wrote extensively, by migraine headaches and by indigestion and other gastric problems that made him pay a high price for departures from the blandest of diets. His problems were compounded by a variety of ailments – dysentery and diphtheria among them – he contracted while serving as an orderly during the Franco-Prussian War, the effects of which continued to plague him. And the syphilis he seems somehow to have acquired (despite leading a virtually celibate life), that was the likely cause of his final collapse a dozen years later, may well have begun to contribute to the deterioration of his health during the gestation period of *Human, All Too Human*.

So Nietzsche went from one health crisis to another, finding the rigours and burdens of his academic position increasingly difficult to bear, despite the fact that he rarely had as many as a dozen students attending his lectures. He often was unable to read or write, and frequently was obliged to take medical leaves from his teaching. His collapses were all too common, and at times he was virtually an invalid. He visited clinics, spas and specialists, whose diagnoses and prescriptions may often have only made things worse. Alternating bouts of blinding headaches and wracking vomiting would last for days; and his lecturing became ever more sporadic and difficult. Finally, in the spring of 1879, he submitted his resignation, receiving a small pension that was his sole income thereafter. He then left Basel and began the nomadic life – moving from boarding-house to boarding-house in search of the right climate and conditions – that he would lead for the decade of active life remaining to him prior to his collapse.

It is miraculous that anyone with such severe problems and living such a life could have written anything at all, let alone the series of brilliant books that Nietzsche managed to complete in this period, beginning with the first volume of *Human, All Too Human*. And to all of this must be added the publication history of these books, which compounds the miracle. This history was troubled by Nietzsche's often strained relations with his publishers and printers, and plagued by such other all-too-human difficulties as his eye problems, requiring him to resort to dictation much of the time, and to reliance on the assistance of others to put his manuscripts together, as well as making proof-reading a torment. But worst of all, Nietzsche's publication history is a veritable chronicle of failure. A recent study by William Schaberg makes all of this painfully clear, setting out the whole long and sorry story in depressing detail.[4] *The Birth of Tragedy* sold modestly well, and attracted a good deal of attention – even if much of it was hostile. But the same cannot be said of any of Nietzsche's subsequent books, during his sentient lifetime. Prior to his collapse, none of them sold more than a few hundred copies, and few of them attracted any attention whatsoever.

Human, All Too Human is a vivid case in point. Of the 1,000 copies in the first printing of the original version, only 120 were sold in 1878; and more than half remained unsold in 1886, when Nietzsche reacquired them and repackaged them with a new introduction as the first volume of the two-volume second edition. The supplement he published in 1879 under the subtitle 'Assorted Opinions and Maxims' sold even more poorly: of the 1,000 copies printed, only a third had been sold by 1886. The second supplement *The Wanderer and His Shadow*, published a year later, fared even worse: fewer than 200 of its initial 1,000 copies had been sold by 1886, when Nietzsche acquired the rights to both supplements and republished them with a new introduction, as the second volume of the second edition of *Human, All Too Human*. There was no true reprinting of additional copies until 1893, when another printing of 1,000 copies of the combined work was run; and its sales remained slow even after his later works began to receive more attention.

Human, All Too Human attained greater circulation and availability as part of the editions of his collected works that began to appear after Nietzsche's death; but it was long eclipsed by *The Birth of Tragedy* before it and by *Thus Spoke Zarathustra* and its sequels after it, both in Europe and in the English-speaking world. The same is true of the other two works in Nietzsche's 'free spirit' series, *Daybreak* and *The Gay Science*. The neglect of *Human, All Too Human* in the English-speaking world is at least partly owing to Walter Kaufmann's lack of interest in it. It was through his translations and his widely read study *Nietzsche: Philosopher, Psychologist, Antichrist*, first published in 1950, that many English-speaking readers after World War II became interested in and acquainted with Nietzsche. Kaufmann translated Nietzsche's first book, *The Birth of Tragedy*, and virtually everything Nietzsche published from *The Gay Science* onward; but he never got around to translating any of the things Nietzsche published in the interval, during the crucial period in which he published not only the three instalments of *Human, All Too Human* but also the four *Untimely Meditations* and *Daybreak*, except for brief excerpts which he inserted in other volumes. Indeed, even Kaufmann's translation of *The Gay Science* was something of an afterthought, appearing long after most of his other translations.[5]

Kaufmann can hardly be blamed for having the interests he did, and for the things he did not choose to do; but they had consequences, since there were no other readily available complete translations of *Human, All Too Human* or *Daybreak* in English until the early 1980s, when Marion Faber translated the first volume of *Human, All Too Human* (published by the University of Nebraska Press) and Hollingdale's Cambridge University Press translations appeared. Their long inaccessibility ensured that these works, and Nietzsche's thinking during the period in which he wrote them, would remain virtually unknown to English-speaking readers during the preceding three decades. (They likewise had been virtually invisible previously, when Nietzsche was known mainly second-hand in the English-speaking world, and was commonly assumed to be the proto-Nazi he had been made out to be by Nazi propaganda.)

The problem was compounded by Kaufmann's treatment of *Human, All Too Human* (and *Daybreak* and *The Gay Science* as well) in his popular intellectual-biographical study, which had little competition for nearly two decades. This entire period, for Kaufmann, was a gestation period in Nietzsche's thought, of little interest in its own right. He appears to have deemed it deserving of comment at all chiefly for the anticipations to be found in some aphorisms of ideas that became prominent in his later thinking, and for the ammunition other aphorisms afford that were useful in combating Nietzsche's Nazi misinterpretation. So *Human, All Too Human* is relegated to a few pages, in a chapter entitled 'Discovery of the Will to Power'. 'There would be little sense', Kaufmann wrote (without explanation), 'in trying here to sample the gems of *Human, all-too-Human* or [*Daybreak*].' He restricted himself to asserting, with a few illustrations, that,

'Proceeding quite unsystematically and considering each problem on its own merits, without a theory to prove or an axe to grind, Nietzsche reverts now and then to explanations in terms of what he was later to call a will to power.'[6] The works of this period, for Kaufmann, were of significance primarily as the record of Nietzsche's development from the author of *The Birth of Tragedy* into a psychological thinker on a par with Freud, with his further transformation into a philosopher coming somewhat later.

There certainly is some truth in this. *Human, All Too Human* undeniably does show us Nietzsche as psychologist both under development and at work, inventing a kind of psychologizing for which he found a wealth of applications all around him – socially, culturally, behaviourally, intellectually, even philosophically – and simultaneously inventing himself as a new kind of thinker capable of employing this sort of analysis to fascinating and important effect. He was not operating in a void. He had some brilliant aphoristic predecessors, the inspiration of such Enlightenment exemplars as Voltaire, and the benefit of reading his 'educator' and philosophical–psychological mentor Schopenhauer. He also had the more immediate example and encouragement of his newfound friend Paul Rée, who had just written a book in a somewhat similar spirit entitled *Psychological Observations*. Rée's influence was readily and profusely acknowledged by Nietzsche, who went so far as to say that his own position at this time could be called 'Réealism'; and it was evident to all who knew him – including the Wagners, who bitterly lamented it (all the more because Rée was Jewish).

But the results were much more than the sum of their influences even here. And they also added up to something that was much more than psychology as well. It is true enough that Nietzsche's thinking continued to develop, even from one book to the next in this period, as well as over the course of the next decade; and that, as Kaufmann maintained, Nietzsche's philosophical maturity was yet some time off. Yet his accomplishment in the three instalments of *Human, All Too Human* is remarkable in its own right, and can stand on its own feet. If he had died without publishing another thing (as might very well have happened), it would have been sufficient to earn him an important place in the intellectual history of the past several centuries – even if a somewhat different one than he has come to have.

The gulf that separates this work from Nietzsche's previous published writings is wide. The enthusiasms, aspirations and assumptions that so strikingly pervade and animate his earlier work are no longer in evidence. It is a much more sober and analytical, colder and wiser thinker who is at work here. Its author is still hopeful of finding both a diagnosis and a cure to what ails our culture and threatens its future, and resists Schopenhauer's pessimism; but he is as disillusioned now with Wagner, the new *Reich* and other pied pipers of modern times as he earlier had been with traditional religious consolations and their philosophical cousins. He has become convinced that only something like a continuation and radicalization of Enlightenment thinking, getting to the bottom of things and ruthlessly exposing all false hopes and dangerous palliatives, can afford us at least the possibility of a future worth having and a life worth living. Nietzsche's dedication to Voltaire was more than a slap at Wagner (although that it surely was). It also was the announcement of a major intellectual re-orientation, placing him squarely in the often calumnied but courageous tradition of Enlightenment thought and effort.

For the Nietzsche of *Human, All Too Human* nothing is beyond criticism – and there is a strong suspicion that (as he would later put it) all 'idols' of our reverence will turn out to be hollow and all-too-human when subjected to critical scrutiny. His new 'psychological' tools are brought to bear upon them, with results that amply support this suspicion. But there is more to the outlook and way of thinking that he is devising and putting into practice here than this. In 'On Truth and Lies in a Nonmoral Sense', some five years earlier, Nietzsche had begun sketching a fundamentally and severely naturalistic picture of our general human condition, in a world over which no benevolent deity reigns and in which no beneficent rationality is at work. We are depicted as alone and adrift in a godless universe, a mere cosmic accident, ill-equipped either to comprehend what is going on or to do much about it; and we are kidding ourselves if we think otherwise – although we seem almost irresistibly drawn to do so. Can we live without such illusions? Nietzsche was at first inclined to doubt it – as one sees in *The Birth of Tragedy*, written at about the same time.

By the time of *Human, All Too Human*, he seems to have resolved to try. The power of myths and illusions to sustain anyone possessed of an un-compromising intellectual conscience is undermined when one sees through them; and so one may have little other choice, if – as for Nietzsche – Kierkegaardian leaps of faith are out of the question, and a Schopenhauerian negation of life is repellent. *Human, All Too Human* is a work of cold passion, in which nothing more is assumed about our humanity than the picture sketched in the 'Truth and Lies' essay, and in which everything in human life that might seem to be of loftier origins is called before the tribunal of scrutiny, with humbling results. Yet the spirit of the investigation is profoundly and pervasively affirmative; for the passion that drives it is not only that of an honesty that will tolerate no nonsense or groundless wishful thinking, but also of a desperate search for enough to work with and ways of doing so to sustain ourselves despite all. To call this 'secular humanism' would be to sell it short; for while Nietzsche's outlook is radically secular, he is far from taking humanity either in general or as embodied in each and every one of us to be the locus of meaning and value. But it is a kind of tough-minded and yet doggedly affirmative naturalism, the upshot of which is that our all-too-human humanity leaves a good deal to be desired, and yet gives us something to work with that is not to be despised.

But if we are to make something worthwhile of ourselves, we have to take a good hard look at ourselves. And this, for Nietzsche, means many things. It means looking at ourselves in the light of everything we can learn about the world and ourselves from the natural sciences – most emphatically including evolutionary biology, physiology and even medical science. It also means looking at ourselves in the light of everything we can learn about human life from history, from the social sciences, from the study of arts, religions, languages, literatures, mores and other features of various cultures. It further means attending closely to human conduct on different levels of human interaction, to the relation between what people say and seem to think about themselves and what they do, to their reactions in different sorts of situations, and to everything else about them that affords clues to what makes them tick. All of this, and more, is what Nietzsche is up to in *Human, All Too Human*. He is at once developing and employing the various perspectival techniques that seem to him to be relevant to the understanding of what we have come to be and what we have it in us to become. This involves gathering materials for a reinterpretation and reassessment of human life, making tentative efforts along those lines and then trying them out on other human phenomena both to put them to the test and to see what further light can be shed by doing so.

This multi-perspectival and multi-directional method, which Nietzsche employed with increasing dexterity and ingenuity throughout the remainder of his productive life, finds its first extended trials and applications in *Human, All Too Human*. The results are uneven, as one might expect – and indeed as is always the case in Nietzsche's writings (or, for that matter, in the case of anyone who engages in such a complex, uncertain and adventuresome sort of interpretive enterprise). Distinguishing between genuine insights and personal preferences, prejudices, over-generalizations, irresistible puns and other such inspirations is not easy. It often can be done better by others than by oneself – even if one's intellectual conscience is as alert and vigorous as Nietzsche's, to whom the all-too-human was no stranger. But by precept and example he invites us to subject him to the same sort of scrutiny to which he subjects others; and that is something many will want to do. He only asks that one be prepared to have one's very objections subjected in turn to the same searching critical assessment – for they too may be questionable.

Nietzsche himself looked back on *Human, All Too Human* twice in print. The final time was in his rather creatively and grandiosely self-interpretive *Ecce Homo*, in 1888, in the course of a review of all of his main publications under the characteristically immodest heading 'Why I Write Such Good Books'. The occasion of his first subsequent retrospective – the reissuing of all three instalments together in 1886 – may itself have had its all-too-human motivations (not the least of which was Nietzsche's hope that by repackaging them with new prefaces he might be able to sell more of them and attract more attention to them). Nonetheless, the two new prefaces he wrote on this occasion are of no little interest; and it is important for readers to bear in mind that they were written long after the material they precede – eight years after the first volume, and six and seven years after the two parts of the second volume. Indeed, the prefaces themselves were written at different times and places – the former in Nice, on the French Mediterranean coast in Spring 1886, and the latter in Sils Maria, in the mountainous Swiss Engadine region, in September of that year. They both deserve close reading, both before and after one has made one's way through the maze of the 1,400 aphorisms.

In the first preface Nietzsche sees himself at the time of the first volume as already burdened with the large and heavy questions that compelled him toward philosophy, and also as struggling to achieve the intellectual and spiritual freedom and resources needed to deal with them, which he feels he had lacked in sufficient measure previously. He also sees himself as having been in a precarious state of health both physically and intellectually, slowly convalescing from the maladies of both sorts that had threatened to engulf him. The same theme is sounded again in the second preface; and there he makes it even clearer what the chief dangers were to which he had to develop resistance and learn to overcome. He refers to these writings as 'a continuation and redoubling of a spiritual cure, namely of the *anti-roman-tic* self-treatment that my still healthy instinct had itself discovered and prescribed for me against a temporary attack of the most dangerous form of romanticism', and as the expressions of a 'courageous pessimism' that is the 'antithesis of all romantic mendacity' (II:P:2, 4).

As Nietzsche observes in the first preface, his determination to resist and reject all such temptations (which for him could be summed up in a single name: Wagner) was still immature here, and was not yet 'that *mature* freedom of spirit which is equally self-mastery and discipline of the heart and permits access to many and contradictory modes of thought', and which he evidently feels he subsequently had come to attain (I: P: 4). But he sees himself in *Human, All Too Human* as having been on the way to it. And it is of no little importance to the understanding of Nietzsche both to observe that he not only places this interpretation upon the direction and outcome of his own intellectual development, and to recognize what is fundamental to it: the repudiation of 'all romantic mendacity', and its replacement by the cultivation of the intellectual conscience and analytical, critical and interpretive abilities of the 'free spirit' he was attempting to become and conjure among his readers by his own example.

Nietzsche thus saw himself here as having turned away from the Wagnerian–Schopenhauerian Romanticism of *The Birth of Tragedy* (of which he was explicitly critical along these very lines in a new preface to that work also written in 1886, entitled 'Attempt at a Self-Criticism'). In doing so, and partly as a way of doing so, he had turned with all the self-discipline and intellect he could muster in an analytical direction, replacing art with science as his new paradigm of high spirituality. Thus, in the preface to the second volume, he refers to the various instalments of *Human, All Too Human* as '*precepts of health* that may be recommended to the more spiritual natures of the generation just coming up as a *disciplina voluntatis* [discipline of the will]' (II:P:2). It is a discipline as much needed today as it was needed by Nietzsche himself and by 'the generation just coming up' in his own time.

This in part answers the question of the intended audience of these volumes. Nietzsche did not think of himself, either at this time or later, as writing primarily for professional philosophers, or even for students in philosophy courses. He clearly was moving in what he conceived to be a philosophical direction; but he was writing first and foremost for inquiring and adventuresome minds of sufficient sophistication to keep pace with him, whoever and wherever they may be – not only in academia but also among the intelligent reading public. He hoped in particular to be able to reach the better minds of the younger generation, who might be more receptive than their elders to challenges to preconceived ideas and assumed values. Yet he also had hopes of having the sort of wider impact Voltaire and other fire-brands of the Enlightenment had had a century earlier.

At the same time Nietzsche worried about what the likes of the Wagners and the few colleagues who had not given up on him would think of it. For a time he even considered publishing the first volume anonymously or under a pseudonym. *Human, All Too Human* may not seem to us today to be scandalously radical, however provocative it may be on some topics; but at the time Nietzsche rightly feared that it would be deeply offensive to many of its readers – not in the ways *The Birth of Tragedy* had been to his fellow philologists, but in an almost opposite way. Now it was those who had been enamoured of Nietzsche the romantic who were offended, by his abandon-ment of Romanticism in favour of a coldly and severely analytical Naturalism – for which he sought the widest possible audience. Beyond the circle of those who already knew of him, however, Nietzsche need not have worried about the scandalousness of his new venture – for, to his dismay, no one else paid the slightest attention. Even today, few recognize it as the gold mine it is, not only as an excellent way of becoming acquainted with his thinking, but also for its wealth of ideas worth thinking about.

It does not do full justice to these ideas to characterize them as 'psycho-logical', let alone as revolving around the 'discovery of the will to power' (as Kaufmann suggests). Nietzsche himself, in his 1886 preface to the first volume, observes that although he may not have realized it at the time, it eventually dawned upon him that 'it is *the problem of order of rank*' – that is, the problem of values and their revaluation and ordering – 'of which we may say it is *our* problem'; and that, to position themselves to address this problem adequately, 'we free spirits' first have to become 'adventurers and circumnavigators of that inner world called "man", as surveyors and [measurers] of that "higher" and "one [above] the other" that is likewise called "man" – penetrating everywhere, almost [!] without fear, disdaining nothing, losing nothing, asking everything, cleansing everything of what is chance and accident in it and as it were thoroughly sifting it…' (1:P:7).

That is a fair characterization of what Nietzsche does in *Human, All Too Human*; and it is in that sense that the term 'psychological' applies to his task and way of going about it. 'Psychology' in his time, after all, was not a discipline in its own right, separate and distinct from philosophy, but rather was conceived both loosely and strictly as a part of it; and in Nietzsche's hands it retained this intimate connection with philosophy as he came to understand and practice it. Philosophy for him revolves around the exploration of things human, and is first and foremost the attempt to comprehend them – even if that comprehension is not an end in itself. It prepares the way for the further comprehension of the whole complex matter of value, as it relates to issues of quality and worth in and about human life, in the service of its enhancement. In *Human, All Too Human*

Nietzsche took (and in his prefaces saw himself as taking) major steps in that direction. He had yet to learn to temper his new enthusiasm for the natural sciences, to figure out how to revisit the perspectives relating to the arts and culture he had known so well without becoming captive once again to them, to supplement both with yet others and to develop the ability to make larger interpretive sense of our humanity in the light of this multiplicity of perspectives upon it. But he was on his way.

This assessment of the place of *Human, All Too Human* in the context of Nietzsche's larger intellectual development has the virtues of acknowledging the great differences between it (and its companion volumes in the 'free spirit' series) and his earlier writings, and also of coherently relating his later writings to both. Many readers – and interpreters – make the mistake of regarding these 'free spirit' works as a kind of interlude between *The Birth of Tragedy* and *Thus Spoke Zarathustra*, and of reading them – if at all – from the perspective of his later writings, in relation to which they are generally found to pale by comparison, both rhetorically and philosophically. It would make a good deal more sense to view his later writings in the perspective of his 'free spirit' works, taking *Human, All Too Human* as one's point of departure, and regarding *Zarathustra* as an interlude between the last of them (the first four-part version of *The Gay Science*) and the continuation of Nietzsche's aphoristic works, beginning with *Beyond Good and Evil* and the expanded version of *The Gay Science* he published a year later. For the continuities between them are strong, even if Nietzsche's arsenal of perspectives grows, his philosophical sophistication increases, his rhetoric sharpens and heats up, and his intellectual pendulum swings back from its scientifically-oriented extreme point in the direction of his artistic and cultural concerns and sensibility (moving subsequently in considerably shorter arcs in the general vicinity of the centre of the spectrum they mark out).

This even applies to the organization of *Human, All Too Human* and the two later works that are not devoted to specific topics or figures, *Beyond Good and Evil* and *Twilight of the Idols*. Like both of them, the first version of *Human, All Too Human* does have an organization, in the form of the division of the volume into parts with headings. Interestingly enough, all three have the same number of major parts – nine – plus an epilogue. And there is a striking similarity among the headings as well. Each starts out with sections on topics relating to philosophers and philosophy; each has a section relating to morality, and another to religious and metaphysical matters; each has a section on social and political matters, and another on cultural and intellectual topics; and each, at some point, contains a collection of one-liners on a variety of sensitive topics guaranteed to offend almost everyone. To be sure, the parallels are not exact; but they are close enough to warrant the suggestion of a continuity of form – and in content there are not only significant differences but also remarkable similarities. One might well ask oneself in what ways Nietzsche's thinking changed on these matters from his initial discussions of them in *Human, All Too Human* to *Beyond Good and Evil* to *Twilight*, what his reasons may have been (if he does not make them explicit) – and whether the changes were invariably for the better.

The two parts of the second volume of *Human, All Too Human* were not supplied with the same sorts of headings, or indeed with any subheadings at all. Most of the aphorisms in them can easily be assigned to one or another of those Nietzsche uses in the first volume, however; for they chiefly range over and fall into the same general topics. An examination of the list of these topics makes it clear both that *Human, All Too Human* is far from being as formless as it is often taken to be, and also that Nietzsche's interests include but are not restricted to issues that are normally deemed 'philosophical'. The first (appropriately enough), 'Of First and Last Things', deals with metaphysical thinking – but in a curiously detached sort of way, more as a phenomenon to be understood than a set of arguments to be engaged head on. The same sort of approach is taken to morality in the second ('On the History of Moral Sensations' – Nietzsche's first go at what he came to call the 'genealogy of morals'); to religion in the third ('The Religious Life'); and to art in the fourth ('From the Souls of Artists and Writers'). In each case Nietzsche is proposing that we make the experiment of looking at these seemingly sublime things as *human* phenomena – experiences and activities of human beings – asking what is going on when such things occur in human life, and shifting the presumption from their sublimity to the suspicion that their appearance of sublimity may well be deceiving.

In the next four sections Nietzsche turns his attention to the domain of cultural, social and interpersonal relationships and types. There is more to culture than art and literature; and he attempts to bring it into focus in the fifth section ('Tokens of Higher and Lower Culture'). Social institutions and relationships are the logical next stop, in the sixth section ('Man in Society'), with family matters coming next ('Woman and Child'), followed by political life ('A Glance at the State'). If in the first four sections he surveys things that claim some sort of transcendent significance, of the sort Hegel sought to express in his characterization of their domain as that of 'absolute spirituality', here Nietzsche surveys those things that flesh out what Hegel had called 'the life of a people' on the level of its 'objective spirituality'. These too are among the chief sorts of things in terms of which our humanity and human meaning and worth are commonly conceived. If one asks what it is that sets us apart from and above other creatures whose existence is merely animal, and is not permitted to give a quick religious or metaphysical answer appealing to transcendent principles and powers, this is a fair inventory of possible answers. That is the larger (and genuinely if unconventionally philosophical) point of these collections of reflections, many of which might not appear to have any philosophical significance whatsoever.

In the final section Nietzsche turns to what he considers to be left after one has considered all of these other dimensions of human life: what we are or can be on our own, as individuals, within or by ourselves ('Man Alone with Himself'). Later he would add another item to the first four on the list, belonging with them, but not yet as problematical in his eyes as he subsequently recognized it to be: scientific thinking, of the very sort he had become so enamoured of and reliant upon here. Like the glasses with which one may be provided to deal with vision problems, and to which one may become so accustomed that one ceases to be aware of them, this sort of thinking can come to be taken for granted beyond the point to which reliance upon it is warranted. To his great credit, Nietzsche was far quicker than most to become sensitive to the limitations of ways of thinking to which he was attracted – and then, having done so, to get past his disappointment with them and ascertain the best uses that might be made of them, their limitations notwithstanding. In *Human, All Too Human*, however, his romance with the sciences was still young, and this process had yet to run its course.

The expression Nietzsche adopted to characterize the kind of thinker and human being he conceived himself to have become – or at any rate to have been on the way to becoming – at the time of *Human, All Too Human* is that which he features in its subtitle: 'free spirit', *Freigeist. Human, All Too Human* is proclaimed in its subtitle to be 'A Book for Free Spirits'. Three years after the publication of its first instalment, when Nietzsche published the first version of *The Gay Science*, he had the following printed on the back cover: 'This book marks the conclusion of a series of writings by FRIEDRICH NIETZSCHE whose common goal it is to erect *a new image and ideal of the free spirit.*' He then went on to list *Human, All Too Human* and its supplements and sequels up to and including *The Gay Science*.[7]

But this did not mark the end of Nietzsche's attachment to the idea of the 'free spirit'. It reappears very significantly in *Beyond Good and Evil*, as the heading of the second part of the book in which, following his largely critical first part 'On the Prejudices of Philosophers', he proceeds to set forth a variety of his own ideas on a broad range of philosophical issues. And it reappears again not only in his retrospective *Ecce Homo*, as one would expect, but also in *Twilight of the Idols*, in a section bearing the heading '*My conception of freedom*'.[8] From first to last it is invoked to convey the double meaning of both liberation from things that have tended to hinder and hobble one, and of determination to undertake tasks requiring independence, strength, courage and imagination. Nietzschean free spirits are not necessarily philosophers; but Nietzschean philosophers are necessarily free spirits. Voltaire, for Nietzsche, was an exemplary free spirit, as the original dedication of *Human, All Too Human* indicated: 'To Voltaire's memory, in commemoration of the day of his death, 30 May 1788.' His example would appear to have taught Nietzsche the erstwhile devoted disciple of Wagner something he came to realize he badly needed to learn.

The 'free spirit' is 'a spirit that has *become free*', as Nietzsche emphasizes in his remarks on *Human, All Too Human* in *Ecce Homo*. In the things that matter most, Rousseau was both right and wrong – right in observing that people are 'everywhere in chains', but wrong in supposing them to be 'born free'. True freedom of the spirit is something that is acquired – if at all – with difficulty, and only by a few. Indeed, in Nietzsche's 1886 preface to the first volume he even goes so far as to allow that he was obliged to *invent* the 'free spirits' to whom the book is addressed, since '"free spirits" of this kind do not exist, did not exist' – although he says 'I had need of them', all the more so because he lacked the kind of actual companionship and comradeship that people of this sort could provide. 'That free spirits of this kind *could* one day exist', on the other hand, and indeed that they *will* one day exist, he does not doubt. 'I see them already *coming*', he optimistically asserts (I: P: 2); and in any event the statement on the back cover of *The Gay Science* makes it clear enough that he hoped and intended *Human, All Too Human* to speed the day, by both precept and example.

But the same could be said for all of Nietzsche's aphoristic works, after as well as before *Thus Spoke Zarathustra*. It is perhaps less true of *Zarathustra* itself, despite Zarathustra's repeated proclamations that he wants no disciples and wants his companions to think for themselves; for it is hard (though not impossible) to read and experience *Zarathustra* as a non-tendentious work. And it likewise is perhaps less true of Nietzsche's polemical later works – against Wagner, against Christianity and even (in *On the Genealogy of Morals*) against the kind of morality he considered to have come to prevail in the Western world. Polemics may have their place in the liberation of fettered spirits from the shackles that bind them, and so in making it possible for some people who might not otherwise do so to become free spirits; but they are far from sufficient to complete the process, and can easily subvert it – as the responses of many people to what they find in some of Nietzsche illustrate well enough.

Unfortunately for Nietzsche's reception, his free-spirited side has all too often been overshadowed and even eclipsed by the appearance of a much more impassioned and seemingly dogmatic side, frightening some and exciting others – for equally dubious reasons in either case. Neither the fact that this appearance has been seen in markedly different (and incompatible) ways, nor the objection that it is only an appearance rather than the dark side of the reality of his thought, has sufficed to keep it from long impeding his interpretation and assessment. The best remedy for this predicament is to direct attention to those works in which Nietzsche is engaged in his free-spirited labours, from *Human, All Too Human* to *The Gay Science* and *Beyond Good and Evil* to *Twilight of the Idols*. This is not to expurgate him; for there is plenty in each of these books to worry about and argue with, and much that is all-too-human in him no less than in his targets. But in these volumes he for the most part carries on in the manner of the kind of 'free spirit' he seeks to evoke and encourage. If one would understand the sort of thing he has in mind in speaking of philosophers and philosophy of the future as he would have them be, one would do well to begin – as he did – with this idea in mind, as the presupposition of anything further that a Nietzschean kind of philosophy might involve.

There is no better commentary in Nietzsche on what free-spiritedness meant to him, as the idea took shape in and beyond *Human, All Too Human*, than the paragraph with which he concludes the part of *Beyond Good and Evil* entitled 'The Free Spirit'. It deserves to be read together with the prefaces to the two volumes of *Human, All Too Human* he shortly went on to write. With them in mind one can turn to *Human, All Too Human* itself and see why Nietzsche was not content to allow it to go unnoticed even after he had gone on to publish a good many other things – and why there may be no better introduction to his thought and thinking.

At home, or at least having been guests, in many countries of the spirit; having escaped again and again from the musty agreeable nooks into which preference and prejudice, youth, origin, the accidents of people and books or even exhaustion from wandering seemed to have banished us; full of malice against the lures of dependence that lie hidden in honors, or money, or offices, or enthusiasms of the senses; grateful even to need and vacillating sickness because they always rid us from some rule and its 'prejudice,' grateful to god, devil, sheep, and worm in us; curious to a vice, investigators to the point of cruelty, with uninhibited fingers for the unfathomable, with teeth and stomachs for the most indigestible, ready for every feat that requires a sense of acuteness and acute senses, ready for every venture, thanks to an excess of 'free will,' with fore- and back-souls into whose ultimate intentions nobody can look so easily, with fore- and backgrounds which no foot is likely to explore to the end; concealed under cloaks of light, conquerors even if we look like heirs and prodigals, arrangers and collectors from morning till late, misers of our riches and our crammed drawers, economical in learning and forgetting, inventive in schemas, occasionally proud of tables of categories, occasionally pedants, occasionally night owls of work even in broad daylight; yes, when it is necessary even scarecrows – and today it is necessary; namely, insofar as we are born, sworn, jealous friends of *solitude*, of our own most profound, most midnightly, most middaily solitude; that is the type of man we are, we free spirits! And perhaps *you* have something of this, too, you that are coming? you *new* philosophers? –[9]

Notes

1 *On the Genealogy of Morals/Ecce Homo*, trans. Walter Kaufmann (New York, 1967), p. 283 ('Why I Write Such Good Books': *Human, All Too Human*, §71).

2 See, e.g., *The Gay Science*, trans. Walter Kaufmann (New York, 1974), §§108, 125 and 343.

3 *Ecce Homo*, p. 283

4 *The Nietzsche Canon: A Publication History and Bibliography* (Chicago, 1995).

5 In 1974 (see note 2).

6 Walter Kaufmann, *Nietzsche: Philosopher, Psychologist, Antichrist*, 4th edn. (Princeton, 1974), pp. 157, 158.

7 *The Gay Science*, trans. Kaufmann, p. 30.

8 *Twilight of the Idols*, in *The Portable Nietzsche*, ed. and trans. Walter Kaufmann (New York, 1954), 'Skirmishes of an Untimely Man', §39.

9 Trans. Walter Kaufmann (New York, 1966), §44.

CHRONOLOGY

1844   Friedrich Wilhelm Nietzsche born on 15 October in Röcken, in the Prussian province of Saxony

1849   His father dies (at the age of 36)

1858–64   Attends the classics-oriented boarding-school Schulpforta; plays the piano and composes

1864   Enters Bonn University to study classical languages and literatures

1869   Associate professor of classical philology (before even completing his Ph.D.) at the Swiss university at Basel

1870   Full professor at Basel; enlists as a medical orderly in the Franco-Prussian War, contracting serious illnesses

1872   First book *The Birth of Tragedy* appears (and is met with scholarly derision) – his only major classical studies publication

1873–4   Publishes the first three *Untimely Meditations*, including the essays *On the Uses and Disadvantages of History for Life* and *Schopenhauer as Educator*

1876   Writes a fourth *Meditation* in homage to Wagner, but his enthusiasm for Wagner cools

1878   The first volume of *Human, All Too Human* (638 aphorisms) appears; Wagner sends him *Parsifal*, and their estrangement deepens

1879   Resigns (with pension) from his position at Basel, incapacitated by health problems; begins spending his summers in the Swiss Engadine region, and his winters in northern Italy, living in boarding-houses

1879–80   Writes two sequels to *Human, All Too Human*, subsequently published as the two parts of its second volume (another 758 aphorisms)

1881   Publishes *Daybreak* (575 aphorisms); alternative periods of depression and exhilaration; first summer in Sils Maria, where the idea of 'eternal recurrence' comes to him

1882   The year of his intense but short-lived relationship with Lou Salome, which ends badly; publishes the initial four-part version of *The Gay Science* (342 aphorisms and reflections)

1883   The first two parts of *Thus Spoke Zarathustra* are written and published; estrangement from family and friends; depression; resolves against living in Germany; Wagner dies

1884	Completes and publishes the third part of *Zarathustra*; breaks with his sister Elizabeth, unable to endure her anti-Semitic, pro-'Teutonic' fiancee Bernard Förster (She marries him the next year, to Nietzsche's disgust and distress, accompanying him to Paraguay where he sought to found a Teutonic colony)
1885	The fourth part of *Zarathustra* is written, but is only privately printed and circulated; condition worsens
1886	*Beyond Good and Evil* (296 aphorisms and reflections in nine parts, plus a poem 'Aftersong') is published; new editions of most pre-*Zarathustra* works are prepared and supplied with prefaces
1886–7	An expanded second edition of *The Gay Science* is prepared and published, with a new preface and fifth part consisting of 41 additional reflections, and an appendix of poetry', 'Songs of Prince Vogelfrei'
1887	*On the Genealogy of Morals* appears, consisting of a preface and three 'essays' (of 17, 25 and 28 numbered sections, respectively); completes orchestral score for *Hymnus an das Leben*; begins working on magnus opus, to be called *The Will to Power*
1888	*The Case of Wagner* is published; and *Twilight of the Idols, The Antichrist, Nietzsche contra Wagner, Dionysian Dithyrambs* (a collection of poems) and *Ecce Homo* are all written; *The Will to Power* project is dropped, in favour of a projected four-part *Revaluation of All Values*; condition deteriorates
1889	Collapses in early January in Turin, at the age of 44 (never recovers, living his final eleven years in invalid insanity in the care of his mother and sister); *Twilight of the Idols* is published in January
1892	First public edition of the fourth part of *Zarathustra* appears
1893	Sister returns from Paraguay, and – under the name Elizabeth Förster-Nietzsche – assists their mother in the management of her brother's affairs
1895	*The Antichrist* and *Nietzsche Contra Wagner* are published
1897	Mother dies, leaving complete control of his care – and of his literary estate – to Elizabeth, who exploits his growing fame and fosters the assimilation of his thought to right-extremist political purposes during the next four decades
1900	Nietzsche dies, on 25 August, in Weimar
1901	Sister publishes an arrangement of selections from his notebooks of 1883–8 under the title *The Will to Power*, and in his name
1908	*Ecce Homo* is finally published
1910–11	First edition of Nietzsche's collected works is published under the supervision of Elizabeth – including a greatly expanded edition of *The Will to Power*

R.S.

FURTHER READING

Intellectual background

The history of philosophy has few chapters as rich and varied as that of German (or Central European) philosophy from Kant to Nietzsche. A superb survey of German philosophy up to and including Kant is Lewis White Beck's *Early German Philosophy: Kant and his Predecessors* (Cambridge, MA, 1969). The next chapters of the story are well told by Frederick C. Beiser in *The Fate of Reason: German Philosophy from Kant to Fichte* (Cambridge, MA, 1987); G. A. Kelly in *Idealism, Politics and History: Sources of Hegelian Thought* (Cambridge, 1969) and Herbert Schnädelbach in *Philosophy in Germany 1831–1933* (Cambridge, 1984).

Two classic studies of German philosophy in the nineteenth century, both first published in 1941, are Herbert Marcuse's *Reason and Revolution: Hegel and the Rise of Social Theory* (Boston, 1960) and Karl Löwith's *From Hegel to Nietzsche: The Revolution in Nineteenth-Century Thought* (New York, 1964). More recent studies include Walter Kaufmann's *From Shakespeare to Existentialism* (Garden City, NY, 1959), Maurice Mandelbaum's *History, Man and Reason* (Baltimore, 1971), and Robert Solomon's *From Rationalism to Existentialism* (New York, 1972).

The two most important figures in Nietzsche's intellectual life and development were Arthur Schopenhauer and Richard Wagner. Useful studies of Schopenhauer include Patrick Gardiner's *Schopenhauer* (Baltimore, 1963), D. W. Hamlyn's *Schopenhauer* (London, 1980) and Christopher Janaway's *Self and World in Schopenhauer* (Oxford, 1989). On Wagner, see Ernest Newman's four-volume biography *The Life of Richard Wagner* (New York, 1933–46), and Geoffrey Skelton's *Wagner at Bayreuth* (London and New York, 1976). The many studies of the Nietzsche–Wagner relationship include Dietrich Fischer-Dieskau's *Wagner and Nietzsche* (New York, 1976) and Frederick Love's *The Young Nietzsche and the Wagnerian Experience* (Chapel Hill, 1963). Roger Hollinrake discusses all three of them in *Nietzsche, Wagner and the Philosophy of Pessimism* (London, 1982).

Nietzsche himself published essays on both Schopenhauer and Wagner, shortly before *Human, All Too Human*, although they both reveal much more about the Nietzsche of that period of his life than they do about Schopenhauer and Wagner themselves. They are the third and fourth of his *Untimely Meditations* (Cambridge, 1983), and bear the titles 'Schopenhauer as Educator' and 'Richard Wagner in Bayreuth'. Late in his productive life (though only fifteen years after the appearance of the latter essay), Nietzsche also published two short books as polemically critical of Wagner as his early essay had been appreciative: *The Case of Wagner* (New York, 1967) and *Nietzsche Contra Wagner*, included in Walter Kaufmann's *The Portable Nietzsche* (New York, 1954).

Nietzsche's life

Perhaps the best recent biography of Nietzsche is Ronald Hayman's *Nietzsche: A Critical Life* (New York, 1980). Another useful and shorter biography is R. J. Hollingdale's *Nietzsche* (London, 1965). Kaufmann's *Nietzsche: Philosopher, Psychologist, Antichrist* (Princeton, 1950; Princeton, 1974), a kind of intellectual biography, is the book that rehabilitated Nietzsche for the post-World War II generation in the English-speaking world, and remains one of the most accessible introductions to his life and thought.

Here again, Nietzsche himself has also supplied a contribution that cannot go unmentioned, even if it is no more reliable and no less tendentious than his writings on Schopenhauer and Wagner. It is his intellectual-autobiographical *Ecce Homo* (New York, 1967), to which he gave the subtitle 'How One Becomes What One Is'. It is the last book he completed before his collapse. Considered by some to be all too clearly indicative of his incipient insanity, it is regarded by others as a work of profound significance. In any event, it is well worth reading.

Nietzsche's writings

Most of Nietzsche's publications have been translated into English in a number of versions, the best of which have long been generally considered to be the translations made by Walter Kaufmann and R. J. Hollingdale (sometimes in collaboration). A monumental critical edition of his writings in German has been published by De Gruyter, edited by Giorgio Colli and Mazzino Montinari; and a translation project intended to result in an English-language counterpart has now begun, under the editorship of Ernst Behler, at Stanford University Press.

Other writings of Nietzsche's that will be of particular interest to readers of the present work certainly include the two similar works following it in what Nietzsche came to think of and refer to as his 'free spirit' series: *Daybreak: Thoughts on the Prejudices of Morality* (Cambridge, 1982), also translated by Hollingdale; and *The Gay Science* (New York, 1974), translated by Kaufmann. Nietzsche's earlier writings are well worth consulting as well, for the indications they provide of the concerns which shaped the direction of his thinking and efforts in this series of aphoristic volumes. Chief among them are his first book (1872), *The Birth of Tragedy* (New York, 1967), translated by Kaufmann, and a series of four essays (first published in the years 1873–6) Nietzsche gathered together in 1886 under the title *Untimely Meditations* (Cambridge, 1983), translated by Hollingdale. They also include a draft of an important early essay Nietzsche never finished or published, which however reveals the starkly naturalistic picture of the human condition that was a part of his point of departure: 'On Truth and Lies in a Nonmoral Sense' (1873), translated by Daniel Breazeale and included in his volume *Nietzsche, Philosophy and Truth* (Atlantic Highlands, NJ, 1979).

Following his 'free spirit' series, Nietzsche turned his attention to a very different sort of project: his extraordinary four-part literary–philosophical experiment and masterpiece, *Thus Spoke Zarathustra* (1883–5), translated (among others) by both Kaufmann (in *The Portable Nietzsche*) and Hollingdale (Harmondsworth, 1961). He then (1886) returned to the publication of volumes of a somewhat aphoristic nature, beginning with *Beyond Good and Evil*, which again has been translated by both Kaufmann (New York, 1966) and Hollingdale (Harmondsworth, 1973), and an expanded version of *The Gay Science*. His next book, *On the Genealogy of Morals* (1887), translated by Kaufmann and Hollingdale together (New York, 1967), joins his aphoristic style to a three-essay format with a more specific focus than any of his previous aphoristic works (published in 1994, trans. Carol Diethe, edited by Keith Ansell-Pierson). In the final year before his collapse (1888) Nietzsche not only published the two polemics against Wagner and the autobiographical *Ecce Homo* mentioned above, but also a polemical critique of Christianity, *The Antichrist*, and a final volume of aphorisms more in the tradition of *Human, All Too Human*, which (parodying Wagner's fourth *Ring* opera) he called *Götzendämmerung*, or *Twilight of the Idols*. Both of these last works have been translated by Kaufmann (in *The Portable Nietzsche*) and also by Hollingdale (Harmondsworth, 1968).

Which of these many things should one read after *Human, All Too Human*? That depends upon one's interests. If one is primarily interested in matters relating to morality, one might look first at *Daybreak*, then at the fifth and ninth parts of *Beyond Good and Evil* and then at *On the Genealogy of Morals*. On religion, *Daybreak* again is a good sequel, together with the sections of *The Gay Science* dealing with God and religion, the third part of *Beyond Good and Evil* and *The Antichrist*. On the many philosophical topics relating to knowledge, our world and ourselves, one might look back to the early essay 'On Truth and Lies', and ahead to *The Gay Science*, the first two parts of *Beyond Good and Evil* and *Twilight of the Idols*; and one might also take a look at the selections from Nietzsche's notebooks from the 1880s published under the title *The Will to Power*, translated by Kaufmann and Hollingdale (New York, 1967). And for an indication of Nietzsche's thinking with respect to the enhancement of life and the possibility of a 'higher humanity' he discerns along with the 'all too human' tendencies he examines here and subsequently, one might look back to his essay 'Schopenhauer as Educator' (the third of his *Untimely Meditations*) as well as to *Thus Spoke Zarathustra*.

Nietzsche's thought

Nietzsche has been so influential in so many ways during the course of the twentieth century, and has been so variously interpreted; that no one account can be considered authoritative. He has been claimed as originator, anticipator, inspiration and kindred spirit by fascists and humanists, existentialists and deconstructionists, critical theorists and analytical philosophers, and by more artists, writers and composers than any other figure in the history of philosophy (at least since Plato). Both his admirers and his critics can make persuasive arguments for and against him; but they all too often fail to take the trouble to read him thoroughly and attentively enough to understand him – or at any rate to earn the right to make their claims.

Walter Kaufmann's classic study *Nietzsche* (mentioned above) offers a readable interpretation of Nietzsche's thought along humanistic existentialist and pragmatist lines. Another early study of enduring value, which explores Nietzsche's thought more systematically, is George Morgan's *What Nietzsche Means* (Cambridge, MA, 1941; New York, 1965). Useful interpretations in the analytic tradition include Arthur Danto's *Nietzsche as Philosopher* (New York, 1965), Alexander Nehamas's *Nietzsche: Life as Literature* (Cambridge, MA, 1985), Maudemarie Clark's *Nietzsche on Truth and Philosophy* (Cambridge, 1990), and Richard Schacht's *Nietzsche* (London and New York, 1983) and *Making Sense of Nietzsche* (Urbana and Chicago, 1995). A sampling of interpretations along post-structuralist and deconstructionist lines may be found in David Allison's collection *The New Nietzsche: Contemporary Styles of Interpretation* (New York, 1977). Helpful recent studies of various aspects of Nietzsche's thought relating to matters he discusses in *Human, All Too Human* include Erich Heller's *The Importance of Nietzsche* (Chicago, 1988), Peter Bergmann's *Nietzsche: The Last Antipolitical German* (Bloomington, IN, 1987) and Lester Hunt's *Nietzsche and the Origin of Virtue* (London, 1991).

R.S.

VOLUME ONE

CONTENTS

PREFACE

1

I have been told often enough, and always with an expression of great surprise, that all my writings, from the *Birth of Tragedy** to the most recently published *Prelude to a Philosophy of the Future*,† have something that distinguishes them and unites them together: they all of them, I have been given to understand, contain snares and nets for unwary birds and in effect a persistent invitation to the overturning of habitual evaluations and valued habits. What? *Everything* only – human, all too human? It is with this sigh that one emerges from my writings, not without a kind of reserve and mistrust even in regard to morality, not a little tempted and emboldened, indeed, for once to play the advocate of the worst things: as though they have perhaps been only the worst slandered? My writings have been called a schooling in suspicion, even more in contempt, but fortunately also in courage, indeed in audacity. And in fact I myself do not believe that anyone has ever before looked into the world with an equally profound degree of suspicion, and not merely as an occasional devil's advocate, but, to speak theologically, just as much as an enemy and indicter of God; and anyone who could divine something of the consequences that lie in that profound suspiciousness, something of the fears and frosts of the isolation to which that unconditional *disparity of view* condemns him who is infected with it, will also understand how often, in an effort to recover from myself, as it were to induce a temporary self-forgetting, I have sought shelter in this or that – in some piece of admiration or enmity or scientificality or frivolity or stupidity; and why, where I could not find what I *needed*, I had artificially to enforce, falsify and invent a suitable fiction for myself (– and what else have poets ever done? and to what end does art exist in the world at all?). What I again and again needed most for my cure and self-restoration, however, was the belief that I was *not* thus isolated, not alone in *seeing* as I did – an enchanted surmising of relatedness and identity in eye and desires, a reposing in a trust of friendship, a blindness in concert with another without suspicion or question-marks, a pleasure in foregrounds, surfaces, things close and closest, in everything possessing colour, skin and apparitionality. Perhaps in this regard I might be reproached with having employed a certain amount of 'art', a certain amount of false-coinage: for

* *Birth of Tragedy:* Nietzsche's first published book (1872)
† *Prelude to a Philosophy of the Future:* the subtitle of *Beyond Good and Evil*, published in 1886

example, that I knowingly-willfully closed my eyes before Schopen-hauer's* blind will to morality at a time when I was already sufficiently clearsighted about morality; likewise that I deceived myself over Richard Wagner'st incurable romanticism, as though it were a beginning and not an end; likewise over the Greeks, likewise over the Germans and their future – and perhaps a whole long list could be made of such likewises? – Supposing, however, that all this were true and that I was reproached with it with good reason, what do *you* know, what *could* you know, of how much cunning in self-preservation, how much reason and higher safeguarding, is contained in such self-deception – or of how much falsity I shall *require* if I am to continue to permit myself the luxury of *my* truthful-ness? . . . Enough, I am still living; and life is, after all, not a product of morality: it *wants* deception, it *lives* on deception . . . but there you are, I am already off again, am I not, and doing what I have always done, old immoralist and bird-catcher that I am – speaking unmorally, extra-morally, 'beyond good and evil'? –

2

–Thus when I needed to I once also *invented* for myself the 'free spirits' to whom this melancholy-valiant book with the title *Human, All Too Human* is dedicated: 'free spirits' of this kind do not exist, did not exist – but, as I have said, I had need of them at that time if I was to keep in good spirits while surrounded by ills (sickness, solitude, unfamiliar places, *acedia*, in-activity): as brave companions and familiars with whom one can laugh and chatter when one feels like laughing and chattering, and whom one can send to the Devil when they become tedious – as compensation for the friends I lacked. That free spirits of this kind *could* one day exist, that our Europe *will* have such active and audacious fellows among its sons of tomorrow and the next day, physically present and palpable and not, as in my case, merely phantoms and hermit's phantasmagoria: *I* should wish to be the last to doubt it. I see them already *coming*, slowly, slowly; and perhaps I shall do something to speed their coming if I describe in advance under what vicissitudes, upon what paths, I *see* them coming? – –

3

One may conjecture that a spirit in whom the type 'free spirit' will one day become ripe and sweet to the point of perfection has had its decisive experience in a *great liberation* and that previously it was all the more a fet-tered spirit and seemed to be chained for ever to its pillar and corner. What fetters the fastest? What bonds are all but unbreakable? In the case of men of a high and select kind they will be their duties: that reverence proper to youth, that reserve and delicacy before all that is honoured and

* Schopenhauer: Arthur Schopenhauer (1788–1860), the philosopher, of whom Nietzsche was in his youth a disciple (see the essay, 'Schopenhauer as Educator' in the *Untimely Medi-tations*)
† Richard Wagner (1813–83), the composer and dramatist who was, like Schopenhauer, an object of the youthful Nietzsche's veneration (see the essay 'Richard Wagner in Bayreuth' in the *Untimely Meditations*)

revered from of old, that gratitude for the soil out of which they have grown, for the hand which led them, for the holy place where they learned to worship – their supreme moments themselves will fetter them the fastest, lay upon them the most enduring obligation. The great liberation comes for those who are thus fettered suddenly, like the shock of an earthquake: the youthful soul is all at once convulsed, torn loose, torn away – it itself does not know what is happening. A drive and impulse rules and masters it like a command; a will and desire awakens to go off, anywhere, at any cost; a vehement dangerous curiosity for an undiscovered world flames and flickers in all its senses. 'Better to die than to go on living *here*' – thus responds the imperious voice and temptation: and this 'here', this 'at home' is everything it had hitherto loved! A sudden terror and suspicion of what it loved, a lightning-bolt of contempt for what it called 'duty', a rebellious, arbitrary, volcanically erupting desire for travel, strange places, estrangements, coldness, soberness, frost, a hatred of love, perhaps a desecrating blow and glance *backwards* to where it formerly loved and worshipped, perhaps a hot blush of shame at what it has just done and at the same time an exultation *that* it has done it, a drunken, inwardly exultant shudder which betrays that a victory has been won – a victory? over what? over whom? an enigmatic, question-packed, questionable victory, but the *first* victory nonetheless: such bad and painful things are part of the history of the great liberation. It is at the same time a sickness that can destroy the man who has it, this first outbreak of strength and will to self-determination, to evaluating on one's own account, this will to *free* will: and how much sickness is expressed in the wild experiments and singularities through which the liberated prisoner now seeks to demonstrate his mastery over things! He prowls cruelly around with an unslaked lasciviousness; what he captures has to expiate the perilous tension of his pride; what excites him he tears apart. With a wicked laugh he turns round whatever he finds veiled and through some sense of shame or other spared and pampered: he puts to the test what these things look like *when* they are reversed. It is an act of willfulness, and pleasure in willfulness, if now he perhaps bestows his favour on that which has hitherto had a bad reputation – if, full of inquisitiveness and the desire to tempt and experiment, he creeps around the things most forbidden. Behind all his toiling and weaving – for he is restlessly and aimlessly on his way as if in a desert – stands the question-mark of a more and more perilous curiosity. 'Can *all* values not be turned round? and is good perhaps evil? and God only an invention and finesse of the Devil? Is everything perhaps in the last resort false? And if we are deceived, are we not for that very reason also deceivers? *must* we not be deceivers?' – such thoughts as these tempt him and lead him on, even further away, even further down. Solitude encircles and embraces him, ever more threatening, suffocating, heart-tightening, that terrible goddess and *mater saeva cupidinum** – but who today knows what *solitude* is? . . .

---

* *mater saeva cupidinum:* wild mother of the passions

4

From this morbid isolation, from the desert of these years of temptation and experiment, it is still a long road to that tremendous overflowing certainty and health which may not dispense even with wickedness, as a means and fish-hook of knowledge, to that *mature* freedom of spirit which is equally self-mastery and discipline of the heart and permits access to many and contradictory modes of thought – to that inner spaciousness and indulgence of superabundance which excludes the danger that the spirit may even on its own road perhaps lose itself and become infatuated and remain seated intoxicated in some corner or other, to that superfluity of formative, curative, moulding and restorative forces which is precisely the sign of *great* health, that superfluity which grants to the free spirit the dangerous privilege of living *experimentally* and of being allowed to offer itself to adventure: the master's privilege of the free spirit! In between there may lie long years of convalescence, years full of variegated, painfully magical transformations ruled and led along by a tenacious *will to health* which often ventures to clothe and disguise itself as health already achieved. There is a midway condition which a man of such a destiny will not be able to recall without emotion: it is characterized by a pale, subtle happiness of light and sunshine, a feeling of bird-like freedom, bird-like altitude, bird-like exuberance, and a third thing in which curiosity is united with a tender contempt. A 'free-spirit' – this cool expression does one good in every condition, it is almost warming. One lives no longer in the fetters of love and hatred, without yes, without no, near or far as one wishes, preferably slipping away, evading, fluttering off, gone again, again flying aloft; one is spoiled, as everyone is who has at some time seen a tremendous number of things *beneath* him – and one becomes the opposite of those who concern themselves with things which have nothing to do with them. Indeed, the free spirit henceforth has to do only with things – and how many things! – with which he is no longer *concerned* . . .

5

A step further in convalescence: and the free spirit again draws near to life – slowly, to be sure, almost reluctantly, almost mistrustfully. It again grows warmer around him, yellower, as it were; feeling and feeling for others acquire depth, warm breezes of all kind blow across him. It seems to him as if his eyes are only now open to what is *close at hand*. He is astonished and sits silent: where *had* he been? These close and closest things: how changed they seem! what bloom and magic they have acquired! He looks back gratefully – grateful to his wandering, to his hardness and self-alienation, to his viewing of far distances and bird-like flights in cold heights. What a good thing he had not always stayed 'at home', stayed 'under his own roof' like a delicate apathetic loafer! He had been *beside* himself: no doubt of that. Only now does he see himself – and what surprises he experiences as he does so! What unprecedented shudders!

What happiness even in the weariness, the old sickness, the relapses of the convalescent! How he loves to sit sadly still, to spin out patience, to lie in the sun! Who understands as he does the happiness that comes in winter, the spots of sunlight on the wall! They are the most grateful animals in the world, also the most modest, these convalescents and lizards again half turned towards life: – there are some among them who allow no day to pass without hanging a little song of praise on the hem of its departing robe. And, to speak seriously: to become sick in the manner of these free spirits, to remain sick for a long time and then, slowly, slowly, to become healthy, by which I mean 'healthier', is a fundamental *cure* for all pessimism (the cancerous sore and inveterate vice, as is well known, of old idealists and inveterate liars). There is wisdom, practical wisdom, in for a long time prescribing even health for oneself only in small doses. –

6

At that time it may finally happen that, under the sudden illumination of a still stressful, still changeable health, the free, ever freer spirit begins to unveil the riddle of that great liberation which had until then waited dark, questionable, almost untouchable in his memory. If he has for long hardly dared to ask himself: 'why so apart? so alone? renouncing everything I once reverenced? renouncing reverence itself? why this hardness, this suspiciousness, this hatred for your own virtues?' – now he dares to ask it aloud and hears in reply something like an answer. 'You shall become master over yourself, master also over your virtues. Formerly *they* were your masters; but they must be only your instruments beside other instruments. You shall get control over your For and Against and learn how to display first one and then the other in accordance with your higher goal. You shall learn to grasp the sense of perspective in every value judgement – the displacement, distortion and merely apparent teleology of horizons and whatever else pertains to perspectivism; also the quantum of stupidity that resides in antitheses of values and the whole intellectual loss which every For, every Against costs us. You shall learn to grasp the *necessary* injustice in every For and Against, injustice as inseparable from life, life itself as *conditioned* by the sense of perspective and its injustice. You shall above all see with your own eyes where injustice is always at its greatest: where life has developed at its smallest, narrowest, neediest, most incipient and yet cannot avoid taking *itself* as the goal and measure of things and for the sake of its own preservation secretly and meanly and ceaselessly crumbling away and calling into question the higher, greater, richer – you shall see with your own eyes the problem of *order of rank*, and how power and right and spaciousness of perspective grow into the heights together. You shall' – enough: from now on the free spirit *knows* what 'you shall' he has obeyed, and he also knows what he now *can*, what only now he – *may* do . . .

7

This is how the free spirit elucidates to himself that enigma of liberation, and inasmuch as he generalizes his own case ends by adjudicating on what he has experienced thus. 'What has happened to me', he says to himself, 'must happen to everyone in whom a *task* wants to become incarnate and "come into the world".' The secret force and necessity of this task will rule among and in the individual facets of his destiny like an unconscious pregnancy – long before he has caught sight of this task itself or knows its name. Our vocation commands and disposes of us even when we do not yet know it; it is the future that regulates our today. Given it is *the problem of order of rank* of which we may say it is *our* problem, we free spirits: it is only now, at the midday of our life, that we understand what preparations, bypaths, experiments, temptations, disguises the problem had need of before it was *allowed* to rise up before us, and how we first had to experience the most manifold and contradictory states of joy and distress in soul and body, as adventurers and circumnavigators of that inner world called 'man', as surveyors and guagers of that 'higher' and 'one upon the other' that is likewise called 'man' – penetrating everywhere, almost without fear, disdaining nothing, losing nothing, asking everything, cleansing everything of what is chance and accident in it and as it were thoroughly sifting it – until at last we had the right to say, we free spirits: 'Here – a *new* problem! Here a long ladder upon whose rungs we ourselves have sat and climbed – which we ourselves have at some time *been*! Here a higher, a deeper, a beneath-us, a tremendous long ordering, an order of rank, which we *see:* here – *our* problem!' – –

8

– No psychologist or reader of signs will have a moment's difficulty in recognizing to what stage in the evolution just described the present book belongs (or has been *placed* –). But where today are there psychologists? In France, certainly; perhaps in Russia; definitely not in Germany. There is no lack of reasons as to why the Germans of today could even regard this fact as redounding to their honour: an ill fate for one who in this matter is by nature and attainment un-German! This *German* book, which has known how to find its readers in a wide circle of lands and peoples – it has been on its way for about ten years – and must be capable of some kind of music and flute-player's art by which even coy foreign ears are seduced to listen – it is precisely in Germany that this book has been read most carelessly and *heard* the worst: why is that? – 'It demands too much', has been the reply, 'it addresses itself to people who are not oppressed by uncouth duties, it wants refined and experienced senses, it needs superfluity, superfluity of time, of clarity in heart and sky, of *otium** in the most audacious sense: – all of them good things that we Ger-

---

* *otium:* leisure, idleness; in Catullus' usage, it denotes a vice or condition of *ennui*.

mans of today do not have and therefore also cannot give'. – After so courteous a reply my philosophy advises me to keep silent and to ask no more questions; especially as in certain cases, as the saying has it, one *remains* a philosopher only by – keeping silent.

Nice
Spring 1886

1

OF FIRST
AND
LAST THINGS

1

Chemistry of concepts and sensations. – Almost all the problems of philosophy once again pose the same form of question as they did two thousand years ago: how can something originate in its opposite, for example rationality in irrationality, the sentient in the dead, logic in unlogic, disinterested contemplation in covetous desire, living for others in egoism, truth in error? Metaphysical philosophy has hitherto surmounted this difficulty by denying that the one originates in the other and assuming for the more highly valued thing a miraculous source in the very kernel and being of the 'thing in itself'.* Historical philosophy, on the other hand, which can no longer be separated from natural science, the youngest of all philosophical methods, has discovered in individual cases (and this will probably be the result in every case) that there are no opposites, except in the customary exaggeration of popular or metaphysical interpretations, and that a mistake in reasoning lies at the bottom of this antithesis: according to this explanation there exists, strictly speaking, neither an unegoistic action nor completely disinterested contemplation; both are only sublimations, in which the basic element seems almost to have dispersed and reveals itself only under the most painstaking observation. All we require, and what can be given us only now the individual sciences have attained their present level, is a *chemistry* of the moral, religious and aesthetic conceptions and sensations, likewise of all the agitations we experience within ourselves in cultural and social intercourse, and indeed even when we are alone: what if this chemistry would end up by revealing that in this domain too the most glorious colours are derived from base, indeed from despised materials? Will there be many who desire to pursue such researches? Mankind likes to put questions of origins and beginnings out of its mind: must one not be almost inhuman to detect in oneself a contrary inclination? –

2

Family failing of philosophers. – All philosophers have the common failing of starting out from man as he is now and thinking they can reach their goal through an analysis of him. They involuntarily think of 'man' as an *aeterna veritas*,† as something that remains constant in the midst of all flux, as a sure measure of things. Everything the philosopher has

---

* thing-in-itself: Kant's term for objects as they are independently of our knowledge of them, contrasted (see section 10) with 'appearances', objects considered as conforming to our modes of knowing them
† *aeterna veritas*: something everlastingly true

declared about man is, however, at bottom no more than a testimony as to the man of a *very limited* period of time. Lack of historical sense is the family failing of all philosophers; many, without being aware of it, even take the most recent manifestation of man, such as has arisen under the impress of certain religions, even certain political events, as the fixed form from which one has to start out. They will not learn that man has become, that the faculty of cognition has become; while some of them would have it that the whole world is spun out of this faculty of cognition. Now, everything *essential* in the development of mankind took place in primeval times, long before the four thousand years we more or less know about; during these years mankind may well not have altered very much. But the philosopher here sees 'instincts' in man as he now is and assumes that these belong to the unalterable facts of mankind and to that extent could provide a key to the understanding of the world in general: the whole of teleology is constructed by speaking of the man of the last four millennia as of an *eternal* man towards whom all things in the world have had a natural relationship from the time he began. But everything has become: there are *no eternal facts*, just as there are no absolute truths. Consequently what is needed from now on is *historical philosophizing*, and with it the virtue of modesty.

3
Estimation of unpretentious truths. – It is the mark of a higher culture to value the little unpretentious truths which have been discovered by means of rigorous method more highly than the errors handed down by metaphysical and artistic ages and men, which blind us and make us happy. At first the former are regarded with scorn, as though the two things could not possibly be accorded equal rights: they stand there so modest, simple, sober, so apparently discouraging, while the latter are so fair, splendid, intoxicating, perhaps indeed enrapturing. Yet that which has been attained by laborious struggle, the certain, enduring and thus of significance for any further development of knowledge is nonetheless the higher; to adhere to it is manly and demonstrates courage, simplicity and abstemiousness. Gradually not only the individual but all mankind will be raised to this manliness, when they have finally become accustomed to valuing viable, enduring knowledge more highly and lost all faith in inspiration and the acquisition of knowledge by miraculous means. – Worshippers of *form*, with their standards of the beautiful and sublime, will, to be sure, at first have good ground for mockery once estimation of unpretentious truths and the scientific spirit begins to dominate: but only because either their eye has not yet discovered the charm of the *simplest* form or because those raised in that spirit are as yet very far from being thoroughly permeated by it, so that they still thoughtlessly imitate old forms (and do so badly, as does everyone to whom a thing no longer matters very much). Formerly the spirit was not engaged in rigorous thinking, its serious occupation was the spinning out of forms and symbols. That has now changed; serious occupation with the symbolic

has become a mark of a lower culture. As our arts themselves grow ever more intellectual, our senses more spiritual, and as for example we now adjudge what is pleasant sounding quite differently from the way we did a hundred years ago: so the forms of our life will grow ever more *spiritual,* perhaps to the eye of earlier ages *uglier,* but only because it is incapable of seeing how the realm of inner, spiritual beauty is continually growing deeper and wider, and to what extent we may all now accord the eye of insight greater value than the fairest structure or the sublimest edifice.

4

Astrology and what is related to it. – It is probable that the objects of the religious, moral and aesthetic sensations belong only to the surface of things, while man likes to believe that here at least he is in touch with the world's heart; the reason he deludes himself is that these things produce in him such profound happiness and unhappiness, and thus he exhibits here the same pride as in the case of astrology. For astrology believes the starry firmament revolves around the fate of man; the moral man, however, supposes that what he has essentially at heart must also constitute the essence and heart of things.

5

Misunderstanding of the dream. – The man of the ages of barbarous primordial culture believed that in the dream he was getting to know a *second real world:* here is the origin of all metaphysics. Without the dream one would have had no occasion to divide the world into two. The dissection into soul and body is also connected with the oldest idea of the dream, likewise the postulation of a life of the soul,* thus the origin of all belief in spirits, and probably also of the belief in gods. 'The dead live on, *for* they appear to the living in dreams': that was the conclusion one formerly drew, throughout many millennia.

6

The spirit of science rules its parts, not the whole. – The separate *smallest* regions of science are treated purely objectively: the great universal sciences, on the other hand, viewed as a whole pose the question – a very unobjective question, to be sure – to what end? of what utility? On account of this regard for utility they are as a whole treated less impersonally than they are in their parts. And when it comes to philosophy, the summit of the entire scientific pyramid, we find the question as to the utility of knowledge as such involuntarily raised, and the unconscious intention of every philosophy is to ascribe to it the *highest* utility. That is why there is in all philosophies so much high-flying metaphysics and such a dread of the explanations offered by physics, which seem so modest and insignificant; for the significance of knowledge for life *has* to appear as great as it possibly can. Here lies the antagonism between the individual regions of science and philosophy. The latter wants, as art does, to bestow on life and action the greatest possible profundity and signifi-

---

* life of the soul: *Seelenscheinleib,* Nietzsche's coinage

cance; in the former one seeks knowledge and nothing further – and does in fact acquire it. There has hitherto been no philosopher in whose hands philosophy has not become an apologia for knowledge; on this point at least each of them is an optimist, inasmuch as he believes that knowledge must be in the highest degree useful. They are all tyrannized over by logic: and logic is by its nature optimism.

7

The mischief-maker in science. – Philosophy separated itself from science when it posed the question: what kind of knowledge of the world and life is it through which man can live happiest? This took place in the Socratic schools: by having in view the objective of happiness one applied a ligature to the arteries of scientific research – and does so still today.

8

Pneumatological elucidation of nature. – Metaphysics elucidates the handwriting of nature as it were *pneumatologically,** as the church and its scholars formerly did the Bible. It requires a great deal of understanding to apply to nature the same kind of rigorous art of elucidation that philologists have now fashioned for all books: with the intention of comprehending what the text intends to say but without sensing, indeed presupposing, a *second* meaning. But as even with regard to books the bad art of elucidation has by no means been entirely overcome and one still continually encounters in the best educated circles remnants of allegorical and mystical interpretations: so it is also in respect to nature – where, indeed, it is even far worse.

9

Metaphysical world. – It is true, there could be a metaphysical world; the absolute possibility of it is hardly to be disputed. We behold all things through the human head and cannot cut off this head; while the question nonetheless remains what of the world would still be there if one had cut it off. This is a purely scientific problem and one not very well calculated to bother people overmuch; but all that has hitherto made metaphysical assumptions *valuable, terrible, delightful* to them, all that has begotten these assumptions, is passion, error and self-deception; the worst of all methods of acquiring knowledge, not the best of all, have taught belief in them. When one has disclosed these methods as the foundation of all extant religions and metaphysical systems, one has refuted them! Then that possibility still remains over; but one can do absolutely nothing with it, not to speak of letting happiness, salvation and life depend on the gossamer of such a possibility. – For one could assert nothing at all of the metaphysical world except that it was a being-other, an inaccessible, incomprehensible being-other; it would be a thing with negative qualities. – Even if the existence of such a world were never so well demonstrated, it is certain that knowledge of it would be the most useless of all

---

* *pneumatologically*: pneumatology is the 'science' of spirits and spiritual beings

15

knowledge: more useless even than knowledge of the chemical composition of water must be to the sailor in danger of shipwreck.

10

Future innocuousness of metaphysics. – As soon as the origin of religion, art and morality is so described that it can be perfectly understood without the postulation of *metaphysical interference* at the commencement or in the course of their progress, the greater part of our interest in the purely theoretical problem of the 'thing in itself' and 'appearance' ceases to exist. For with religion, art and morality we do not touch upon the 'nature of the world in itself'; we are in the realm of ideas, no 'intuition' can take us any further. The question of how our conception of the world could differ so widely from the disclosed nature of the world will with perfect equanimity be relinquished to the physiology and history of the evolution of organisms and concepts.

11

Language as putative science. – The significance of language for the evolution of culture lies in this, that mankind set up in language a separate world beside the other world, a place it took to be so firmly set that, standing upon it, it could lift the rest of the world off its hinges and make itself master of it. To the extent that man has for long ages believed in the concepts and names of things as in *aeternae veritates* he has appropriated to himself that pride by which he raised himself above the animal: he really thought that in language he possessed knowledge of the world. The sculptor of language was not so modest as to believe that he was only giving things designations, he conceived rather that with words he was expressing supreme knowledge of things; language is, in fact, the first stage of the occupation with science. Here, too, it is the *belief that the truth has been found* out of which the mightiest sources of energy have flowed. A great deal later – only now – it dawns on men that in their belief in language they have propagated a tremendous error.* Happily, it is too late for the evolution of reason, which depends on this belief, to be again put back. – *Logic* too depends on presuppositions with which nothing in the real world corresponds, for example on the presupposition that there are identical things, that the same thing is identical at different points of time: but this science came into existence through the opposite belief (that such conditions do obtain in the real world). It is the same with *mathematics*, which would certainly not have come into existence if one had known from the beginning that there was in nature no exactly straight line, no real circle, no absolute magnitude.

12

Dream and culture. – The function of the brain that sleep encroaches upon most is the memory: not that it ceases altogether – but it is reduced to a condition of imperfection such as in the primeval ages of mankind may have been normal by day and in waking. Confused and capricious as it is,

---

* Nietzsche had described this error in detail in *Truth and Falsehood in the Extra-Moral Sense* (1873).

it continually confuses one thing with another on the basis of the most fleeting similarities: but it was with the same confusion and capriciousness that the peoples composed their mythologies, and even today travellers observe how much the savage is inclined to forgetfulness, how his mind begins to reel and stumble after a brief exertion of the memory and he utters lies and nonsense out of mere enervation. But in dreams we all resemble this savage; failure to recognize correctly and erroneously supposing one thing to be the same as another is the ground of the false conclusions of which we are guilty in dreams; so that, when we clearly recall a dream, we are appalled to discover so much folly in ourselves. – The perfect clarity of all the images we see in dreams which is the precondition of our unquestioning belief in their reality again reminds us of conditions pertaining to earlier mankind, in whom hallucination was extraordinarily common and sometimes seized hold on whole communities, whole peoples at the same time. Thus: in sleep and dreams we repeat once again the curriculum of earlier mankind.*

13
Logic of the dream. – In sleep our nervous system is continually agitated by a multiplicity of inner events, almost all our organs are active, our blood circulates vigorously, the position of the sleeper presses on individual limbs, his bedcovers influence his sensibilities in various ways, his stomach digests and its motions disturb other organs, his intestines are active, the position of his head involves unusual muscular contortions, his feet, unshod and not pressing against the floor, produce an unfamiliar feeling, as does the difference in the way his whole body is clad – all this, through its unusualness and to a differing degree each day, excites the entire system up to the functioning of the brain; and so there are a hundred occasions for the mind to be involved in puzzlement and to look for *grounds* for this excitation: the dream is the *seeking and positing of the causes* of this excitement of the sensibilities, that is to say the supposed causes. If, for example, you tie two straps about your feet you may well dream that your feet are coiled round by snakes: this is first a hypothesis, then a belief, with an accompanying pictorial representation and the supposition: 'these snakes must be the *causa* of those sensations that I, the sleeper, feel' – thus the sleeper's mind judges. The immediate past he has thus inferred becomes through his aroused imagination the present to him. Everyone knows from experience how quickly a dreamer entwines with his dream a sound that strongly impinges upon him from without, the ringing of bells or the firing of cannon, for example; that is to say, he accounts for the sound in terms of the dream, so that he *believes* he experiences the cause of the sound first, then the sound itself. – But how does it come about that the dreamer's mind always blunders like this,

* In *The Interpretation of Dreams*, ch. VII (B), Freud writes: 'We can guess how much to the point is Nietzsche's assertion that in dreams "some primeval relic of humanity is at work which we can now scarcely reach any longer by a direct path"; and we may expect that the analysis of dreams will lead us to a knowledge of man's archaic heritage, of what is psychologically innate in him.'

when the same mind is accustomed to be so sober, cautious and so sceptical with regard to hypotheses while it is awake? – so that the first plausible hypothesis for explaining a sensation that occurs to him is at once accepted as the truth? (For in dreams we believe in the dream as though it were reality, that is to say we regard our hypothesis as completely proved.) – In my opinion, the conclusions man still draws in dreams to the present day for many millennia mankind also drew *when awake*: the first *causa* that entered the mind as an explanation of anything that required explaining satisfied it and was accounted truth. (According to travellers' tales savages still do this today.) In the dream this piece of primeval humanity continues to exercise itself, for it is the basis upon which higher rationality evolved and continues to evolve in every human being: the dream takes us back again to remote stages of human culture and provides us with a means of understanding them better. We now find dream-thinking* so easy because it is in precisely this imaginative and agreeable form of explanation by means of the first plausible idea that strikes us that we have been so well drilled over such enormous periods of human evolution. To this extent the dream is a relaxation for the brain, which has had enough of the strenuous demands in the way of thinking such as are imposed by our higher culture during the day. – A related occurrence which stands as portal and entrance-hall of the dream can actually be observed in full wakefulness. If we close our eyes, the brain produces a host of light-impressions and colours, probably as a kind of after-play and echo of those effects of light which crowd in upon it during the day. Now, however, the reason (in alliance with the imagination) at once assembles these in themselves formless colour-impressions into definite figures, shapes, landscapes, moving groups. What is actually occurring is again a kind of inferring of the cause from the effect; the mind asks where these light-impressions and colours come from and supposes these shapes and figures are their causes: it regards them as occasioning these lights and colours because, by day and with eyes open, it is accustomed to finding that every colour, every light-impression does in fact have a cause that occasions it. Here, then, the imagination is continually providing the mind with images borrowed from the sight-impressions of the day, and this is precisely the way in which it fashions the dream-fantasy: – that is to say, the supposed cause is inferred from the effect and introduced *after* the effect: and all with extraordinary rapidity, so that, as with a conjurer, a confusion of judgement can here arise and successive events appear as simultaneous events or even with the order of their occurrence reversed. – These facts show us *how late* more rigorous logical thinking, a clear perception of the nature of cause and effect, must have been evolved if our faculties of reason and understanding *even now* involuntarily grasp at those primitive forms of conclusion and inference and we still live about half of our life in this condition. – The poet and the artist, too, *foists upon* his moods and states of mind causes which are cer-

---

* dream-thinking: *Traumdenken*

tainly not the true ones; to this extent he recalls an earlier humanity and can aid us to an understanding of it.

14

Sympathetic resonance. – All *stronger* moods bring with them a sympathetic resonance on the part of related sensations and moods: they as it were root up the memory. Something in us is provoked to recollection and becomes aware of similar states and their origins. Thus there come to be constructed habitual rapid connections between feelings and thoughts which, if they succeed one another with lightning speed, are in the end no longer experienced as complexes but as *unities*. It is in this sense that one speaks of the moral feelings, of the religious feelings, as though these were simple unities: in truth, however, they are rivers with a hundred tributaries and sources. Here too, as so often, the unity of the word is no guarantee of the unity of the thing.

15

No inner and outer in the world. – As Democritus* transferred the concepts Above and Below to infinite space, where they make no sense, so philosophers in general transfer the concept 'inner and outer' to the essence and phenomena of the world; they believe that profound feelings take one deep into the interior, close to the heart of nature. But such feelings are profound only insofar as when they occur certain complex groups of thoughts which we call profound are, scarcely perceptibly, regularly aroused with them; a feeling is profound because we regard the thoughts that accompany it as profound. But a profound thought can nonetheless be very distant from the truth, as, for example, every metaphysical thought is; if one deducts from the profound feeling the element of thought mixed in with it, what remains is the *strong* feeling, and this has nothing to do with knowledge as such, just as strong belief demonstrates only its strength, not the truth of that which is believed.

16

Appearance and thing in itself. – Philosophers are accustomed to station themselves before life and experience – before that which they call the world of appearance – as before a painting that has been unrolled once and for all and unchangeably depicts the same scene: this scene, they believe, has to be correctly interpreted, so as to draw a conclusion as to the nature of the being that produced the picture: that is to say, as to the nature of the thing in itself, which it is customary to regard as the sufficient reason† for the existence of the world of appearance. As against this, more rigorous logicians, having clearly identified the concept of the metaphysical as that of the unconditioned, consequently also unconditioning, have disputed any connection between the unconditioned (the metaphysical world) and the world we know: so that what appears in

* Democritus (c. 460 to c. 370 BC): Greek philosopher, one of the latest of the so-called 'pre-Socratic' philosophers

† The principle of sufficient reason's various formulations include 'every existent has a ground' and 'every event has a cause'; Schopenhauer discussed the history and justification of the principle in *The Fourfold Root of the Principle of Sufficient Reason* (1813).

appearance is precisely *not* the thing in itself, and no conclusion can be drawn from the former as to the nature of the latter. Both parties, however, overlook the possibility that this painting – that which we humans call life and experience – has gradually *become*, is indeed still fully in course of *becoming*, and should thus not be regarded as a fixed object on the basis of which a conclusion as to the nature of its originator (the sufficient reason) may either be drawn or pronounced undrawable. Because we have for millennia made moral, aesthetic, religious demands on the world, looked upon it with blind desire, passion or fear, and abandoned ourselves to the bad habits of illogical thinking, this world has gradually *become* so marvellously variegated, frightful, meaningful, soulful, it has acquired colour – but we have been the colourists: it is the human intellect that has made appearance appear and transported its erroneous basic conceptions into things. Late, very late – it has reflected on all this: and now the world of experience and the thing in itself seem to it so extraordinarily different from one another and divided apart that it rejects the idea that the nature of one can be inferred from the nature of the other – or invites us in a chillingly mysterious fashion to *abandon* our intellect, our personal will: so as to attain to the real by *becoming real* oneself. Others again have assembled all the characteristic traits of our world of appearance – that is to say, the idea of the world spun out of intellectual errors we have inherited – and, *instead of indicting the intellect as the guilty party*, have charged the essence of things with being the cause of the very uncanny character this world in fact possesses and have preached redemption from being. – With all these conceptions the steady and laborious process of science, which will one day celebrate its greatest triumph in a *history of the genesis of thought*, will in the end decisively have done; for the outcome of this history may well be the conclusion: That which we now call the world is the outcome of a host of errors and fantasies which have gradually arisen and grown entwined with one another in the course of the overall evolution of the organic being, and are now inherited by us as the accumulated treasure of the entire past – as treasure: for the value of our humanity depends upon it. Rigorous science is capable of detaching us from this ideational world only to a limited extent – and more is certainly not to be desired – inasmuch as it is incapable of making any essential inroad into the power of habits of feeling acquired in primeval times: but it can, quite gradually and step by step, illuminate the history of the genesis of this world as idea – and, for brief periods at any rate, lift us up out of the entire proceeding. Perhaps we shall then recognize that the thing in itself is worthy of Homeric laughter: that it appeared to be so much, indeed everything, and is actually empty, that is to say empty of significance.

17

Metaphysical explanations. – The young person values metaphysical explanations because they reveal to him something in the highest degree significant in things he found unpleasant or contemptible; and if he is

discontented with himself this feeling is alleviated when he comes to recognize the innermost enigma or misery of the universe in that which he
so much condemns in himself. To feel more irresponsible and at the same
time to find things more interesting – that is the twofold benefit for which
he believes he has metaphysics to thank. Later on, to be sure, he acquires
mistrust of the whole metaphysical mode of explanation; then perhaps
he sees that the effects he has experienced are to be attained equally well
and more scientifically by another route: that physical and historical explanations produce that feeling of irresponsibility at least as well, and
that interest in life and its problems is perhaps enflamed even more by
them.

18

Fundamental questions of metaphysics. – When one day the history of the
genesis of thought comes to be written, the following sentence by a distinguished logician will also stand revealed in a new light: 'The primary
universal law of the knowing subject consists in the inner necessity of
recognizing every object in itself as being in its own essence something
identical with itself, thus self-existent and at bottom always the same and
unchanging, in short as a substance'. This law, too, which is here called
'primary', evolved: one day it will be shown how gradually, in the lower
organisms, this tendency comes into being: how the purblind mole's eyes
of this organization at first never see anything but the same thing; how
then, when the various pleasurable and unpleasurable stimuli become
more noticeable, various different substances are gradually distinguished, but each of them with one attribute, that is to say a single relationship with such an organism. – The first stage of the logical is the
judgement: and the essence of the judgement consists, according to the
best logicians, in belief. At the bottom of all belief there lies the *sensation of
the pleasurable or painful* in respect to the subject experiencing the sensation. A new, third sensation as a product of two preceding single sensations is the judgement in its lowest form. – In our primary condition, all
that interests us organic beings in any thing is its relationship to us in
respect of pleasure and pain. Between the moments in which we become
conscious of this relationship, the states of awareness of sensation, lie
those of repose, of non-sensation: then the world and every thing is
devoid of interest to us, we notice no alteration in it (just as now anyone
absorbed with interest in something will still not notice someone walking
by him). To the plants all things are usually in repose, eternal, every
thing identical with itself. It is from the period of the lower organisms
that man has inherited the belief that there are *identical things* (only
knowledge educated in the highest scientificality contradicts this proposition). It may even be that the original belief of everything organic was
from the very beginning that all the rest of the world is one and unmov-
ing. – What lies farthest from this primeval stage of the logical is the
notion of *causality*: even now, indeed, we believe at bottom that all sensations and actions are acts of free will; when the sentient individuum

observes itself, it regards every sensation, every change, as something *isolated*, that is to say unconditioned, disconnected: it emerges out of us independently of anything earlier or later. We are hungry, but originally we do not think that the organism wants to sustain itself; this feeling seems to be asserting itself *without cause or purpose*, it isolates itself and considers itself *willful*. Thus: belief in freedom of will is a primary error committed by everything organic, as old as the impulse to the logical itself; belief in unconditioned substances and in identical things is likewise a primary, ancient error committed by everything organic. Insofar, however, as all metaphysics has had principally to do with substance and freedom of will, one may designate it the science that treats of the fundamental errors of mankind – but does so as though they were fundamental truths.

19

Number. – The invention of the laws of numbers was made on the basis of the error, dominant even from the earliest times, that there are identical things (but in fact nothing is identical with anything else); at least that there are things (but there is no 'thing'). The assumption of plurality always presupposes the existence of *something* that occurs more than once: but precisely here error already holds sway, here already we are fabricating beings, unities which do not exist. – Our sensations of space and time are false, for tested consistently they lead to logical contradictions. The establishment of conclusions in science always unavoidably involves us in calculating with certain false magnitudes: but because these magnitudes are at least *constant*, as for example are our sensations of time and space, the conclusions of science acquire a complete rigorousness and certainty in their coherence with one another; one can build on them – up to that final stage at which our erroneous basic assumptions, those constant errors, come to be incompatible with our conclusions, for example in the theory of atoms. Here we continue to feel ourselves compelled to assume the existence of a 'thing' or material 'substratum' which is moved, while the whole procedure of science has pursued the task of resolving everything thing-like (material) in motions: here too our sensations divide that which moves from that which is moved, and we cannot get out of this circle because our belief in the existence of things has been tied up with our being from time immemorial. – When Kant says 'the understanding does not draw its laws from nature, it prescribes them to nature', this is wholly true with regard to the *concept of nature* which we are obliged to attach to nature (nature = world as idea, that is as error), but which is the summation of a host of errors of the understanding. – To a world which is *not* our idea the laws of numbers are wholly inapplicable: these are valid only in the human world.

20

A few steps back. – One, certainly very high level of culture has been attained when a man emerges from superstitious and religious concepts and fears and no longer believes in angels, for example, or in original sin, and has ceased to speak of the salvation of souls: if he is at this level of liberation he now has, with the greatest exertion of mind, to overcome metaphysics. *Then*, however, he needs to take a *retrograde step*: he has to grasp the historical justification that resides in such ideas, likewise the psychological; he has to recognize that they have been most responsible for the advancement of mankind and that without such a retrograde step he will deprive himself of the best that mankind has hitherto produced. – In regard to philosophical metaphysics, I see more and more who are making for the negative goal (that all positive metaphysics is an error), but still few who are taking a few steps back; for one may well want to look out over the topmost rung of the ladder, but one ought not to want to stand on it. The most enlightened get only as far as liberating themselves from metaphysics and looking back on it from above: whereas here too, as in the hippodrome, at the end of the track it is necessary to turn the corner.

21

Probable victory of scepticism. – Let us for once accept the validity of the sceptical point of departure: if there were no other, metaphysical world and all explanations of the only world known to us drawn from metaphysics were useless to us, in what light would we then regard men and things? This question can be thought through, and it is valuable to do so, even if we do for once ignore the question whether the existence of anything metaphysical has been scientifically demonstrated by Kant and Schopenhauer. For the historical probability is that one day mankind will very possibly become in general and on the whole *sceptical* in this matter; thus the question becomes: what shape will human society then assume under the influence of such an attitude of mind? Perhaps the *scientific demonstration* of the existence of any kind of metaphysical world is already so *difficult* that mankind will never again be free of a mistrust of it. And if one has a mistrust of metaphysics the results are by and large the same as if it had been directly refuted and one no longer had the *right* to believe in it. The historical question in regard to an unmetaphysical attitude of mind on the part of mankind remains the same in both cases.

22

Disbelief in the 'monumentum aere perennius'. * – An essential disadvantage which the cessation of the metaphysical outlook brings with it lies in the fact that the attention of the individual is too firmly fixed on his own brief span of life and receives no stronger impulse to work at the construction of enduring institutions intended to last for centuries; he wants to pluck the fruit himself from the tree he plants, and he is therefore no longer interested in planting those trees which demand constant tending for a century and are intended to provide shade for long successions of generations. For the metaphysical outlook bestows the belief that it offers the last, ultimate foundation upon which the whole future of mankind is then invited to establish and construct itself; the individual is promoting

* *'monumentum aere perennius'*: a memorial longer lasting than bronze (Horace)

his salvation when, for example, he founds a church or a convent, he thinks it will be accounted to his credit and rewarded in the eternal future life of his soul, it is a contribution to the eternal salvation of the soul. – Can science, too, awaken such faith in its conclusions? The fact is that science needs doubt and distrust for its closest allies; nonetheless, the sum of unimpeachable truths – truths, that is, which have survived all the assaults of scepticism and disintegration – can in time become so great (in the dietetics of health, for example) that on the basis of them one may resolve to embark on 'everlasting' works. In the meanwhile, the *contrast* between our agitated ephemeral existence and the slow-breathing repose of metaphysical ages is still too strong, because the two ages are still too close together; the individual human being himself now runs through far too many inner and outer evolutions for him to venture to establish himself securely and once and for all even for so short a span as his own lifetime. A completely modern man who wants, for example, to build himself a house has at the same time the feeling he is proposing to immure himself alive in a mausoleum.

23

Age of comparison. – The less men are bound by tradition, the greater is the fermentation of motivations within them, and the greater in consequence their outward restlessness, their mingling together with one another, the polyphony of their endeavours. Who is there who now still feels a strong compulsion to attach himself and his posterity to a particular place? Who is there who still feels any strong attachment at all? Just as in the arts all the genres are imitated side by side, so are all the stages and genres of morality, custom, culture. – Such an age acquires its significance through the fact that in it the various different philosophies of life, customs, cultures can be compared and experienced side by side; which in earlier ages, when, just as all artistic genres were attached to a particular place and time, so every culture still enjoyed only a localized domination, was not possible. Now an enhanced aesthetic sensibility will come to a definitive decision between all these forms offering themselves for comparison: most of them – namely all those rejected by this sensibility – it will allow to die out. There is likewise now taking place a selecting out among the forms and customs of higher morality whose objective can only be the elimination of the lower moralities. This is the age of comparison! It is the source of its pride – but, as is only reasonable, also of its suffering. Let us not be afraid of this suffering! Let us rather confront the task which the age sets us as boldly as we can: and then posterity will bless us for it – a posterity that will know itself to be as much beyond the self-enclosed original national cultures as it is beyond the culture of comparison, but will look back upon both species of culture as upon venerable antiquities.

24

Possibility of progress. – When a scholar of the old culture swears to have nothing more to do with people who believe in progress he is right. For the old culture has its goods and greatness behind it and history compels one to admit that it can never be fresh again; one needs to be intolerably stupid or fanatical to deny this. But men are capable of *consciously* resolving to evolve themselves to a new culture, whereas formerly they did so unconsciously and fortuitously: they can now create better conditions for the propagation of men and for their nutrition, education and instruction, manage the earth as a whole economically, balance and employ the powers of men in general. This new, conscious culture destroys the old, which viewed as a whole has led an unconscious animal- and plant-life; it also destroys mistrust of progress – it is *possible*. It would, of course, be rash and almost nonsensical to believe that progress must *necessarily* follow; but how could it be denied that progress is possible? On the other hand, progress in the sense and along the paths of the old culture is not even thinkable. If romantic fantasizings still do designate their goals (e.g. self-contained original national cultures) as 'progress', they nonetheless borrow their image of it from the past: in this domain their thinking and imagining lacks all originality.

25
Private and public morality. – Since the belief has ceased that a God broadly directs the destinies of the world and that, all the apparent twists and turns in its path notwithstanding, is leading mankind gloriously upward, man has to set himself ecumenical goals embracing the whole earth. The former morality, namely Kant's, demanded of the individual actions which one desired of all men: that was a very naive thing; as if everyone knew without further ado what mode of action would benefit the whole of mankind, that is, what actions at all are desirable; it is a theory like that of free trade, presupposing that universal harmony *must* result of itself in accordance with innate laws of progress. Perhaps some future survey of the requirements of mankind will show that it is absolutely not desirable that all men should act in the same way, but rather that in the interest of ecumenical goals whole tracts of mankind ought to have special, perhaps under certain circumstances even evil tasks imposed upon them. – In any event, if mankind is not to destroy itself through such conscious universal rule, it must first of all attain to a hitherto altogether unprecedented *knowledge of the preconditions of culture* as a scientific standard for ecumenical goals. Herein lies the tremendous task facing the great spirits of the coming century.

26
Reaction as progress. – Sometimes there appear blunt and forceful spirits capable of exciting great enthusiasm whose development is nonetheless retarded, so that they conjure up again an earlier phase of mankind: they serve to prove that the modern tendencies against which they act are not yet strong enough, that there is something lacking in them: otherwise the latter would be able to offer better resistance to these conjurers. Thus Luther's Reformation, for example, witnesses that in his century all the impulses to freedom of spirit were still uncertain, tender and youthful; science was as yet unable to raise its head. The whole Renaissance,

indeed, seems like an early spring almost snowed away again. But in our century, too, Schopenhauer's metaphysics demonstrates that even now the scientific spirit is not yet sufficiently strong: so that, although all the dogmas of Christianity have long since been demolished, the whole medieval Christian conception of the world and of the nature of man could in Schopenhauer's teaching celebrate a resurrection. Much science resounds in his teaching, but what dominates it is not science but the old familiar 'metaphysical need'. One of the greatest, indeed quite invaluable advantages we derive from Schopenhauer is that through him our sensibilities are for a time compelled to return to older ways of contemplating the world and mankind that once held sway which we would otherwise have no easy access to. The gain for historical justice is very great: I believe that no one would find it easy to do justice to Christianity and its Asiatic relations without Schopenhauer's assistance: on the basis of present-day Christianity alone it would be quite impossible. Only after this great *triumph of justice*, only after we have corrected the mode of historical interpretation introduced by the Age of Enlightenment on so essential a point as this, may we bear the banner of the Enlightenment – the banner bearing the three names Petrach,* Erasmus,† Voltaire – further onward. Out of reaction we have created progress.

27

Substitute for religion. – One believes one is commending a philosophy when one presents it as a popular substitute for religion. The economy of the spirit does indeed occasionally require transitional orders of ideas; thus the passage from religion to a scientific mode of thought is a violent and perilous leap, something to be advised against. To that extent this recommendation of a philosophy is justified. But in the end one also has to understand that the needs which religion has satisfied and philosophy is now supposed to satisfy are not immutable; they can be *weakened* and *exterminated.* Consider, for example, that Christian distress of mind that comes from sighing over one's inner depravity and care for one's salvation – all conceptions originating in nothing but errors of reason and deserving, not satisfaction, but obliteration. A philosophy can be employed either to *satisfy* such needs or to *set them aside;* for they are acquired, time-bound needs resting on presuppositions that contradict those of science. To effect a transition here, to relieve the heart overladen with feeling, it is much more useful to employ *art;* for those conceptions we have spoken of will be nourished far less by art than they will be by a metaphysical philosophy. From art it will then be easier to go over to a truly liberating philosophical science.

28

Words in bad odour. – Away with those overused words optimism and pessimism! We have had enough of them. Occasion for using them is growing less day by day; it is only idle chatterers who still have such an

---

* Petrach: Francesco Petrach (1304–74): Italian poet and scholar
† Erasmus: Desiderius Erasmus (1466–1536): Dutch humanist

indispensable need of them. For why in the world should anyone want to be an optimist if he does not have to defend a God who *has* to have created the best of worlds if he himself is goodness and perfection – but what thinker still has need of the hypothesis of a God? – But any occasion for a pessimistic creed is likewise lacking, unless one has an interest in provoking the advocates of God, the theologians or the theologizing philosophers, and forcefully asserting the opposite point of view: that evil reigns, that there exists more pain than pleasure, that the world is an artifice, the apparition of an evil will to live. But who still bothers about theologians – except other theologians? – Disregarding theology and opposition to theology, it is quite obvious that the world is neither good nor evil, let alone the best of all or the worst of all worlds, and that these concepts 'good' and 'evil' possess meaning only when applied to men, and perhaps even here are, as they are usually employed, unjustified: in any event, we must cast off both that conception of the world that inveighs against it and that which glorifies it.

29
Drunk with the odour of blossoms. – The ship of mankind has, one believes, a deeper and deeper draught the more heavily it is laden; one believes that the more profoundly a man thinks, the more tenderly he feels, the more highly he rates himself, the greater the distance grows between him and the other animals – the more he appears as the genius among animals – the closer he will get to the true nature of the world and to a knowledge of it: this he does in fact do through science, but he *thinks* he does so even more through his arts and religions. These are, to be sure, a blossom of the world, but they are certainly not *closer to the roots of the world* than the stem is: they provide us with no better understanding of the nature of things at all, although almost everyone believes they do. It is *error* that has made mankind so profound, tender, inventive as to produce such a flower as the arts and religions. Pure knowledge would have been incapable of it. Anyone who unveiled to us the nature of the world would produce for all of us the most unpleasant disappointment. It is not the world as thing in itself, it is the world as idea (as error) that is so full of significance, profound, marvellous, and bearing in its womb all happiness and unhappiness. This consequence leads to a philosophy of *logical world-denial*: which can, however, be united with a practical world-affirmation just as easily as with its opposite.

30
Bad habits in drawing conclusions. – The commonest erroneous conclusions drawn by mankind are these: a thing exists, therefore it has a right to. Here the conclusion is from the capacity to live to the fitness to live, from the fitness to live to the right to live. Then: an opinion makes happy, therefore it is a true opinion, its effect is good, therefore it itself is good and true. Here the effect is accorded the predicate beneficent, good, in the sense of useful, and then the cause is furnished with the same predicate good, but here in the sense of the logically valid. The reverse of these

propositions is: a thing cannot prevail, preserve itself, therefore it is wrong; an opinion causes pain and agitation, therefore it is false. The free spirit, who is all too often acquainted with the erroneousness of this kind of reasoning and has to suffer from its consequences, often succumbs to the temptation to draw the opposite conclusions, which are of course in general equally erroneous: a thing cannot prevail, therefore it is good; an opinion causes pain and distress, therefore it is true.

31

The illogical necessary. – Among the things that can reduce a thinker to despair is the knowledge that the illogical is a necessity for mankind, and that much good proceeds from the illogical. It is implanted so firmly in the passions, in language, in art, in religion, and in general in everything that lends value to life, that one cannot pull it out of these fair things without mortally injuring them. Only very naive people are capable of believing that the nature of man could be transformed into a purely logical one; but if there should be degrees of approximation to this objective, what would not have to be lost if this course were taken! Even the most rational man from time to time needs to recover nature, that is to say his *illogical original relationship with all things.*

32

Injustice necessary. – All judgements as to the value of life have evolved illogically and are therefore unjust. The falsity of human judgement derives firstly from the condition of the material to be judged, namely very incomplete, secondly from the way in which the sum is arrived at on the basis of this material, and thirdly from the fact that every individual piece of this material is in turn the outcome of false knowledge, and is so with absolute necessity. Our experience of another person, for example, no matter how close he stands to us, can never be complete, so that we would have a logical right to a total evaluation of him; all evaluations are premature and are bound to be. Finally, the standard by which we measure, our own being, is not an unalterable magnitude, we are subject to moods and fluctuations, and yet we would have to know ourselves as a fixed standard to be able justly to assess the relation between ourself and anything else whatever. Perhaps it would follow from all this that one ought not to judge at all; if only it were possible to *live* without evaluating, without having aversions and partialities! – for all aversion is dependent on an evaluation, likewise all partiality. A drive to something or away from something divorced from a feeling one is desiring the beneficial or avoiding the harmful, a drive without some kind of knowing evaluation of the worth of its objective, does not exist in man. We are from the very beginning illogical and thus unjust beings *and can recognize this*: this is one of the greatest and most irresolvable discords of existence.

33

Error regarding life necessary to life. – Every belief in the value and dignity of life rests on false thinking; it is possible only through the fact that empathy with the universal life and suffering of mankind is very feebly developed in the individual. Even those rarer men who think beyond themselves at all have an eye, not for this universal life, but for fenced-off portions of it. If one knows how to keep the exceptions principally in view, I mean the greatly gifted and pure of soul, takes their production for the goal of world-evolution and rejoices in the effects they in turn produce, one may believe in the value of life, because then one is *overlooking* all other men: thinking falsely, that is to say. And likewise if, though one does keep in view all mankind, one accords validity only to *one* species of drives, the less egoistical, and justifies them in face of all the others, then again one can hope for something of mankind as a whole and to this extent believe in the value of life: thus, in this case too, through falsity of thinking. Whichever of these attitudes one adopts, however, one is by adopting it an *exception* among men. The great majority endure life without complaining overmuch; they *believe* in the value of existence, but they do so precisely because each of them exists for himself alone, refusing to step out of himself as those exceptions do: everything outside themselves they notice not at all or at most as a dim shadow. Thus for the ordinary, everyday man the value of life rests solely on the fact that he regards himself more highly than he does the world. The great lack of imagination from which he suffers means he is unable to feel his way into other beings and thus he participates as little as possible in their fortunes and sufferings. *He,* on the other hand, who really could participate in them would have to despair of the value of life; if he succeeded in encompassing and feeling within himself the total consciousness of mankind he would collapse with a curse on existence – for mankind has as a whole *no* goal, and the individual man when he regards its total course cannot derive from it any support or comfort, but must be reduced to despair. If in all he does he has before him the ultimate goallessness of man, his actions acquire in his own eyes the character of useless squandering. But to feel thus *squandered,* not merely as an individual but as humanity as a whole, in the way we behold the individual fruits of nature squandered, is a feeling beyond all other feelings. – But who is capable of such a feeling? Certainly only a poet: and poets always know how to console themselves.

34
In mitigation. – But will our philosophy not thus become a tragedy? Will truth not become inimical to life, to the better man? A question seems to lie heavily on our tongue and yet refuses to be uttered: whether one *could* consciously reside in untruth? or, if one were *obliged* to, whether death would not be preferable? For there is no longer any 'ought'; for morality, insofar as it was an 'ought', has been just as much annihilated by our mode of thinking as has religion. Knowledge can allow as motives only pleasure and pain, utility and injury: but how will these motives come to terms with the sense for truth? For they too are in contact with errors (insofar as inclination and aversion and their very unjust assessments

are, as we said, the essential determinants of pleasure and pain). The whole of human life is sunk deeply in untruth; the individual cannot draw it up out of this well without thereby growing profoundly disillusioned about his own past, without finding his present motives, such as that of honour, absurd, and pouring mockery and contempt on the passions which reach out to the future and promise happiness in it. Is it true, is all that remains a mode of thought whose outcome on a personal level is despair and on a theoretical level a philosophy of destruction? – I believe that the nature of the after-effect of knowledge is determined by a man's *temperament*: in addition to the after-effect described I could just as easily imagine a different one, quite possible in individual instances, by virtue of which a life could arise much simpler and emotionally cleaner than our present life is: so that, though the old motives of violent desire produced by inherited habit would still possess their strength, they would gradually grow weaker under the influence of purifying knowledge. In the end one would live among men and with oneself as in *nature*, without praising, blaming, contending, gazing contentedly, as though at a spectacle, upon many things for which one formerly felt only fear. One would be free of emphasis, and no longer prodded by the idea that one is only nature or more than nature. For this to happen one would, to be sure, have to possess the requisite temperament, as has already been said: a firm, mild and at bottom cheerful soul, a temper that does not need to be on its guard against malice or sudden outbursts and in whose utterances there is nothing of snarling and sullenness – those familiar tedious qualities of old dogs and men who have long been kept on the leash. A man from whom the ordinary fetters of life have fallen to such an extent that he continues to live only so as to know better must, rather, without envy or vexation be able to forgo much, indeed almost everything upon which other men place value; that free, fearless hovering over men, customs, laws and the traditional evaluations of things must *suffice* him as the condition he considers most desirable. He is happy to communicate his joy in this condition, and he *has*, perhaps, nothing else to communicate – which involves, to be sure, one more privation and renunciation. If more is nonetheless desired of him, he will, with a benevolent shake of the head, point to his brother, the free man of action, and perhaps not conceal a certain mockery in doing so: for of his 'freedom' there is a curious tale still to be told.

2

ON THE HISTORY
OF THE
MORAL SENSATIONS

35

Advantages of psychological observation. – That reflection on the human, all too human – or, as the learned expression has it: psychological observation – is among the expedients by means of which one can alleviate the burden of living, that practice in this art lends presence of mind in difficult situations and entertainment in tedious circumstances, that one can, indeed, pluck useful maxims from the thorniest and most disagreeable stretches of one's own life and thereby feel a little better: that was believed, that was known – in former centuries. Why has it been forgotten by this century, in which, at least in Germany, indeed in all Europe, poverty in psychological observation is apparent through a hundred signs? Not especially in novels, novellas or philosophical writings – these are the work of exceptional men; it is already more evident, however, in assessments made of public events and personalities: but the art of psychological dissection and computation is lacking above all in the social life of all classes, in which, while there may be much talk about people, there is none at all about *man*. But why is the richest and most inoffensive material for conversation neglected in this way? Why does one not even read the great masters of the psychological maxim any more? – for it can be said without any exaggeration that it is hard to find any educated person in Europe who has read Larochefoucauld* or those related to him in style and spirit, and very much harder to find one who has read them and does not revile them. Even this uncommon reader, however, will probably derive much less pleasure from them than the form they employ ought to give him; for even the most refined head is not in a position to appreciate the art of polishing maxims as it ought to be appreciated if he himself is not drawn to it and has not competed in it. In the absence of such practical instruction, one takes the creation and shaping of maxims to be easier than it is, one does not feel intensely enough the charm and sense of achievement in it. That is why present-day readers of maxims find relatively little to satisfy them, indeed hardly more than a mouthful of pleasantries; so that it is with them as it usually is with observers of cameos: who praise because they cannot love, and are quick to admire but even quicker to go away.

36

Objection. – Or is there a debit side to this proposition that psychological

* Larochefoucauld: François, Duc de Larochefoucauld (1613–80): French writer and aphorist.

observation is one of the means of bestowing charm on existence and relieving and mollifying it? Ought one not to have been sufficiently convinced of the unpleasant consequences of this art to want now deliberately to direct the eyes of anyone in process of formation away from it? A certain blind faith in the goodness of human nature, an innate aversion to the dissection of human actions, a kind of modesty in regard to the nakedness of the soul may indeed be more desirable things for the total happiness of an individual than that psychological perspicacity which may be helpful in particular cases; and perhaps belief in goodness, in virtuous men and actions, in an abundance of impersonal benevolence in the world has in fact made men better, inasmuch as it has made them less mistrustful. If one enthusiastically imitates Plutarch's* heroes and feels a repugnance towards suspiciously probing the motives of their actions, one may not be serving truth but one may well be furthering the wellbeing of human society: psychological error and insensibility in this domain in general promotes humanity, while knowledge of truth perhaps gains for us one more hypothesis such as Larochefoucauld placed before the first edition of his *Sentences et maximes morales*: '*Ce que le monde nomme vertu n'est d'ordinaire qu'un fantôme formé par nos passions à qui on donne un nom honnête pour faire impunément ce qu'on veut.*'† Larochefoucauld and the other French masters of psychical examination (to whom there has lately been added a German, the author of the *Psychological Observations*)‡ are like skilful marksmen who again and again hit the bullseye – but it is the bullseye of human nature. Their skill evokes amazement, but in the end a spectator inspired not by the spirit of science but that of philanthropy execrates an art that appears to implant a sense of suspicion and reductionism into the souls of men.

37
Nevertheless. – However credit and debit balance may stand: at its present state as a specific individual science the awakening of moral observation has become necessary, and mankind can no longer be spared the cruel sight of the moral dissecting table and its knives and forceps. For here there rules that science which asks after the origin and history of the so-called moral sensations and which as it progresses has to pose and solve the sociological problems entangled with them: – the older philosophy knows nothing of the latter and has, with paltry evasions, always avoided investigation of the origin and history of the moral sensations. With what consequences is now very clearly apparent, since it has been demonstrated in many instances how the errors of the "greatest philosophers usually have their point of departure in a false explanation of certain human actions and sensations; how on the basis of an erroneous

* Plutarch: Greek biographer and essayist (c. 46 to c. 127); his *Lives* contain characterizations of eminent Greeks and Romans.
† '*Ce que ... qu'on veut*': That which the world calls virtue is usually nothing but a phantom formed by our passions to which we give an honest name so as to do what we wish with impunity.
‡ The author of the *Psychological Observations*: Paul Rée, with whom Nietzsche was closely acquainted (the book appeared in 1875).

analysis, for example that of the so-called unegoistic actions, a false ethics is erected, religion and mythological monsters are then in turn called upon to buttress it, and the shadow of these dismal spirits in the end falls across even physics and the entire perception of the world. If, however, it is certain that superficiality in psychological observation has laid the most dangerous traps for human judgement and reasoning and continues to lay them, so now what is required is that perseverance in labour that does not weary of heaping stone upon stone, brick upon brick, what is required is the abstemious courage not to be ashamed of such modest labour and to defy every attempt to disparage it. It is true that countless individual observations regarding the human and all too human have first been discovered and expressed in circles of society accustomed to sacrifice, not to scientific knowledge, but to intellectual coquetry; and the odour of that ancient home of the moral maxim – a very seductive odour – has continued to adhere almost inextricably to the whole genre: so that on account of it the scientific man involuntarily evidences a certain distrust of this genre and of its seriousness. But it suffices to point to the · consequences: for already it is becoming apparent what results of the most serious description are emerging from the ground of psychological observation. For what is the principle which one of the boldest and coldest of thinkers, the author of the book *On the Origin of the Moral Sensations*,* arrived at by virtue of his incisive and penetrating analyses of human action? 'Moral man', he says, 'stands no closer to the intelligible (metaphysical) world than does physical man'. This proposition, hardened and sharpened beneath the hammer-blow of historical knowledge, may perhaps at some future time serve as the axe which is laid at the root of the 'metaphysical need' of man – whether as *more* of a blessing than a curse to the general wellbeing, who can say? – but in any event as a proposition with the weightiest consequences; at once fruitful and fearful and looking out upon the world with that Janus-face possessed by all great perceptions.

38

To what extent useful. – Thus: whether psychological observation is more advantageous or disadvantageous to man may remain undecided; what is certain, however, is that it is necessary, because science cannot dispense with it. Science, however, knows no regard for final objectives, just as nature knows nothing of it: but, as the latter occasionally brings into existence things of the greatest appropriateness and usefulness without having willed them, so genuine science, *as the imitation of nature in concepts*, will also occasionally, indeed frequently promote the wellbeing of mankind and achieve what is appropriate and useful – but likewise *without having willed it.*

He who finds the breath of such a way of thinking too wintry for him perhaps has merely too little fire in him: if he cares to look around him,

---

* The author of the book *On the Origin of the Moral Sensations*: again Paul Rée; the book, which is Rée's chief work, was written during 1876–7 in the house in Sorrento in which Nietzsche was at the same time writing *Human, All Too Human.*

however, he will perceive illnesses that require icepacks, and people so 'compounded together' of fire and spirit they are hard put to it to find air cold and cutting enough for them. Moreover: just as individuals and nations too much given to seriousness have a need of frivolity, just as others too excitable and emotional require from time to time the pressure of a heavy burden if they are to stay healthy, ought *we*, the *more spiritual* men of an age which is visibly becoming more and more ignited, not to seize hold on every means there is of extinguishing and cooling, so that we can remain at least as steady, inoffensive and moderate as we still are, and thus perhaps one day be able to serve this age as its mirror and self-reflection? –

39

*The fable of intelligible freedom.** – The principal stages in the history of the sensations by virtue of which we make anyone accountable for his actions, that is to say, of the moral sensations, are as follows. First of all, one calls individual actions good or bad quite irrespective of their motives but solely on account of their useful or harmful consequences. Soon, however, one forgets the origin of these designations and believes that the quality 'good' and 'evil' is inherent in the actions themselves, irrespective of their consequences: thus committing the same error as that by which language designates the stone itself as hard, the tree itself as green – that is to say, by taking for cause that which is effect. Then one consigns the being good or being evil to the motives and regards the deeds in themselves as morally ambiguous. One goes further and accords the predicate good or evil no longer to the individual motive but to the whole nature of a man out of whom the motive grows as the plant does from the soil. Thus one successively makes men accountable for the effects they produce, then for their actions, then for their motives, and finally for their nature. Now one finally discovers that this nature, too, cannot be accountable, inasmuch as it is altogether a necessary consequence and assembled from the elements and influence of things past and present: that is to say, that man can be made accountable for nothing, not for his nature, nor for his motives, nor for his actions, nor for the effects he produces. One has thereby attained to the knowledge that the history of the moral sensations is the history of an error, the error of accountability, which rests on the error of freedom of will. – Schopenhauer concluded otherwise, thus: because certain actions bring after them a feeling of *displeasure* ('consciousness of guilt'), there must exist a sense of accountability; for there would be *no ground* for this feeling of displeasure if not only were all the actions of man determined by necessity – which is in fact the case, a view also held by this philosopher – but man himself acquired his entire *nature* with this same necessity – which Schopenhauer denies. From the fact of that feeling of displeasure Schopenhauer believes he can demonstrate a freedom which man must have acquired somehow, not in

* Schopenhauer adhered to Kant's concept of intelligible freedom and defends it in *On the Basis of Morality*, ch. 2 section 10.

respect of his actions but in respect to his nature: freedom to *be* thus or thus, that is to say, not to *act* thus or thus. From the *esse*,* the sphere of freedom and accountability, there follows in his opinion the *operari*† – the sphere of strict causality, necessity and unaccountability. That feeling of displeasure appears to relate to the *operari*, to be sure – to that extent it is in error – in truth, however, to the *esse*, which is the deed of the free will, the basic cause of the existence of an individual: man becomes that which he *wills* to become, his willing precedes his existence. – Here the erroneous conclusion is drawn that from the fact of a feeling of displeasure there can be inferred the justification, the rational *admissibility* of this feeling of displeasure; and from this erroneous conclusion Schopenhauer arrives at his fantastic concept of so-called intelligible freedom. But a feeling of displeasure after a deed is absolutely not obliged to be rational; on the contrary, it cannot be, since it rests precisely on the erroneous presupposition that that deed need *not* have taken place of necessity. Thus: it is because man *regards* himself as free, not because he is free, that he feels remorse and pangs of conscience. – This feeling is, moreover, something one can disaccustom oneself to, and many people do not feel it at all in respect of actions which evoke it in others. It is a very changeable thing, tied to the evolution of morality and culture and perhaps present in only a relatively brief span of world-history. – No one is accountable for his deeds, no one for his nature; to judge is the same thing as to be unjust. This also applies when the individual judges himself. The proposition is as clear as daylight, and yet here everyone prefers to retreat back into the shadows and untruth: from fear of the consequences.

40

The over-animal. – The beast in us wants to be lied to; morality is an official lie told so that it shall not tear us to pieces. Without the errors that repose in the assumptions of morality man would have remained animal. As it is, he has taken himself for something higher and imposed sterner laws upon himself. That is why he feels a hatred for the grades that have remained closer to animality: which is the explanation of the contempt formerly felt for the slave as a non-man, as a thing.

41

The unalterable character.‡ – That the character is unalterable is not in the strict sense true; this favourite proposition means rather no more than that, during the brief lifetime of a man, the effective motives are unable to scratch deeply enough to erase the imprinted script of many millennia. If one imagines a man of eighty-thousand years, however, one would have in him a character totally alterable: so that an abundance of different individuals would evolve out of him one after the other. The brevity of human life misleads us to many erroneous assertions regarding the qualities of man.

---

* *esse*: being
† *operari*: action, manner of acting
‡ The view that character is unalterable was held insistently by Schopenhauer; see his *Essay on the Freedom of the Will*, ch. 3.

42

The order of desirable things and morality. – The accepted order of rank of desirable things, according to whether a low, higher or highest egoism desires the one or the other, now determines whether one is moral or immoral. To prefer a low-esteemed thing (sensual pleasure, for example) to a more highly valued one (health, for example) counts as immoral; as does preferring luxury to freedom. But the order of rank of desirable things is not firm and the same at all times; if someone prefers revenge to justice, according to the standard of an earlier culture he is moral, according to that of ours immoral. 'Immoral' therefore means that one is not yet, or not yet sufficiently sensible of the higher, more refined, more spiritual motives which a new culture has introduced: it designates one who is retarded, has remained behind, though always it is only a matter of degree. – The order of rank of desirable things itself is not erected or altered in accordance with moral considerations; but once it has been established it then determines whether an action is moral or immoral.

43

Cruel men as retarded men. – We have to regard men who are cruel as stages of *earlier cultures* which have remained behind: the deeper formations in the mountain of mankind which are otherwise hidden are here for once laid open. They are retarded men whose brain has, through some chance or other in the course of hereditary transmission, failed to develop in as sensitive and multifarious a way as is normal. They show us what we all *were*, and fill us with horror: but they themselves are as little accountable for it as a piece of granite is for being granite. Just as certain human organs recall the stage of evolution of the fish, so there must also be in our brain grooves and convolutions that correspond to that cast of mind: but these grooves and convolutions are no longer the riverbed along which the stream of our sensibility runs.

44

Gratitude and revenge. – The reason the man of power is grateful is this. His benefactor has, through the help he has given him, as it were laid hands on the sphere of the man of power and intruded into it: now, by way of requital, the man of power in turn lays hands on the sphere of his benefactor through the act of gratitude. It is a milder form of revenge. If he did not have the compensation of gratitude, the man of power would have appeared unpowerful and thenceforth counted as such. That is why every community of the good, that is to say originally the powerful, places gratitude among its first duties. Swift suggested that men are grateful in the same degree as they are revengeful.

45

Twofold prehistory of good and evil. – The concept good and evil has a twofold prehistory: *firstly* in the soul of the ruling tribes and castes. He who has the power to requite, good with good, evil with evil, and also actually practises requital – is, that is to say, grateful and revengeful – is called good; he who is powerless and cannot requite counts as bad. As a good man one belongs to the 'good', a community which has a sense of belonging together because all the individuals in it are combined with one another through the capacity for requital. As a bad man one belongs to the 'bad', to a swarm of subject, powerless people who have no sense of belonging together. The good are a caste, the bad a mass like grains of sand. Good.and bad is for a long time the same thing as noble and base, master and slave. On the other hand, one does not regard the enemy as evil: he can requite. In Homer the Trojan and the Greek are both good. It is not he who does us harm but he who is contemptible who counts as bad. In the community of the good goodness is inherited; it is impossible that a bad man could grow up out of such good soil. If, however, one of the good should do something unworthy of the good, one looks for excuses; one ascribes the guilt to a god, for example, by saying he struck the good man with madness and rendered him blind. – *Then* in the soul of the subjected, the powerless. Here every *other* man, whether he be noble or base, counts as inimical, ruthless, cruel, cunning, ready to take advantage. Evil is the characterizing expression for man, indeed for every living being one supposes to exist, for a god, for example; human, divine mean the same thing as diabolical, evil. Signs of goodness, benevolence, sympathy are received fearfully as a trick, a prelude with a dreadful termination, a means of confusing and outwitting, in short as refined wickedness. When this disposition exists in the individual a community can hardly arise, at best the most rudimentary form of community: so that wherever this conception of good and evil reigns the downfall of such individuals, of their tribes and races, is near. – Our present morality has grown up in the soil of the *ruling* tribes and castes.

46

Sympathy more painful than suffering. – There are cases in which sympathy for suffering is more painful than actual suffering. We find it more painful, for example, when one of our friends makes himself guilty of something shameful than when we do so ourselves. For we believe, firstly, in the purity of his character more than he does: then, probably precisely on account of this belief, our love for him is stronger than his own love for himself. Even if his egoism really does suffer more than our egoism does, inasmuch as he has to endure the evil consequences of his act more than we do, nonetheless the unegoistic in us – this word is never to be taken in a strict sense but only as a simplified form of expression – is affected more strongly by his guilt than is the unegoistic in him.

47

Hypochondria. – There are people who out of empathy with and concern for another person become hypochondriac; the species of sympathy that arises in this case is nothing other than an Illness. Thus there is also a Christian hypochondria such as overcomes those solitary, religiously inclined people who have the suffering and death of Christ continually before their eyes.

48

Economy of goodness. – Goodness and love as the most salutary medicine in traffic between men are such precious inventions one could well wish they might be employed as economically as possible: but this is impossible. Economy of goodness is the dream of the boldest utopians.

49

Benevolence. – Among the little but immeasurably frequent and thus very influential things to which science ought to pay more attention than to the great, rare things, benevolence too is to be reckoned; I mean those social expressions of a friendly disposition, those smiles of the eyes, those handclasps, that comfortable manner with which almost all human action is as a rule encompassed. Every teacher, every official brings this addition to what he does as a matter of duty; it is the continual occupation of humanity, as it were its light-waves in which everything grows; especially within the narrowest circle, within the family, is life made to flourish only through this benevolence. Good-naturedness, friendliness, politeness of the heart are never-failing emanations of the unegoistic drive and have played a far greater role in the construction of culture than those much more celebrated expressions of it called pity, compassion and self-sacrifice. But usually they are neglected and undervalued; and there is, indeed, very little of the unegoistic in them. The *sum* of these small doses is nonetheless enormous; their collective force is among the mightiest of forces. – One can likewise discover much more happiness in the world than clouded eyes can see: one can do so if one calculates correctly and does not overlook all those moments of pleasure in which every day of even the most afflicted human life is rich.

50

The desire to excite pity. – Larochefoucauld is certainly right when, in the most noteworthy passage of his self-portrait (first printed 1658), he warns all those who possess reason against pity, when he advises that it be left to those people of the commonality who (because their actions are not determined by reason) require the passions if they are to be brought to the point of aiding a sufferer or energetically intervening in a case of misfortune; while pity, in his (and Plato's) judgement, enfeebles the soul. One should, to be sure, *manifest* pity, but take care not to possess it; for the unfortunate are so *stupid* that the manifestation of pity constitutes for them the greatest good in the world. – Perhaps one can warn even more strongly against this having pity if one understands this need felt by the unfortunate, not precisely as stupidity and intellectual deficiency, as a kind of mental disturbance that misfortune brings with it (that, indeed, is how Larochefoucauld seems to conceive it), but as something quite different and more suspicious. Observe children who weep and wail *in order that* they shall be pitied, and therefore wait for the moment when their condition will be noticed; live among invalids and the mentally afflicted and ask yourself whether their eloquent moaning and complaining, their displaying of misfortune, does not fundamentally have the objective of *hurting* those who are with them: the pity which these then express is a consolation for the weak and suffering, inasmuch as it shows them that, all their weakness notwithstanding, they possess at any rate *one power*: the *power to hurt*. In this feeling of superiority of which the manifestation of pity makes him conscious, the unfortunate man gains a sort of pleasure; in the conceit of his imagination he is still of sufficient importance to cause affliction in the world. The thirst for pity is thus a thirst for self-enjoyment, and that at the expense of one's fellow men; it displays man in the whole ruthlessness of his own dear self: but not precisely in his 'stupidity', as Larochefoucauld thinks. – In the conversations of social life, three-quarters of all questions are asked, three-quarters of all answers given, in order to cause just a little pain to the other party; that is why many people have such a thirst for social life: it makes them aware of their strength. In such countless but very small doses in which malice makes itself felt it is a powerful stimulant to life: just as benevolence, disseminated through the human world in the same form, is the ever available medicine. – But will there be many honest men prepared to admit that causing pain gives pleasure? that one not seldom entertains oneself – and entertains oneself well – by mortifying other people, at least in one's own mind, and by firing off at them the grapeshot of petty malice? Most are too dishonest, and a few too good, to know anything of this *pudendum*;* and they are welcome to deny if they like that Prosper Meriméet is right when he says: '*Sachez aussi qu'il n'y a rien de plus commun que de faire le mal pour le plaisir de le faire.*'‡

51

How appearance becomes being. – Even when in the deepest distress, the actor ultimately cannot cease to think of the impression he and the whole scenic effect is making, even for example at the burial of his own child; he will weep over his own distress and the ways in which it expresses itself, as his own audience. The hypocrite who always plays one and the same role finally ceases to be a hypocrite; for example priests, who as young men are usually conscious or unconscious hypocrites, finally become natural and then really are priests without any affectation; or if the father fails to get that far then perhaps the son does so, employing his father's start and inheriting his habits. If someone obstinately and for a long time wants to *appear* something it is in the end hard for him to *be* anything else. The profession of almost every man, even that of the artist, begins with hypocrisy, with an imitation from without, with a copying of what is most effective. He who is always wearing a mask of a friendly countenance must finally acquire a power over benevolent moods without which

---

* *pudendum*: shameful part

† Prosper Merimée (1803–70): French writer, the author of *Carmen*

‡ '*Sachez aussi . . . de le faire*': Know, too, that there is nothing more common than to do evil for the pleasure of doing it.

the impression of friendliness cannot be obtained – and finally these acquire power over him, he *is* benevolent.

52

The point of honesty in deception. – With all great deceivers there is a noteworthy occurrence to which they owe their power. In the actual act of deception, with all its preparations, its enthralling in voice, expression and gesture, in the midst of the scenery designed to give it effect, they are overcome by *belief in themselves*: it is this which then speaks so miraculously and compellingly to those who surround them. The founders of religions are distinguished from these great deceivers by the fact that they never emerge from this state of self-deception: or very rarely they experience for once that moment of clarity when doubt overcomes them; usually, however, they comfort themselves by ascribing these moments of clarity to the evil antagonist. Self-deception has to exist if a grand *effect* is to be produced. For men believe in the truth of that which is plainly strongly believed.

53

Supposed stages of truth. – One of the commonest false conclusions is this: because someone is true and honest towards us, he speaks the truth. Thus a child believes in the judgements of its parents, the Christian in the assertions of the founder of the Church. There is likewise a disinclination to admit that all that which men have defended in earlier centuries with sacrifice of happiness and life were nothing but errors: perhaps one says they were stages of truth. But what one thinks at bottom is that, if someone has honestly believed in something and has fought and died for his belief, it would be altogether too *unfair* if what had inspired him had actually been no more than an error. Such an event seems to go against eternal justice; which is why the heart of sensitive people again and again contradicts their head, and decrees: there absolutely must exist a necessary connection between moral action and intellectual insight. Unhappily it is otherwise; for there is no such thing as eternal justice.

54

The lie. – Why do almost all people tell the truth in ordinary everyday life? – Certainly not because a god has forbidden them to lie. The reason is, firstly because it is easier; for lying demands invention, dissimulation and a good memory. (Which is why Swift says that he who tells a lie seldom realizes what a heavy burden he has assumed; for, in order to maintain a lie, he has to invent twenty more.) Then because, in straightforward relationships, it is advantageous to say: I want this, I have done that, and things of that kind; because, that is to say, the route of authority and compulsion is more certain than that of cunning. – If, however, a child should have been brought up in complicated domestic circumstances, it is just as natural for him to employ the lie and involuntarily always to say that which serves his interests; a sense of truth, an aversion to lying as such, is quite foreign and inaccessible to him, and thus he lies in all innocence.

55

Casting suspicion on morality on account of faith. – No power could maintain itself if its advocates were nothing but hypocrites; however many 'worldly' elements it may possess, the strength of the Catholic Church rests on those priestly natures, still very numerous, whose lives are hard and full of meaning and whose glance and wasted bodies speak of night-watches, fasting, fervent prayer, perhaps even of flagellation; these men deeply affect other men and inspire them with fear: what if it were *needful* to live thus? – that is the dreadful question the sight of them lays on the tongue. By propagating this doubt they continually establish further pillars of their power; even the free-thinkers do not dare to confront the man selfless in this way with a harsh sense of truth and say to him: 'Deceived yourself, cease to deceive!' – It is only difference in insight that divides them from him, certainly no difference as regards goodness or badness; but what one does not like one usually also treats unjustly. Thus one speaks of the cunning and infamous arts of the Jesuits, but overlooks what self-overcoming every individual Jesuit imposes upon himself and that the alleviated practice of life preached by the Jesuit textbooks is intended for the benefit of the laity, not for their own. One may ask, indeed, whether, given quite the same tactics and organization, we children of the Enlightenment would be equally good instruments or equally admirable in self-conquest, indefatigability or devotedness.

56

Victory of knowledge over radical evil. – He who wants to become wise will profit greatly from at some time having harboured the idea that mankind is fundamentally evil and corrupt: it is a false idea, as is its opposite; but it enjoyed dominance throughout whole ages of history, and its roots have branched out even into us ourselves and our world. To understand *ourselves* we must understand *it*; but if we are then ourselves to rise higher, we must rise up above it. We then come to recognize that there is no such thing as sin in the metaphysical sense; but, in the same sense, no such thing as virtue either; that this whole domain of moral ideas is in a state of constant fluctuation, that there exist higher and deeper conceptions of good and evil, of moral and immoral. He who desires little more of things than knowledge of them easily finds repose of soul and if he blunders (or, as the world puts it, sins), it will at most be through ignorance but hardly out of covetousness. He will no longer want to decry the desires as heretical and to exterminate them; but the only goal which completely dominates him, at all times to *know* as fully as possible, will make him cool and soothe everything savage in his disposition. Moreover, he will have got free of a host of tormenting ideas, the expressions 'pains of Hell', 'sinfulness', 'incapacity for good' will no longer have any effect on him: he will recognize in them only the hovering phantoms of false ways of viewing life and the world.

57

Morality as the self-division of man. – A good author whose heart is really in his subject wishes that someone would come and annihilate him by presenting the same subject with greater clarity and resolving all the questions contained in it. A girl in love wishes the faithfulness and devotion of her love could be tested by the faithlessness of the man she loves. A soldier wishes he could fall on the battlefield for his victorious fatherland; for his supreme desire is victor in the victory of his fatherland. A mother gives to her child that of which she deprives herself, sleep, the best food, if need be her health, her strength. – But are these all unegoistic states? Are these deeds of morality *miracles* because they are, in Schopenhauer's words, 'impossible and yet real'? Is it not clear that in all these instances man loves *something of himself*, an idea, a desire, an offspring, more than *something else of himself*, that he thus *divides* his nature and sacrifices one part of it to the other? Is it something *essentially* different from when some obstinate man says: 'I would rather be shot down than move an inch out of that fellow's way?' – The *inclination for something* (wish, impulse, desire) is present in all the above-mentioned instances; to give in to it, with all the consequences, is in any event not 'unegoistic'. – In morality man treats himself not as *individuum* but as *dividuum*.*

58
What one can promise. – One can promise actions but not feelings; for the latter are involuntary. He who promises someone he will always love him or always hate him or always be faithful to him, promises something that does not reside in his power; but he can certainly promise to perform actions which, though they are usually the consequences of love, hatred, faithfulness, can also derive from other motives: for several paths and motives can lead to the same action. To promise always to love someone therefore means: for as long as I love you I shall render to you the actions of love; if I cease to love you, you will continue to receive the same actions from me, though from other motives: so that in the heads of our fellow men the appearance will remain that love is still the same and unchanged. – One therefore promises the continuation of the appearance of love when one swears to someone ever-enduring love without self-deception.

59
Intellect and morality. – One has to have a good memory if one is to keep a promise. One has to have a powerful imagination if one is to feel sympathy. So closely is morality tied to the quality of the intellect.

60
Revenge and the desire to revenge. – To desire to revenge and then to carry out revenge means to be the victim of a vehement attack of fever which then, however, passes: but to desire to revenge without possessing the strength and courage to carry out revenge means to carry about a chronic illness, a poisoning of body and soul. Morality, which looks only at inten-

* Terms of Scholastic philosophy: *individuum*: that which cannot be divided without destroying its essence, *dividuum*: that which is composite and lacks an individual essence

tions, assesses both cases equally; in the ordinary way the former case is assessed as being the worse (on account of the evil consequences which the act of revenge will perhaps produce). Both evaluations are short-sighted.

61

The ability to wait. – Ability to wait is so difficult an accomplishment that the greatest poets have not disdained to make inability to wait a motif of their poems. Thus did Shakespeare in *Othello*, Sophocles in *Ajax*: if the latter had only allowed his feelings to cool for one more day his suicide would no longer have appeared necessary, as is indicated by the oracle; probably he would have snapped his fingers at the horrible promptings of his wounded vanity and said to himself: who in my situation would not have mistaken a sheep for a hero? is it something so very terrible? On the contrary, it is something anyone would do: Ajax could console him-self with such a reflection as that. Passion will not wait; the tragic element in the life of great men often lies not in their conflicts with their age and with the lowness of their fellow men, but in their inability to put off their work for a year or two years; they cannot wait. – In all cases of duels, the seconds have the duty to determine whether the contestants cannot wait: if they cannot then a duel is reasonable, inasmuch as each of them says to himself: 'either I live on, in which event he dies this instant, or the other way round'. In such a case waiting would mean protracting the torments of wounded honour in the face of him who has wounded it, and this can be more painful than life is worth.

62

Revelling in revenge. – Uncultivated people who feel insulted are accus-tomed to set the degree of insultingness as high as possible and to recount the cause of the insult in strongly exaggerated terms, so as to be able really to revel in the feeling of hatred and revengefulness thus engendered.

63

Value of diminution. – There are not a few people (perhaps it is even most people) who, in order to maintain in themselves a sense of self-respect and a certain efficiency in action, are obliged to disparage and diminish in their minds all the other people they know. Since, however, petty natures are in the majority, and it matters very much whether they pos-sess or lose this efficiency, it follows –

64

The rager. – We should beware of someone raging at us as of one who would like to take our life: for *that* we are still alive is due to the absence of the power to kill; if looks sufficed it would long since have been all up with us. It is a piece of a ruder stage of culture to reduce a person to silence by making a visible presentation of physical savagery and thus inspiring fear in him. – Likewise, that cold glance that the noble reserve for their servants is a remnant of ancient caste-divisions between man and man, a piece of rude antiquity; women, the custodians of the ancient, have preserved this relic too more faithfully.

65

Whither honesty can lead. – Someone had the bad habit of occasionally examining the motives of his actions, which were as good and bad as the motives of everyone else, and honestly saying what they were. He excited at first revulsion, then suspicion, gradually became altogether proscribed and declared an outlaw in society, until finally the law took notice of this infamous being on occasions when usually it closed its eyes. Lack of ability to keep silent about the universal secret, and the irresponsible tendency to see what no one wants to see – himself – brought him to prison and a premature death.

66

Punishable, never punished. – Our crime against criminals consists in the fact that we treat them like scoundrels.

67

Sancta simplicitas *of virtue.** – Every virtue has its privileges: for example, that of bringing to a condemned man's stake its own little bundle of wood.

68

Morality and success. – It is not only the spectators of an act who usually assess its morality or immorality according to whether or not it is successful: no, the performer himself does so. For the motives and intentions behind it are seldom sufficiently clear and simple, and sometimes even the memory seems to be muddled by the success of an act, so that one foists false motives upon one's act oneself, or treats inessential motives as essential. Success often bestows upon an act the whole honest lustre of the good conscience, a failure casts the shadow of pangs of conscience over the most estimable deed. From this there follows the familiar practice of the politician, who thinks: 'only give me success: if I have success I shall also have brought every honest soul over to my side – and made myself honest in my own eyes too'. – In a similar way, success is supposed to be a substitute for greater validity. Even today many educated people think that the victory of Christianity over Greek philosophy is a proof of the superior truth of the former – although in this case it was only the coarser and more violent that conquered the more spiritual and delicate. So far as superior truth is concerned, it is enough to observe that the awakening sciences have allied themselves point by point with the philosophy of Epicurus but point by point rejected Christianity.†

69

Love and justice. – Why is love overestimated as compared with justice,

---

* *sancta simplicitas*: holy simplicity

† Epicurus (341–270 BC): Greek philosopher, the founder of the philosophy named after him which shared with Stoicism the allegiance of the Graeco-Roman world during the centuries preceding the rise of Christianity. See *The Gay Science*, book I, section 45, and Kaufmann's commentary (New York: Vintage Books, 1974, p. 110).

and the fairest things said of it, as though it were of a far higher nature than the latter? For is it not obviously the stupider of the two? – Certainly, but for precisely that reason so much more *pleasant* for everybody. It is stupid and possesses a rich cornucopia; out of this it distributes its gifts, and does so to everyone, even when he does not deserve them, indeed does not even thank it for them. It is as impartial as the rain, which, according to the Bible and in accordance too with experience, soaks not only the unjust man but, in certain circumstances, also the just man to the skin.

70
Execution. – How is it that every execution offends us more than a murder? It is the coldness of the judges, the scrupulous preparation, the insight that here a human being is being used as a means of deterring others. For it is not the guilt that is being punished, even when it exists: this lies in educators, parents, environment, in us, not in the murderer – I mean the circumstances that caused him to become one.

71
Hope. – Pandora brought the box containing the evils and opened it. It was the gift of the gods to mankind, outwardly a fair, seductive gift and named the 'box of good fortune'. Then all the evils, living winged creatures, flew out: since then they have been hovering about doing harm to men by day and night. A single evil had not yet slipped out of the box: then, by the will of Zeus, Pandora shut the lid, and thus it remained within. Now man has the box of good fortune forever in the house and is amazed at the treasure he possesses in it; it stands at his service, he reaches for it when he desires to do so; for he does not know that the box Pandora brought was the box of evil and regards the evil that has remained behind as the greatest piece of good fortune – it is hope. – For what Zeus wanted was that man, though never so tormented by the other evils, should nonetheless not throw life away but continue to let himself be tormented. To that end he gives men hope: it is in truth the worst of all evils, because it protracts the torment of men.

72
Degree of moral inflammability unknown. – Whether or not our passions glow red hot and direct the whole course of our life depends on whether or not we have had certain painfully affecting sights and impressions – a father unjustly condemned, killed or tortured, for example, an unfaithful wife, a cruel attack by an enemy. No one knows whither circumstances, pity, indignation may drive him, no one knows the degree of his inflammability. Paltry little circumstances make one paltry oneself; it is usually not the quality of his experiences but their quantity that distinguishes the lower from the higher man, in both good and evil.

73
The unwilling martyr. – In a party there was a man who was too fearful and

cowardly ever to contradict his comrades: they employed him in every kind of service, they demanded everything of him, because he was more afraid of the ill opinion of his companions than he was of death; he was a miserably feeble soul. They recognized this and on the basis of the qualities mentioned made of him a hero and finally even a martyr. Although the cowardly man inwardly always said No, with his lips he always said Yes, even on the scaffold when he died for the views of his party: for beside him there stood one of his old party comrades, who by word and glance so tyrannized over him that he actually suffered death without flinching and has since then been celebrated as a martyr and a man of great character.

74
Everyday standard. – One will seldom go wrong if one attributes extreme actions to vanity, moderate ones to habit and petty ones to fear.

75
Misunderstanding of virtue. – He who has come to know unvirtue in association with pleasure – such as he who has a dissolute youth behind him – imagines that virtue must be associated with the unpleasurable. He, on the contrary, who is much tormented by his passions and vices longs for peace and happiness of soul in the practice of virtue. It is thus possible that two virtuous people completely misunderstand one another.

76
The ascetic. – The ascetic makes of virtue a state of distress.

77
Honour transferred from the person to the thing. – Acts of love and self-sacrifice for the good of one's neighbour are generally held in honour in whatever circumstances they may be performed. In this way one augments the *value of the things* which are loved in this fashion or for which someone sacrifices himself: even though in themselves they may perhaps not be worth very much. A brave army is a convincing argument for the cause for which it fights.

78
Ambition a surrogate for moral feeling. – Moral feeling must not be lacking in those natures that have no ambition. The ambitious contrive to get on even without it, and with almost equal success. – That is why, if they should ever lose moral feeling, the sons of modest families that know nothing of ambition decline very rapidly into complete good-for-nothings.

79
Vanity enriches. – How poor the human spirit would be without vanity! But for this reason it resembles a well-stocked and continually restocked department store that entices customers of every kind: they can find

almost anything, have almost anything, provided they bring with them the valid coin (admiration).

80

Old age and death. – Disregarding the demands made by religion one might well ask: why should it be more laudable for an old man who senses the decline of his powers to await his slow exhaustion and dissolution than in full consciousness to set himself a limit? Suicide is in this case a wholly natural and obvious action, which as a victory for reason ought fairly to awaken reverence: and did awaken it in those ages when the heads of Greek philosophy and the most upright Roman patriots were accustomed to die by suicide. On the other hand, the desire to carry on existing from day to day, anxiously consulting physicians and observing scrupulous rules of conduct, without the strength to get any closer to the actual goal of one's life, is much less respectworthy. – The religions are rich in excuses for evading the demand of suicide: in this way they ingratiate themselves with those who are in love with life.

81

Errors of the sufferer and the doer. – When a rich man takes a possession from a poor one (for example, a prince robs a plebeian of his beloved) an error arises in the poor man: he thinks the rich man must be utterly infamous to take from him the little that he has. But the rich man does not feel nearly so deeply the value of a *single* possession because he is used to having many: thus he cannot transport himself into the soul of the poor man and has not committed nearly so great an injustice as the latter supposes. Both have a false idea of one another. The injustice of the powerful which arouses most indignation in history is not nearly as great as it seems. The inherited sense of being a higher type of creature with higher claims already makes such a man fairly cold and leaves his conscience at rest: we all, indeed, lose all feeling of injustice when the difference between ourselves and other creatures is very great, and will kill a gnat, for example, without the slightest distress of conscience. Thus it is no sign of baseness in Xerxes (whom even the Greeks depict as being outstandingly noble) when he takes a son from his father and has him dismembered because he has expressed fearful and ominous misgivings about the whole campaign they are engaged on: in this instance the individual is disposed of like an annoying insect: he is too lowly to be allowed to go on upsetting a world-ruler. Indeed, no cruel man is *so* cruel as he whom he has misused believes; the idea of pain is not the same thing as the suffering of it. The same applies to the unjust judge, to the journalist who misleads public opinion with petty untruths. Cause and effect are in all these cases surrounded by quite different groups of thoughts and sensations; while one involuntarily presupposes that doer and sufferer think and feel the same and, in accordance with this presupposition, assesses the guilt of the one by the pain of the other.

82

Skin of the soul. – Just as the bones, flesh, intestines and blood vessels are enclosed in a skin that makes the sight of man endurable, so the agitations and passions of the soul are enveloped in vanity: it is the skin of the soul.

83

Sleep of virtue. – When virtue has slept it will arise more vigorous.

84

Refinement of shame. – Men are not ashamed of thinking something dirty, but they are when they imagine they are credited with this dirty thought.

85

Wickedness is rare. – Most people are much too much occupied with themselves to be wicked.

86

The index of the scales. – We praise or blame according to whether the one or the other offers a greater opportunity for our power of judgement to shine out.

87

Luke 18, 14 improved.* – He that humbleth himself wants to be exalted.

88

Prevention of suicide. – There exists a right by which we take a man's life but none by which we take from him his death: this is mere cruelty.

89

Vanity. – We have an interest in the good opinion of others, firstly because it is useful to us, then because we want to give them pleasure (children their parents, pupils their teacher, and benevolent people all other people in general). Only where the good opinion of others is important to someone quite apart from advantage or the desire to give pleasure do we speak of vanity. In this case a person wants to give pleasure to himself but at the expense of his fellow men, inasmuch as he either seduces them to a false opinion regarding himself or even aims at a degree of 'good opinion' that is bound to be painful to others (through the arousal of envy). As a rule, the individual wants through the opinion of others to confirm the opinion he has of himself and to ratify himself in his own eyes; but our mighty habituation to authority – a habituation that is as old as mankind itself – also impels many to rely on authority for their belief in themself, that is to say to acquire it only at the hands of others: they trust the judgement of others more than they do their own. – Interest in oneself, the desire to feel pleasure, attains in the vain person to such an intensity that he seduces others to a false, much too high assessment of himself, yet then submits to the authority of these others: that is to say, he induces error and then believes in this error. – One is therefore bound to see that vain people desire to please not so much other people

---

* Luke 18, 14: 'for every one that exalteth himself shall be abased; and he that humbleth himself shall be exalted'.

as themselves, and that they go so far as to neglect their own advantage in doing so; for they are then obliged to arouse in their fellow men ill-will, hostility and envy, simply so as to be able to take pleasure in themselves.

90
Boundary of philanthropy. – Anyone who has declared another to be an idiot, an unpleasant fellow, is annoyed if in the end he demonstrates that he is not one.

91
*Moralité larmoyante.** – How much entertainment morality provides! Think only what an ocean of delicious tears has flowed, for instance, at the telling of tales of noble, magnanimous deeds! – This embellishment of life would disappear if belief in total unaccountability came to prevail.

92
Origin of justice. – Justice (fairness) originates between parties of approximately *equal power*, as Thucydides† correctly grasped (in the terrible colloquy between the Athenian and Melian ambassadors): where there is no clearly recognizable superiority of force and a contest would result in mutual injury producing no decisive outcome the idea arises of coming to an understanding and negotiating over one another's demands: the characteristic of *exchange* is the original characteristic of justice. Each satisfies the other, inasmuch as each acquires what he values more than the other does. One gives to the other what he wants to have, to be henceforth his own, and in return receives what one oneself desires. Justice is thus requital and exchange under the presupposition of an approximately equal power position: revenge therefore belongs originally within the domain of justice, it is an exchange. Gratitude likewise. – Justice goes back naturally to the viewpoint of an enlightened self-preservation, thus to the egoism of the reflection: 'to what end should I injure myself uselessly and perhaps even then not achieve my goal?' – so much for the *origin* of justice. Since, in accordance with their intellectual habit, men have *forgotten* the original purpose of so-called just and fair actions, and especially because children have for millennia been trained to admire and imitate such actions, it has gradually come to appear that a just action is an unegoistic one: but it is on this appearance that the high value accorded it depends; and this high value is, moreover, continually increasing, as all valuations do: for something highly valued is striven for, imitated, multiplied through sacrifice, and grows as the worth of the toil and zeal expended by each individual is added to the worth of the valued thing. – How little moral would the world appear without forgetfulness! A poet could say that God has placed forgetfulness as a doorkeeper on the threshold of the temple of human dignity.

93
Of the rights of the weaker. – If someone, a besieged town for instance,

---

* *moralité larmoyante*: tearful morality
† Thucydides (c. 460–394 BC): Greek historian, principally of the Peloponnesian War

submits under conditions to a stronger force, the counter-condition is that one is able to destroy oneself, burn the town down, and thus inflict a great loss upon the stronger. For this reason there here arises a kind of *equalization* on the basis of which rights can be established. The enemy derives advantage from preserving them. – To this extent there also exist rights as between slaves and masters, that is to say to precisely the extent that the possession of the slave is useful and important to his master. *Rights* originally extend *just as far* as one *appears* valuable, essential, unlosable, unconquerable and the like, to the other. In this respect the weaker too possess rights, but more limited ones. Thence the celebrated *unusquisque tantum juris habet, quantum potentia valet* (or more exactly: *quantum potentia valere creditur*).*

94

The three phases of morality hitherto. – It is the first sign that animal has become man when his actions are no longer directed to the procurement of momentary wellbeing but to enduring wellbeing, that man has thus become attuned to *utility* and *purpose*: it is then that the free domination of reason first breaks forth. An even higher stage is attained when he acts according to the principle of *honour*; in accordance with this he orders himself with regard to others, submits to common sensibilities, and that raises him high above the phase in which he is diverted only by utility understood in a purely personal sense: he accords others respect and wants them to accord respect to him, that is to say: he conceives utility as being dependent on what he thinks of others and what they think of him. Finally, at the highest stage of morality *hitherto*, he acts in accordance with *his own* standard with regard to men and things: he himself determines for himself and others what is honourable and useful; he has become the lawgiver of opinion, in accordance with an ever more highly evolving conception of usefulness and honourableness. Knowledge qualifies him to prefer the most useful, that is to say general and enduring utility, to personal utility, general and enduring honour and recognition to momentary honour and recognition: he lives and acts as a collective-individual.

95

Morality of the mature individual. – Hitherto the impersonal has been regarded as the actual distinguishing mark of the moral action; and it has been proved that at first it was on account of their general utility that impersonal actions were universally commended and accorded distinction. Ought a significant alteration in this point of view not to lie just ahead, now when it is realized more and more that it is in precisely the most *personal* possible considerations that the degree of utility is at its greatest also for the generality: so that it is the strictly personal action that corresponds to the current conception of morality (as general utility)? To make of oneself a complete *person*, and in all that one does to have in view the *highest*

---

* *unusquisque . . . valet*: each man has as much right as he has power; *quantum . . . creditur*: as he is believed to have power; Spinoza, *Tractatus Politicus*, ch. 2, section 8.

good of this person – that gets us further than those pity-filled agitations and actions for the sake of others. We all of us, to be sure, still suffer from the all-too-little regard paid to the personal in us, it has been badly cultivated – let us admit to ourselves that our minds have, rather, been drawn forcibly away from it and offered as a sacrifice to the state, to science, to those in need, as though what would have to be sacrificed was in any case what was bad. Even now let us work for our fellow men, but only to the extent that we discover our own highest advantage in this work: no more, no less. All that remains is what it is one understands by *one's advantage*; precisely the immature, undeveloped, crude individual will understand it most crudely.

96

Custom and what is in accordance with it. – To be moral, to act in accordance with custom, to be ethical means to practise obedience towards a law or tradition established from of old. Whether one subjects oneself with effort or gladly and willingly makes no difference, it is enough that one does it. He is called 'good' who does what is customary as if by nature, as a result of a long inheritance, that is to say easily and gladly, and this is so whatever what is customary may be (exacts revenge, for example, when exacting revenge is part of good custom, as it was with the ancient Greeks). He is called good because he is good 'for something'; since, however, benevolence, sympathy and the like have throughout all the changes in customs always been seen as 'good for something', as useful, it is now above all the benevolent, the helpful who are called 'good'. To be evil is 'not to act in accordance with custom', to practise things not sanctioned by custom, to resist tradition, however rational or stupid that tradition may be; in all the laws of custom of all times, however, doing injury to one's neighbour has been seen as injurious above all else, so that now at the word 'evil' we think especially of voluntarily doing injury to one's neighbour. 'Egoistic' and 'unegoistic' is not the fundamental antithesis which has led men to make the distinction between 'in accordance with custom' and 'in defiance of custom', between good and evil, but adherence to a tradition, a law, and severance from it. How the tradition has *arisen* is here a matter of indifference, and has in any event nothing to do with good and evil or with any kind of immanent categorical imperative;* it is above all directed at the preservation of a *community*, a people; every superstitious usage which has arisen on the basis of some chance event mistakenly interpreted enforces a tradition which it is in accordance with custom to follow; for to sever oneself from it is dangerous, and even more injurious to the *community* than to the individual (because the gods punish the community for misdeeds and for every violation of their privileges and only to that extent punish the individual). Every tradition now continually grows more venerable the farther away its origin lies and the more this origin is forgotten; the respect paid to it increases from

* Kant considered the categorical imperative – defined in the *Groundwork for a Metaphysic of Morals* as 'Act as if the maxim of your action were to become through your will a universal natural law' – to derive from the nature of rationality.

generation to generation, the tradition at last becomes holy and evokes awe and reverence; and thus the morality of piety is in any event a much older morality than that which demands unegoistic actions.

97

Pleasure in custom. – An important species of pleasure, and thus an important source of custom, originates in habit. One does what is habitual better and more easily and thus prefers to do it, one derives a sense of pleasure from it and knows from experience that the habitual has proved itself and is thus useful; a custom one can live with is demonstrated as salutary, beneficial, in contrast to all novel experimentations that have not yet proved themselves. Custom is consequently the union of the pleasant and the useful, and in addition it demands no cogitation. As soon as man is in a position to exercise compulsion he exercises it to introduce and impose his *customs*, for to him they are demonstrated practical wisdom. A community of individuals likewise compels each separate individual to observe the same custom. Here there is the false conclusion: because one feels happy with a custom, or at least can preserve one's existence by means of it, this custom is necessary, for it counts as the *sole* condition under which one can feel happy; a happy life seems to derive from this custom alone. This conception of the customary as a condition of existence is conveyed into the minutest particulars of custom: since insight into actual causality is very slight among the lower peoples and cultures, one sees to it with superstitious fear that everything continues on in the way it has always gone; even when custom is hard, rigorous, burdensome, it is preserved on account of its apparent supreme utility. One does not know that the same degree of wellbeing can also exist under different customs or that even higher degrees are attainable. But one does perceive that all customs, even the harshest, grow milder and more pleasant in course of time, and that even the strictest mode of life can become habitual and thus a source of pleasure.

98

Pleasure and social instinct. – From his relations with other men, man adds a new species of *pleasure* to those pleasurable sensations he derives from himself; whereby he significantly enlarges the domain of pleasurable sensations in general. Perhaps he has already inherited much that has its place here from the animals, who plainly feel pleasure when they play with one another, especially the mothers with the young. Then consider sexual relations, through which more or less every female appears interesting to every male with regard to the prospect of pleasure, and the reverse. To feel sensations of pleasure on the basis of human relations on the whole makes men better; joy, pleasure, is enhanced when it is enjoyed together with others, it gives the individual security, makes him good-natured, banishes distrust and envy: for one feels a sense of wellbeing and sees that others are likewise feeling a sense of wellbeing. *Similar expressions of pleasure* awaken the fantasy of empathy, the feeling of being like something else: the same effect is produced by common sufferings, by experiencing bad weather, dangers, enemies in common. It is no doubt upon this that the oldest form of alliance is based: the sense of which is that to act together to ward off and dispose of a threatening displeasure is of utility to each individual. And thus the social instinct grows out of the feeling of pleasure.

99

The innocent element in so-called evil acts. – All 'evil' acts are motivated by the drive to preservation or, more exactly, by the individual's intention of procuring pleasure and avoiding displeasure; so motivated, however, they are not evil. 'Procuring pain as such' *does not exist*, except in the brains of philosophers, neither does 'procuring pleasure as such' (pity in the Schopenhauerian sense). In conditions obtaining *before* the existence of the state we kill the creature, be it ape or man, that seeks to deprive us of a fruit of the tree if we happen to be hungry and are making for the tree ourself: as we would still do to the animals even now if we were travelling in inhospitable regions. – The evil acts at which we are now most indignant rest on the error that he who perpetrates them against us possesses free will, that is to say, that he could have *chosen* not to cause us this harm. It is this belief in choice that engenders hatred, revengefulness, deceitfulness, all the degrading our imagination undergoes, while we are far less censorious towards an animal because we regard it as unaccountable. To do injury not from the drive to preservation but as requital – is the consequence of a mistaken judgement and therefore likewise innocent. In conditions obtaining before the existence of the state the individual can act harshly and cruelly for the purpose of *frightening* other creatures: to secure his existence through such fear-inspiring tests of his power. Thus does the man of violence, of power, the original founder of states, act when he subjugates the weaker. His right to do so is the same as the state now relegates to itself; or rather, there exists no right that can prevent this from happening. The ground for any kind of morality can then be prepared only when a greater individual or a collective-individuality, for example society, the state, subjugates all other individuals, that is to say draws them out of their isolation and orders them within a collective. Morality is preceded by *compulsion*, indeed it is for a time itself still compulsion, to which one accommodates oneself for the avoidance of what one regards as unpleasurable. Later it becomes custom, later still voluntary obedience, finally almost instinct: then, like all that has for a long time been habitual and natural, it is associated with pleasure – and is now called *virtue*.

100

Shame. – Shame exists wherever there exists a 'mystery'; this, however, is a religious concept which in earlier ages of human culture was of wide compass. Everywhere there were enclosed domains to which divine right denied entry except under certain conditions: in the first instance these were simply areas of ground, inasmuch as certain places were not to be stepped upon by the feet of the uninitiated, who were seized with fear and trembling when they approached them. This feeling was transferred to many other regions, for example to that of sexual relations, from which, as a privilege and adytum* of maturity, the gaze of youth must for its own advantage be directed away: relations for whose protection and the preservation of whose sanctity many divinities were thought of as active and set up as guardians of the marriage chamber. (That is why this chamber is called in Turkish the harem, the 'sanctuary', the same word, that is to say, normally used to designate the forecourt of a mosque.) Thus kinghood is, as a centre from which power and glory radiate, a mystery full of shame and secrecy to those subject to it: the force of which is still perceptible among nations otherwise in no way noted for being ashamed and abashed. The whole world of interior states, the so-called 'soul', is likewise still a mystery to all non-philosophers; through endless ages it has been believed that the 'soul' was of divine origin and worthy of traffic with the gods: consequently it is an adytum and evokes shame.

101

Judge not. – When considering earlier periods of history one must take care not to fall into an unjust condemnation of them. The injustice involved in slavery, the cruelty involved in the subjugation of persons and nations is not to be measured by our own standards. For in those days the instinct for justice had not yet been so far developed. Who dare reproach the Genevan Calvin for having burned the physician Serveto?† It was a consistent action that flowed from his convictions, and the Inquisition too was equally justified; only the views that then predominated were false and led to consequences that seem to us harsh because those views have become alien to us. And what in any event is the burning of a single individual compared with everlasting punishment in Hell for almost everybody! And yet this idea dominated all the world at that time without its much greater horrors doing any essential damage to the idea of a God. With us, too, political sectarians are treated harshly and cruelly, but because one has learned to believe in the necessity of the state one is not as sensible of the cruelty as one is in the former case, where we repudiate the ideas behind it. The cruelty towards animals exhibited by children and Italians is attributable to want of understanding; the animal has, especially in the interest of ecclesiastical teaching, been placed too far below man. – Much that is horrific and inhuman in history in which one can hardly bear to believe is likewise ameliorated when we consider that he who ordered it and he who carried it out are different people: the former does not see it and his imagination therefore receives no strong impression of it, the latter obeys one set above him and does not feel responsible. From lack of imagination most princes and military leaders can easily seem cruel and harsh without being so. – *Egoism is not evil*, because the idea of one's 'neighbour' – the expression is of Christian origin and does not correspond with truth – is very weak in us; and we feel almost as

---

* adytum: innermost chamber of a temple, where oracles are delivered
† Miguel Serveto (1511–53): Spanish doctor and theologian. Calvin allegedly denounced him to the Inquisition as a unitarian; he was burned in Geneva.

free of responsibility for him as we do for plants and stones. That the other suffers has to be *learned*; and it can never be learned fully.

102

'*Man's actions are always good.*' – We do not accuse nature of immorality when it sends us a thunderstorm and makes us wet: why do we call the harmful man immoral? Because in the latter case we assume a voluntarily commanding free will, in the former necessity. But this distinction is an error. And then: we do not call even intentional harming immoral under all circumstances; one unhesitatingly kills a fly intentionally, for example, merely because one does not like its buzzing, one punishes the criminal intentionally and does him harm so as to protect ourselves and society. In the first instance it is the individual who, to preserve himself or even merely to avoid displeasure, intentionally does harm; in the second it is the state. All morality allows the intentional causing of harm in the case of self-defence: that is, when it is a matter of *self-preservation*. But these two points of view *suffice* to explain all evil acts perpetrated by men against men: one desires pleasure or to ward off displeasure; it is always in some sense a matter of self-preservation. Socrates and Plato are right: whatever man does he always does the good, that is to say: that which seems to him good (useful) according to the relative degree of his intellect, the measure of his rationality.

103

The innocent element in wickedness. – Wickedness does not have the suffering of another as such as its objective, but our own enjoyment, for example the enjoyment of the feeling of revenge or of a powerful excitation of the nerves. Even teasing demonstrates what pleasure it gives to vent our power on others and to produce in ourselves the pleasurable feeling of ascendancy. Is the *immoral* element, then, the *deriving of pleasure from the displeasure of others*? Is *Schadenfreude** devilish, as Schopenhauer says it is? Well, in the midst of nature we procure pleasure for ourselves by breaking off branches, loosening stones, fighting with wild animals, and do so in order to become aware of our strength. Is it the *knowledge* that another suffers because of us that is here supposed to make immoral the same thing in respect of which we otherwise feel unaccountable? But if one did not know this, one would also experience no pleasure in one's superiority, which can *reveal itself* only in the suffering of the other, for example in the case of teasing. Pleasure in oneself is neither good nor bad; whence is the stipulation supposed to come that one may not excite displeasure in others in order to have pleasure in oneself? Only from the point of view of utility, that is to say with regard to the *consequences*, to the displeasure that may eventuate if the person harmed, or in his place the state, should demand requital and revenge: originally only this can have offered a reason for denying oneself such acts. – Pity has the pleasure of the other as its objective just as little as wickedness has the pain of the other as such. For it conceals within itself at least two (perhaps many

* *Schadenfreude*: pleasure in another's suffering

more) elements of a personal pleasure and is to that extent self-enjoyment: first as the pleasure of the emotion, which is the kind represented by pity in tragedy, and then, when it eventuates in action, as the pleasure of gratification in the exercise of power. If, in addition to this, a suffering person is very close to us, we remove from ourselves the suffering we ourselves feel by performing an act of pity. – With the exception of a few philosophers, men have always placed pity fairly low in the order of rank of the moral sensations: and rightly.

104

Self-defence. – If one is to allow that self-defence is morally justified, then one must also allow that almost all expressions of so-called immoral egoism are morally justified: one causes suffering, robs or kills, in order to preserve or protect oneself, to ward off personal harm; one lies when cunning and dissimulation is the proper means of self-preservation. *To harm intentionally* when it is a question of our existence or security (preservation of our wellbeing) is conceded as being morally justified; the state itself does harm from this point of view when it imposes punishments. In unintentional harm there can, of course, be nothing immoral, for here chance rules. Is there then a species of intentional harm where our existence, the preservation of our wellbeing, are *not* in question? Is there such a thing as doing harm out of pure *wickedness*, for example in an act of cruelty? When one does not know how much pain an act causes, it is not an act of wickedness; thus a child is not wicked, not evil, with regard to an animal: it investigates and destroys it as though it were a toy. But does one ever fully *know* how much pain an act causes another? As far as our nervous system extends we guard ourselves against pain: if it extended further, namely into our fellow men, we would never do harm to another (except in such cases as when we do it to ourselves, that is to say when we cut ourselves for the purpose of a cure, exert and weary ourselves for the sake of our health). We *conclude* by analogy that something causes someone pain, and through recollection and strength of imagination we can ourselves suffer as a consequence. But what a difference there nonetheless remains between a toothache and the ache (pity) that the sight of a toothache evokes. Thus: in the case of doing harm out of so-called wickedness the *degree* of pain produced is in any event unknown to us; insofar, however, as the act is accompanied by *pleasure* (feeling of one's own power, of one's own strong excitation), it occurs for the purpose of preserving the wellbeing of the individual, and thus comes under a similar heading to self-defence and lying under duress. Without pleasure no life; the struggle for pleasure is the struggle for life. Whether an individual pursues this struggle in such a way that people call him *good*, or in such a way that they call him *evil*, is determined by the degree and quality of his intellect.

105

Justice that rewards. – He who has fully grasped the theory of total unaccountability can no longer accommodate so-called justice that punishes and rewards under the concept of justice at all: provided, that is, that this consists in giving to each what is his own. For he who is punished does not deserve the punishment: he is merely being employed as the means of henceforth deterring others from certain actions; likewise, he who is rewarded does not deserve this reward: for he could not have acted otherwise than he did. Thus the reward possesses only the sense of an encouragement, to him and others, and the provision of a motive for subsequent actions; commendation is called out to the runner who is still on the track, not to him who has reached the finishing-line. Neither punishment nor reward are something due to a person as *his*; they are given him for reasons of utility without his being able to lay any just claim to them. One thus has to say: 'the wise man does not reward because a good deed has been done', just as one has already said: 'the wise man does not punish because a bad deed has been done but so that bad deeds shall not be done'. If punishment and reward were abolished, the strongest motives for performing certain acts and not performing certain acts would also be abolished; mankind's utility requires their continuance; and insofar as punishment and reward, blame and praise, operate most effectively upon vanity, this same utility also requires the continuance of vanity.

106

By the waterfall. – At the sight of a waterfall we think we see in the countless curvings, twistings and breakings of the waves capriciousness and freedom of will; but everything here is necessary, every motion mathematically calculable. So it is too in the case of human actions; if one were all-knowing, one would be able to calculate every individual action, likewise every advance in knowledge, every error, every piece of wickedness. The actor himself, to be sure, is fixed in the illusion of free will; if for one moment the wheel of the world were to stand still, and there were an all-knowing, calculating intelligence there to make use of this pause, it could narrate the future of every creature to the remotest ages and describe every track along which this wheel had yet to roll. The actor's deception regarding himself, the assumption of free-will, is itself part of the mechanism it would have to compute.

107

Unaccountability and innocence. – The complete unaccountability of man for his actions and his nature is the bitterest draught the man of knowledge has to swallow if he has been accustomed to seeing in accountability and duty the patent of his humanity. All his evaluations, all his feelings of respect and antipathy have thereby become disvalued and false: his profoundest sentiment, which he accorded to the sufferer, the hero, rested upon an error; he may no longer praise, no longer censure, for it is absurd to praise and censure nature and necessity. As he loves a fine work of art but does not praise it since it can do nothing for itself, as he stands before the plants, so must he stand before the actions of men and before his own. He can admire their strength, beauty, fullness, but he may not find any merit in them: the chemical process and the strife of the elements, the torment of the sick man who yearns for an end to his sickness, are as little merits as are those states of distress and psychic convulsions which arise when we are torn back and forth by conflicting motives until we finally choose the most powerful of them – as we put it (in truth, however, until the most powerful motive chooses us). But all these motives, whatever exalted names we may give them, have grown up out of the same roots as those we believe evilly poisoned; between good and evil actions there is no difference in kind, but at the most one of degree. Good actions are sublimated evil ones; evil actions are coarsened, brutalized good ones. It is the individual's sole desire for self-enjoyment (together with the fear of losing it) which gratifies itself in every instance, let a man act as he can, that is to say as he must: whether his deeds be those of vanity, revenge, pleasure, utility, malice, cunning, or those of sacrifice, sympathy, knowledge. Degrees of intelligent judgement decide whither each person will let his desire draw him; every society, every individual always has present an order of rank of things considered good, according to which he determines his own actions and judges those of others. But this standard is continually changing, many actions are called evil but are only stupid, because the degree of intelligence which decided for them was very low. Indeed, in a certain sense *all* present actions are stupid, for the highest degree of human intelligence which can now be attained will certainly be exceeded in the future: and then all our actions and judgements will seem in retrospect as circumscribed and precipitate as the actions and judgements of still existing primitive peoples now appear to us. To perceive all this can be very painful, but then comes a consolation: such pains are birth-pangs. The butterfly wants to get out of its cocoon, it tears at it, it breaks it open: then it is blinded and confused by the unfamiliar light, the realm of freedom. It is in such men as are *capable* of that suffering – how few they will be! – that the first attempt will be made to see whether mankind could *transform itself from a moral to a knowing mankind*. The sun of a new gospel is casting its first beam on the topmost summits in the soul of every individual: there the mists are gathering more thickly than ever, and the brightest glitter and the gloomiest twilight lie side by side. Everything is necessity – thus says the new knowledge; and this knowledge itself is necessity. Everything is innocence: and knowledge is the path to insight into this innocence. If pleasure, egoism, vanity are *necessary* for the production of the moral phenomena and their finest flower, the sense for truth and justice in knowledge; if error and aberration of the imagination was the only means by which mankind was able gradually to raise itself to this degree of self-enlightenment and self-redemption – who could venture to denigrate those means? Who could be despondent when he becomes aware of the goal to which those paths lead? It is true that everything in the domain of morality has become and is changeable, unsteady, everything is in flux: but *everything is also flooding forward*, and towards *one* goal. Even if the inherited habit of erroneous evaluation, loving, hating does continue to rule in us, under the influence of increas-

58

ing knowledge it will grow weaker: a new habit, that of comprehending, not-loving, not-hating, surveying is gradually implanting itself in us on the same soil and will in thousands of years' time perhaps be strong enough to bestow on mankind the power of bringing forth the wise, innocent (conscious of innocence) man as regularly as it now brings forth – *not his antithesis but necessary preliminary* – the unwise, unjust, guilt-conscious man.

3

THE RELIGIOUS
LIFE

108

The twofold struggle against an ill. – When we are assailed by an ill we can dispose of it either by getting rid of its cause or by changing the effect it produces on our sensibilities: that is to say by reinterpreting the ill into a good whose good effects will perhaps be perceptible only later. Religion and art (and metaphysical philosophy too) endeavour to bring about a change of sensibility, partly through changing our judgement as to the nature of our experiences (for example with the aid of the proposition: 'whom God loveth he chastiseth'), partly through awakening the ability to take pleasure in pain, in emotion in general (from which the art of tragedy takes its starting-point). The more a man inclines towards re-interpretation, the less attention he will give to the cause of the ill and to doing away with it; the momentary amelioration and narcoticizing, such as is normally employed for example in a case of toothache, suffices him in the case of more serious sufferings too. The more the domination of the religions and all the arts of narcosis declines, the stricter attention men pay to the actual abolition of the ill: which is, to be sure, a bad lookout for the writers of tragedies – for there is less and less material for tragedy, because the realm of inexorable, implacable destiny is growing narrower and narrower – but an even worse one for the priests: for these have hitherto lived on the narcoticizing of human ills.

109

Sorrow is knowledge. – How one would like to exchange the false assertions of the priests that there is a God who desires that we do good, is the guardian and witness of every action, every moment, every thought, who loves us and in every misfortune wants only what is best for us – how one would like to exchange these for truths that would be as salutary, pacifying and beneficial as those errors are! Yet such truths do not exist; the most philosophy can do is to set against them other metaphysical plausibilities (at bottom likewise untruths). The tragedy, however, lies in the fact that one cannot *believe* these dogmas of religion and metaphysics if one has in one's heart and head the rigorous methods of acquiring truth, while on the other hand one has, through the development of humanity, grown so tender, sensitive and afflicted one has need of means of cure and comfort of the most potent description; from which there thus arises the danger that man may bleed to death from knowledge of truth. This was expressed by Byron in immortal verse:

> Sorrow is knowledge: they who know the most
> Must mourn the deepest o'er the fatal truth:
> The tree of knowledge is not that of life.*

For such cares there is no better antidote, at least for the worst hours and eclipses of the soul, than to conjure up the solemn frivolity of Horace, and with him to say to oneself:

> quid aeternis minorem
> consiliis animum fatigas?
> cur non sub alta vel platano vel hac
> pinu jacentes –†

What is certain, however, is that any degree of frivolity or melancholy is better than a romantic return and desertion, an approach to Christianity in any form: for, given the current state of knowledge, one can no longer have any association with it without incurably dirtying one's intellectual conscience and prostituting it before oneself and others. Those agonies may be painful enough: but without agonies one cannot become a leader and educator of mankind; and woe to him who wants to attempt it but no longer possesses this clean conscience!

110

Truth in religion. – In the period of the Enlightenment the significance of religion was not adequately appreciated, of that there can be no doubt: but it is just as certain that in the reaction to the Enlightenment that followed it was appreciated much too highly, inasmuch as the religions were treated with love, almost amorously indeed, and were for example adjudged to possess a profound, indeed the profoundest possible understanding of the world; science had only to remove their dogmatic dress in order to possess the 'truth' in mythical form. The religions were thus – such was the assertion of all opponents of the Enlightenment – supposed to express *sensu allegorico*,‡ having regard to the understanding of the masses, that primeval wisdom which was wisdom as such, inasmuch as all true science of modern times had always led us towards it and not away from it: so that between the oldest sages of mankind and all the most recent there reigned a harmony, indeed an identity of insights, and a progress in knowledge – assuming one wished to speak of such a thing – could apply, not to the nature of knowledge, but only to the form in which it was communicated. This whole conception of religion and science is erroneous through and through; and no one would still venture to adhere to it if Schopenhauer's eloquence had not taken it under its protection: an eloquence that rings loud and clear yet had to wait a generation before it reached its audience. Certainly one can gain very much towards an understanding of Christianity and other religions from

---

* Sorrow is . . . that of life: from Byron's *Manfred*, Act I Scene I

† *quid aeternis . . . pinu jacentes*: why torment your mind, which is unequal to it, with counsel for eternity; why not come and lie under this tall plane tree, or this pine. . . ? (Horace: *Odes* II 11).

‡ *sensu allegorico*: with the sense of an allegorical representation

Schopenhauer's religio-moral interpretation of men and the world; but it is just as certain that he blundered over the *value of religion with respect to knowledge*. In this he himself was an all too docile pupil of the scientific teachers of his time, who one and all paid homage to romanticism and had renounced the spirit of the Enlightenment; born into our own time, he could not possibly have spoken of the *sensus allegoricus* of religion; he would, rather, have done honour to truth after his usual fashion with the words: *a religion has never yet, either directly or indirectly, either as dogma or as parable, contained a truth.* For every religion was born out of fear and need, it has crept into existence along paths of aberrations of reason; once, perhaps, when imperilled by science, it lyingly introduced some philosophical teaching or other into its system, so that later it could be discovered there: but this is a theologian's artifice from the time when a religion is already doubting itself. It is these artifices of theology – which in Christianity, as the religion of a scholarly age saturated with philosophy, were, to be sure, already being practised very early – that have led to that superstition of a *sensus allegoricus*, but it has been even more the habit of philosophers (and especially those half-creatures the poetizing philosophers and philosophizing artists) of treating all the sensations they discovered in *themselves* as fundamental qualities of mankind in general and therewith to permit their own religious sensations too to exert a significant influence on the intellectual structure of their systems. Because philosophers have frequently philosophized within a religious tradition, or at least under the inherited power of the celebrated 'metaphysical need', they have achieved hypotheses which have in fact been very similar to Jewish or Christian or Indian religious dogmas – similar, that is to say, in the way children are usually similar to their mothers, except that in this case the fathers were not aware of this fact of motherhood, a thing that does no doubt happen – yet have fabled on in innocent astonishment of a family resemblance between all religion and science. In reality there exists between religion and true science neither affinity, nor friendship, nor even enmity: they dwell on different stars. Every philosophy that exhibits a gleaming religious comet-tail in the darkness of its ultimate conclusions thereby casts suspicion on everything in it that is presented as science: all of that, too, is presumably likewise religion, even if it is dressed up as science. – For the rest, even if all the peoples were in agreement over certain religious matters, for example the existence of a God (which, by the way, is not the case in regard to this particular point), this would in fact be no more than a *counter-argument* against the thing asserted, for example the existence of a God: the *consensus gentium* and *hominum** in general can fairly be considered only a piece of folly. On the other hand, there exists no *consensus omnium sapientium*† whatever in regard to any single thing, with the exception of that of which Goethe's lines speak:

---

* *consensus gentium* and *hominum*: unanimous opinion of all mankind
† *consensus omnium sapientium*: unanimous opinion of all the wise

Alle die Weisesten aller der Zeiten
Lächeln und winken und stimmen mit ein:
Töricht, auf Bessrung der Toren zu harren!
Kinder der Klugheit, o habet die Narren
Eben zum Narren auch, wie sichs gehört!*

Expressed without metre and rhyme, and applied to our case: the *consensus sapientium* is that the *consensus gentium* is a piece of folly.

111

Origin of the religious cult. – If we transport ourselves back to the ages in which the religious life flourished most vigorously we discover a fundamental conviction which we no longer share and on account of which we see the door to the religious life once and for all closed to us: it concerns nature and our traffic with nature. In those ages one as yet knows nothing of natural laws; neither earth nor sky are constrained by any compulsion; a season, sunshine, rain can come or they can fail to come. Any conception of *natural* causality is altogether lacking. When one rows it is not the rowing which moves the ship: rowing is only a magical ceremony by means of which one compels a demon to move the ship. All illness, death itself is the result of magical influences. Becoming ill and dying never occur naturally; the whole conception of a 'natural occurrence' is lacking – it first dawns with the older Greeks, that is to say in a very late phase of mankind, in the conception of a *moira†* enthroned above the gods. When someone shoots with the bow, there is still an irrational hand and force at work in it; if the wells suddenly dry up, one thinks first of all of subterranean demons and their knavery; it must be the arrow of a god through whose invisible action a man suddenly sinks down. In India (according to Lubbock)‡ a carpenter is accustomed to make sacrifices to his hammer, his axe and his other tools; a Brahman treats the crayon with which he writes, a soldier the weapon he employs in the field, a mason his trowel, a labourer his plough in the same way. The whole of nature is in the conception of religious men a sum of actions by conscious and volitional beings, a tremendous complex of *arbitrarinesses*. In regard to everything external to us no conclusion can be drawn that something *will* be thus or thus, *must* happen thus or thus; it is *we* who are the more or less secure and calculable; man is the *rule*, nature is *irregularity* – this proposition contains the fundamental conviction which dominates rude, religiously productive primitive cultures. We men of today feel precisely the opposite: the richer a man feels within himself, the more polyphonic his subjectivity is, the more powerfully is he impressed by the uniformity of nature; with Goethe, we all recognize in nature the great means of composure for the modern soul, we listen to the beat of the pendulum of this mightiest of clocks with a longing for rest, for becoming settled and still, as though we could imbibe this uniformity into ourselves and thereby at

---

* 'All the wisest of every age are in agreement: it is foolish to wait for fools to be cured of their folly! The proper thing to do is to make fools of the fools!' From Goethe's 'Kophtisches Lied', lines 3–7.
† *moira*: fate
‡ Sir John Lubbock (1834–1913), English historian

last come to an enjoyment of ourselves. Formerly the reverse was the case: if we think back to rude, primitive conditions of peoples, or if we look closely at present-day savages, we find them determined in the strongest way by the *law*, by *tradition*: the individual is tied to them almost automatically and moved with the regularity of a pendulum. To him, nature – uncomprehended, dreadful, mysterious nature – must seem the *domain of freedom*, of caprice, of a higher power, indeed, as it were a superhuman stage of existence, a god. But every individual living in such ages and conditions feels how his existence, his happiness, that of the family and the state, the success of any undertaking depends on these arbitrarinesses of nature: certain natural events must occur at the right time, others fail to occur. How can one exercise an influence over these terrible unknown powers, how can one fetter the domain of freedom? thus he asked himself, thus he anxiously seeks: are there then no means of regulating these powers through a tradition and law in just the way you are regulated by them? – The believer in magic and miracles reflects on how to *impose a law on nature* – : and, in brief, the religious cult is the outcome of this reflection. The problem these men pose themselves is intimately related to this one: how can the *weaker* tribe nonetheless dictate laws to the *stronger*, dispose of it, regulate its actions (so far as they affect the weaker)? One will think first of that mildest kind of constraint, that constraint one exercises when one has gained the *affection* of someone. It is thus also possible to exercise a constraint on the powers ·of nature through prayers and pleadings, through submission, through engaging regularly to give presents and offerings, through flattering glorifications, inasmuch as by doing so one obtains their affection: love binds and is bound. Then one can conclude *treaties* under which both parties commit themselves to a certain course of conduct, pledge securities and exchange oaths. But much more important than this is a species of more violent constraint through magic and sorcery. Just as man is able with the aid of the sorcerer to harm an enemy stronger than himself, just as the sorcery of love can operate at a distance, so the weaker man believes he can influence the mightier spirits of nature too. The chief means employed by all sorcery is that of getting into one's power something belonging to another: hair, nail, food from his table, even his picture or his name. Thus equipped one can then practise sorcery; for the basic presupposition is that to everything spiritual there pertains something corporeal; with its aid one is able to bind, harm, destroy the spirit; the corporeal provides the handle with which one can grasp the spiritual. So that, as man thus influences other men, so he also influences some spirit of nature; for the latter too has its corporeal aspect by which it can be grasped. The tree and, compared with it, the seed from which it originated – this enigmatic juxtaposition seems to demonstrate that one and the same spirit has incorporated itself in both forms, one small, one big. A stone that suddenly rolls away is the body in which a spirit is active; if a rock lies on a lonely heath and it seems impossible that human strength could ever have sufficed to take it there, it must have moved there itself, that is to say it must harbour a spirit. Everything that has a body is accessible to sorcery, thus the spirits of nature are so too. If a god is actually tied to his image then one can also exercise quite direct constraint upon him (through denial of sacrificial food, scourging, flattering and the like). To force from their god the goodwill he is denying them, the common people in China wind ropes around his image, pull it down, and drag it along the streets through the mud and dung; 'you dog of a spirit', they say, 'we let you live in a splendid temple, we covered you with gold, we fed you well, we sacrificed to you, and yet you are so ungrateful'. Similar violent measures have been taken against images of saints and of the Virgin in Catholic lands even in the present century when they have refused to do their duty in times of pestilence or drought.

All these magical relationships with nature called countless ceremonies into existence: and finally, when their confusion had grown too great, an effort was made to order and systematize them; so that one came to believe that the favourable progress of the whole course of nature, and especially of the great succession of the seasons of the year, was guaranteed by a corresponding progress of a system of procedures. The meaning of the religious cult is to determine and constrain nature for the benefit of mankind, that is to say *to impress upon it a regularity and rule of law which it does not at first possess*; while in the present age one seeks to *understand* the laws of nature so as to accommodate oneself to them. In brief, the religious cult rests on the ideas of sorcery as between man and man; and the sorcerer is older than the priest. But it *likewise* rests on other and nobler ideas; it presupposes relations of sympathy between man and man, the existence of goodwill, gratitude, the hearing of petitions, treaties between enemies, the bestowal of pledges, the claim to protection of property. Even at very low stages of culture man does not stand towards nature as its impotent slave, he is *not* necessarily its will-less servant: at the stage of religion attained by the Greeks, especially in relation to the gods of Olympus, it is even as though two castes lived side by side, a nobler and mightier and one less noble; but both somehow belong together in their origins and are of *one* species, they have no need to be ashamed of one another. That is the element of nobility in Greek religiosity.

112

On viewing certain antique sacrificial implements. – How many sensations have been lost us can be seen, for example, in the union of the farcical, even the obscene, with the religious feeling: our sense of the possibility of this combination dwindles, we comprehend that it existed only historically, in the festivals of Demeter and Dionysus, in the Christian Easter and mystery plays: but we too still know the sublime in concert with the burlesque and the like, the moving blended with the ludicrous: which a later age will in turn perhaps no longer comprehend.

113

Christianity and antiquity. – When on a Sunday morning we hear the bells ringing we ask ourselves: is it possible! this is going on because of a Jew crucified 2000 years ago who said he was the son of God. The proof of such an assertion is lacking. – In the context of our age the Christian religion is certainly a piece of antiquity intruding out of distant ages past, and that the above-mentioned assertion is believed – while one is otherwise so rigorous in the testing of claims – is perhaps the most ancient piece of this inheritance. A god who begets children on a mortal woman; a sage who calls upon us no longer to work, no longer to sit in judgement, but to heed the signs of the imminent end of the world; a justice which accepts an innocent man as a substitute sacrifice; someone who bids his disciples drink his blood; prayers for miraculous interventions; sin perpetrated against a god atoned for by a god; fear of a Beyond to which death is the gateway; the figure of the Cross as a symbol in an age which no longer knows the meaning and shame of the Cross – how gruesomely all this is wafted to us, as if out of the grave of a primeval past! Can one believe that things of this sort are still believed in?

114

The un-Hellenic in Christianity. – The Greeks did not see the Homeric gods as set above them as masters, or themselves set beneath the gods as servants, as the Jews did. They saw as it were only the reflection of the most successful exemplars of their own caste, that is to say an ideal, not an antithesis of their own nature. They felt inter-related with them, there existed a mutual interest, a kind of symmetry. Man thinks of himself as noble when he bestows upon himself such gods, and places himself in a relationship to them such as exists between the lower aristocracy and the higher; while the Italic peoples have a real peasant religion, with continual anxiety over evil and capricious powers and tormenting spirits. Where the Olympian gods failed to dominate, Greek life too was gloomier and more filled with anxiety. – Christianity, on the other hand, crushed and shattered man completely and buried him as though in mud: into a feeling of total depravity it then suddenly shone a beam of divine mercy, so that, surprised and stupefied by this act of grace, man gave vent to a cry of rapture and for a moment believed he bore all heaven within him. It is upon this pathological excess of feeling, upon the profound corruption of head and heart that was required for it, that all the psychological sensations of Christianity operate: it desires to destroy, shatter, stupefy, intoxicate, the one thing it does not desire is *measure*: and that is why it is in the profoundest sense barbaric, Asiatic, ignoble, un-Hellenic.

115

Advantage of being religious. – There are sober and industrious people to whom religion adheres like a bordering of higher humanity: such people do well to remain religious, it beautifies them. – All men incapable of wielding some kind of weapon or other – mouth and pen included as weapons – become servile: for these Christianity is very useful, for within Christianity servility assumes the appearance of a virtue and is quite astonishingly beautified. – People whose daily life appears to them too empty and monotonous easily become religious: this is understandable and forgivable; only they have no right to demand religiosity of those whose daily life is not empty and monotonous.

116

The everyday Christian. – If the Christian dogmas of a revengeful God, universal sinfulness, election by divine grace and the danger of everlasting damnation were true, it would be a sign of weakmindedness and lack of character *not* to become a priest, apostle or hermit and, in fear and trembling, to work solely on one's own salvation; it would be senseless to lose sight of one's eternal advantage for the sake of temporal comfort. If we may assume that these things are at any rate *believed* true, then the everyday Christian cuts a miserable figure; he is a man who really cannot count to three, and who precisely on account of his spiritual imbecility does not deserve to be punished so harshly as Christianity promises to punish him.

117

Of the prudence of Christianity. – Among the artifices of Christianity is that of proclaiming the complete unworthiness, sinfulness and despicableness of man in general so loudly that to despise one's fellow man becomes impossible. 'Let him sin as he may, he is nonetheless not essentially different from me: it is I who am in every degree unworthy and despicable': thus says the Christian to himself. But this feeling too has lost its sharpest sting, because the Christian does not believe in his individual despicableness: he is evil as a man as such and quietens his mind a little with the proposition: we are all of *one* kind.

118

Change of cast. – As soon as a religion comes to dominate it has as its opponents all those who would have been its first disciples.

119

Destiny of Christianity. – Christianity came into existence in order to lighten the heart; but now it has first to burden the heart so as afterwards to be able to lighten it. Consequently it will perish.

120

Proof by pleasure. – The pleasant opinion is taken to be true: this is the proof by pleasure (or, as the church puts it, the proof by power) of which all religions are so proud, though they ought to be ashamed of it. If the belief did not make blessed it would not be believed: how little, then, will it be worth!

121

Dangerous game. – Anyone who now again makes room for religious sensibility within himself will then have to allow it to grow: he cannot do otherwise. As a consequence his nature will gradually change, it will come to prefer that which adheres to and dwells beside the religious

element, the entire horizon of his judgement and sensibility will be clouded round and religious shadows will flit across it. Sensibility cannot stand
still; therefore let us take care.

122

Blind pupils. – As long as a man knows very well the strength and weakness of his teaching, his art, his religion, its power is still slight. The pupil
and apostle who, blinded by the authority of the master and by the piety
he feels towards him, pays no attention to the weaknesses of a teaching, a
religion, and so on, usually has for that reason more power than the
master. The influence of a man and his work has never yet grown great
without his blind pupils. To help a perception to achieve victory often
means merely to unite it with stupidity so intimately that the weight of
the latter also enforces the victory of the former.

123

Demolition of the churches. – There is not enough of religion in the world
even to destroy the religions.

124

Sinlessness of man. – When one has grasped how 'sin came into the world',
namely through errors of reason by virtue of which men mistake one
another – indeed, the individual man mistakes himself – to be much
blacker and more evil than is actually the case, then all one's feelings are
very much relieved and lightened, and man and world sometimes appear
in a halo of harmlessness the sight of which fills one with a thorough
sense of wellbeing. In the midst of nature man is always the child in itself.
This child does once dream a dismal, fear-inspiring dream it is true, but
when it opens its eyes it sees it is still in Paradise.

125

Irreligiosity of artists. – Homer is so much at home among his gods, and as
a poet takes such pleasure in them, that he at any rate must have been
profoundly unreligious; with that with which popular belief presented
him – a paltry, crude, in part horrible superstition – he trafficked as freely
as a sculptor with his clay, that is to say with the same ease and impar-
tiality as that possessed by Aeschylus and Aristophanes and which in
more recent times distinguishes the great artists of the Renaissance, as it
does Shakespeare and Goethe.

126

Art and force of false interpretation. – All the visions, terrors, states of
exhaustion and rapture experienced by the saint are familiar pathological
conditions which, on the basis of rooted religious and psychological
errors, he only *interprets* quite differently, that is to say not as illnesses. –
Thus the daemon of Socrates too was perhaps an ear-infection which, in
accordance with the moralizing manner of thinking that dominated him,
he only *interpreted* differently from how it would be interpreted now. It is
not otherwise with the madness and ravings of the prophets and oracular

priests; it is always the degree of knowledge, imagination, exertion, morality in the head and heart of the *interpreters* that has *made* so much of
them. For those men called geniuses and saints to produce their greatest
effect they have to have constrained to their side interpreters who for the
good of mankind *misunderstand* them.

127
Reverence for madness. – Because it was noticed that a state of excitement
often made the head clearer and called up happy inspirations, it was believed that through the extremest states of excitement one would participate in the happiest of inspirations: and thus the mad were revered as the
wise and propounders of oracles. What lies at the bottom of this is a false
conclusion.

128
What science promises. – Modern science has as its goal: as little pain as
possible, as long life as possible – thus a kind of eternal bliss, though a
very modest kind in comparison with the promises of the religions.

129
Forbidden generosity. – There is not enough love and goodness in the
world for us to be permitted to give any of it away to imaginary things.

130
Continuance of the religious cult in the heart. – The Catholic Church, and
before it all the cults of antiquity, had command of the whole domain of
the means by which man is transported into unfamiliar states and robbed
of the ability to calculate coolly or to think clearly. A church trembling
with deep sounds; dull, regular, repressed calls from a company of
priests who involuntarily transmit their tension to the congregation and
excite them to listen almost in fear, as though a miracle were about to
occur; the breath of the architecture, which, as the abode of a divinity,
reaches up into obscurity, in the dark spaces of which the divinity may at
any moment make evident his dreaded presence – who would want mankind to experience such things again, now that the presuppositions
behind them are no longer believed in? But the consequences of all this
are nonetheless still present: the inner world of the sublime, affected,
tremulous, contrite, expectant states was born in man principally
through the religious cult; that of it which still remains in the soul was, in
the days of its germination and growth, tended and cultivated by it.

131
Religious after-pains. – However much one may believe one has weaned
oneself from religion, the weaning has not been so complete that one
does not enjoy encountering religious moods and sentiments without
conceptual content, for example in music; and when a philosophy
demonstrates to us the justification of metaphysical hopes and the profound peace of soul to be attained through them, and speaks for example
of 'the whole sure evangel in the glance of Raphael's Madonna', we go

out to meet such assertions and expositions with particular warmth of feeling; the philosopher here has an easier task of demonstration, for he here encounters a heart eager to take what he has to offer. From this it is apparent that the less thoughtful free spirits are really taking exception only to the dogmas, but are very well acquainted with the magic of the religious sensations; it hurts them to let the latter go on account of the former. – Scientific philosophy has to be very much on its guard against smuggling in errors on the basis of this need (a need that has come into existence and consequently also a transient one): even logicians speak of 'presentiments' of truth in morality and art (for example of the presentiment 'that the essence of things is one'): which is something that should be forbidden them. Between truths that are the outcome of cautious reasoning and these products of 'presentiment' there lies the unbridgable gulf created by the fact that we owe the former to the intellect and the latter to a need. Hunger is no proof that the food that would satisfy it *exists*, though it desires the food. 'Presentiment' does not signify any degree of knowledge of the existence of a thing, it signifies regarding it as possible, inasmuch as one desires or fears it: 'presentiment' does not advance a single step into the land of certainty. – One involuntarily believes that the religiously coloured departments of a philosophy are better established than the others; but at bottom the case is the reverse; one only has the inner desire it may *be* so – that is to say, that what makes happy should also be what is true. This desire misleads us into purchasing bad reasons for good ones.

132

On the Christian need of redemption. – Careful reflection ought to be able to yield an explanation of the occurrence in the soul of a Christian called need of redemption which is free of mythology: that is to say, a purely psychological explanation. It is true that psychological explanation of religious states and occurrences has hitherto stood in a certain ill-repute, insofar as a theology calling itself free has been pursuing its unprofitable business in this domain: for its purpose was from the first, as the spirit of its founder, Schleiermacher,* leads us to suppose, the preservation of the Christian religion and the continuance of Christian theology; in which regard psychological analysis of the 'facts' of religion was supposed to afford a new anchorage and above all a new occupation. Undeterred by these events we venture to offer the following interpretation of the said phenomenon. – Man is conscious of certain actions which stand low in the customary order of rank of actions; indeed, he discovers in himself a tendency to actions of this sort which seems to him almost as immutable as his whole nature. How much he would like to attempt that other species of actions which in the general estimation are accounted the highest, how much he would like to feel full of that good consciousness which is supposed to attend a selfless mode of thought! Unhappily he

---

* Schleiermacher: Friedrich Schleiermacher (1768–1834), the leading Protestant theologian of his age

gets no further than desiring this: his discontent at his insufficiency is added to all the other kinds of discontent which his lot in life in general or the consequences of those other actions called wicked have engendered in him; so that there arises a profound depression of spirits, together with a watching-out for a physician who might be able to alleviate this condition and all its causes. – This condition would not be felt so bitterly if man compared himself only with other men: for then he would have no reason to be especially discontented with himself, since he would see he was only bearing the general burden of human dissatisfaction and imperfection. But he compares himself with a being which alone is capable of those actions called unegoistic and lives continually in the consciousness of a selfless mode of thought, with God; it is because he looks into this brilliant mirror that his own nature seems to him so dismal, so uncommonly distorted. Then again, the thought of this same being makes him fearful insofar as it appears to his imagination as chastising justice: in all possible experiences, great and small, he believes he recognizes its anger and menaces, indeed that he feels already in advance the whiplash of this judge and executioner. Who can help him in this peril, which, inasmuch as the term of punishment is to be unending, exceeds in horror anything else he can imagine?

133
Before we go on to exhibit this condition in its further consequences let us confess to ourselves that the man in this condition has got into it, not through his 'guilt' and 'sin', but through a succession of errors of reason, that it was the fault of the mirror if his nature appeared to him dark and hateful to such a degree, and that this mirror was *his* work, the very imperfect work of human imagination and judgement. Firstly, a being capable of nothing but unegoistic actions is more fabulous than the phoenix; it cannot even be imagined clearly, if only because under strict examination the whole concept 'unegoistic action' vanishes into thin air. No man has ever done anything that was done wholly for others and with no personal motivation whatever; how, indeed, should a man be *able* to do something that had no reference to himself, that is to say lacked all inner compulsion (which would have its basis in a personal need)? How could the ego act without the ego? – On the other hand, a God who was *wholly* love, as is occasionally supposed, would be incapable of a single unegoistic action: in connection with which one should recall a thought of Lichtenberg's, though it was, to be sure, taken from a somewhat lower sphere: 'It is impossible, as is commonly said, for us to *feel* for others; we feel only for ourselves. The proposition sounds hard, but is not if it is correctly understood. One loves neither father, nor mother, nor wife, nor child, one loves the pleasant sensations they produce in us', or as La Rochefoucauld says: *'si on croit aimer sa maîtresse pour l'amour d'elle, on est bien trompé'*.* As to why actions performed out of love are *evaluated* more highly than others, namely not on account of their nature but on account

* 'if we believe we love our mistress for love of her we are very much mistaken'

of their utility, one should consult the investigations 'On the Origin of the Moral Sensations' previously referred to. If, however, a man should wish to be, like that God, wholly love, and to do and desire everything for others and nothing for himself, then the latter is impossible simply because he has to do a *great deal* for himself if he is to be able to do anything whatever for the sake of others. Moreover, such a thing presupposes that the other is sufficiently egoistical to accept this sacrifice, this life lived for his sake, over and over again: so that men of love and self-sacrifice would have to have an interest in the continuance of the loveless egoist incapable of self-sacrifice, and the highest morality would, if it was to continue to exist, have to downright *compel* the existence of immorality (whereby it would, to be sure, abolish itself). – Further: the idea of a God is disturbing and humiliating as long as it is believed, but how it *originated* can at the present stage of comparative ethnology no longer admit of doubt; and with the insight into this origination that belief falls away. The Christian who compares his nature with that of God is like Don Quixote, who under-estimated his own courage because his head was filled with the miraculous deeds of the heroes of chivalric romances: the standard of comparison applied in both cases belongs in the domain of fable. But if the idea of God falls away, so does the feeling of 'sin' as a transgression against divine precepts, as a blemish on a creature consecrated to God. Then there probably still remains over that feeling of depression which is very much entwined with and related to fear of punishment by secular justice or the disapprobation of other men; the depression caused by the pang of conscience, the sharpest sting in the feeling of guilt, is nonetheless abolished when one sees that, although one may by one's actions have offended against human tradition, human laws and ordinances, one has not therewith endangered the 'eternal salvation of the soul' and its relationship to the divinity. If a man is, finally, able to attain to the philosophical conviction of the unconditional necessity of all actions and their complete unaccountability and to make it part of his flesh and blood, then that remainder of the pang of conscience also disappears.

134

Now if, as has been said, the Christian has got into the feeling of self-contempt through certain errors, that is to say through a false, unscientific interpretation of his actions and sensations, he also notices with the highest astonishment that this condition of contempt, the pang of conscience, displeasure in general, does not persist, but that occasionally there are hours when all this is wafted away from his soul and he again feels free and valiant. What has happened is that his pleasure in himself, his contentment at his own strength, has, in concert with the weakening which every profound excitation must necessarily undergo, carried off the victory: he loves himself again, he feels it – but precisely this love, this new self-valuation seems to him incredible, he can see in it only the wholly undeserved flowing down of a radiance of mercy from on high. If he earlier believed he saw in every event warnings, menaces, punishments and every sort of sign of divine wrath, he now *interprets* divine goodness *into* his experiences: this event appears to him to exhibit kindness, that is like a helpful signpost, a third and especially the whole joyful mood he is in seems to him proof that God is merciful. If he earlier in a condition of depression interpreted his actions falsely, now he does the same with his experiences; he conceives his mood of consolation as the effect upon him of an external power, the love with which fundamentally he loves himself appears as divine love; that which he calls mercy and the prelude to redemption is in truth self-pardon, self-redemption.

135

Thus: a certain false psychology, a certain kind of fantasy in the interpretation of motives and experiences is the necessary presupposition for becoming a Christian and for feeling the need of redemption. With the insight into this aberration of reason and imagination one ceases to be a Christian.

136

Of Christian asceticism and holiness. – However much individual thinkers have exerted themselves to represent those strange phenomena of morality usually called asceticism and holiness as a marvel and miracle to attempt a rational explanation of which is almost a sacrilege and profanation: the urge to commit this sacrilege is, on the other hand, every bit as strong. A mighty drive of *nature* has at all times prompted a protest against these phenomena as such; science, insofar as it is, as aforesaid, an imitation of nature, permits itself at least to register a protest against the alleged inexplicability, indeed inapproachability, of the said phenomena. So far, to be sure, it has done so in vain: they are still unexplained, a fact that gives great satisfaction to the above-mentioned votaries of the morally miraculous. For, speaking quite generally, the unexplained is to be altogether inexplicable, the inexplicable altogether unnatural, supernatural, miraculous – thus sounds the demand in the souls of all religious people and metaphysicians (in those of the artists, too, when they are also thinkers); while the scientific man sees in this demand the 'evil principle'. – The first general probability one arrives at when reflecting on holiness and asceticism is that its nature is a *complex* one: for almost everywhere, within the physical world as well as in the moral, the supposedly marvellous has successfully been traced back to the complex, to the multiply caused. Let us therefore venture first to isolate individual drives in the soul of the saint and ascetic and then conclude by thinking of them entwined together.

137

There is a *defiance of oneself* of which many forms of asceticism are among the most sublimated expressions. For certain men feel so great a need to exercise their strength and lust for power that, in default of other objects or because their efforts in other directions have always miscarried, they at last hit upon the idea of tyrannizing over certain parts of their own nature, over, as it were, segments or stages of themselves. Thus some thinkers confess to views which are plainly not calculated to increase or improve their reputation; some downright call down the disrespect of others upon themselves when by keeping silent they could easily have remained respected men; others retract earlier opinions and are not afraid of henceforth being called inconsistent: on the contrary, they strive to be called so, and behave like high-spirited riders who like their steed best only when it has grown savage, is covered with sweat, and is tamed. Thus a man climbs on dangerous paths in the highest mountains so as to mock at his fears and trembling knees; thus a philosopher adheres to views of asceticism, humility and holiness in the light of which his own image becomes extremely ugly. This division of oneself, this mockery of one's own nature, this *spernere se sperni** of which the religions have made so much, is actually a very high degree of vanity. The entire morality of the Sermon on the Mount belongs here: man takes a real delight in oppressing himself with excessive claims and afterwards idolizing this tyrannically demanding something in his soul. In every ascetic morality man worships a part of himself as God and for that he needs to diabolize the other part. –

138
Man is not equally moral all the time, that fact is well known: if one judges his morality according to his capacity for great self-sacrificing res- olution and self-denial (which, protracted and grown to a habit, consti- tutes holiness), then it is in his *affects* that he is most moral; higher excitation presents him with quite novel motivations which, in his more usual cold and sober state, he would perhaps not even believe himself capable of. How does this come about? Probably through the proximity to one another of all great and highly exciting things; once a man has been brought to a state of extraordinary tension, he can resolve equally well to take a fearful revenge or to break himself of his thirst for revenge. Under the influence of violent emotion he desires in any event the great, tremen- dous, prodigious, and if he happens to notice that the sacrifice of himself satisfies him as much as, or even more than the sacrifice of another, he chooses it. All he is really concerned with, therefore, is the discharge of his emotion; to relieve his state of tension he seizes the spears of his enemies and buries them in his own breast. That there is something great in self-denial, and not only in revenge, must have been inculcated into man only through long habituation; a divinity who sacrifices himself was the strongest, most effective symbol of this kind of greatness. As the overcoming of the foe hardest to conquer, the sudden mastering of an affect – that is how this denial *appeared*; and to this extent it counted as the summit of the moral. In reality what is involved is the exchange of one idea for another, with the feelings remaining at the same level of elev- ation and flood. When they are grown sober again and are resting from this affect, men no longer understand the morality of those moments, but

* *spernere se sperni*: answer contempt with contempt

the general admiration of all who also experienced it sustains and supports them; pride is their consolation when the affect and an understanding of their deed fades away. Thus: these acts of self-denial also are at bottom not moral, insofar as they are not performed strictly for the sake of others; the case, rather, is that the other only offers the highly tensed heart an opportunity to relieve itself through this self-denial.

139

In many respects the ascetic too seeks to make life easier for himself: and he does so as a rule by complete subordination to the will of another or to a comprehensive law and ritual; somewhat in the way in which the Brahman decides nothing whatever for himself but is guided every moment by holy writ. This subordination is a powerful means of becoming master of oneself; one is occupied and thus not bored, and yet one's own willfulness and passions are not in any way involved; after one has acted there is no feeling of responsibility and therefore no pangs of remorse. One has renounced one's own will once and for all, and this is easier than renouncing it only now and again; just as it is easier to relinquish a desire altogether than to enjoy it in moderation. If we recall the relationship between man and state now obtaining, we discover that there too unconditional obedience is more comfortable than conditional. The saint thus makes his life easier through this complete surrender of his personality, and one deceives oneself if one admires in this phenomenon the supreme heroic feat of morality. It is in any event harder to maintain one's personality without vacillation or dissimulation than it is to free oneself of it in the way described; and it demands, moreover, a lot more spirit and reflection.

140

After having discovered in many actions more difficult to explain that pleasure in *emotion as such*, I would also recognize in regard to the self-contempt which is one of the characteristics of saintliness, and likewise in acts of self-torture (through hunger and flagillation, dislocation of limbs, simulation of madness), a means by which these natures combat the general enervation of their will to live (their nerves): they employ the most painful stimulants and cruelties so as, at least for a time, to emerge out of that boredom and torpor into which their great spiritual indolence and their subordination to the will of another just described so often plunges them.

141

The most usual means the ascetic and saint employs to make his life nonetheless endurable and enjoyable consists in occasionally waging war and in the alternation of victory and defeat. To this end he requires an opponent, and he finds him in the so-called 'enemy within'. He exploits especially his tendency to vanity, to a thirst for honours and domination, then his sensual desires, in an attempt to see his life as a continual battle and himself as a battlefield upon which good and evil spirits wrestle with alternating success. It is well known that sensual fantasy is moderated, indeed almost suppressed, by regularity in sexual intercourse, while it is on the other hand unfettered and dissolute when such intercourse is disorderly or does not take place at all. The fantasy of many Christian saints has been dirty to an uncommon degree; by virtue of the theory that these desires are actually demons raging within them they do not feel any very great sense of responsibility for this state of things; it is to this feeling that we owe the instructive candidness of their self-confessions. It has been in their interest that this struggle should be in progress all the time to some degree, since, as already said, it provides entertainment for their tedious life. But so that this struggle should seem sufficiently momentous to excite the continuing interest and admiration of the non-saints, sensuality had to be more and more stigmatized as heretical, indeed the danger of everlasting damnation was associated so closely with these things that it is highly probable that throughout whole ages Christians even begot children with a bad conscience; whereby a great injury has certainly been done to mankind. And yet here truth is stood completely on its head: which is in the case of truth particularly unbecoming. Christianity had indeed said: every man is conceived and born in sin; and in the insupportable superlative Christianity of Calderón* this idea was again knotted and wound together, so that he ventured on the most perverse paradox there is in the well-known lines:

> the greatest guilt of man
> is that he was born.

In all pessimistic religions the act of procreation is felt as being bad in itself, but this feeling is by no means common to all mankind and even the pessimists are not unanimous in the matter. Empedocles,† for example, knows nothing whatever of the disgraceful, diabolical, sinful in erotic things; on the contrary, he sees upon the great field of misfortune only one apparition that promises hope and salvation, Aphrodite; to him she is a guarantee that strife will not rule for ever but will one day hand over the sceptre to a gentler daemon. The Christian practical pessimists had, as aforesaid, an interest in seeing that a different opinion remained dominant; they required for the solitude and the spiritual wasteland of their life an enemy always on the alert: and an enemy, moreover, that was universally recognized through the combating and overcoming of whom they could repeatedly appear to the non-saints as half incomprehensible, supernatural beings. If, as a consequence of their mode of life and the ruination of their health, this enemy finally took flight for ever, they at once knew how to *see* their inner world populated by new demons. The rise and fall of the scales called pride and humility entertained their brooding heads just as well as did the alternation of desire and repose of soul. In those days psychology served the end, not only of casting suspicion on everything human, but of oppressing, scourging

---

* Calderón: Pedro Calderón de la Barca (1600–81): Spanish dramatist
† Empedocles (d.c. 433 BC): 'pre-Socratic' philosopher

and crucifying it; one *wanted* to believe oneself as bad and evil as possible, one sought fear for the salvation of one's soul, despair of one's own strength. Everything natural to which one attaches the idea of the bad and sinful (as for example is done even now in regard to the erotic) oppresses the imagination and makes it gloomy, because frightening to look upon, causes men to haggle with themselves and deprives them of security and trust; even their dreams acquire a flavour of tormented conscience. And yet this suffering from the natural in the reality of things is completely groundless: it is only the consequence of opinions *about* things. It is easy to see how designating the ineluctably natural as bad, and then invariably finding it so, makes men themselves worse than they need be. The artifice practised by religion and by those metaphysicians who will have man evil and sinful by nature is to make him suspicious of nature and thus *make* him himself bad: this being a consequence of his inability to divest himself of nature's garb. If he lives long in this natural dress he gradually comes to feel weighed down by such a burden of sins that supernatural powers are needed to lift it; and with that the need for redemption we have already discussed steps upon the scene, answering to no actual but only to an imaginary sinfulness. Go through the moral demands exhibited in the documents of Christianity one by one and you will find that in every case they are exaggerated, so that man *could* not live up to them; the intention is not that he should *become* more moral, but that he should feel *as sinful as possible*. If man had failed to find this feeling *pleasant* – why should he have engendered such an idea and adhered to it for so long? Just as in the world of antiquity an immeasurable quantity of spirit and inventiveness had been expended on augmenting joy in life through festive cults, so in the era of Christianity an immeasurable amount of spirit has likewise been sacrificed to another endeavour: man was by every means to be made to feel sinful and thereby become excited, animated, enlivened in general. To excite, animate, enliven at any price – is that not the watchword of an enervated, over-ripe, over-cultivated age? The circle of all natural sensations had been run through a hundred times, the soul had grown tired of them: thereupon the saint and the ascetic invented a new species of stimulant. They presented themselves before all eyes, not really so that many might imitate them, but as a frightful and yet delightful spectacle, performed on that borderline between world and over-world where in those days everyone believed they beheld now rays of heavenly light, now uncanny tongues of flame flickering up from the depths. The eye of the saint, directed upon the dreadful significance of the brevity of earthly life, upon the proximity of the final decision in regard to endless new vistas of life, this burning eye in a body half destroyed, made the men of the ancient world tremble in their very depths; to gaze at him, suddenly to look away, to feel again the attraction of the spectacle, to surrender to it, to satiate oneself with it until the soul was convulsed with fire and icy fevers – this was the last *pleasure antiquity invented* after it had grown apathetic even to the sight of animal and human combats.

142

To summarize what has been said: that condition of the soul in which the saint or one becoming a saint rejoices is composed of elements with which we are all very familiar; except that in the light of other conceptions than the religious they appear in other colours and then they usually incur the censure of mankind as surely as, garnished with religion and the ultimate meaning of existence, they can count on admiration or, indeed, worship – or at least could count on them in earlier ages. Now the saint practises that defiance of oneself that is a close relation of lust for power and bestows the feeling of power even upon the hermit; now his distended sensibility leaps out of the desire to allow his passions free rein over into the desire to break them like wild horses under the mighty impress of a proud soul; now he desires a complete cessation of sensations of a disturbing, tormenting, stimulating kind, a waking sleep, a lasting repose in the womb of a dull, beast- and plant-like indolence; now he seeks conflict and ignites it in himself, because boredom has shown him its yawning face: he scourges his self-idolatry with self-contempt and cruelty, he rejoices in the wild riot of his desires, in the sharp sting of sin, indeed in the idea that he is lost, he knows how to lay a trap for his affects, for example that of the extremest lust for power, so that he passes over into the extremest abasement and his hunted soul is wrenched utterly out of joint by this contrast; and when, finally, he comes to thirst for visions, for colloquies with the dead or divine beings, it is at bottom a rare kind of voluptuousness he desires, but perhaps that voluptuousness within which all other kinds are knotted together. Novalis, one of the authorities in questions of saintliness by experience and instinct, once blurted out the whole secret with naive rapture: 'It is sufficiently marvellous that not long ago the association of voluptuousness, religion and cruelty called the attention of men to their inner relatedness and common tendency.'

143

It is not what the saint *is*, but what he *signifies* in the eyes of the non-saints, that gives him his world-historic value. Because he was mistaken for what he was not, because his psychological states were interpreted falsely and he was set as far apart as possible from everyone else as though he were something altogether incomparable, strange and supra-human: that is how he acquired the extraordinary power with which he was able to dominate the imagination of whole nations and whole ages. He himself did not know himself; he himself deciphered the characters of his moods, inclinations and actions by means of an art of interpretation that was as exaggerated and artificial as the pneumatical interpretation of the Bible. What was perverse and pathological in his nature, with its coupling together of spiritual poverty, deficient knowledge, ruined health and over-excited nerves, was concealed from his own sight just as it was from that of his spectators. He was not an especially good man, even less an especially wise one: but he *signified* something that exceeded the ordinary human portion of goodness and wisdom. Belief in him lent support to belief in the divine and miraculous, in a religious meaning of existence, in an imminent Day of Judgement. In the evening glow of the sun of the coming end of the world that shone over all Christian peoples the shadow of the saint grew to monstrous size: to such a height, indeed, that even in our own age, which no longer believes in God, there are still thinkers who believe in the saints.

144
It goes without saying that this depiction of the saint, which is sketched after the average profile of the whole species, can be countered by many depictions which might evoke more pleasant feelings. Individual exceptions stand apart from the species in general, either through great gentleness and philanthropy or through the charm of an uncommon degree of energy; others are in the highest degree attractive because their whole being is flooded with the light of certain delusions: as for example was the case with the celebrated founder of Christianity, who regarded himself as the innate son of God and as a consequence felt himself to be sinless; so that, through this conceit – which ought not to be judged too harshly, since the whole of antiquity swarmed with sons of gods – he attained the same goal, the feeling of complete sinlessness, complete unaccountability, which nowadays everyone can acquire through scientific study. – I have likewise taken no account of the Indian saints, who occupy an intermedite position between the Christian saint and the Greek philosopher and to this extent do not represent a pure type: knowledge, science – insofar as there was any – elevation above other men through logical discipline and schooling have been demanded by the Buddhists as a sign of sainthood to the same extent as these qualities are rejected and denounced as signs of unholiness in the Christian world.

FROM THE SOULS OF
ARTISTS
AND WRITERS

145

What is perfect is supposed not to have become. – In the case of everything perfect we are accustomed to abstain from asking how it became: we rejoice in the present fact as though it came out of the ground by magic. Here we are probably still standing under the after-effect of a primeval mythological invention. We still *almost* feel (for example in a Greek temple such as that at Paestum) that a god must one morning have playfully constructed his dwelling out of these tremendous weights: at other times that a stone suddenly acquired by magic a soul that is now trying to speak out of it. The artist knows that his work produces its full effect when it excites a belief in an improvisation, a belief that it came into being with a miraculous suddenness; and so he may assist this illusion and introduce those elements of rapturous restlessness, of blindly groping disorder, of attentive reverie that attend the beginning of creation into his art as a means of deceiving the soul of the spectator or auditor into a mood in which he believes that the complete and perfect has suddenly emerged instantaneously. – The science of art has, it goes without saying, most definitely to counter this illusion and to display the bad habits and false conclusions of the intellect by virtue of which it allows the artist to ensnare it.

146

The artist's sense of truth. – In regard to knowledge of truths, the artist possesses a weaker morality than the thinker; he does not wish to be deprived of the glittering, profound interpretations of life and guards against simple and sober methods and results. He appears to be fighting on behalf of the greater dignity and significance of man; in reality he refuses to give up the presuppositions which are *most efficacious* for his art, that is to say the fantastic, mythical, uncertain, extreme, the sense for the symbolical, the over-estimation of the person, the belief in something miraculous in genius: he thus considers the perpetuation of his mode of creation more important than scientific devotion to the true in any form, however plainly this may appear.

147

Art as necromancer. – Among the subsidiary duties of art is that of conserving, and no doubt also of taking extinguished, faded ideas and restoring to them a little colour: when it performs this task it winds a band around different ages and makes the spirits that inform them return. It is only a phantom life that here arises, to be sure, such as appears about graves or like the return of the beloved dead in dreams; but the old emotions are again aroused, if only for a few moments, and the heart beats to a rhythm it had forgotten. On account of this useful function of art one must overlook it in the artist himself if he does not stand in the foremost ranks of the Enlightenment and the progressive *masculinization* of man: he has remained a child or a youth all his life, stuck at the point at which he was first assailed by his drive to artistic production; feelings belonging to the first stages of life are, however, admitted to be closer to those of earlier times than to those of the present century. Without his knowing it, his task becomes that of making mankind childlike; this is his glory and his limitation.

148
Poets as alleviators of life. – Insofar as they want to alleviate the life of men, poets either turn their eyes away from the toilsome present or they procure for the present new colours through a light which they direct upon it from the past. To be able to do this, they themselves have to be in many respects backward-looking creatures: so that they can be employed as bridges to quite distant ages and conceptions, to dead or dying religions and cultures. They are, in fact, always and necessarily *epigones*. There are, to be sure, several things to be said against their means of alleviating life: they soothe and heal only provisionally, only for a moment; they even hinder men from working for a real improvement in their conditions by suspending and discharging in a palliative way the very passion which impels the discontented to action.

149
The slow arrow of beauty. – The noblest kind of beauty is not that which suddenly transports us, which makes a violent and intoxicating assault upon us (such beauty can easily excite disgust), but that which slowly infiltrates us, which we bear away with us almost without noticing and encounter again in dreams, but which finally, after having for long lain modestly in our heart, takes total possession of us, filling our eyes with tears and our heart with longing. – What is it we long for at the sight of beauty? To be beautiful ourself: we imagine we would be very happy if we were beautiful. – But that is an error.

150
Animation of art. – Art raises its head where the religions relax their hold. It takes over a host of moods and feelings engendered by religion, lays them to its heart and itself grows more profound and soulful, so that it is now capable of communicating exultation and enthusiasm as it formerly could not. The wealth of religious feelings, swollen to a torrent, breaks forth again and again and seeks to conquer new regions: but the growth of the Enlightenment undermined the dogmas of religion and inspired a fundamental distrust of them: so that the feelings expelled from the sphere of religion by the Enlightenment throw themselves into art; in individual cases into political life as well, indeed even straight into the sciences. Wherever we perceive human endeavours to be tinted with a

higher, gloomier colouring, we can assume that dread of spirits, the odour of incense and the shadows of churches are still adhering to them.

151

How metre beautifies. – Metre lays a veil over reality: it effectuates a certain artificiality of speech and unclarity of thinking; by means of the shadows it throws over thoughts it now conceals, now brings into prominence. As beautification requires shadows, so clarification requires 'vagueness'. – Art makes the sight of life bearable by laying over it the veil of unclear thinking.

152

Art of the ugly soul. – One imposes far too narrow limitations on art when one demands that only well-ordered, morally balanced souls may express themselves in it. As in the plastic arts, so in music and poetry too there is an art of the ugly soul beside the art of the beautiful soul; and the mightiest effects of art, that which tames souls, moves stones and humanizes the beast, have perhaps been mostly achieved by precisely that art.

153

Art makes the thinker's heart heavy. – How strong the metaphysical need is, and how hard nature makes it to bid it a final farewell, can be seen from the fact that even when the free spirit has divested himself of everything metaphysical the highest effects of art can easily set the metaphysical strings, which have long been silent or indeed snapped apart, vibrating in sympathy; so it can happen, for example, that a passage in Beethoven's Ninth Symphony will make him feel he is hovering above the earth in a dome of stars with the dream of *immortality* in his heart: all the stars seem to glitter around him and the earth seems to sink farther and farther away. – If he becomes aware of being in this condition he feels a profound stab in the heart and sighs for the man who will lead him back to his lost love, whether she be called religion or metaphysics. It is in such moments that his intellectual probity is put to the test.

154

Playing with life. – The facility and frivolity of the Homeric fantasy was necessary for soothing the immoderately passionate disposition and over-subtle intellect of the Greeks and temporarily banishing them. When their intellect speaks, how cruel and bitter life appears! They do not deceive themselves, but they deliberately and playfully embellish life with lies. Simonides* advised his compatriots to take life as a game; they were only too familiar with its painful seriousness (for the misery of mankind is among the favourite themes for song among the gods), and they knew that even misery could become a source of enjoyment solely through art. As a punishment for this insight, however, they were so plagued by a delight in telling stories that it was hard for them to desist from lies and deception in the course of everyday life – just as all poetical

* Simonides (c. 556 to c. 468 BC), Greek poet

people take a delight in lying, a delight that is moreover quite innocent. The neighbouring nations were no doubt sometimes reduced to despair by it.

155

Belief in inspiration. – Artists have an interest in the existence of a belief in the sudden occurrence of ideas, in so-called inspirations; as though the idea of a work of art, a poem, the basic proposition of a philosophy flashed down from heaven like a ray of divine grace. In reality, the imagination of a good artist or thinker is productive continually, of good, mediocre and bad things, but his *power of judgement*, sharpened and practised to the highest degree, rejects, selects, knots together; as we can now see from Beethoven's notebooks how the most glorious melodies were put together gradually and as it were culled out of many beginnings. He who selects less rigorously and likes to give himself up to his imitative memory can, under the right circumstances, become a great improviser; but artistic improvisation is something very inferior in relation to the serious and carefully fashioned artistic idea. All the great artists have been great workers, inexhaustible not only in invention but also in rejecting, sifting, transforming, ordering.

156

Inspiration again. – If productive power has been blocked for a time and prevented from flowing out by an obstruction, there occurs in the end an effusion so sudden it appears that an immediate inspiration without any preliminary labour, that is to say a miracle, has taken place. This constitutes the familiar deception with whose continuance the interest of all artists is, as aforesaid, a little too much involved. The capital has only been accumulated, it did not fall from the sky all at once. Similar apparent inspiration is also to be found in other domains, for example in that of goodness, virtue, vice.

157

The sufferings of genius and their value. – The artistic genius wants to give pleasure, but if he stands on a very high level there can easily be a lack of others to enjoy it; he offers food but no one wants it. This sometimes bestows upon him a moving and ludicrous pathos; for fundamentally he has no right to compel people to enjoy themselves. He sounds his pipe but no one wants to dance: can that be tragic? – Perhaps it can. After all, he has, as a compensation for this privation, more enjoyment in creating than other people have in any other species of activity. His sufferings are felt to be exaggerated because the sound of his lamentations is louder, his mouth more persuasive; and *sometimes* his sufferings really are great, but only because his ambition and envy are so great. The genius of knowledge, such as Kepler and Spinoza, is usually not so covetous and does not make such a commotion over his sufferings and privations, which are actually greater. He can be more certain of posterity and divest himself of the present; whereas an artist who does this is always playing a desperate game which must fill him with trepidation. In very rare cases – when the genius of ability and of knowledge is amalgamated with moral genius in the same individual – there is added to the sufferings referred to a species of suffering that one must take to be the most singular exception in the world: an extra- and supra-personal sensibility attuned to a nation, to mankind, to a whole culture, to all suffering existence: which acquires its value through its connection with very difficult and remote forms of knowledge (pity in itself is of little value). – But by what standard, on what scales can we measure whether or not it is genuine? Is it not almost obligatory to mistrust all who *speak* of possessing sensibilities of this sort?

158

Fatality of greatness. – Every great phenomenon is succeeded by degeneration, especially in the domain of art. The example of greatness incites all vainer natures to extreme imitation or attempts to outdo; in addition to which, all great talents have the fatal property of suppressing many weaker shoots and forces and as it were laying nature waste all around them. The most fortunate thing that can happen in the evolution of an art is that several geniuses appear together and keep one another in bounds; in the course of this struggle the weaker and tenderer natures too will usually be granted light and air.

159

Art dangerous to the artist. – When art seizes violently on an individual it draws him back to the conceptions of those ages in which art flourished most mightily, and then it effects a retrogression in him. The artist acquires increasing reverence for sudden excitations, believes in gods and demons, instils a soul into nature, hates the sciences, becomes changeable of mood as were the men of antiquity and longs for an overthrowing of everything unfavourable to art, and he does this with all the vehemence and unreasonableness of a child. The artist is in himself already a retarded being, inasmuch as he has halted at games that pertain to youth and childhood: to this there is now added his gradual retrogression to earlier times. Thus there at last arises a violent antagonism between him and the men of his period, of his own age, and his end is gloomy; just as, according to the tales told in antiquity, Homer and Aeschylus at last lived and died in melancholia.

160

Created people. – When we say the dramatist (and the artist in general) actually *creates* characters, this is a nice piece of deception and exaggeration in the existence and dissemination of which art celebrates one of its unintentional and as it were superfluous triumphs. In reality we understand very little of an actual living person and generalize very superficially when we attribute to him this or that character: well, the poet adopts the same *very imperfect* posture towards man as we do, in that his sketches of men are just as *superficial* as is our knowledge of men. There is much illusion involved in these created characters of the artists; they are in no way living products of nature, but, like painted people, a little too thin, they cannot endure inspection from close to. And if one should even venture to say that the character of the ordinary living man is often self-contradictory and that created by the dramatist the ideal that hovered dimly before the eye of nature, this would be quite wrong. An actual human being is something altogether *necessary* (even in those so-called contradictions), but we do not always recognize this necessity. The invented human being, the phantasm, desires to signify something necessary, but only in the eyes of those who comprehend even an actual human being only in a crude, unnatural simplification: so that a couple of striking, often repeated characteristics, with a great deal of light on them and a great deal of shadow and twilight around them, suffice to meet all their demands. They are thus quite ready to treat phantasms as actual, necessary human beings because they are accustomed when dealing with actual human beings to take a phantasm, a silhouette, an arbitrary abridgement for the whole. – That the painter and the sculptor, of all people, give expression to the 'idea' of the human being is mere fantasizing and sense-deception: one is being tyrannized over by the eye when one says such a thing, since this sees even of the human body only the surface, the skin; the inner body, however, is just as much part of the idea. Plastic art wants to make characters visible on the outside; the art of speech employs the word to the same end, it delineates the character in sounds. Art begins from the natural *ignorance* of mankind as to his interior (both bodily and as regards character): it does not exist for physicists or philosophers.

161

Self-overestimation in the belief in artists and philosophers. – We all think that a work of art, an artist, is proved to be of high quality if it seizes hold on us and profoundly moves us. But for this to be so our *own high quality* in judgement and sensibility would first have to have been proved: which is not the case. Who in the realm of the plastic arts has moved and enraptured more than Bernini, who has produced a mightier effect than that post-Demosthenes rhetor* who introduced the Asiatic style and caused it to predominate for two centuries? Such a predomination over entire centuries proves nothing in regard to the quality or lasting validity of a style; that is why one should never be too firm in one's faith in any artist: for such a faith is not only faith in the veracity of our sensibility but also in the infallibility of our judgement, while our judgement or sensibility, or both of them, can themselves be too coarse or too refined, exaggerated or gross. The blessings and raptures conferred by a philosophy or a religion likewise prove nothing in regard to their truth: just as little as the happiness the madman enjoys from his *idée fixe* proves anything in regard to its rationality.

162

Cult of the genius out of vanity. – Because we think well of ourselves, but

* Hegesias of Magnesia (c. 250 BC), of the school of Cyrenaic philosophers

nonetheless never suppose ourselves capable of producing a painting like one of Raphael's or a dramatic scene like one of Shakespeare's, we convince ourselves that the capacity to do so is quite extraordinarily marvellous, a wholly uncommon accident, or, if we are still religiously inclined, a mercy from on high. Thus our vanity, our self-love, promotes the cult of the genius: for only if we think of him as being very remote from us, as a *miraculum*, does he not aggrieve us (even Goethe, who was without envy, called Shakespeare his star of the most distant heights; in regard to which one might recall the line: 'the stars, these we do not desire'). But, aside from these suggestions of our vanity, the activity of the genius seems in no way fundamentally different from the activity of the inventor of machines, the scholar of astronomy or history, the master of tactics. All these activities are explicable if one pictures to oneself people whose thinking is active in *one* direction, who employ everything as material, who always zealously observe their own inner life and that of others, who perceive everywhere models and incentives, who never tire of combining together the means available to them. Genius too does nothing except learn first how to lay bricks then how to build, except continually seek for material and continually form itself around it. Every activity of man is amazingly complicated, not only that of the genius: but none is a 'miracle'. – Whence, then, the belief that genius exists only in the artist, orator and philosopher? that only they have 'intuition'? (Whereby they are supposed to possess a kind of miraculous eyeglass with which they can see directly into 'the essence of the thing'!) It is clear that people speak of genius only where the effects of the great intellect are most pleasant to them and where they have no desire to feel envious. To call someone 'divine' means: 'here there is no need for us to compete'. Then, everything finished and complete is regarded with admiration, everything still becoming is under-valued. But no one can see in the work of the artist how it has *become;* that is its advantage, for wherever one can see the act of becoming one grows somewhat cool. The finished and perfect art of representation repulses all thinking as to how it has become; it tyrannizes as present completeness and perfection. That is why the masters of the art of representation count above all as gifted with genius and why men of science do not. In reality, this evaluation of the former and undervaluation of the latter is only a piece of childishness in the realm of reason.

163

The serious workman. – Do not talk about giftedness, inborn talents! One can name great men of all kinds who were very little gifted. They *acquired* greatness, became 'geniuses' (as we put it), through qualities the lack of which no one who knew what they were would boast of: they all possessed that seriousness of the efficient workman which first learns to construct the parts properly before it ventures to fashion a great whole; they allowed themselves time for it, because they took more pleasure in making the little, secondary things well than in the effect of a dazzling whole. The recipe for becoming a good novelist, for example, is easy to give, but to carry it out presupposes qualities one is accustomed to overlook when one says 'I do not have enough talent.' One has only to make a hundred or so sketches for novels, none longer than two pages but of such distinctness that every word in them is necessary; one should write down anecdotes each day until one has learned how to give them the most pregnant and effective form; one should be tireless in collecting and describing human types and characters; one should above all relate things to others and listen to others relate, keeping one's eyes and ears open for the effect produced on those present, one should travel like a landscape painter or costume designer; one should excerpt for oneself out of the individual sciences everything that will produce an artistic effect when it is well described, one should, finally, reflect on the motives of human actions, disdain no signpost to instruction about them and be a collector of these things by day and night. One should continue in this many-sided exercise some ten years: what is then created in the workshop, however, will be fit to go out into the world. – What, however, do most people do? They begin, not with the parts, but with the whole. Perhaps they chance to strike a right note, excite attention and from then on strike worse and worse notes, for good, natural reasons. – Sometimes, when the character and intellect needed to formulate such a life-plan are lacking, fate and need take their place and lead the future master step by step through all the stipulations of his trade.

164

Peril and profit in the cult of the genius. – The belief in great, superior, fruitful spirits is not necessarily, yet nonetheless is very frequently associated with that religious or semi-religious superstition that these spirits are of supra-human origin and possess certain miraculous abilities by virtue of which they acquire their knowledge by quite other means than the rest of mankind. One ascribes to them, it seems, a direct view of the nature of the world, as it were a hole in the cloak of appearance, and believes that, by virtue of this miraculous seer's vision, they are able to communicate something conclusive and decisive about man and the world without the toil and rigorousness required by science. As long as there continue to be those who believe in the miraculous in the domain of knowledge one can perhaps concede that these people themselves derive some benefit from their belief, inasmuch as through their unconditional subjection to the great spirits they create for their own spirit during its time of development the finest form of discipline and schooling. On the other hand, it is at least questionable whether the superstitious belief in genius, in its privileges and special abilities, is of benefit to the genius himself if it takes root in him. It is in any event a dangerous sign when a man is assailed by awe of himself, whether it be the celebrated Caesar's awe of Caesar or the awe of one's own genius now under consideration; when the sacrificial incense which is properly rendered only to a god penetrates the brain of the genius, so that his head begins to swim and he comes to regard himself as something supra-human. The consequences that slowly result are: the feeling of irresponsibility, of exceptional rights, the belief that he confers a favour by his mere presence, insane rage when anyone attempts even to compare him with others, let alone to rate him beneath them, or to draw attention to lapses in his work. Because he ceases to practise criticism of himself, at last one pinion after the other falls out of his plumage: that superstitious belief eats at the roots of his powers and perhaps even turns him into a hypocrite after his powers have fled from him. For the great spirits themselves it is therefore probably more beneficial if they acquire an insight into the nature and origin of their powers, if they grasp, that is to say, what purely human qualities have come together in them and what fortunate circumstances attended them: in the first place undiminishing energy, resolute application to individual goals, great personal courage, then the good fortune to receive an upbringing which offered in the early years the finest teachers, models and methods. To be sure, when their goal is the production of the greatest possible *effect*, unclarity with regard to oneself and that semi-insanity superadded to it has always achieved much; for what has been admired and envied at all times has been that power in them by virtue of which they render men will-less and sweep them away into the delusion that the leaders they are following are supra-natural. Indeed, it elevates and inspires men to believe that someone is in possession of supra-natural powers: to this extent Plato was right to say that madness has brought the greatest of blessings upon mankind. – In rare individual cases this portion of madness may, indeed, actually have been the means by which such a nature, excessive in all directions, was held firmly together: in the life of individuals, too, illusions that are in themselves poisons often play the role of healers; yet, in the end, in the case of every 'genius' who believes in his own divinity the poison shows itself to the same degree as his 'genius' grows old: one may recall, for example, the case of Napoleon, whose nature certainly grew into the mighty unity that sets him apart from all men of modern times precisely through his belief in himself and his star and through the contempt for men that flowed from it; until in the end, however, this same belief went over into an almost insane fatalism, robbed him of his acuteness and swiftness of perception, and became the cause of his destruction.

165
Genius and nullity. – It is precisely the original heads among the artists, those who draw on resources that are their own, who can sometimes produce the empty and hollow, while the more dependent natures, the so-called talents, full of recollections of everything imaginable are able even when they are at their weakest to produce something tolerable. If the originals are deserted by themselves recollection renders them no aid: they become empty.

166
The public. – The people really demands of tragedy no more than to be

thoroughly moved so as for once to have a good cry; the artist who sees a new tragedy, on the other hand, takes pleasure in the ingenious technical inventions and artifices, in the handling and apportionment of the material, in the new application of old motifs and old ideas. – His attitude is the aesthetic attitude to the work of art, that of the creator; the one first described, which pays attention only to the material, is that of the people. Of the man between them there is nothing to be said; he is neither people nor artist and does not know what he wants: thus his pleasure, too, is obscure and slight.

167

Artistic education of the public. – If the same motif has not been treated in a hundred different ways by various masters, the public never learns to get beyond interest in the material alone; but once it has come to be familiar with the motif from numerous versions of it, and thus no longer feels the charm of novelty and anticipation, it will then be able to grasp and enjoy the nuances and subtle new inventions in the way it is treated.

168

The artist and his following must keep in step. – Progress from one stylistic level to the next must proceed so slowly that not only the artists but the auditors and spectators too can participate in this progress and know exactly what is going on. Otherwise there suddenly appears that great gulf between the artist creating his works on a remote height and the public which, no longer able to attain to that height, at length disconsolately climbs back down again deeper than before. For when the artist no longer raises his public up, it swiftly sinks downwards, and it plunges the deeper and more perilously the higher a genius has borne it, like the eagle from whose claws the tortoise it has carried up into the clouds falls to its death.

169

Origin of the comic. – If one considers that man was for many hundreds of thousands of years an animal in the highest degree accessible to fear and that everything sudden and unexpected bade him prepare to fight and perhaps to die; that even later on, indeed, in social relationships all security depended on the expected and traditional in opinion and action; then one cannot be surprised if whenever something sudden and unexpected in word and deed happens without occasioning danger or injury man becomes wanton, passes over into the opposite of fear: the anxious, crouching creature springs up, greatly expands – man laughs. This transition from momentary anxiety to short-lived exuberance is called the *comic*. In the phenomenon of the tragic, on the other hand, man passes swiftly from great, enduring wantonness and high spirits into great fear and anguish; since, however, great, enduring wantonness and high spirits is much rarer among mortals than occasions for fear, there is much more of the comic than the tragic in the world; we laugh much more often than we are profoundly shaken.

170

Artist's ambition. – The Greek artists, the tragedians for example, poetized in order to conquer; their whole art cannot be thought of apart from contest: Hesiod's good Eris,* ambition, gave their genius its wings. Now this ambition demands above all that their work should preserve the highest excellence in *their own eyes*, as *they* understand excellence, that is to say, without reference to a dominating taste or the general opinion as to what constitutes excellence in a work of art; and thus Aeschylus and Euripides were for a long time unsuccessful until they had finally *educated* judges of art who assessed their work according to the standards they themselves laid down. It is thus they aspire to victory over their competitors as they understand victory, a victory before their own seat of judgement, they want actually to *be* more excellent; then they exact agreement from others as to their own assessment of themselves and confirmation of their own judgement. To aspire to honour here means: 'to make oneself superior and to wish this superiority to be publicly acknowledged'. If the former is lacking and the latter nonetheless still demanded, one speaks of *vanity*. If the latter is lacking and its absence not regretted, one speaks of *pride*.

171

The necessary in a work of art. – Those who talk so much of the necessary in a work of art exaggerate, if they are artists, *in majorem artis gloriam*,† or, if they are laity, out of ignorance. The forms of a work of art which express the ideas contained in it, its mode of speech that is to say, always have something easy-going about them, like all forms of speech. The sculptor can add many little details or leave them out: the performer likewise, whether he be an actor or, in the realm of music, a virtuoso or conductor. These many little details and elaborations today appeal to him, tomorrow not; they exist for the sake of the artist rather than for that of the art, for he too, given the rigorousness and self-constraint the representation of his principal idea demands of him, occasionally requires sweetmeats and playthings if he is not to grow sullen and morose.

172

Causing the master to be forgotten. – The pianist who performs the work of a master will have played best when he makes his listeners forget the master, when it seems as though he is relating a tale from his own life or is experiencing something at that very moment. To be sure, if he himself *is* nothing of consequence his listeners will execrate the loquacity with which he tells us about himself. He thus has to know how to engage the imagination of his listeners on his own behalf. Conversely, it is this which accounts for all the weaknesses and follies of 'the virtuoso'.

173

Corriger la fortune.‡ Evil chances occur in the lives of great artists such as

* Hesiod (c. 800 BC), Greek poet, distinguishes Eris as a goddess of peaceable competition from 'terrible Eris', bringer of war and strife. Also referred to in 'The wanderer and his shadow', section 29.

† *in majorem artis gloriam*: to the greater glory of art

‡ *Corriger la fortune*: to compensate for the deliverances of fate

compel a painter, for instance, to leave his finest picture in the form of mere hurried sketches, or which compelled Beethoven, for example, to leave behind to us in many great sonatas (as in the case of the great B major)* only an unsatisfactory piano arrangement of a symphony. Here the artist coming after ought to try posthumously to amend the life of the master: which is what he would do, for example, who, as a master of orchestration, should waken to life for us that symphony now lying in the death-trance of the piano.

174

Diminution. – There are many things, events or people which cannot endure being reduced in scale. The Laokoon group† cannot be reduced to a trinket; it needs to be large. But it is much rarer for something small by nature to be able to endure enlargement; which is why biographers will always have better success in diminishing the size of a great man than in enlarging that of a small one.

175

Sensuality in contemporary art. – Artists nowadays often go wrong when they labour to make their works of art produce a sensual effect; for their spectators or auditors are no longer in possession of a full sensuality and the effect which, quite contrary to his intention, the artist's work produces upon them is a feeling of 'saintliness' closely related to boredom. – Their sensuality perhaps commences just where the artist's ceases; thus they encounter one another at *one* point at the most.

176

Shakespeare as moralist. – Shakespeare reflected a great deal on the passions and from his temperament probably had very intimate access to many of them (dramatists are in general somewhat wicked men). But, unlike Montaigne,‡ he was incapable of discoursing on them; instead of which he placed observations *about* the passions into the mouths of impassioned characters: a practice which, though counter to nature, makes his plays so full of ideas they make all others seem empty and can easily arouse in us a repugnance to them. – The maxims of Schiller§ (which are almost always based on ideas either false or trite) are designed purely for the theatre, and as such they are extremely effective: while Shakespeare's do honour to his model, Montaigne, and contain entirely serious ideas in a polished form, but are for that reason too remote and subtle for the theatre public and thus ineffective.

177

Getting oneself heard well. – One has to know, not only how to play well,

---

* Beethoven's piano sonata no. 29 in B flat major, Op. 106, 'Hammerklavier'
† Laokoon group: Hellenistic statue, from the Golden House of Nero, representing the Trojan priest Laokoon and his two sons being crushed by giant serpents
‡ Montaigne: Michel de Montaigne (1533–92): French essayist
§ Schiller: Friedrich von Schiller (1759–1805): German poet, dramatist and historian

but also how to get oneself heard well. The violin in the hands of the greatest master will emit only a chirp if the room is too big; and then the master sounds no better than any bungler.

178

The effectiveness of the incomplete. – Just as figures in relief produce so strong an impression on the imagination because they are as it were on the point of stepping out of the wall but have suddenly been brought to a halt, so the relief-like, incomplete presentation of an idea, of a whole philosophy, is sometimes more effective than its exhaustive realization: more is left for the beholder to do, he is impelled to continue working on that which appears before him so strongly etched in light and shadow, to think it through to the end, and to overcome even that constraint which has hitherto prevented it from stepping forth fully formed.

179

Against originality. – When art dresses itself in the most worn-out material it is most easily recognized as art.

180

Collective spirit. – A good writer possesses not only his own spirit but also the spirit of his friends.

181

Twofold misjudgement. – The misfortune suffered by clear-minded and easily understood writers is that they are taken for shallow and thus little effort is expended on reading them: and the good fortune that attends the obscure is that the reader toils at them and ascribes to them the pleasure he has in fact gained from his own zeal.

182

Relationship to science. – They lack a true interest in a science who begin to become enthusiastic about it only when they themselves have made discoveries in it.

183

The key. – A man of significance may set great store by an idea and all the insignificant laugh and mock at him for it: to him it is a key to hidden treasure-chambers, while to them it is no more than a piece of old iron.

184

Untranslatable. – It is neither the best nor the worst in a book that is untranslatable in it.

185

Author's paradoxes. – The so-called paradoxes of an author to which a reader takes exception very often stand not at all in the author's book but in the reader's head.

186

Wit. – The wittiest authors evoke the least perceptible smile.

187
The antithesis. – The antithesis is the narrow gateway through which error most likes to creep into truth.

188
Thinkers as stylists. – Most thinkers write badly because they communicate to us not only their thoughts but also the thinking of their thoughts.

189
Thought in poetry. – The poet conducts his thoughts along festively, in the carriage of rhythm: usually because they are incapable of walking on foot.

190
Sin against the spirit of the reader. – If the author denies his talent merely so as to place himself on a level with his reader, he commits the only mortal sin the latter will never forgive him – supposing, that is, he notices it. One may say anything ill of a man one likes: but in the *way* one says it one must know how to restore his vanity again.

191
Limit of honesty. – Even the most honest writer lets fall a word too many when he wants to round off a period.

192
The best author. – The best author will be he who is ashamed to become a writer.

193
Draconian law against writers. – Writers ought to be treated as malefactors who deserve to be freed or pardoned only in the rarest cases: this would be a way of preventing the proliferation of books.

194
The licensed fools of modern culture. – The licensed fools of the courts of the Middle Ages have their counterpart in our *feuilletonists:** they are the same species of man, half-rational, witty, extravagant, silly, sometimes in attendance only to ameliorate heaviness of mood and to drown down the all too weighty solemn clangour of great events; formerly in the service of princes and the nobility, now in the service of the parties (just as a good deal of the ancient submissiveness of the people in their commerce with princes still lives on in party feeling and party discipline). The whole modern literary world, however, stands very near to the *feuilletonists;* they are the 'licensed fools of modern culture', who are judged more gently when they are taken to be not wholly of sound mind. To regard writing as a lifetime's profession ought fairly to be considered a kind of folly.

195
After the Greeks. – Knowledge is at present very much obstructed by the fact that all words have, through centuries of exaggerated feeling,

* *feuilletonists*: writers of pieces of light literature and criticism for French newspapers

become vaporous and inflated. The higher level of culture that places itself under the domination (if not indeed under the tyranny) of knowledge has need of a great sobriety of feeling and a strong concentration of all words; in which matter the Greeks of the age of Demosthenes have preceded us.* All modern writing is characterized by exaggeratedness; and even when it is written simply the words it contains are *felt* too eccentrically. Rigorous reflection, terseness, coldness, simplicity, deliberately pursued even to their limit, self-containment of the feelings and silence in general – that alone can help us. – Moreover, this cold manner of writing and feeling is now, as a contrast, very stimulating: and in that there lies, to be sure, a great danger. For biting coldness is just as much a stimulant as a high degree of warmth.

196

Good narrators, bad explainers. – Many good storytellers possess an admirable psychological certainty and consistency so long as it applies itself to the actions of their characters, in a downright ludicrous contrast to the ineptitude of their psychological thinking: so that the degree of their culture seems at one moment exceptionally high and the next regrettably low. It happens all too often that the explanations they give of their heroes and their actions are palpably *false* – there can be no doubt about it, however improbable it may sound. Perhaps the greatest pianist has reflected very little on technical matters and the particular virtue, vice, utility and educability of each finger (dactylic ethics), and blunders badly whenever he speaks of such things.

197

Writings of acquaintances and their readers. – We read the writings of our acquaintances (friends and foes) in a twofold sense, inasmuch as our knowledge continually whispers to us: 'this is by him, a sign of his inner nature, his experiences, his talent', while another kind of knowledge at the same time seeks to determine what his work is worth in itself, what evaluation it deserves apart from its author, what enrichment of knowledge it brings with it. As goes without saying, these two kinds of reading and evaluating disturb one another. Even a conversation with a friend will bring the fruits of knowledge to maturity only if both finally think only of the matter in hand and forget they are friends.

198

Sacrifice of rhythm. – Good writers alter the rhythm of many periods merely because they do not acknowledge in the ordinary reader the capacity to grasp the measure followed by the period in its first version: they make it easier for him by giving preference to the more familiar rhythms. – This consideration for the rhythmic incapacity of the present-day reader has already evoked many a sigh, for much has already been sacrificed to it. – Is something similar not perhaps happening to good musicians?

* Demosthenes (385–322 BC): Greek orator

199

The incomplete as artistic stimulant. – The incomplete is often more effective than completeness, especially in the case of the eulogy: the aim of which requires precisely an enticing incompleteness as an irrational element which presents to the hearer's imagination the illusion of a dazzling sea and obscures the coast on the other side, that is to say the limitations of the object to be eulogized, as though in a fog. When one refers to the known merits of a man and does so in detail and at length, it always gives rise to the suspicion that these are his only merits. The complete eulogist sets himself above the person eulogized, he appears to *survey* him. That is why the complete produces a diminishing effect.

200

Warning to writers and teachers. – He who has once written, and feels in himself the passion of writing, acquires from almost all he does and experiences only that which can be communicated through writing. He no longer thinks of himself but of the writer and his public: he desires insight, but not for his own private use. He who is a teacher is usually incapable of any longer doing anything for his own benefit, he always thinks of the benefit of his pupils, and he takes pleasure in knowledge of any kind only insofar as he can teach it. He regards himself in the end as a thoroughfare of knowledge and as a means and instrument in general, so that he has ceased to be serious with regard to himself.

201

Bad writers necessary. – There will always have to be bad writers, for they answer to the taste of the immature, undeveloped age-group; these have their requirements as well as do the mature. If human life were longer, the number of mature individuals would preponderate or at least be equal to that of the immature; as things are, however, most by far die too young, that is to say there are always many more undeveloped intellects with bad taste. These, moreover, desire that their requirements be satisfied with the greater vehemence of youth, and they *demand* bad authors and get them.

202

Too near and too far. – The reader and the author often fail to understand one another because the author knows his theme too well and almost finds it boring, so that he dispenses with the examples and illustrations of which he knows hundreds; the reader, however, is unfamiliar with the subject and can easily find it ill-established if examples and illustrations are withheld from him.

203

A vanished preparation for art. – Of all the grammar school did, the most valuable thing was the practice it afforded in Latin style: for this was a *practice in art*, whereas all its other undertakings had only knowledge as their objective. To accord German composition a premier position is barbarism, for we have no model German style evolved out of public eloquence; if one wants to promote practice in thinking through German composition, however, it is certainly better for the time being to forget about style altogether, to discriminate, that is to say, between practice in thinking and practice in presentation. The latter ought to apply itself to the production of manifold versions of a given content and not to the invention of this content itself. The mere presentation of a given content was the task of Latin style, for which the teachers of antiquity possessed a subtlety of hearing which has long since been lost. Formerly whoever learned to write well in a modern language had this practice to thank for it (now one is compelled to send oneself to school with the older French writers); but even more: he acquired an idea of elevated and difficult form and was prepared for art in the only proper way, through practice.

204

Dark and too bright side by side. – Writers who in general are unable to express their thoughts with clarity will in individual instances take pleasure in employing the strongest, most exaggerated designations and superlatives: thus producing a light-effect like torches flaring on confused forest pathways.

205

Painting in writing. – An object of significance will be best represented if, like a chemist, one takes the colours for the painting from the object itself, and then employs them like a painter: so that the outline is allowed to grow out of the boundaries and shadings of the colours. Thus the painting will acquire something of the ravishing element of nature which makes the object itself significant.

206

Books which teach one to dance. – There are writers who, by representing the impossible as possible and speaking of morality and genius as though both were merely a matter of wanting them, a mere whim and caprice, evoke a feeling of high-spirited freedom, as though man were standing on tiptoe and compelled to dance for sheer joy.

207

Uncompleted thoughts. – Just as it is not only adulthood but youth and childhood too that possess value *in themselves* and not merely as bridges and thoroughfares, so incomplete thoughts also have their value. That is why one must not torment a poet with subtle exegesis but content oneself with the uncertainty of his horizon, as though the way to many thoughts still lay open. Let one stand on the threshold; let one wait as at the excavation of a treasure: it is as though a lucky find of profound import were about to be made. The poet anticipates something of the joy of the thinker at the discovery of a vital idea and makes us desire it, so that we snatch at it; he, however, flutters by past our heads, displaying the loveliest butterfly-wings – and yet he eludes us.

208

The book become almost human. – Every writer is surprised anew how, once a book has detached himself from him, it goes on to live a life of its own; it is to him as though a part of an insect had come free and was now going its own way. Perhaps he almost forgets it, perhaps he raises himself above the views he has set down in it, perhaps he no longer even understands it and has lost those wings upon which he flew when he thought out that book: during which time it seeks out its readers, enkindles life, makes happy, terrifies, engenders new works, becomes the soul of new designs and undertakings – in short, it lives like a being furnished with soul and spirit and is yet not human. – That author has drawn the happiest lot who as an old man can say that all of life-engendering, strengthening, elevating, enlightening thought and feeling that was in him lives on in his writings, and that he himself is now nothing but the grey ashes, while the fire has everywhere been rescued and borne forward. – If one now goes on to consider that, not only a book, but every action performed by a human being becomes in some way the cause of other actions, decisions, thoughts, that everything that happens is inextricably knotted to everything that will happen, one comes to recognize the existence of an actual *immortality*, that of motion: what has once moved is enclosed and eternalized in the total union of all being like an insect in amber.

209

Joy in age. – The thinker, and the artist likewise, whose better self has taken refuge in his work, feels an almost malicious joy when he sees how his body and his spirit are being slowly broken down and destroyed by time: it is as though he observed from a corner a thief working away at his money-chest, while knowing that the chest is empty and all the treasure it contained safe.

210

Quiet fruitfulness. – The born aristocrats of the spirit are not too zealous: their creations appear and fall from the tree on a quiet autumn evening unprecipitately, in due time, not quickly pushed aside by something new. The desire to create continually is vulgar and betrays jealousy, envy, ambition. If one is something one really does not need to make anything – and one nonetheless does very much. There exists above the 'productive' man a yet higher species.

211

Achilles and Homer. – It is always as between Achilles and Homer: the one *has* the experience, the sensation, the other *describes* it. A true writer only bestows words on the emotions and experiences of others, he is an artist so as to divine much from the little he himself has felt. Artists are by no means men of great passion but they often *pretend* to be, in the unconscious feeling that their painted passions will seem more believable if their own life speaks for their experience in this field. One has only to let oneself go, to abandon self-control, to give rein to one's anger or desires:

at once all the world cries: how passionate he is! But deep-rooted passion, passion which gnaws at the individual and often consumes him, is a thing of some consequence: he who experiences such passion certainly does not describe it in dramas, music or novels. Artists are often *unbridled* individuals to the extent that they are not artists: but that is something else.

212

Old doubts over the effect of art. – Are fear and pity really discharged by tragedy, as Aristotle has it, so that the auditor goes home colder and more placid? Do ghost stories make one less fearful and superstitious? It is true in the case of certain physical events, the enjoyment of love for example, that with the satisfaction of a need an alleviation and temporary relaxation of the drive occurs. But fear and pity are not in this sense needs of definite organs which want to be relieved. And in the long run a drive is, through practice in satisfying it, *intensified*, its periodical alleviation notwithstanding. It is possible that in each individual instance fear and pity are mitigated and discharged: they could nonetheless grow greater as a whole through the tragic effect in general, and Plato could still be right when he says that through tragedy one becomes generally more fearful and emotional. The tragic poet himself would then necessarily acquire a gloomy, disheartened view of the world and a soft, susceptible, tearful soul, and it would likewise accord with Plato's opinion of the matter if the tragic poet and with him whole city communities which take especial delight in him should degenerate to ever greater unbridledness and immoderation. – But what right has our age to offer an answer to Plato's great question concerning the moral influence of art at all? Even if we possessed art – what influence *of any kind* does art exercise among us?

213

Pleasure in nonsense. – How can man take pleasure in nonsense? For wherever in the world there is laughter this is the case; one can say, indeed, that almost everywhere there is happiness there is pleasure in nonsense. The overturning of experience into its opposite, of the purposive into the purposeless, of the necessary into the arbitrary, but in such a way that this event causes no harm and is imagined as occasioned by high spirits, delights us, for it momentarily liberates us from the constraint of the necessary, the purposive and that which corresponds to our experience, which we usually see as our inexorable masters; we play and laugh when the expected (which usually makes us fearful and tense) discharges itself harmlessly. It is the pleasure of the slave at the Saturnalia.

214

Ennoblement of reality. – The fact that men saw in the aphrodisiac drive a divinity, and felt its operation within them with reverential gratitude, has over the course of time saturated that affect with a series of exalted notions and actually very greatly ennobled it. In the same way, several nations have by virtue of this art of idealization created for themselves mighty aids to culture out of sicknesses: for example the Greeks, who in earlier centuries suffered from great nervous epidemics (in the form of epilepsy and St Vitus' dance) and fashioned from them the glorious type of the bacchante. – For the Greeks were certainly not possessed of a square and solid healthiness; – their secret was to honour even sickness as a god if only it had *power*.

215

Music. – Music is, of and in itself, not so significant for our inner world, nor so profoundly exciting, that it can be said to count as the *immediate* language of feeling; but its primeval union with poetry has deposited so much symbolism into rhythmic movement, into the varying strength and volume of musical sounds, that we now *suppose* it to speak directly *to* the inner world and to come *from* the inner world. Dramatic music becomes possible only when the tonal art has conquered an enormous domain of symbolic means, through song, opera and a hundred experiments in tone-painting. 'Absolute music' is either form in itself, at a primitive stage of music in which sounds made in tempo and at varying volume gave pleasure as such, or symbolism of form speaking to the understanding without poetry after both arts had been united over a long course of evolution and the musical form had finally become entirely enmeshed in threads of feeling and concepts. Men who have remained behind in the evolution of music can understand in a purely formalistic way the same piece of music as the more advanced understand wholly symbolically. In itself, no music is profound or significant, it does not speak of the 'will' or of the 'thing in itself'; the intellect could suppose such a thing only in an age which had conquered for musical symbolism the entire compass of the inner life. It was the intellect itself which first *introduced* this significance into sounds: just as, in the case of architecture, it likewise introduced a significance into the relations between lines and masses which is in itself quite unknown to the laws of mechanics.

216

Gesture and language. – Older than language is the mimicking of gestures, which takes place involuntarily and is even now, when the language of gesture is universally restrained and control of the muscles has been achieved, so strong that we cannot see a mobile face without an innervation of our own face (one can observe that feigned yawning will evoke real yawning in one who sees it). The imitated gesture leads him who imitates it back to the sensation which it expressed in the face or body of the person imitated. That is how people learned to understand one another: that is how a child still learns to understand its mother. In general, painful sensations may well also be expressed by gestures which in turn occasion pain (for example by pulling hair out, beating the breast, violent distortions and strainings of the facial muscles). Conversely, gestures of pleasure were themselves pleasurable and could thus easily convey their meaning (laughter as an expression of being tickled, which is pleasurable, again served as an expression of other pleasurable sensations). – As soon as the meaning of gestures was understood, a *symbolism* of gestures could arise: I mean a sign-language of sounds could be so agreed that at first one produced sound *and* gesture (to which it was symbolically joined), later only the sound. – It appears here that in earlier ages there often occurred that which now takes place before our eyes and ears in the evolution of music, especially of dramatic music: while music was at first empty noise without explanatory dance and mime (gesture-language), the ear was, through long habituation to the juxtaposition of music and movement, schooled to an instantaneous interpretation of the total figurations and has at last attained to a height of rapid understanding at which it no longer has any need of the visible movement and *understands* the tone-poet without it. One then speaks of absolute music, that is to say of music in which everything is at once understood symbolically without further assistance.

217

The desensualization of higher art. – By virtue of the extraordinary exercise the intellect has undergone through the artistic evolution of modern music, our ears have grown more and more intellectual. We can now endure a much greater volume, much more 'noise', than our forefathers could because we are much more practised in listening for the *reason in it* than they were. Because they at once inquire after the reason, the 'meaning', and are no longer content to know that a thing 'is', all our senses have in fact become somewhat blunted: a fact betrayed by, for example, the complete dominance of the well-tempered tonal system; for ears that can still hear the subtle distinction between for example C sharp and D flat are now exceptional. In this matter our ears have become coarser. Then, the ugly side of the world, the side originally hostile to the senses, has now been conquered for music; its sphere of power especially in the domain of the sublime, dreadful and mysterious has therewith increased astonishingly: our music now brings to utterance things which formerly had no tongue. In a similar way, some of our painters have made our eyes more intellectual and have gone far beyond that which was formerly called pleasure in form and colour. Here too the side of the world that originally counted as ugly has been conquered by artistic reason. – What will be the consequence of all this? The more capable of thought eye and ear become, the closer they approach the point at which they become unsensual: pleasure is transferred to the brain, the sense-organs themselves grow blunt and feeble, the symbolic increasingly replaces the simple being – and along this path we thus attain to barbarism as certainly as along any other. For the moment we still believe: the world is uglier than ever, but it *signifies* a more beautiful world than there has ever been. But the more attenuated the fragrant odour of 'significance' becomes, the fewer there will be still able to perceive it: and the rest will finally be left with the ugly, which they will try to enjoy directly – an endeavour in which they are bound to fail. Thus there is in Germany a twofold current of musical evolution: on the one hand a host of ten thousand with ever higher, more refined demands, listening ever more intently for the 'meaning', and on the other the enormous majority growing every year more and more incapable of comprehending the meaningful even in the form of the sensually ugly and therefore learning to seize with greater and greater contentment the ugly and disgusting in itself, that is to say the basely sensual, in music.

218

Stone is more stony than it used to be. – In general we no longer understand architecture; at least we do not do so nearly as well as we understand music. We have grown out of the symbolism of lines and figures, just as we have weaned ourselves from the sound-effects of rhetoric, and no longer imbibe this kind of cultural mother's milk from the first moment of our lives. Everything in a Greek or Christian building originally signified something, and indeed something of a higher order of things: this feeling of inexhaustible significance lay about the building like a magical veil. Beauty entered this sytem only incidentally, without essentially encroaching upon the fundamental sense of the uncanny and exalted, of consecration by magic and the proximity of the divine; at most beauty *mitigated* the *dread* – but this dread was everywhere the presupposition. – What is the beauty of a building to us today? The same thing as the beautiful face of a mindless woman: something mask-like.

219

Religious origin of modern music. – Music of feeling comes into being within the restored Catholicism that followed the Council of Trent,* through Palestrina,† who assisted the newly awakened spirit to find utterance; later, with Bach, it extended to Protestantism too, insofar as Protestantism had been deepened by the Pietists‡ and detached from its original dogmaticism. The presupposition and necessary preliminary for both developments is the occupation with music such as was practised during the Renaissance and before it, and especially that scholarly concern with it, at bottom scientific, that takes pleasure in the artifices of harmony and counterpoint. On the other hand, opera was also a necessary preliminary: for in opera the laity promulgated its protest against a cold music grown too learned and sought to restore to Polyhymnia§ her soul. – Without that profoundly religious conversion, without that resounding of the deeply agitated heart, music would have remained scholarly or operatic; the spirit of the Counter-reformation is the spirit of modern music (for that Pietism in Bach's music is also a kind of Counter-reformation). This is how profoundly indebted we are to the religious

* Council of Trent: opened in 1545, it produced the reform of the Roman church known as the Counter-reformation.
† Palestrina (1525–94): Italian composer of nearly a hundred masses who eventually entered the priesthood. In Pfitzner's opera, *Palestrina*, he is represented as divinely inspired to write a mass that persuaded the Council of Trent not to ban polyphonic music.
‡ Pietists: Lutheran followers of Phillip Jakob Spener, whose movement began in Frankfurt in about 1670 and accorded to the individual immediate experience of the divine.
§ Polyhymnia: the muse of vocal music

life. – Music was the *Counter-renaissance* in the domain of art; to it belongs the later painting of Murillo,* perhaps the Baroque style does too: more so, at any rate, than the architecture of the Renaissance or of antiquity. And now one may go on to ask: if our modern music could move stones, would it set them together in the manner of the architecture of antiquity? I doubt very much that it would. For that which reigns in music, the affect, joy in enhanced, wide-ranging moods, the desire for liveliness at any cost, the rapid change of sensations, strong relief-effects in light and shadow, the juxtaposition of the ecstatic and the naive – all this reigned once before in the plastic arts and created new stylistic laws: – but it was neither in antiquity nor in the time of the Renaissance.

220

The Beyond in art. – It is not without profound sorrow that one admits to oneself that in their highest flights the artists of all ages have raised to heavenly transfiguration precisely those conceptions which we now recognize as false: they are the glorifiers of the religious and philosophical errors of mankind, and they could not have been so without believing in the absolute truth of these errors. If belief in such truth declines in general, if the rainbow-colours at the extreme limits of human knowledge and supposition grow pale, that species of art can never flourish again which, like the *Divina Commedia*, the pictures of Raphael, the frescoes of Michelangelo, the Gothic cathedrals, presupposes not only a cosmic but also a metaphysical significance in the objects of art. A moving tale will one day be told how there once existed such an art, such an artist's faith.

221

The revolution in poetry. – The stern constraint the French dramatists imposed upon themselves in regard to unity of action, of place and of time, to style, to construction of verse and sentence, to choice of words and ideas, was as vital a schooling as that of counterpoint and fugue in the development of modern music or as the Gorgian tropes in Greek rhetoric. To fetter oneself in this way can seem absurd; nonetheless there is no way of getting free of naturalization than that of first limiting oneself to what is most severe (perhaps also most capricious). Thus one gradually learns to walk with poise even upon narrow bridges spanning dizzying abysses and brings the highest suppleness of movement home as booty: as has been demonstrated to the eyes of everyone now living by the history of music. Here we see how the fetters grow looser step by step, until in the end it can appear as though they have been wholly thrown off: this *appearance* is the supreme outcome of a necessary evolution in art. No such gradual emergence out of self-imposed fetters has occurred in the case of modern poetry. Lessing made French form,† that is to say the only modern artistic form, into a laughing-stock in Germany and pointed to Shakespeare, and thus we forewent the steady continuity of that unfettering and made a leap into naturalism – that is to say, back to

* Murillo: Bartolomé Murillo (1618–82): Spanish painter
† Lessing: Gotthold Ephraim Lessing (1729–81): German dramatist, critic and aesthetician

the beginnings of art. Goethe attempted to rescue himself from this situation through his ability again and again to impose differing kinds of constraint upon himself; but even the most gifted can achieve only a continual experimentation once the thread of evolution has been broken. Schiller owed his relative firmness of form to having modelled himself on French tragedy, which, though he repudiated, he involuntarily respected, and maintained a degree of independence of Lessing (whose dramatic experiments he is known to have rejected). After Voltaire the French themselves were suddenly lacking in the great talents who could have led the evolution of tragedy out of constraint on to that appearance of freedom; later they too copied the Germans and made the leap into a kind of Rousseauesque state of nature in art and experimented. One only has to read Voltaire's *Mahomet* from time to time to bring clearly before one's soul what European culture has lost once and for all through this breach with tradition. Voltaire was the last great dramatist to subdue through Greek moderation a soul many-formed and equal to the mightiest thunderstorms of tragedy – he was able to do what no German has yet been able to do because the nature of the Frenchman is much more closely related to the Greek than is the nature of the German – just as he was also the last great writer to possess a Greek ear, Greek artistic conscientiousness, Greek charm and simplicity in the treatment of prose speech; just as he was, indeed, one of the last men able to unite in himself the highest freedom of spirit and an altogether unrevolutionary disposition without being inconsistent and cowardly. Since his time the modern spirit, with its restlessness, its hatred for bounds and moderation, has come to dominate in every domain, at first let loose by the fever of revolution and then, when assailed by fear and horror of itself, again laying constraints upon itself – but the constraints of logic, no longer those of artistic moderation. It is true that for a time this unfettering enables us to enjoy the poetry of all peoples, all that has grown up in hidden places, the primitive, wild-blooming, strangely beautiful and gigantically irregular, from the folksong up to the 'great barbarian' Shakespeare; we taste the joys of local colour and costumes such as all artistic nations have hitherto been strangers to; we make abundant employment of the 'barbaric advantages' of our age that Goethe urged against Schiller's objections so as to set the formlessness of his *Faust* in the most favourable light. But for how much longer? The inbreaking flood of poetry of all styles of all peoples *must* gradually sweep away the soil in which a quiet, hidden growth would still have been possible; all poets *must* become experimenting imitators and foolhardy copiers, however great their powers may have been at first; the public, finally, which has forgotten how to see in the harnessing of the powers of representation, in the mastering of all the expedients of art and their organization, the actual artistic deed, *must* increasingly value artistic power for its own sake, indeed colour for its own sake, the idea for its own sake, inspiration for its own sake, will consequently no longer enjoy the elements and terms of the work of art if not in *isolation*, and in the long run make the natural demand that the artist *must* also present them to it in isolation. One has indeed thrown off the 'unreasonable' fetters of Franco-Hellenic art, but without noticing it has accustomed oneself to finding all fetters, all limitation unreasonble; and thus art moves towards its *dissolution* and in doing so ranges – which is extremely instructive, to be sure – through all the phases of its beginnings, its childhood, its imperfection, its former hazardous enterprises and extravagances: in going down to destruction it interprets its birth and becoming. One of the great upon whose instinct one can no doubt rely and whose theory lacked nothing except thirty years *more* of practice – Lord Byron once said: 'So far as poetry is concerned, the more I reflect on it, the more firmly am I convinced that we are all on the wrong path, every one of us. We all pursue a revolutionary system inwardly false – our own or the next generation will arrive at the same conviction.' It is this same Byron who says: 'I regard Shakespeare as the worst of models, even though the most extraordinary of poets.' And does the mature artistic insight that Goethe achieved in the second half of his life not at bottom say exactly the same thing? – that insight with which he gained such a start of a whole series of generations that one can assert that on the whole Goethe has not yet produced any effect at all and that his time is still to come? It is precisely because his nature held him for a long time on the path of the poetical revolution, precisely because he savoured most thoroughly all that had been discovered in the way of new inventions, views and expedients through that breach with tradition and as it were dug out from beneath the ruins of art, that his later transformation and conversion carries so much weight: it signifies that he felt the profoundest desire to regain the traditional ways of art and to bestow upon the ruins and colonnades of the temple that still remained their ancient wholeness and perfection at any rate with the eye of imagination if strength of arm should prove too weak to construct where such tremendous forces were needed even to destroy. Thus he lived in art as in recollection of true art: his writing had become an aid to recollection, to an understanding of ancient, long since vanished artistic epochs. His demands were, to be sure, having regard to the powers possessed by the modern age unfulfillable; the pain he felt at that fact was, however, amply counterbalanced by the joy of knowing that they once *had* been fulfilled and that we too can still participate in this fulfilment. Not individuals, but more or less idealized masks; no actuality, but an allegorical universalization; contemporary characters, local colour evaporated almost to invisibility and rendered mythical; present-day sensibility and the problems of present-day society compressed to the simplest forms, divested of their stimulating, enthralling, pathological qualities and rendered *ineffectual* in every sense but the artistic; no novel material or characters, but the ancient and long-familiar continually reanimated and transformed: this is art as Goethe later *understood* it, as the Greeks and, yes, the French *practised* it.

222

What is left of art. – It is true, certain metaphysical presuppositions bestow much greater value upon art, for example when it is believed that the character is unalterable and that all characters and actions are a continual expression of the nature of the world: then the work of the artist becomes an image of the *everlastingly steadfast,* while with our conceptions the artist can bestow upon his images validity only for a time, because man as a whole has become and is changeable and even the individual man is not something firm and steadfast. – The same would be so in the case of another metaphysical presupposition: supposing our visible world were only appearance, as the metaphysicians assume, then art would come to stand quite close to the real world, for there would then be only too much similarity between the world of appearance and the illusory world of the artist; and the difference remaining would even elevate the significance of art above the significance of nature, because art would represent the uniform, the types and prototypes of nature. – These presuppositions are, however, false: after this knowledge what place still remains for art? Above all, it has taught us for thousands of years to look upon life in any of its forms with interest and pleasure, and to educate our sensibilities so far that we at last cry: 'life, however it may be, is good!'* This teaching imparted by art to take pleasure in life and to regard the human life as a piece of nature, as the object of regular evolution, without being too violently involved in it – this teaching has been absorbed into us, and it now reemerges as an almighty requirement of knowledge. One could give up art, but would not thereby relinquish the capacity one has learned from it: just as one has given up religion but not the enhancement of feeling and exaltations one has acquired from it. As the plastic arts and music are the measure of the wealth of feelings we have actually gained and ·obtained through religion, so if art disappeared the intensity and multifariousness of the joy in life it has implanted would still continue to demand satisfaction. The scientific man is the further evolution of the artistic.

223

Evening twilight of art. – Just as in old age one remembers one's youth and celebrates festivals of remembrance, so will mankind soon stand in relation to art: it will be a moving recollection of the joys of youth. Perhaps art has never before been comprehended so profoundly or with so much feeling as it is now, when the magic of death seems to play around it. Recall that Greek city in south Italy which on *one* day of the year continued to celebrate their Greek festival and did so with tears and sadness at the fact that foreign barbarism was triumphing more and more over the customs they had brought with them; it is to be doubted whether the Hellenic has ever been so greatly savoured, or its golden nectar imbibed with so much relish, as it was among these declining Hellenes. The artist will soon be regarded as a glorious relic, and we shall bestow upon him, as a

---

* The closing line of Goethe's 'Der Bräutigam': 'Wie es auch sei, das Leben, es ist gut.'

marvellous stranger upon whose strength and beauty the happiness of former ages depended, honours such as we do not grant to others of our own kind. The best in us has perhaps been inherited from the sensibilities of earlier ages to which we hardly any longer have access by direct paths; the sun has already set, but the sky of our life still glows with its light, even though we no longer see it.

5

TOKENS OF HIGHER
AND
LOWER CULTURE

224

Ennoblement through degeneration. – History teaches that the branch of a nation that preserves itself best is the one in which most men have, as a consequence of sharing habitual and undiscussable principles, that is to say as a consequence of their common belief, a living sense of community. Here good, sound custom grows strong, here the subordination of the individual is learned and firmness imparted to character as a gift at birth and subsequently augmented. The danger facing these strong communities founded on similarly constituted, firm-charactered individuals is that of the gradually increasing inherited stupidity such as haunts all stability like its shadow. It is the more unfettered, uncertain and morally weaker individuals upon whom *spiritual progress* depends in such communities: it is the men who attempt new things and, in general, many things. Countless numbers of this kind perish on account of their weakness without producing any very visible effect; but in general, and especially when they leave posterity, they effect a loosening up and from time to time inflict an injury on the stable element of a community. It is precisely at this injured and weakened spot that the whole body is as it were *innoculated* with something new; its strength must, however, be as a whole sufficient to receive this new thing into its blood and to assimilate it. Degenerate natures are of the highest significance wherever progress is to be effected. Every progress of the whole has to be preceded by a partial weakening. The strongest natures *preserve* the type, the weaker help it to *evolve*. – Something similar occurs in the case of the individual human being; rarely is a degeneration, a mutilation, even a vice and physical or moral damage in general without an advantage in some other direction. The more sickly man, for example, will if he belongs to a warlike and restless race perhaps have more inducement to stay by himself and thereby acquire more repose and wisdom, the one-eyed will have *one* stronger eye, the blind will see more deeply within themselves and in any event possess sharper hearing. To this extent the celebrated struggle for existence does not seem to me to be the only theory by which the progress or strengthening of a man or a race can be explained. Two things, rather, must come together: firstly the augmentation of the stabilizing force through the union of minds in belief and communal feeling; then the possibility of the attainment of higher goals through the occurrence of degenerate natures and, as a consequence of them, partial weakenings and injurings of the stabilizing force; it is precisely the weaker nature, as the tenderer and more refined, that makes any progress possible at all. A people that becomes somewhere weak and fragile but is as a whole still strong and healthy is capable of absorbing the infection of the new and in-corporating it to its own advantage. In the case of the individual human being, the task of education is to imbue him with such firmness and cer-tainty he can no longer as a whole be in any way deflected from his path. Then, however, the educator has to inflict injuries upon him, or employ the injuries inflicted on him by fate, and when he has thus come to experi-ence pain and distress something new and noble can be innoculated into the injured places. It will be taken up into the totality of his nature, and later the traces of its nobility will be perceptible in the fruits of his nature. – So far as the state is concerned, Macchiavelli says that 'the form of government signifies very little, even though semi-educated people think otherwise. The great goal of statecraft should be *duration*, which outweighs everything else, inasmuch as it is much more valuable than freedom.' Only when there is securely founded and guaranteed long dur-ation is a steady evolution and ennobling innoculation at all possible: though the dangerous companion of all duration, established authority, will, to be sure, usually resist it.

225

Free spirit a relative concept. – He is called a free spirit who thinks differ-ently from what, on the basis of his origin, environment, his class and profession, or on the basis of the dominant views of the age, would have been expected of him. He is the exception, the fettered spirits are the rule; the latter reproach him that his free principles either originate in a desire to shock and offend or eventuate in free actions, that is to say in actions incompatible with sound morals. Occasionally it is also said that this or that free principle is to be attributed to perversity and mental over-excitation; but this is merely the voice of malice, which does not believe what it says but desires only to wound: for the superior quality and sharpness of his intellct is usually written on the face of the free spirit in characters clear enough even for the fettered spirit to read. But the two other derivations of free spiritedness are honestly meant; and many free spirits do in fact come to be what they are in one or other of these ways. But the principles they arrive at along these paths could nonetheless be truer and more reliable than those favoured by the fettered spirits. In the case of the knowledge of truth the point is whether or not one *possesses* it, not from what motives one sought it or along what paths one found it. If the free spirits are right, the fettered spirits are wrong, regardless of whether the former have arrived at the truth by way of immorality or the latter have hitherto cleaved to untruth out of morality. – In any event, however, what characterizes the free spirit is not that his opinions are the more correct but that he has liberated himself from tradition, whether the outcome has been successful or a failure. As a rule, though, he will none-theless have truth on his side, or at least the spirit of inquiry after truth: he demands reasons, the rest demand faith.

226

Origin of faith. – The fettered spirit takes up his position, not for reasons, but out of habit; he is a Christian, for example, not because he has knowledge of the various religions and has chosen between them; he is an Englishman, not because he has decided in favour of England: he encountered Christianity and Englishness and adopted them without reasons, as a man born in wine-producing country becomes a wine-drinker. Later, when he was a Christian and Englishman, he may perhaps have also devised a couple of reasons favourable to his habits; but if one refutes these reasons one does not therewith refute him in his general position. Oblige a fettered spirit to present his reasons for opposing bigamy, for example, and you will discover whether his holy zeal for monogamy rests on reasons or on acquired habit. Acquired habituation to spiritual principles without reasons is called faith.

227

Reasons judged a posteriori *on the basis of consequences.* – All states and orderings within society – classes, marriage, education, law – all these derive their force and endurance solely from the faith the fettered spirits have in them: that is to say in the absence of reasons, or at least in the warding off of the demand for reasons. The fettered spirits are unwilling to admit this: they recognize that it constitutes a *pudendum* Christianity, which was very innocent in its intellectual notions, noticed nothing of this *pudendum*, demanded faith and nothing but faith and passionately repulsed the desire for reasons; it pointed to the success enjoyed by faith: you will soon see the advantage to be derived from faith, it intimated, it shall make you blessed. The state in fact does the same thing, and every father raises his son in the same fashion: only regard this as true, he says, and you will see how much good it will do you. What this means, however, is that the personal *utility* of an opinion is supposed to demonstrate its *truth*, the advantageousness of a theory is supposed to guarantee its intellectual soundness and well-foundedness. It is as though a defendant said to the court: my counsel is telling the whole truth, for just see what follows from what he says: I shall be acquitted. – Because the fettered spirits harbour their principles on account of their utility, they suppose that the views of the free spirit are likewise held for utilitarian ends and that he regards as true only that which profits him. Since, however, this seems to be the opposite of that which is profitable to their country or class, they assume that the principles of the free spirit are dangerous to them; they say, or sense: he must not be right, for he is harmful to us.

228

The good, strong character. – Narrowness of views, through habit become instinct, conducts to what is called strength of character. When someone acts from a few but always the same motives, his actions attain to a great degree of energy; if those actions are in accord with the principles held by the fettered spirits they receive recognition and produce in him who does them the sensation of the good conscience. Few motives, energetic action and good conscience constitute what is called strength of character. The man of strong character lacks knowledge of how many possibilities of action there are and how many directions it can take; his intellect is unfree, fettered, because in any given case it presents to him perhaps only two possibilities; between these he must, in accordance with his whole nature, necessarily make a selection, and he does so easily and quickly because he does not have fifty possibilities to choose from. The environment in which he is educated seeks to make every man unfree, inasmuch as it presents to him the smallest range of possibilities. The individual is treated by his educators as though, granted he is something new, what he ought to become is a *repetition*. If a man at first appears as something unfamiliar, never before existent, he is to be made into something familiar, often before existent. A child is said to have a good character when it is visibly narrowly determined by what is already existent; by placing itself on the side of the fettered spirits the child first proclaims its awakening sense of community; it is on the basis of this sense of community, however, that it will later be useful to its state or its class.

229

The fettered spirits' measure of things. – Of four species of things the fettered spirits say they are in the right. Firstly: all things that possess duration are in the right; secondly: all things that do not inconvenience us are in the right, thirdly: all things that bring us advantage are in the right; fourthly: all things for which we have made a sacrifice are in the right. This last explains why, for example, a war started against the will of the nation is carried on with enthusiasm once sacrifices have been made. – The free spirits who urge their cause before the forum of the fettered spirits have to demonstrate that there have always been free spirits, that is to say that free spiritedness possesses duration, then that they do not desire to inconvenience, and finally that on the whole they bring advantage to the fettered spirits; but because they cannot convince the fettered spirits of this last it is of no use to them to have demonstrated the first and second points.

230

Esprit fort. – Compared with him who has tradition on his side and requires no reasons for his actions, the free spirit is always weak, especially in actions; for he is aware of too many motives and points of view and therefore possesses an uncertain and unpractised hand. What means are there of nonetheless rendering him *relatively strong*, so that he shall at least make his way and not ineffectually perish? How does the strong spirit (*esprit fort*) come into being? This is in the individual case the question how genius is produced. Whence comes the energy, the inflexible strength, the endurance with which the individual thinks, in opposition to tradition, to attain to a wholly individual perception of the world?

231

The origin of genius. – The way in which a prisoner uses his wits in the

search for a means of escape, the most cold-blooded and tedious employment of every little advantage, can teach us what instrument nature
sometimes makes use of to bring into existence genius – a word I ask to be
understood without any flavour of the mythological or religious: it takes
it and shuts it in a prison and excites in it the greatest possible desire to
free itself. – Or, to employ a different image: someone who has completely lost his way in a forest but strives with uncommon energy to get
out of it again sometimes discovers a new path which no one knows: that
is how those geniuses come about who are famed for originality. – It has
already been remarked that a mutilation, crippling, a serious deficiency
in an organ offers the occasion for an uncommonly successful development of another organ, the reason being that it has to discharge not only
its own function but another as well. It is in this way one can suppose
many a glittering talent to have originated. – Now apply these general indications as to the origin of genius to the specific case of the origin of the
perfect free spirit.

232
Conjecture as to the origin of free spiritedness. – Just as the glaciers increase
when in the equatorial regions the sun burns down upon the sea with
greater heat than before, so it may be that a very strong and aggressive
free spiritedness is evidence that somewhere the heat of sensibility has
sustained an extraordinary increase.

233
The voice of history. – In general history *seems* to furnish the following
instruction regarding the production of genius: mistreat and torment
men – thus it cries to the passions of envy, hatred and contest – drive
them to the limit, one against the other, nation against nation, and do it
for centuries on end; then perhaps, a spark as it were thrown off by the
fearful energy thus ignited, the light of genius will suddenly flare up; the
will, made wild like a horse under the rider's spur, will then break out
and leap over into another domain. – He who became aware of how
genius is produced, and desired to proceed in the manner in which
nature usually does in this matter, would have to be exactly as evil and
ruthless as nature is. – But perhaps we have misheard.

234
Value of the middle of the way. – Perhaps the production of genius is reserved to only a limited period in the life of mankind. For one cannot
expect of the future of mankind that it will produce all at the same time
things which required for their production quite definite conditions belonging to some period or other of the past; we cannot, for example,
expect to see the astonishing effects of the religious feeling. This itself has
had its time and many very good things can never thrive again because it
was only out of it they could grow. Thus there will never again be a life
and culture bounded by a religiously determined horizon. Perhaps even
the type of the saint is possible only with a certain narrowness of intellect

which, as it seems, is now done with for all future time. And thus the high point of intelligence has perhaps been reserved for a single age of mankind: it appeared – and continues to appear, for we are still living in this age – when an extraordinary, long accumulated energy of will exceptionally transferred itself through inheritance to *spiritual* goals. This high point will be past when that wildness and energy have ceased to be cultivated. Perhaps mankind will approach closer to its actual goals at the middle of its way, in the mid-period of its existence, than at its end. Forces such as condition the production of art, for example, could simply die out; delight in lying, in the vague, in the symbolic, in intoxication, in ecstasy could fall into disrepute. Indeed, if life were ever to be ordered within the perfect state, there would no longer exist in the present any motive whatever for poetry and fiction, and it would be only the retarded who still had a desire for poetical unreality. These would in any case look back in longing to the times of the imperfect state, of society still half barbaric, to *our* times.

235

Genius incompatible with the ideal state. – The Socialists desire to create a comfortable life for as many as possible. If the enduring homeland of this comfortable life, the perfect state, were really to be attained, then this comfortable life would destroy the soil out of which great intellect and the powerful individual in general grows: by which I mean great energy. If this state is achieved mankind would have become too feeble still to be able to produce the genius. Ought one therefore not to desire that life should retain its violent character and savage forces and energies continue to be called up again and again? The warm, sympathizing heart will, of course, desire precisely the *abolition* of that savage and violent character of life, and the warmest heart one can imagine would long for it the most passionately: and yet precisely this passion would nonetheless have derived its fire, its warmth, indeed its very existence from that savage and violent character of life; the warmest heart thus desires the abolition of its own foundation, the destruction of itself, which is to say it desires something illogical, it lacks intelligence. The highest intelligence and the warmest heart cannot coexist in the same person, and the sage who pronounces judgement on life places himself above goodness as well and regards it only as something to be taken into account together with everything else in the total assessment of life. The sage has to resist these extravagant desires of unintelligent goodness, because his concern is the continuance of his type and the eventual creation of the supreme intellect; at the least he will refrain from promoting the foundation of the 'perfect state', inasmuch as only enfeebled individuals can have any place in it. Christ, on the contrary, whom we may think of as possessing the warmest heart, promoted the stupidifying of man, placed himself on the side of the poor in spirit and retarded the production of the supreme intellect: and in this he was consistent. His antithesis, the perfect sage – this one may venture to prophesy – will just as necessarily obstruct the production of a Christ. – The state is a prudent institution for the protection of individuals against one another: if it is completed and perfected too far it will in the end enfeeble the individual and, indeed, dissolve him – that is to say, thwart the original purpose of the state in the most thorough way possible.

236

The zones of culture. – One can say metaphorically that the ages of culture correspond to the various climatic belts, except that they are ranged one after the other and not, as in the case of the geographic zones, side by side. In comparison with the temperate zone of culture into which it is our task to pass over, that of the past produces, taken as a whole, the impression of a *tropical* climate. Violent antitheses, the abrupt transition of day to night and night to day, heat and vivid colour, reverence for everything sudden, mysterious, terrible, the swiftness with which a storm breaks, everywhere a prodigal overflowing of the cornucopias of nature: and, on the other hand, in our culture a bright yet not radiant sky, a clear, more or less unchanging air, sharp, occasionally cold: thus are the two zones distinguished one from another. When we behold in that other zone how the most raging passions are brought down and destroyed by the uncanny force of metaphysical conceptions, we feel as though we were witnessing the crushing of tropical tigers in the coils of monstrous serpents; such events are lacking in our spiritual climate, our imagination has been quietened; even in dreams we do not experience what earlier peoples beheld while awake. But should we not be permitted to rejoice at this change, even allowing that the artists have suffered badly through the disappearance of tropical culture and find us non-artists a little too sober? To this extent artists are no doubt right to deny that there has been any 'progress', for it is at least open to doubt whether the past three millennia evidence a course of progress in the arts, while a metaphysical philosopher such as Schopenhauer would likewise have no cause to recognize any progress if he surveyed the past four millennia with regard to metaphysical philosophy and religion. – To us, however, the very *existence* of the temperate zone of culture counts as progress.

237

Renaissance and Reformation. – The Italian Renaissance contained within it all the positive forces to which we owe modern culture: liberation of thought, disrespect for authorities, victory of education over the arrogance of ancestry, enthusiasm for science and the scientific past of mankind, unfettering of the individual, a passion for truthfulness and an aversion to appearance and mere effect (which passion blazed forth in a whole host of artistic characters who, in an access of moral rectitude, demanded of themselves perfection in their work and nothing but perfection); indeed, the Renaissance possessed positive forces which have *up to now* never reappeared in our modern culture with such power as they had then. All its blemishes and vices notwithstanding, it was the golden age of this millennium. In contrast to it there stands the German

Reformation: an energetic protest by retarded spirits who had by no means had enough of the world-outlook of the Middle Ages and greeted the signs of its dissolution, the extraordinary transformation of the religious life into something shallow and merely external, not with rejoicing, as would have been appropriate, but with profound ill-humour. With their stiff-necked northern forcefulness they reversed the direction in which men were going, with a violence appropriate to a state of siege they compelled the Counter-reformation, that is to say a Catholic Christianity of self-defence, and, just as they delayed the complete awakening and hegemony of the sciences for two or three hundred years, so they perhaps rendered the complete growing-together of the spirit of antiquity and the modern spirit impossible for ever. The great task of the Renaissance could not be brought to completion, the protestation of German nature grown retarded (for in the Middle Ages it had had sufficient sense to cross over the Alps again and again for the sake of its salvation) prevented it. It was an extraordinary chance political constellation that preserved Luther and lent force to that protestation: for the Emperor protected him so as to employ his innovation as an instrument of pressure against the Pope, while the Pope likewise secretly befriended him so as to employ the Protestant princes of the Holy Roman Empire as a counterweight to the Emperor. Without this curious combination of motives Luther would have been burned like Huss* – and the Enlightenment perhaps have dawned somewhat sooner than it did and with a fairer lustre than we can now even imagine.

238

Justice towards the evolving god. – When the entire history of culture opens up before our gaze as a confusion of evil and noble, true and false conceptions, and at the sight of this surging of the waves we come to feel almost seasick, we are then able to grasp what comfort there lies in the idea of an *evolving god*: the transformations and destinies of mankind are, according to this idea, the ever increasing self-revelation of this god, it is not all a blind mechanism, a senseless, purposeless confused play of forces. The deification of becoming is a metaphysical outlook – as though from a lighthouse down on to the sea of history – in which a generation of scholars too much given to historicizing found their consolation; one ought not to get annoyed at it, however erroneous that idea may be. Only he who, like Schopenhauer, denies the fact of evolution, will likewise feel nothing of the wretchedness of this surging of the waves of history, and because he knows and feels nothing of that evolving god or of the need to suppose his existence may fairly give vent to his mockery.

239

Fruit out of season. – That better future which one wishes for mankind must necessarily be in some respects a worse future: for it is folly to believe that a new higher stage of mankind will unite in itself all the excellences of earlier stages and be obliged, for example, to include the highest

* John Huss, religious teacher condemned for heresy and burned at Constance in 1415.

114

phase of art. What is the case, rather, is that every season has its own particular charm and excellencies and excludes those of the other seasons.
That which grew up out of religion and in proximity to it cannot grow
again if this is destroyed; at the most, stray, late-sprouting shoots can put
in a deceptive appearance, as can brief outbreaks of recollection of the art
of former times: a condition which may well betray a sense of loss and
deprivation, but which is no evidence of the existence of any force out of
which a new art could be born.

240

The world's increasing severity. – The higher a man's culture ascends, the
less space there is for humour and mockery. Voltaire was grateful to
heaven from his very heart for the invention of marriage and the church:
it showed how well amusement had been taken care of. But he and his
age, and before him the sixteenth century, mocked these themes to
exhaustion; in these domains all witticism is now belated and above all
too cheap to attract the buyer's curiosity. Nowadays one asks after
causes: it is the age of seriousness. Who is now interested in seeing the
differences between reality and presumptuous appearance, between
what a man is and what he seeks to represent, in a humorous light? The
feeling evoked by this contrast produces a quite different effect as soon as
one looks for the reasons. The more profoundly anyone understands life
the less he will give vent to mockery, unless perhaps he comes at last to
mock at the 'profundity of his understanding'.

241

Genius of culture. – If anyone wanted to imagine a genius of culture, what
would the latter be like? He would manipulate falsehood, force, the most
ruthless self-interest as his instruments so skilfully he could only be
called an evil, demonic being; but his objectives, which here and there
shine through, would be great and good. He would be a centaur, half
beast, half man, and with angel's wings attached to his head in addition.

242

Miraculous education. – Interest in education will become genuinely
intense only from the moment when belief in a God and his loving care is
abandoned: just as the art of medicine could begin to flourish only when
belief in miraculous cures ceased. To the present day, however, all the
world continues to believe in miraculous education: for the greatest disorder, confusion of objectives, unfavourable circumstances have succeeded in producing the most fruitful and capable men, and how could
there not be something uncanny in that? – Soon these cases too will be ex-
amined more closely and tested more carefully: no miracles will ever be
discovered. Under the same circumstances countless men continually
perish, the single individual who has been saved usually grows stronger
as a consequence because, by virtue of an inborn, indestructible strength,
he has endured these ill circumstances and in doing so exercised and augmented this strength: that is the explanation of the miracle. An education

that no longer believes in miracles will have to pay attention to three things: firstly, how much energy is inherited? secondly, how can new energy be ignited? thirdly, how can the individual be adapted to the enormously diversified demands of culture without being distracted by them and his individuality dispersed – in short, how can the individual be set in place within the counterpoint of private and public culture, how can he play the main theme and at the same time the subordinate theme as well?

243

The future of the physician. – There is at present no profession capable of being so greatly advanced as is that of the physician; especially now that the spiritual physicians, the so-called curers of souls, may no longer carry on their sorceries to the sound of public approval and are avoided by all educated people. A physician has not now attained the highest degree of training of which he is capable when he knows the best and most recent remedies and is practised in applying them, and can draw those quick conclusions from effects to causes that make the celebrated diagnostician: he also has to possess an eloquence adapted to every individual and calculated to touch him to the very heart, a manliness at the sight of which all timorousness (the wormrot that undermines all invalids) takes flight, a diplomat's flexibility in mediating between those who require joy if they are to become well and those who for reasons of health must (and can) make others joyful, the subtlety of an agent of police or an advocate in comprehending the secrets of a soul without betraying them – in short, a good physician now needs the artifices and privileges of all the other professions; thus equipped he is then in a position to become a benefactor to the whole of society through the augmentation of good works, spiritual joy and fruitfulness, through the prevention of evil thoughts, intentions, acts of roguery (whose revolting source is so often the belly), through the production of a spiritual-physical aristocracy (as promoter and preventer of marriages), through the benevolent amputation of all so-called torments of soul and pangs of conscience: only thus will he cease to be a 'medicine-man' and become a saviour, to which end he will nonetheless require no miracles, nor will he need to have himself crucified.

244

In the proximity of madness. – The sum of sensations, items of knowledge, experiences, the whole burden of culture, that is to say, has become so great that an over-excitation of the nervous and thinking powers is now a universal danger; indeed, the cultivated classes of Europe have in fact become altogether neurotic, and almost every one of its great families has come close to lunacy in any rate one of its branches. It is true that health is nowadays sought by all available means; but what is chiefly needed is an abatement of that tension of feeling, that crushing cultural burden which, even if it has to be purchased at a heavy cost, nonetheless gives ground for high hopes of a *new Renaissance*. We have Christianity, the philosophers, poets, musicians to thank for an abundance of profound sensations: if these are not to stifle us we must conjure up the spirit of science, which on the whole makes one somewhat colder and more sceptical and in especial cools down the fiery stream of belief in ultimate definitive truths; it is principally through Christianity that this stream has grown so turbulent.

245
Bell-founding of culture. – Culture is fashioned as a bell is, inside a casing of coarser, commoner stuff: untruth, violence, unlimited expansion of every individual ego, of every individual nation, have been this casing. Has the time now come to remove it? Has what was molten become solid, have the good, advantageous drives, the habits of the nobler disposition, grown so secure and general that there is no longer any need to lean on metaphysics and the errors of the religions, acts of severity and violence are no longer the strongest cement binding man to man and nation to nation? – There is no longer a god to aid us in answering this question: our own insight must here decide. Man himself has to take in hand the rule of man over the earth, it is his 'omniscience' that has to watch over the destiny of culture with a sharp eye in future.

246
The cyclops of culture. – When we behold those deeply-furrowed hollows in which glaciers have lain, we think it hardly possible that a time will come when a wooded, grassy valley, watered by streams, will spread itself upon the same spot. So it is, too, in the history of mankind: the most savage forces beat a path, and are mainly destructive; but their work was nonetheless necessary, in order that later a gentler civilization might raise its house. The frightful energies – those which are called evil – are the cyclopean architects and road-makers of humanity.

247
Circular orbit of humanity. – Perhaps the whole of humanity is no more than a stage in the evolution of a certain species of animal of limited duration: so that man has emerged from the ape and will return to the ape, while there will be no one present to take any sort of interest in this strange comic conclusion. Just as, with the decline of Roman culture and its principal cause, the spread of Christianity, a general uglification of man prevailed within the Roman Empire, so an eventual decline of the general culture of the earth could also introduce a much greater uglification and in the end animalization of man to the point of apelikeness. – Precisely because we are able to visualize this prospect we are perhaps in a position to prevent it from occurring.

248
Words of consolation of a progress grown desperate. – Our age gives the impression of being an interim state; the old ways of thinking, the old cultures are still partly with us, the new not yet secure and habitual and thus lacking in decisiveness and consistency. It looks as though everything is becoming chaotic, the old becoming lost to us, the new proving useless

and growing ever feebler. But the same thing is experienced by the soldier learning to march: for a time he is more insecure and awkward than ever, because he is moving his muscles now according to the old method, now according to the new, and as yet neither has carried off the victory. We are faltering, but we must not let it make us afraid and perhaps surrender the new things we have gained. Moreover, we *cannot* return to the old, we *have* burned our boats; all that remains is for us to be brave, let happen what may. – Let us only *go forward*, let us only make a move! Perhaps what we do will present the aspect of *progress*; but if not, let us heed the words of Friedrich the Great and take consolation from them: '*Ah, mon cher Sulzer, vous ne connaissez pas assez cette race maudite, à laquelle nous appartenons.*'*

249

Suffering from the cultural past. – He who has come to a clear understanding of the problem of culture suffers from a feeling similar to that suffered by one who has inherited a fortune dishonestly acquired or by a prince who reigns by virtue of an act of violence on the part of his forebears. He thinks with sorrow of his origins and is often ashamed, often sensitive about them. The whole sum of the energy, will and joy he expends on his property is often balanced by a profound weariness: he cannot forget his origins. He gazes sadly into the future: he knows in advance that his posterity will suffer from the past as he does.

250

Manners. – Good manners disappear in proportion to the slackening of the influence of the court and of a closed aristocracy: one can clearly observe this decline from decade to decade if one keeps an eye on public behaviour, which is plainly growing more and more plebeian. The art of flattering and paying homage in a witty and elegant way has been entirely lost; from this emerges the ludicrous fact that in cases where homage *has* to be paid today (for example to a great statesman or artist) people borrow the language of deep feeling, of honest, true-hearted probity – out of embarrassment and lack of wit and elegance. Thus it is that formal public encounters between men seem ever more awkward but more sincere and honest without, however, being so. – But must manners continue to go downhill for ever? It seems to me, rather, that manners are describing a curve and that we are approaching its nadir. Once society has grown more certain of its objectives and principles, so that they act constructively (whereas now the manners we have acquired, constructed as they were by circumstances that have ceased to exist, are being acquired and inherited ever more feebly), manners and deportment in social intercourse will necessarily be as natural and simple as these objectives and principles are. An improvement in the division of time and work, gymnastic exercise transformed into an accompaniment to leisure, a power of reflection augmented and grown more rigorous that

---

* 'Ah, my dear Sulzer, you have too little understanding of this wicked race to which we belong.'

bestows prudence and flexibility even upon the body, will bring all this with it. – Here, to be sure, one might pause to wonder whether our men of learning, who desire to be the forerunners of this new culture, are in fact distinguished by the quality of their manners? They are not, of course: though their spirit may be willing enough, their flesh is weak. The past still lives too powerfully in their muscles: they still stand in a constricted posture, and are half worldly clerics, half the dependent tutors of the nobility, and in addition to this crippled and enervated by pedantry and antiquated procedures. They are thus, at any rate as regards their body and often also as regards three-quarters of their mind, still the court servants of an old, indeed senile culture, and as such themselves senile; the new spirit that can occasionally be heard buffeting about in these ancient containers for the present serves only to make them more fearful and insecure. Within them there walk the ghosts of the past as well as the ghosts of the future: is it any wonder if they fail to produce the most pleasing possible impression?

251

Future of science. – Science bestows upon him who labours and experiments in it much satisfaction, upon him who *learns* its results very little. As all the important truths of science must gradually become common and everyday, however, even this little satisfaction will cease: just as we have long since ceased to take pleasure in learning the admirable two-times-table. But if science provides us with less and less pleasure, and deprives us of more and more pleasure through casting suspicion on the consolations of metaphysics, religion and art, then that mightiest source of joy to which mankind owes almost all its humanity will become impoverished. For this reason a higher culture must give to man a double-brain, as it were two brain-ventricles, one for the perceptions of science, the other for those of non-science: lying beside one another, not confused together, separable, capable of being shut off; this is a demand of health. In one domain lies the power-source, in the other the regulator: it must be heated with illusions, onesidednesses, passions, the evil and perilous consequences of overheating must be obviated with the aid of the knowledge furnished by science. – If this demand of higher culture is not met, then the future course of human evolution can be foretold almost with certainty: interest in truth will cease the less pleasure it gives: because they are associated with pleasure, illusion, error and fantasy will regain step by step the ground they formerly held: the ruination of science, a sinking back into barbarism, will be the immediate consequence; mankind will have to begin again at the weaving of its tapestry, after having, like Penelope, unwoven it at night. But who can guarantee to us that it will always find the strength for it?

252

Pleasure in knowledge. – Why is knowledge, the element of the scholar and philosopher, associated with pleasure? Firstly and above all, because one here becomes conscious of one's strength; for the same reason, that is to say, that gymnastic exercises are pleasurable even when there are no spectators. Secondly, because in the course of acquiring knowledge one goes beyond former conceptions and their advocates and is victor over them, or at least believes oneself to be. Thirdly, because through a new piece of knowledge, however small, we become superior to *all* and feel ourselves as the only ones who in this matter know aright. These three causes of pleasure are the most important, though there are many other subsidiary causes, according to the nature of the man who acquires knowledge. – A comprehensive catalogue of these is offered, in a place where it would hardly be expected, in my parenthetic essay on Schopenhauer:* with this exhibition any experienced servant of knowledge can rest content, though he may deprecate the trace of irony that seems to lie on these pages. For if it is true that, if the scholar is to come into existence 'a host of very human drives, great and small, have to be moulded together', that the scholar, though a very noble metal, is not a pure one and 'consists of a tangled network of very various motives and stimuli', the same likewise applies to the artist, the philosopher, the moral genius – and whatever the great names glorified in that essay are called. *Everything* human deserves to be viewed ironically so far as its *origin* is concerned: that is why irony is so *superfluous* in the world.

253
Loyalty as proof of soundness. – It is sound evidence for the validity of a theory if its originator remains true to it for *forty years;* but I assert that there has never yet been a philosopher who has not in the end looked down on the philosophy of his youth with contempt, or at the least with mistrust. – Perhaps, however, he has never spoken publicly of this change of heart, out of a care for his reputation or – as is more likely in the case of nobler natures – out of a tender regard for his adherents.

254
Increasing interest. – During the course of a man's higher education everything becomes interesting to him, he knows how to discover the instructive side of a subject quickly and to specify the point where it will fill a gap in his thinking or an idea can be confirmed by it. Boredom vanishes more and more, as does excessive excitability of feeling. In the end he goes among men as a naturalist does among plants, and perceives even himself as a phenomenon that stimulates strongly only his drive to knowledge.

255
Superstition in simultaneity. – Things that happen simultaneously are connected with one another – that is the general opinion. A distant relation dies, at the same time we dream of him – there you are! But countless relations die without our dreaming of them. It is as with the shipwrecked who take vows: the votive tablets of those who perished are not afterwards observed in the temple. – A man dies, an owl hoots, a clock stops,

* The third of Nietzsche's *Untimely Meditations*: 'Schopenhauer as educator' (1874).

all in the *same* night hour: must there not be a connection? So intimate a relationship with nature as is assumed in this supposition is also encountered in a more refined form among historians and depicters of culture, who usually suffer from a kind of hydrophobia in regard to all the meaningless juxtapositions in which the life of the individual and of nations is nonetheless so rich.

256

Science furthers ability, not knowledge. – The value of having for a time rigorously pursued a *rigorous science* does not derive precisely from the results obtained from it: for in relation to the ocean of things worth knowing these will be a mere vanishing droplet. But there will eventuate an increase in energy, in reasoning capacity, in toughness of endurance; one will have learned how *to achieve an objective by the appropriate means*. To this extent it is invaluable, with regard to everything one will afterwards do, once to have been a man of science.

257

Youthful charm of science. – The search for truth still possesses the charm of standing everywhere in stark contrast to grey and tedious error; but this charm is in continual decline. Now, to be sure, we are still living in truth's youthful era and are accustomed to pursue truth as though she were a beautiful girl; but what of that day when she shall have become a scowling old woman? In almost every science the fundamental insight is either discovered in its earliest years or it continues to be sought; how different a charm it then exerts from when everything essential has been discovered and only a pitiful late remainder is left for the seeker to cull (a sensation one can experience in certain historical disciplines).

258

The statue of humanity. – The genius of culture does as Cellini* did when he cast his statue of Perseus: the liquefied mass seemed to be insufficient, but he was *determind* to produce enough: so he threw into it keys and plates and whatever else came to hand. And just so does that genius throw in errors, vices, hopes, delusions and other things of baser as well as nobler metal, for the statue of humanity must emerge and be completed; what does it matter if here and there inferior material is employed?

259

A masculine culture. – Greek culture of the classical era is a masculine culture. As regards women, Pericles says it all in the funeral oration with the words: they are at their best when men talk about them as little as possible. – The erotic relationship of the men with the youths was, to a degree we can no longer comprehend, the sole and necessary presupposition of all male education (somewhat in the way in which with us all higher education was for a long time introduced to women only through love-affairs and marriage); all the practical idealism of the Hellenic nature threw itself

* Cellini: Benvenuto Cellini (1500–71): Italian sculptor and goldsmith

upon this relationship, and young people have probably never since been treated with so much attention and kindness or so completely with a view to enhancing their best qualities (*virtus*) as they were in the sixth and fifth centuries – in accordance, that is, with Hölderlin's* fine maxim 'for the mortal gives of his best when loving'.† The greater the regard paid to this relationship, the less was paid to commerce with woman: considerations of child-begetting and sensual pleasure – that was all that counted here; there was no spiritual commerce, not even an actual love-affair. When one further considers that they were excluded from contests and spectacles of every kind, only the religious cults are left as the sole form of higher entertainment for women. – If the figures of Electra and Antigone were nonetheless presented on the tragic stage, this was *endurable* in art, though in life one would not want it: just as we now could not bear in *life* all the pathos we are happy enough to witness in art. – The women had no other task than to bring forth handsome, powerful bodies in which the character of the father lived on as uninterruptedly as possible and therewith to counteract the nervous over-excitation that was gaining the upper hand in so highly developed a culture. It was this that kept Greek culture young for so relatively long a time; for in the Greek mothers the Greek genius again and again returned to nature.

260

The prejudice in favour of bigness. – It is plain that men overvalue everything big and conspicuous. This originates in the conscious or unconscious insight that they find it very useful if one throws all one's force into *one* domain and makes of oneself as it were *one* monstrous organ. For the individual himself a *uniform* development of his powers is certainly more useful and productive of happiness; for every talent is a vampire that sucks blood and strength from the other powers, and an exaggerated production can reduce even the most gifted man almost to madness. In the arts, too, the extreme natures attract much too much attention; but one must also have a much lower culture to allow oneself to be captivated by them. Men subject themselves from habit to everything that wants power.

261

The tyrants of the spirit. – Only where the radiance of the myth falls is the life of the Greeks bright; elsewhere it is gloomy. Now, the Greek philosophers deprived themselves of precisely this myth: is it not as if they wanted to move out of the sunshine into shadows and gloom? But no plant avoids the light; fundamentally these philosophers were only seeking a *brighter* sun, the myth was not pure, not lucid enough for them. They discovered this light in their knowledge, in that which each of them called his 'truth'. But in those days knowledge still possessed a greater lustre; it was still young and as yet knew little of the perils and difficulties of its path; it could still hope to reach the midpoint of being with a single

---

* Friedrich Hölderin (1770–1843): German poet
† From *Der Tod des Empedokles*, first version, lines 1569–70

leap and thence solve the riddle of the universe. These philosophers possessed a firm belief in themselves and their 'truth' and with it they overthrew all their contemporaries and predecessors; each of them was a warlike brutal *tyrant*. Perhaps happiness in the belief that one was in possession of the truth has never been greater in the history of the world, but nor, likewise, has the severity, arrogance, tyrannical and evil in such a belief. They were tyrants, that is to say that which every Greek wanted to be and what everyone was when he *could* be. Perhaps Solon* alone constitutes an exception; he says in his poems how he disdained personal tyranny. But he did it for love of his work, of his lawgiving; and to be a lawgiver is a more sublimated form of tyranny. Parmenides also gave laws, Pythagoras and Empedocles probably did so; Anaximander founded a city.† Plato was the incarnate desire to become the supreme philosophical lawgiver and founder of states; he appears to have suffered terribly from the non-fulfilment of his nature, and towards the end of his life his soul became full of the blackest gall. The more the power of the Greek philosophers declined, the more they inwardly suffered from this bitterness and vituperativeness; when the various sects came to the point of battling for their truths in the open street the souls of all these wooers of truth were totally choked with jealousy and spleen, the tyrannical element now raged as poison through their own bodies. These many petty tyrants would have liked to have eaten one another raw; not a spark of love was left in them, and all too little joy in their own knowledge. – In general, the rule that tyrants are usually murdered and that their posterity has but a brief existence also applies to the tyrants of the spirit. Their history is brief and violent, their posthumous influence ceases abruptly. Of almost all the great Hellenes it can be said that they seem to have come too late: such is the case with Aeschylus, with Pindar, with Demosthenes, with Thucydides; one further generation – and it is all over. This is what is uncanny and violent about Greek history. Nowadays, to be sure, we adhere to the gospel of the tortoise. To think historically today is almost to believe that at all times history has been made according to the principle: 'as little as possible in the longest possible time!' Alas, Greek history moves so fast! Life has never since been lived so prodigally, so exorbitantly. I cannot convince myself that the history of the Greeks pursued that *natural* course for which it is so celebrated. They were much too multifariously gifted to have proceeded *gradually* in the step-by-step manner of the tortoise in its race with Achilles: and that is what is meant by natural evolution. With the Greeks everything goes quickly forwards, but it likewise goes quickly downwards; the movement of the whole machine is so accelerated that a single stone thrown into its wheels makes it fly to pieces. Socrates, for example, was such a stone; in a single night the evolution of philosophical science, hitherto so wonderfully

* Solon (638–558 BC): Athenian lawgiver
† Parmenides (b.c. 510 BC), Pythagoras (c. 582–500 BC), Anaximander (611–547 BC): pre-Socratic philosophers. Nietzsche discusses the pre-Socratics in his early *Philosophy in the Tragic Age of the Greeks*, trans. M. Cowan (Chicago: Gateway, 1962).

regular if all too rapid, was destroyed. It is no idle question whether, if he had not come under the spell of Socrates, Plato might not have discovered an even higher type of philosophical man who is now lost to us for ever. We gaze into the ages that preceded him as into a sculptor's workshop of such types. The sixth and fifth centuries seem, however, to promise even more and higher things than they actually brought forth; it remained only a promise and proclamation. And yet there can hardly be a more grievous loss than the loss of a type, of a new, hitherto undiscovered highest *possibility of the philosophical life*. Even the older realized types have mostly come down to us ill-defined; all the philosophers from Thales to Democritus seem to me extraordinarily hard to discern; but whoever succeeded in recreating these figures would move among forms of the mightiest and purest type. This capacity is rare, to be sure; even the later Greeks who took notice of the older philosophy lacked it; Aristotle especially seems to have no eyes in his head whenever he stands before those we have named. And so it seems as though these glorious philosophers had lived in vain, or as though their only function had been to prepare the way for the quarrelsome and loquacious hordes of the Socratic schools. Here, as aforesaid, there is a gap, a breach in evolution; some great disaster must have occurred and the only statue from which we could have perceived the purpose and meaning of that great preparatory exercise in sculpting have miscarried or been shattered: what actually happened must for ever remain a secret of the workshop. – That which eventuated among the Greeks – every great thinker, in the belief that he was the possessor of absolute truth, became a tyrant, so that in the case of the Greeks the history of the spirit exhibits the same violent, precipitate and perilous character as does their political history – this kind of event was not therewith exhausted: many things of the same sort have occurred right up to the most recent times, though they have gradually grown rarer and can hardly occur now with the same naive clarity of conscience as they did among the philosophers of Greece. For on the whole contradiction and scepticism now speak too powerfully and too loudly. The period of the tyrants of the spirit is past. In the spheres of higher culture there will always have to be a sovereign authority, to be sure – but this sovereign authority will hereafter lie in the hands of the *oligarchs of the spirit*. Their spatial and political division notwithstanding, they constitute a close-knit society whose members *know* and *recognize* one another, a thing which public opinion and the judgements of the writers for the popular papers may circulate as expressions of favour and disfavour. The spiritual superiority which formerly divided and created hostility now tends to *unite*: how could the individual keep himself aloft and, against every current, swim along his own course through life if he did not see here and there others of his own kind living under the same conditions and take them by the hand, in struggle against both the ochlocratic character of the half-spirited and the half-educated and the attempts that occasionally occur to erect a tyranny with the aid of the masses? The oligarchs have need of one another, they have joy in one another, they understand the signs of one another – but each of them is nonetheless free, he fights and conquers in his *own* place, and would rather perish than submit.

262

Homer. – The greatest fact in the cultivation of Greece remains that Homer became pan-Hellenic so early. All the spiritual and human freedom the Greeks attained to goes back to this fact. But it was also the actual fatality of Greek cultivation, for Homer by centralizing made everything level and dissolved the more serious instincts for independence. From time to time a resistance to Homer arose from out of the deepest foundations of the Hellenic; but *he* was always victorious. All great spiritual forces exercise beside their liberating effect also a repressive one; but it makes a difference, to be sure, whether it is Homer or the Bible or science that tyrannizes over mankind.

263

Talent. – In as highly developed a humanity as ours now is everyone acquires from nature access to many talents. Everyone *possesses inborn talent*, but few possess the degree of inborn and acquired toughness, endurance and energy actually to become a talent, that is to say to *become* what he *is*: which means to discharge it in works and actions.

264

The gifted either over-valued or under-valued. – Men who are gifted but unscientific value every token of spirit, whether it is on the right track or not; they desire above all that the man who has commerce with them should entertain them with his spiritual capacities, should spur them on, inflame them, carry them away into undertakings serious and jesting, and in any event protect them as the mightiest amulet against boredom. Scientific natures, on the other hand, know that the talent for having ideas of all kinds must be rigorously curbed by the spirit of science; not that which glitters, shines, excites, but often insignificant seeming truth is the fruit he wishes to shake down from the tree of knowledge. Like Aristotle, he may not draw a distinction between 'boring' and 'gifted', his daemon leads him through the desert as well as through tropical vegetation, so that he may everywhere take pleasure only in the real, valid, genuine. – This is why insignificant scholars harbour a distrust and suspicion of giftedness in general, and why, on the other hand, gifted people frequently harbour an aversion to science: as do, for example, almost all artists.

265

Reason in school. – The school has no more important task than to teach rigorous thinking, cautious judgement and consistent reasoning; therefore it has to avoid all those things that are of no use for these operations, for example religion. For it can be sure that, if the bow of thought has been stretched too tight, human unclarity, habit and need will afterwards relax it again. But so long as it exerts influence it ought to extort that which distinguishes and is the essence of man: 'reason and science, the *supremest* powers of man' – as Goethe at least judges. – The great naturalist von Baer* sees the superiority of all Europeans when compared with Asiatics to lie in their inculcated ability to give reasons for what they believe, an ability the latter totally lack. Europe has attended the school of consistent and critical thinking, Asia still does not know how to distinguish between truth and fiction and is unaware whether its convictions stem from observation and correct thinking or from fantasies. – Reason in school has made Europe Europe: in the Middle Ages it was on the way to becoming again a piece and appendage of Asia – that is to say losing the scientific sense which it owed to the Greeks.

266

Under-valued effect of grammar-school teaching. – The value of the grammar school is seldom sought in the things that are actually learned and safely brought home there, but in those that are taught but which the pupil acquires only with reluctance and shakes off again as quickly as he dares. The reading of the classics – every educated person admits this – is, wherever it is carried on, a monstrous procedure: before young people who are in no way whatever ripe for it, by teachers whose every word, often whose mere appearance, lays a blight on a good writer. But herein lies the value that usually goes unrecognized – that these teachers speak the *abstract language of higher culture*, ponderous and hard to understand but nonetheless a higher gymnastics for the head; that concepts, technical terms, methods, allusions continually occur in their language such as young people almost never hear in the conversation of their relations or in the street. If the pupils merely *listen*, their intellect will be involuntarily prepared for a scientific mode of thinking. It is not possible for them to emerge from this discipline as a pure child of nature quite untouched by the power of abstraction.

267

Learning many languages. – Learning many languages fills the memory with words instead of facts and ideas, while the memory is a receptacle which in the case of each man can take only a certain limited content. Then the learning of many languages is harmful insofar as it invites belief that one is in possession of complete accomplishments, and in fact also lends one a certain seductive esteem in social intercourse; it is also harmful indirectly in that it stands in the way of the acquisition of thorough knowledge and any ambition to deserve the respect of others by honest means. Finally, it is the axe that is laid at the roots of a feeling for the nuances of one's own mother tongue: it incurably injures and destroys any such feeling. The two nations which produced the greatest stylists, the Greeks and the French, learned no foreign languages. – Because, however, commerce between men is bound to grow ever more cosmopolitan and an efficient merchant in London, for example, already has to make himself understood, in speech and writing, in eight languages, the

* Karl Ernst von Baer (1792–1876)

learning of many languages is, to be sure, a necessary *evil*; but it is one for which mankind will sooner or later be compelled to find a cure: and at some distant future there will be a new language for all – first as a commercial language, then as the language of intellectual intercourse in general – just as surely as there will one day be air travel. To what other end has the science of language studied the laws of language for the past hundred years and determined what is necessary, valuable and successful in each individual language!

268

On the war history of the individual. – In an individual human life which passes through several cultures we find compressed together the conflict which is otherwise played out between two generations, between father and son: the closeness of the relationship *aggravates* this conflict, because each of the parties pitilessly draws into it the inner self of the other party that it knows so well; and this conflict will thus be fought most bitterly within the single individual; here each new phase will trample over the earlier with cruel injustice and lack of understanding of its capacities and objectives.

269

A quarter-of-an-hour earlier. – Occasionally we discover someone whose views are in advance of their time, but only to the extent that he anticipates the commonplace views of the next decade. He adheres to public opinion before it is public, that is to say he has fallen into the arms of a view that deserves to become trivial a quarter-of-an-hour earlier than others have. His fame, however, usually tends to be much noisier than the fame of the truly great and superior.

270

The art of reading. – Every strong course is onesided; it approaches the course of a straight line and like this is exclusive; that is to say, it does not touch many other courses, as weak parties and natures do in their wavelike swayings back and forth: one must thus forgive the philologists too for being onesided. Production and preservation of texts, together with their elucidation, pursued in a guild for centuries, has now finally discovered the correct methods; the entire Middle Ages was profoundly incapable of a strict philological elucidation, that is to say of a simple desire to understand what the author is saying – to have discovered these methods was an achievement, let no one undervalue it! It was only when the art of correct reading, that is to say philology, arrived at its summit that science of any kind acquired continuity and constancy.

271

The art of drawing conclusions. – The greatest advance mankind has made lies in its having learned to draw correct conclusions. This is by no means so natural an accomplishment as Schopenhauer assumes when he says: 'all are capable of drawing conclusions, few of judging'; on the contrary, it was learned late and has even now not yet attained to dominance. The

drawing of false conclusions was in earlier ages the rule: and the mythologies of all nations, their magic and their superstition, their religious
cults, their law are inexhaustible sources of proof of this proposition.

272

Annual rings of individual culture. – The strengths and weaknesses of spiritual productivity depend far less on inherited talent than they do on the
power of expansion bestowed with it. Most educated young people of thirty
go back at around this early solstice of their lives and are from then on disinclined to make new spiritual changes. That is why an ongrowing culture at once needs for its salvation another new generation, which in its
turn, however, does not get very far: for to *overtake* the culture of his
father the son must consume almost all the inherited energy the father
himself possessed at the stage of life at which he begot his son; it is with
the little bit left over that he goes past him (for, because the path is here
being traversed a second time, progress is a little quicker; the son does
not need to expend quite as much strength on learning what the father
has learned). Men possessed of great power of expansion, such as
Goethe for example, traverse as much as four successive generations
would hardly be able to equal; for that reason, however, they advance
ahead too quickly, so that other men overtake them only in the next century, and perhaps do not even completely overtake them, because the
chain of culture, the smooth consistency of its evolution, is frequently
weakened and interrupted. – The ordinary phases of spiritual culture
attained to in the course of history are overtaken more and more speedily. Men at present begin by entering the realm of culture as children
affected religiously and these sensations are at their liveliest in perhaps
their tenth year, then pass over into feebler forms (pantheism) while at
the same time drawing closer to science; they put God, immortality and
the like quite behind them but fall prey to the charms of a metaphysical
philosophy. At last they find this, too, unbelievable; art, on the other
hand, seems to promise them more and more, so that for a time metaphysics continues just to survive transformed into art or as a mood of
artistic transfiguration. But the scientific sense grows more and more
imperious and leads the man away to natural science and history and
especially to the most rigorous methods of acquiring knowledge, while
art is accorded an ever gentler and more modest significance. All this
nowadays usually takes place within a man's first thirty years. It is the re-
capitulation of a curriculum at which mankind has been labouring for
perhaps thirty thousand years.

273

Retrogressed, not retarded. – He who nowadays still commences his evolution from religious sensations, and perhaps after that lives for a time in
metaphysics and art, has in any event gone back quite a distance and
begins his race with other modern men under unfavourable circumstances: he appears to be at a disadvantage as regards both space and
time. But because he has sojourned in those regions where heat and

energy are unchained and power flows continually as a volcanic stream out of inexhaustible wells, provided he quits these domains at the proper time he moves forward all the faster, his feet have wings, his breast has learned to breathe more placidly, with longer and more enduring breath. – He went back only so as to have sufficient ground for his leap: thus there can be even something fearful and threatening in this retrogression.

274

A segment of our self as artistic object. – It is a sign of superior culture consciously to retain certain phases of development which lesser men live through almost without thinking and then wipe from the tablet of their soul, and to draft a faithful picture of it: for this is the higher species of the art of painting which only a few understand. To this end it will be necessary artificially to isolate those phases. Historical studies cultivate the ability for this painting, for they constantly challenge us, when faced with a piece of history, of the life of a nation or of a man, to conjure up a quite distinct horizon of ideas, a distinct strength of sensations, the predomination of this, the stepping-back of that. It is in this ability rapidly to reconstruct such systems of ideas and sensations on any given occasion, as for example the impression of a temple on the basis of a few pillars and pieces of wall that chance to remain standing, that the historical sense consists. The first result of it is that we comprehend our fellow men as being determined by such systems and representatives of different cultures, that is to say as necessary, but as alterable. And conversely, that we are able to segregate parts of our own development and exhibit them in isolation.

275

Cynic and Epicurean. – The Cynic recognizes the connection between the augmented and enhanced sufferings of the more highly cultivated man and the abundance of his needs; he grasps, that is to say, that the host of opinions that exists as regards the beautiful, appropriate, becoming, pleasurable must give rise not only to sources of enjoyment but also of repugnance. In accordance with this insight he reverses his development, inasmuch as he gives up many of these opinions and evades certain of the demands of culture; he therewith gains a feeling of freedom and invigoration, and, once habit has rendered his mode of life endurable to him, he gradually in fact comes to feel sensations of repugnance less often and less acutely and to approach the condition of the domestic animal; in addition, however, he feels all that lies in the charm of contrast and can in any event scold and grumble to his heart's content: so that in this way he again raises himself high above the world of sensations of the animal. – The Epicurean has the same viewpoint as the Cynic; between the two there usually exists only a difference of temperament. The Epicurean likewise employs his higher culture to make himself independent of dominating opinions; only he lifts himself above them, while the Cynic remains at the stage of negation. It is as though he wanders along still, sheltered, twilight pathways, while above him the tops of the trees whirl about in the wind and betray to him how violently buffetted the world outside is. In the case of the Cynic, on the other hand, it is as though he walks abroad naked in the teeth of the wind and hardens himself to the point of feeling nothing.

276

Microcosm and macrocosm of culture. – The finest discoveries concerning culture are made by the individual man within himself when he finds two heterogeneous powers ruling there. Supposing someone is as much in love with the plastic arts or music as he is enraptured by the spirit of science and he regards it as impossible to resolve this contradiction by annihilating the one and giving the other free rein, the only thing for him to do is to turn himself into so large a hall of culture that both powers can be accommodated within it, even if at opposite ends, while between them there reside mediating powers with the strength and authority to settle any contention that might break out. Such a hall of culture within the single individual would, however, bear the strongest resemblance to the cultural structure of entire epochs and provide continual instruction regarding them by means of analogy. For wherever grand cultural architecture has developed, its purpose has been to effect a harmony and concord between contending powers through the agency of an overwhelming assemblage of the other powers, but without the need to suppress them or clap them in irons.

277

Happiness and culture. – The sight of the surroundings of our childhood moves us deeply: the garden-house, the church with the graveyard, the pond and the wood – we see all these with a sense of suffering. We are seized with pity for ourselves, for what have we not gone through since those days! And here everything is still standing there so motionless and eternal: it is only we who are so different, so affected; we even rediscover certain people upon whom time has whetted its teeth as *little* as it has on an oaktree: peasants, fishermen, forest-dwellers – they are the same. – To be moved and to feel self-pity in face of lower culture is a sign of a higher culture; from which it follows that happiness at any rate has not been augmented by the latter. He who wants to harvest happiness and contentment from life has only to avoid acquiring a higher culture.

278

Parable of the dance. – Nowadays it is to be regarded as the decisive sign of greater culture when anyone possesses sufficient strength and flexibility to be as clear and rigorous in the domain of knowledge as at other times he is capable of as it were giving poetry, religion and metaphysics a hundred paces advantage and entering into their power and beauty. Such a situation between two so different demands is very hard to maintain, for science presses for the absolute dominance of its methods, and if this pressure is not relaxed there arises the other danger of a feeble vacillation back and forth between different drives. To indicate the way towards a resolution of this difficulty, however, if only by means of a parable, one might recall that the *dance* is not the same thing as a languid reeling back and forth between different drives. High culture will resemble an audacious dance: which is, as aforesaid, why one needs a great deal of strength and suppleness.

279

On the alleviation of life. – A principal means of alleviating one's life is to idealize everything that occurs in it; but first, however, one has to make clear to oneself from the art of painting what idealizing means. The painter desires that the viewer shall not observe too precisely, too sharply, he compels him to retreat a certain distance and view the painting from there; he is obliged to presuppose that the viewer will be some quite definite distance from the picture; he must, indeed, even assume an equally definite degree of sharpness of eyesight in his viewer! He must be in no way irresolute in such matters. Everyone who wants to idealize his life must therefore not desire to see it too precisely, he must always banish his view of it back to a certain distance away. This artifice was understood by, for example, Goethe.

280

Aggravation as alleviation and the reverse. – Much that is aggravation of life to a certain level of mankind serves a higher level as alleviation, because such men have become acquainted with sterner aggravations of life. The reverse likewise occurs: thus religion, for example, has a double face, according to whether a man gazes up to it so that it may take from him his burdens and distress, or looks down on it as on the fetters fastened to him so that he may not rise too high into the air.

281

Higher culture is necessarily misunderstood. – He who has furnished his instrument with only two strings – like the scholars, who apart from the *drive to knowledge* have only an acquired *religious* drive – cannot understand those men who are able to play on more strings than two. It lies in the nature of higher, *many-stringed* culture that it should always be falsely interpreted by the lower; as happens, for example, when art is counted a disguised form of religiousness. Indeed, people who are only religious understand even science as a seeking on the part of the religious feeling, just as the deaf-and-dumb do not know what music is if it is not visible movement.

282

Lamentation. – It is perhaps the advantages of our age that bring with them a decline in and occasionally an undervaluation of the *vita contemplativa*.* But one has to admit to oneself that our age is poor in great moralists, that Pascal, Epictetus, Seneca and Plutarch† are little read now, that

* *vita contemplativa*: contemplative life
† Pascal (1623–62), Epictetus (c. 55–135), Seneca (4 BC to AD 65), Plutarch (c. 46–120)

work and industry – formerly adherents of the great goddess health – sometimes seem to rage like an epidemic. Because time for thinking and quietness in thinking are lacking, one no longer ponders deviant views: one contents oneself with hating them. With the tremendous acceleration of life mind and eye have become accustomed to seeing and judging partially or inaccurately, and everyone is like the traveller who gets to know a land and its people from a railway carriage. An independent and cautious attitude towards knowledge is disparaged almost as a kind of derangement, the free spirit is brought into disrepute, especially by scholars, who miss in his art of reflecting on things their own thoroughness and antlike industry and would dearly love to banish him to a solitary corner of science: whereas he has the quite different and higher task of commanding from a lonely position the whole militia of scientific and learned men and showing them the paths to and goals of culture. – Such a lament as has just been sung will probably one day have had its time and, when the genius of meditation makes a mighty reappearance, fall silent of its own volition.

283
Principal deficiency of active men. – Active men are generally wanting in the higher activity: I mean that of the individual. They are active as officials, businessmen, scholars, that is to say as generic creatures, but not as distinct individual and unique human beings; in this regard they are lazy. – It is the misfortune of the active that their activity is always a little irrational. One ought not to ask the cash-amassing banker, for example, what the purpose of his restless activity is: it is irrational. The active roll as the stone rolls, in obedience to the stupidity of the laws of mechanics. – As at all times, so now too, men are divided into the slaves and the free; for he who does not have two-thirds of his day to himself is a slave, let him be what he may otherwise: statesman, businessman, official, scholar.

284
In favour of the idle. – One sign that the valuation of the contemplative life has declined is that scholars now compete with men of action in a kind of precipitate pleasure, so that they seem to value this kind of pleasure more highly than that to which they are really entitled and which is in fact much more pleasurable. Scholars are ashamed of *otium*.* But there is something noble about leisure and idleness. – If idleness really is the *beginning* of all vice, then it is at any rate in the closest proximity to all virtue; the idle man is always a better man than the active. – But when I speak of leisure and idleness, you do not think I am alluding to you, do you, you sluggards? –

285
Modern restlessness. – Modern agitatedness grows greater the farther west we go, so that to the Americans the inhabitants of Europe seem one and

---

* *otium:* see Preface, section 8, and note

all ease-loving and epicurean creatures, though in fact they are swarming among one another like bees and wasps. This agitatedness is growing so great that higher culture can no longer allow its fruits to mature; it is as though the seasons were following upon one another too quickly. From lack of repose our civilization is turning into a new barbarism. At no time have the active, that is to say the restless, counted for more. That is why one of the most necessary corrections to the character of mankind that have to be taken in hand is a considerable strengthening of the contemplative element in it. Yet even now every individual who is calm and steady in head and heart has the right to believe not only that he has a good temperament but also that he is in possession of a universally useful virtue and even that, by preserving this virtue, he is fulfilling a higher task.

286

The extent to which the man of action is lazy. – I believe that everyone must have his own individual opinion concerning everything about which an opinion is possible, because he himself is an individual, unique thing which adopts a new posture towards all other things such as has never been adopted before. But the laziness that lies in the depths of the soul of the man of action prevents man from drawing the water up from his own well. – Freedom of opinion is like health: both are individual, from neither can a universally valid concept be set up. That which one individual needs for his health is to another a cause of sickness, and many ways and means to freedom of spirit may to more highly developed natures count as ways and means to unfreedom.

287

*Censor vitae.** – For a long time the inner condition of a man who wants to exercise his own unfettered judgement regarding life is characterized by the alternation of love and hate; he forgets nothing and keeps a faithful account of all things, good and evil. Finally, when the tablet of his soul is wholly written over with experiences, he will not hate and despise existence, but neither will he love it: he will hover above it, now with the eye of joy, now with that of sorrow, and, like nature itself, be now in a summery, now in an autumnal mood.

288

Incidental success. – He who seriously wants to become free will at the same time unconstrainedly lose any tendency to faults and vices; he will likewise be assailed by annoyance and ill-humour less and less often. For his will will desire nothing more earnestly than knowledge and the means to it, that is to say the enduring condition in which he is at his most efficient in acquiring knowledge.

289

Value of illness. – The man who lies ill in bed sometimes discovers that what he is ill from is usually his office, his business or his society and that

* *Censor vitae:* censor of life

through them he has lost all circumspection with regard to himself: he acquires this wisdom from the leisure to which his illness has compelled him.

290

Country sensibility. – If a man has not drawn firm, restful lines along the horizon of his life, like the lines drawn by mountain and forest, his innermost will itself grows restless, distracted and covetous, as is the nature of the city-dweller: he has no happiness himself and bestows none on others.

291

Prudence of free spirits. – The liberal minded, men who live for the sake of knowledge alone, will find they soon attain the external goal of their life, their definitive position in relation to society and the state, and will easily be content with, for example, a minor office or an income that just enables them to live; for they will organize their life in such a way that a great transformation of external circumstances, even an overturning of the political order, does not overturn their life with it. Upon all these things they expend as little energy as possible, so that they may dive down into the element of knowledge with all their accumulated strength and as it were with a deep breath. Thus they may hope to dive deep and perhaps get a view of the ground at the bottom. – Of whatever happens to him such a spirit will want to appropriate only the tip; he has no love for things in their entirety, in all the breadth and prolixity of their convolutions, for he has no wish to get himself entangled with them. – He too knows the weekdays of unfreedom, of dependence, of servitude. But from time to time he has to have a Sunday of freedom, or he will find life unendurable. – It is probable that even his love for other people will be prudent and somewhat short-breathed, for he wants to become involved with the world of affection and blindness only insofar as it is necessary for acquiring knowledge. He must trust that the genius of justice will put in a word on behalf of his disciple and protégé if accusing voices should call him poor in love. – There is in his way of living and thinking a *refined heroism* which disdains to offer itself to the veneration of the great masses, as his coarser brother does, and tends to go silently through the world and out of the world. Whatever labyrinths he may stray through, among whatever rocks his stream may make its tortuous way – if he emerges into the open air he will travel his road bright, light and almost soundlessly and let the sunshine play down into his very depths.

292

Forward. – And with that, forward on the path of wisdom with a bold step and full of confidence! However you may be, serve yourself as your own source of experience! Throw off discontent with your nature, forgive yourself your own ego, for in any event you possess in yourself a ladder with a hundred rungs upon which you can climb to knowledge. The age in which with regret you feel yourself thrown counts you happy on account of this good fortune; it calls to you to participate in experiences that men of a later age will perhaps have to forgo. Do not underestimate the value of having been religious; discover all the reasons by virtue of which you have still had a genuine access to art. Can you not, precisely with aid of these experiences, follow with greater understanding tremendous stretches of the paths taken by earlier mankind? Is it not on precisely *this* soil, which you sometimes find so displeasing, the soil of unclear thinking, that many of the most splendid fruits of more ancient cultures grew up? One must have loved religion and art like mother and nurse – otherwise one cannot grow wise. But one must be able to see beyond them, outgrow them; if one remains under their spell, one does not understand them. You must likewise be on familiar terms with history and with playing the cautious game with the scales 'on one hand – on the other hand'. Turn back and trace the footsteps of mankind as it made its great sorrowful way through the desert of the past: thus you will learn in the surest way whither all later mankind can and may not go again. And by your desiring with all your strength to see ahead how the knot of the future is going to be tied, your own life will acquire the value of an instrument and means of knowledge. You have it in your hands to achieve the absorption of all you experience – your experiments, errors, faults, delusions, passions, your love and your hope – into your goal without remainder. This goal is yourself to become a necessary chain of rings of culture and from this necessity to recognize the necessity inherent in the course of culture in general. When your gaze has become strong enough to see to the bottom of the dark well of your nature and your knowledge, perhaps you will also behold in its mirror the distant constellations of future cultures. Do you believe that such a life with such a goal is too laborious, too much lacking in everything pleasant? Then you have not yet learned that no honey is sweeter than that of knowledge, or that the clouds of affliction hovering over you will yet have to serve you as udders from which you will milk the milk for your refreshment. Only when you grow old will you come to realize how you have given ear to the voice of nature, that nature which rules the whole world through joy: the same life that has its apex in old age also has its apex in wisdom, in that gentle sunshine of a constant spiritual joyousness; both of them, old age and wisdom, you will encounter on the *same* mountain ridge of life: so did nature will it. Then it is time, and no cause for anger, that the mists of death should approach. Towards the light – your last motion; a joyful shout of knowledge – your last sound.

6

MAN
IN
SOCIETY

293
Benevolent dissimulation. – When trafficking with men we often need to practise a benevolent dissimulation; we have to pretend we do not see through the motives of their actions.

294
Copies. – We quite often encounter copies of significant men; and, as also in the case of paintings, most people prefer the copies to the originals.

295
The speaker. – One can speak very much to the purpose and yet in such a way that all the world cries out the opposite: that happens when one is not speaking to all the world.

296
Lack of confidence. – Lack of confidence among friends is a fault that cannot be reprimanded without becoming incurable.

297
On the art of giving. – To be obliged to decline a gift simply because it was not offered in the proper way incenses one against the giver.

298
The most dangerous party member. – In every party there is one who through his all too credulous avowal of the party's principles incites the others to apostasy.

299
Adviser of an invalid. – He who offers his advice to an invalid acquires a feeling of superiority over him, whether his advice is accepted or rejected. That is why proud and sensitive invalids hate advisers even more than they do their illness.

300
Two kinds of equality. – The thirst for equality can express itself either as a desire to draw everyone down to oneself (through diminishing them, spying on them, tripping them up) or to raise oneself and everyone else up (through recognizing their virtues, helping them, rejoicing in their success).

301
Against embarrassment. – The best means of coming to the aid of people

who suffer greatly from embarrassment and of calming them down is to single them out for praise.

302

Preference for specific virtues. – We do not place especial value on the possession of a virtue until we notice its total absence in our opponent.

303

Why we contradict. – We often contradict an opinion for no other reason than that we do not like the tone in which it is expressed.

304

Trust and intimacy. – He who deliberately seeks to establish an intimacy with another person is usually in doubt as to whether he possesses his trust. He who is sure he is trusted sets little value on intimacy.

305

Equilibrium of friendship. – Sometimes in our relations with another person the right equilibrium of friendship is restored when we place in our own balance of the scales a few grains of injustice.

306

The most dangerous physicians. – The most dangerous physicians are those who, as born actors, employ a perfect art of deception to imitate the born physician.

307

When paradoxes are in order. – One sometimes needs witty people so as to win them over to a proposition so that they may exhibit it only in the form of a tremendous paradox.

308

How brave people are won over. – One can persuade brave people to participate in an action by representing it as being more dangerous than it is.

309

Civilities. – Acts of civility towards us by people we do not like we account offences on their part.

310

Keeping waiting. – A sure means of irritating people and putting evil thoughts into their heads is to keep them waiting a long time. To have this happen makes one immoral.

311

Against the trusting. – People who give us their complete trust believe they have thus acquired a right to ours. This is a false conclusion; gifts procure no rights.

312

Means of compensation. – When we have done a person harm, it often provides him with sufficient satisfaction – makes him, indeed, well disposed towards us – if we offer him an opportunity to make us the subject of a witticism.

313
Vanity of the tongue. – Whether a man conceals his bad qualities and vices or openly admits them, in both cases his vanity is seeking its advantage: one has only to observe how subtly he distinguishes before whom he conceals these qualities, before whom he is honest and open-hearted.

314
Considerate. – To desire to offend no one and injure no one can be the mark of a just disposition as well as of a timorous one.

315
Requisite for disputing. – He who does not know how to put his thoughts on ice ought not to enter into the heat of battle.

316
Society and arrogance. – One unlearns arrogance when one knows one is always among deserving people; being alone implants presumptuousness. Young people are arrogant, for they live in the society of their own kind, who are all nothing but like to seem much.

317
Motive of attack. – One attacks someone not only so as to harm him or to overpower him but perhaps only so as to learn how strong he is.

318
Flattery. – Persons who wish to deaden our caution when we associate with them by flattering us are employing a dangerous expedient: it is like a sleeping-draught which, if it does not put us to sleep, only keeps us more wakeful.

319
Good letter-writers. – He who does not write books, thinks a great deal and lives in inadequate company will usually be a good letter-writer.

320
The ugliest. – It is to be doubted whether a traveller will find anywhere in the world regions uglier than the human face.

321
Sympathizers. – Natures full of sympathy and always ready to assist in misfortune are rarely at the same time willing to join in rejoicing: when others are fortunate they have nothing to do, are superfluous, feel they have lost their position of superiority and thus can easily exhibit displeasure.

322
A suicide's relatives. – The relatives of a suicide hold it against him that out of regard for their reputation he did not remain alive.

323
Ingratitude to be expected. – He who bestows something great receives no gratitude; for the recipient is already overburdened by the act of taking.

324
In company lacking esprit. – No one is grateful for the politeness the man of *esprit* exhibits when he accommodates himself to a company in which it is not polite to exhibit *esprit*.

325
Presence of witnesses. – One is twice as glad to leap after a man who has fallen into the water when there are people present who dare not do so.

326
Silence. – The way of replying to a polemical attack the most unpleasant for both parties is to get annoyed and stay silent: for the attacker usually interprets the silence as a sign of contempt.

327
A friend's secret. – There will be few who, when they are in want of matter for conversation, do not reveal the more secret affairs of their friends.

328
Humanity. – The humanity of celebrities of the spirit when they traffic with those who are not celebrated consists in being courteously in the wrong.

329
The embarrassed. – People who do not feel secure in society employ every opportunity afforded by the presence of someone to whom they are superior of publicly exhibiting this superiority at his expense before the company, for example by teasing.

330
Obligation. – It oppresses a refined soul to know that anyone is under an obligation, a coarse one to be under an obligation to anyone.

331
Sign of estrangement. – The most obvious token of an estrangement of views between two men is that both inject a certain irony into their remarks but neither feels the irony of it.

332
Arrogance of the meritorious. – Arrogance on the part of the meritorious is even more offensive to us than the arrogance of those without merit: for merit itself is offensive.

333
The danger in our own voice. – Sometimes in the course of conversation the sound of our own voice disconcerts us and misleads us into making assertions which in no way correspond to our opinions.

334
In conversation. – Whether in conversation one generally acknowledges or
denies that another is in the right is altogether a matter of what one is accustomed to: both make good sense.

335
Fear of one's neighbour. – We fear the hostility of our neighbour because we
are apprehensive that through such a mood he will get to know our private secrets.

336
To distinguish through reprimanding. – Very prominent persons apportion
even their reprimands as though they were distinguishing us by them.
The warmth with which they concern themselves with us ought to put us
on our guard. We completely misunderstand them if we take their reprimands objectively and defend ourselves against them; we annoy them
and estrange them from us if we do so.

337
Vexation at another's goodwill. – We are mistaken as to the degree to which
we believe ourselves hated or feared: we ourselves may know very well
the degree to which we differ from a person, tendency, party, but others
know us only very superficially and therefore hate us only superficially.
We often encounter goodwill that we find inexplicable; when we understand it, however, it offends us, because it shows we are not being taken
with sufficient seriousness.

338
Clashing vanities. – When two people who are equally vain meet they
afterwards retain a poor impression of one another, because each was so
much concerned with the impression he wished to make on the other that
the other made no impression on him; both eventually come to realize
their efforts are in vain, and each puts the blame on the other.

339
Bad manners as a good sign. – The superior spirit takes pleasure in the acts
of tactlessness, arrogance, even hostility perpetrated against him by ambitious youths; they are the bad manners of fiery steeds who have as yet
carried no rider and yet will before long be so proud to carry one.

340
When it is advisable to be in the wrong. – We do well to tolerate accusations
against us without refuting them even when we are wronged by them,
when it is the case that our accuser would consider us even more in the
wrong if we contradicted him, let alone refuted him. It is true, of course,
that in this way a man can be always in the wrong and always appear to
be in the right, and in the end become with the clearest conscience in the
world the most unendurable tyrant and bore; and what applies to the individual can also apply to entire classes of society.

341

Too little honoured. – Very conceited people who have received less consideration than they expected to receive try hard to mislead themselves and others on the matter and become ingenious psychologists in their efforts to make out that they have in fact been sufficiently honoured: if they fail to obtain their objective, if the veil of deception is rent, they abandon themselves to all the greater ill-humour.

342

Echoes of primal conditions in speech. – In the way in which men now advance assertions in society one often recognizes an echo of the ages when they knew how to handle weapons better than they knew anything else: they wield their assertions like marksmen taking aim, or we seem to hear the ringing and whistling of blades; and with some men an assertion comes battering down like a club. – Women, on the other hand, speak like creatures who have for millennia sat at the loom, or plied the needle, or been childish with children.

343

The narrator. – He who narrates something soon reveals whether he is doing so because the subject interests him or whether by doing so he hopes to arouse interest. In the latter case he will exaggerate, employ superlatives and the like. He will then usually narrate badly, because he is thinking not so much of the subject as of himself.

344

The reciter. – He who recites dramatic poems in public makes discoveries about his character: he finds that his voice is more naturally suited to certain moods and scenes, for example to pathos or scurrility, while perhaps in everyday life he had simply had no opportunity of exhibiting pathos or scurrility.

345

A scene of comedy that happens in real life. – Someone devises a witty opinion on a subject in order to utter it in social company. Now, in a comedy we would listen to him and see how he would try to sail full ahead and to transport the company to the point at which he can make his remark: how he continually nudges the conversation towards *one* goal, occasionally loses his direction, recovers it, at last attains the vital moment: his breath almost fails him – and then someone else in the company takes the remark out of his mouth. What will he do? Oppose his own opinion?

346

Involuntarily impolite. – If someone involuntarily treats another impolitely, for example fails to greet him because he does not recognize him, he is vexed by the fact, even though he is unable to reproach himself for it; he grieves at the ill-opinion of him he has aroused in the other, or he fears the consequences of any discord that may follow, or it pains him to have offended the other – vanity, fear or pity can be set in motion, that is to say, and perhaps all of them together.

347
Betrayer's masterpiece. – To express to a fellow conspirator the grievous suspicion that one is going to be betrayed by him, and to do so at precisely the moment one is oneself engaged in betrayal, is a masterpiece of malice, because it keeps the other occupied with himself and compels him for a time to behave very openly and unsuspiciously, thus giving the actual betrayer full freedom of action.

348
To offend and to be offended. – It is much more pleasant to offend and later ask forgiveness than to be offended and forgive. He who does the former gives a token of power and afterwards of quality of character. The latter, if he does not wish to be thought inhumane, *has* to forgive; pleasure in the humbling of the other is, on account of this constraint, slight.

349
In a disputation. – When one contradicts another opinion and at the same time develops one's own, continual consideration of that other opinion usually disturbs the natural posture of one's own: it appears more deliberate, more rigorous, perhaps a little exaggerated.

350
Artifice. – He who wants to demand something hard of another must not conceive the matter as any kind of problem but simply present his plan as though it were the only possibility; if objection or contradiction begin to dawn in the eye of his opponent, he must know how to break off quickly and allow him no time to develop them.

351
Pangs of conscience after social gatherings. – Why after the usual sort of social gatherings do we suffer from pangs of conscience? Because we have taken important things lightly, because in discussing people we have spoken without complete loyalty or because we have kept silent when we should have spoken, because occasionally we have not leaped up and run off, in short because we have behaved in society as though we belonged to it.

352
One is judged falsely. – Whoever listens to how he is being judged is always vexed. For even those who stand closest to us ('know us best') judge us falsely. Even good friends sometimes give vent to their ill-feeling in an ill-judged word; and would they be our friends if they knew us well? – The judgements of those who are indifferent to us are very painful, because they sound so unprejudiced and almost objective. But if we notice that someone who is hostile to us knows us on some point we have kept secret as well as we know it ourselves, how great is our chagrin then!

353
Tyranny of the portrait. – Artists and statesmen who speedily put together a complete picture of a man or an event out of a few individual traits are usually unjust inasmuch as they afterwards demand that the event or the man must actually be as they have painted it or him; they demand, in fact, that one shall be as talented, as cunning, as unjust as one is in their representation.

354
The relative as the best friend. – The Greeks, who knew so well what a friend is – of all peoples they alone often and repeatedly ventilated the subject of friendship, so that they were the first, and so far the last, to whom the friend has appeared a problem worth solving – these same Greeks designated *relatives* by an expression which is the superlative of the word 'friend'. I find this inexplicable.

355
Misunderstood honesty. – When in conversation someone quotes himself ('as I said then', 'as I usually say'), this gives an impression of presumptuousness, whereas it often arises from the opposite source, or at least from honesty, which does not wish to deck and embellish the moment with ideas that rightly belong to an earlier one.

356
The parasite. – It indicates a complete lack of nobility of disposition when someone prefers to live in dependency, at the expense of others, merely so as not to have to work and usually with a secret animosity towards those he is dependent on. – Such a disposition is much more frequent among women than among men, also much more excusable (for historical reasons).

357
On the altar of reconciliation. – There are circumstances under which one can obtain something from a man by offending and falling out with him: the feeling of having an enemy so torments him that he employs the first sign of a softening of hostility to effect a reconciliation and sacrifices on the altar of this reconciliation that thing on which he at first set such store he refused to relinquish it at any price.

358
Demanding pity as a sign of presumption. – There are people who, when they fly into a rage and offend others, demand firstly that it should not be held against them, and secondly that they should be pitied for being subject to such violent paroxysms. Such is the extent of human presumption.

359
Bait. – 'Everyone has his price' – this is not true. But there surely exists for everyone a bait he cannot help taking. Thus to win many people over to a cause one needs only to put on it a gloss of philanthropy, nobility,

charitableness, self-sacrifice – and on to what cause can one not put it?–: these are the sweetmeats and dainties for *their* soul; others have others.

360

Attitude towards praise. – When good friends praise a talented nature he will often exhibit pleasure at it, though he does so out of politeness and benevolence: in truth he is indifferent to it. His real being is quite languid in its presence and it cannot drag him a single step out of the sunshine or shadow in which he lies; but men want to give pleasure when they praise and one would grieve them if one did not rejoice at their praise.

361

The experience of Socrates. – If one has become a master in one thing one usually for that very reason remains a complete bungler in most other things; but one thinks precisely the opposite, a fact experienced already by Socrates. This is the drawback that makes association with masters unpleasant.

362

Means of brutalizing. – To fight against stupidity in the long run makes even the fairest and gentlest men brutal. Perhaps this means they are on the right path to their own self-defence, for the just argument against a stupid head is a clenched fist. But because, as aforesaid, they are gentle and fair of character, the suffering they inflict on others through this means of defence is less than the suffering they inflict on themselves.

363

Curiosity. – If there were no curiosity little would be done to further the wellbeing of one's neighbour. But curiosity creeps into the house of the unfortunate and needy under the name of duty or pity. – Perhaps even much lauded mother-love contains a goodly portion of curiosity.

364

Miscalculation in society. – This one wishes to arouse interest through his judgements, that through his inclinations and disinclinations, a third through his acquaintanceships, a fourth through his isolation – and they all miscalculate. For he before whom the spectacle is enacted himself believes he is the only spectacle that comes into consideration.

365

Duel. – In favour of all affairs of honour and duels it can be said that, if someone has so susceptible a sensibility that he cannot endure to live if this or that person says or thinks this or that about him, he has a right to make the matter an issue of life or death for one or the other. That he is in fact so susceptible must be considered outside the domain of dispute: it is part of our inheritance from the past, whose greatness could never have existed without its excesses. If, however, there has been created a code of honour which admits blood in place of death, so that the heart is lightened after a duel fought according to rules, this is a great blessing, since otherwise many human lives would be placed in danger. – Such an institution, moreover, educates men into being cautious about what they say and makes it possible to associate with them.

366
Nobility and gratitude. – A noble soul will be glad to feel obligated to gratitude and will not anxiously avoid those occasions on which such obligation arises; it will likewise also subsequently be composed in the expression of gratitude; whereas baser souls resist all becoming obligated or are afterwards excessive and all too sedulous in their expressions of gratitude. The latter is also to be found in people of baser origin or lowly position: a favour shown to *them* seems to them a miracle of grace.

367
Hours of eloquence. – In order to speak well, one man needs someone who is decidedly and recognizedly his superior, another can find full freedom of eloquence and happy turns of phrase only before someone he excels: the reason is the same in both cases; each of them speaks well only when he speaks *sans gêne*,* the one because before the more elevated person he feels no urge to contest and competition, the other likewise in face of the person more lowly. – Now, there exists a quite different species of men who speak well only when they speak in contest with the intention of winning. Which of these two species is the more ambitious: he who speaks well out of thirst for honour or he who, if he speaks with that motive in view, speaks badly or not at all?

368
The talent for friendship. – Among men who possess a particular gift for friendship two types predominate. One is in a state of continual ascent and for each phase of his development finds a friend precisely appropriate to it. The succession of friends he acquires in this way are seldom at one with one another and sometimes in dissonance and discord: which is quite in accord with the fact that the later phases of his development abolish or infringe upon the earlier. Such a man may be jocularly *called* a ladder. – The other type is represented by him who exercises an attraction on very various characters and talents, so that he gains a whole circle of friends; they, however, establish friendly relations between one another, their differences notwithstanding, on account of being his friend. One can call such a man a *circle*: for in him this solidarity between such different natures and dispositions must in some way be prefigured. – For the rest, the gift of having good friends is in many men much greater than the gift of being a good friend.

369
Tactics in conversation. – After a conversation with anyone one is best placed to speak of the partner in the conversation if one has had the opportunity of displaying one's wit and amiability before him in all their splendour. It is a tactic that has been employed by shrewd people who wanted to prejudice someone in their favour and did so by offering him

---

* *sans gêne*: without shame or inhibition

the opportunity for a good witticism and the like. A merry conversation could be imagined between two very shrewd people each of whom wanted to prejudice the other in his favour and to this end tossed the fairest opportunities back and forth while neither accepted them: so that the conversation would be on the whole unwitty and unamiable because each assigned the opportunity for wit and amiability to the other.

370

Discharge of ill-humour. – The man who experiences failure prefers to attribute this failure to the ill-will of another rather than to chance. His incensed feelings are relieved if he imagines a person, and not a thing, to be the cause of his failure; for one can revenge oneself on people, while the iniquities of chance must be swallowed down. That is why, when a prince experiences a failure, his attendance is accustomed to point out one sole man as the supposed cause and to sacrifice him in the interest of the whole court; for, since he can take no revenge on the goddess of destiny herself, the prince's displeasure would otherwise be visited on them all.

371

Receiving the colour of the environment. – Why are inclination and aversion so contagious that it is hard to live in the proximity of a person of strong feelings without being filled like a barrel with his For and Against? Firstly, it is very hard for us wholly to refrain from exercising judgement; sometimes, indeed, our vanity finds it altogether unendurable to do so; it here wears the same colours as poverty of thought and feeling or timidity and unmanliness: and thus we are at last impelled to take sides, perhaps against the tendency of our environment if this posture is more satisfying to our pride. Usually, however – this is the second point – our transition from indifference to inclination or aversion is in no way conscious; we gradually accustom ourself to the sensibility of our environment, and because sympathetic agreement and accommodation is so pleasant we soon bear all the marks and party colours of this environment.

372

Irony. – Irony is in place only as a pedagogic tool, employed by a teacher in dealing with any kind of pupil: its objective is humiliation, making ashamed, but of that salutary sort which awakens good resolutions and inspires respect and gratitude towards him who treats us thus of the kind we feel for a physician. The ironist poses as unknowing, and does so so well that the pupils in discussion with him are deceived, grow bold in their belief they know better and expose themselves in every way; they abandon circumspection and reveal themselves as they are – up to the moment when the lamp they have been holding up to the face of the teacher sends its beams very humiliatingly back on to them themselves. – Where such a relationship as that between teacher and pupil does not obtain, irony is ill-breeding, a vulgar affectation. All ironical writers depend on the foolish species of men who together with the author would like to feel themselves superior to all others and who regard the author as the mouthpiece of their presumption. – Habituation to irony, moreover, like habituation to sarcasm, spoils the character, to which it gradually lends the quality of a malicious and jeering superiority: in the end one comes to resemble a snapping dog which has learned how to laugh but forgotten how to bite.

373
Presumptuousness. – One should guard against nothing more than against the efflorescence of that weed which is called presumptuousness and which ruins in us every good harvest, for there is a presumptuousness in cordiality, in respectfulness, in benevolent familiarity, in endearment, in friendly advice, in the admission of error, in sympathy for others, and all these fair things excite aversion when that weed flourishes among them. The presumptuous person, that is to say the person who wants to signify more than he is *or counts for*, always makes a false calculation. He enjoys a momentary success, it is true, inasmuch as the people before whom he is presumptuous usually mete out to him the measure of respect he demands, out of fear or because it is the easiest thing to do; but they take a vile revenge for it, inasmuch as they subtract the excess measure he has demanded from the value they previously accorded him. There is nothing for which men demand higher payment than humiliation. The presumptuous person can make his actual merits, which may be great, seem so suspect and small in the eyes of others that they are trampled in the dust. – One should permit oneself even a proud demeanour only where one can be quite sure one will not be misunderstood and regarded as presumptuous, for example in the presence of friends and wives. For in traffic with men there is no greater folly than to acquire a reputation for presumptuousness; it is worse than having failed to learn how to tell polite lies.

374
Dialogue. – The dialogue is the perfect conversation, because everything one of the parties says acquires its particular colour, its sound, its accompanying gestures *strictly with reference to the other* to whom he is speaking, and thus resembles a correspondence in which the forms of expression vary according to whom the correspondent is writing to. In a dialogue there is only a single refraction of the thought: this is produced by the partner in the dialogue, as the mirror in which we desire to see our thoughts reflected as perfectly as possible. But what happens when there are two, three or more fellow participants? The conversation necessarily loses its subtle individuality, different intentions clash with and disrupt one another; a turn of phrase that appeals to one offends the disposition of another. That is why in converse with several people one will be compelled to draw back into oneself, to present the facts as they are but to deduct from the subjects of converse that opalescent ether of humanity that makes of a conversation one of the pleasantest things in the world. One has only to listen to the tone men tend to adopt when speaking to whole groups of men; it is as though the fundamental note of all speech

were: 'this is what *I* am, this is what *I* say, you can make of it what you will!' This is the reason intelligent women usually leave behind on him who has encountered them in society an alienating, painful, forbidding impression: it is speaking to many, before many, that robs her of all intellectual amiability and throws a harsh light only on her conscious concern with herself, her tactics and her objective of a public victory: whereas the same women become female again and rediscover their intellectual charm in a dialogue for two.

375
Posthumous fame. – To hope for the recognition of a distant future makes sense if one assumes that mankind will remain essentially unchanged and that all greatness is bound to be felt as great not only in a single age but in all ages. This, however, is an error; mankind undergoes great transformations in its feeling for and judgement of what is good and beautiful; it is fantasizing to believe of oneself that one is a mile further on in advance and that all mankind is going along *our* road. In addition: a scholar who fails to gain recognition may be quite sure that his discovery will also be made by others and that at the best some future historian will acknowledge that he already knew this or that but was not able to obtain general acquiescence in the matter. Failure to gain recognition will always be interpreted by posterity as lack of vigour. – In short, one should not be too ready to speak up for proud isolation. There are of course exceptions; but as a rule it is our faults, weaknesses and follies that hinder recognition of our great qualities.

376
Of friends. – Only reflect to yourself how various are the feelings, how divided the opinions, even among your closest acquaintances, how even the same opinions are of a quite different rank or intensity in the heads of your friends than they are in yours; how manifold are the occasions for misunderstanding, for hostility and rupture. After reflecting on all this you must tell yourself: how uncertain is the ground upon which all our alliances and friendships rest, how close at hand are icy downpours or stormy weather, how isolated each man is! When one realizes this, and realizes in addition that all the opinions of one's fellow men, of whatever kind they are and with whatever intensity they are held, are just as necessary and unaccountable as their actions; if one comes to understand this inner necessity of opinions originating in the inextricable interweaving of character, occupation, talent, environment – perhaps one will then get free of that bitterness of feeling with which the sage cried: 'Friends, there are no friends!' One will, rather, avow to oneself: yes, there are friends, but it is error and deception regarding yourself that led them to you; and they must have learned how to keep silent in order to remain your friend; for such human relationships almost always depend upon the fact that two or three things are never said or even so much as touched upon: if these little boulders do start to roll, however, friendship follows after them and shatters. Are there not people who would be mort-

ally wounded if they discovered what their dearest friends actually know about them? – Through knowing ourselves, and regarding our own nature as a moving sphere of moods and opinions, and thus learning to despise ourself a little, we restore our proper equilibrium with others. It is true we have good reason to think little of each of our acquaintances, even the greatest of them; but equally good reason to direct this feeling back on to ourself. – And so, since we can endure ourself, let us also endure other people; and perhaps to each of us there will come the more joyful hour when we exclaim:

> 'Friends, there are no friends!' thus said the dying sage;
> 'Foes, there are no foes!' say I, the living fool.

7
WOMAN
AND
CHILD

377
The perfect woman. – The perfect woman is a higher type of human being than the perfect man: also something much rarer. – The natural science of the animals offers a means of demonstrating the truth of this proposition.

378
Friendship and marriage. – The best friend will probably acquire the best wife, because a good marriage is founded on the talent for friendship.

379
Continuance of the parents. – The unresolved dissonances between the characters and dispositions of the parents continue to resound in the nature of the child and constitute the history of his inner sufferings.

380
From the mother. – Everyone bears within him a picture of woman derived from his mother: it is this which determines whether, in his dealings with women, he respects them or despises them or is in general indifferent to them.

381
Correcting nature. – If one does not have a good father one should furnish oneself with one.

382
Fathers and sons. – Fathers have much to do to make amends for having sons.

383
Error of noble women. – Noble women think that a thing does not exist if it is not possible to speak about it in company.

384
A male sickness. – For the male sickness of self-contempt the surest cure is to be loved by a clever woman.

385
A kind of jealousy. – Mothers are easily jealous of the friends of their sons when these enjoy particular success. Usually a mother loves *herself* in her son more than she does her actual son.

386
Rational irrationality. – In the maturity of his life and understanding a man is overcome by the feeling his father was wrong to beget him.

387
Motherly goodness. – Some mothers need happy, respected children, others unhappy ones: otherwise she has no chance to exhibit her goodness as a mother.

388
Diverse sighs. – Some men have sighed over the abduction of their wives, most however over the fact that no one wanted to abduct them.

389
Love-matches. – Marriages contracted from love (so-called love-matches) have error for their father and need for their mother.

390
Friendship with women. – Women are quite able to make friends with a man; but to preserve such a friendship – that no doubt requires the assistance of a slight physical antipathy.

391
Boredom. – Many people, especially women, never feel boredom because they have never learned to work properly.

392
An element of love. – In every kind of womanly love there also appears something of motherly love.

393
Unity of place and action. – If married couples did not live together good marriages would be more common.

394
Usual consequences of marriage. – All society that does not elevate one draws one down, and conversely; that is why men usually sink a little when they take wives, while their wives are elevated a little. Men who are too intellectual have great need of marriage, though they resist it as they would a foul-tasting medicine.

395
Teaching to command. – Children of modest families need to be taught how to command as other children need to be taught obedience.

396
The desire to become loved. – Engaged people who have been brought together by convenience often strive to *become* loved, so as to do away with the reproach of acting out of cold, calculating utility. Those who have adopted Christianity for the sake of advantage likewise strive to become genuinely devout; it makes the religious pantomime easier for them.

397
No standstill in love. – A musician who *loves* slow tempo will take a piece of

music more and more slowly. In the same way there is no standstill in any kind of love.

398

Modesty. – Generally speaking, the more beautiful a woman is the more modest she is.

399

Marriage with stability. – A marriage in which each of the parties seeks to achieve an individual goal through the other will stand up well; for example when the wife seeks to become famous through the husband, the husband liked through the wife.

400

Proteus nature. – Women in love come to be just as they are in the image that the men by whom they are loved have of them.

401

Love and possession. – Women mostly love a man of consequence as though they want to have him for themselves alone. They would gladly keep him under lock and key if their vanity did not dissuade them: for this desires him to appear of consequence before others as well.

402

Test of a good marriage. – A marriage proves itself a good marriage by being able to endure an occasional 'exception'.

403

Means of getting anyone to do anything. – Anyone can be so fatigued and weakened by agitation, fears, overloading with work and thinking that he will no longer resist anything that appears complicated but yield to it – a fact known to diplomats and to women.

404

Respectability and honesty. – Every girl who thinks to employ her youthful charms alone to provide for her entire life, and whose cunning is in addition prompted by a wise mother, has precisely the same objective as a courtesan, only she pursues it more shrewdly and less honestly.

405

Masks. – There are women who, however you may search them, prove to have no content but are purely masks. The man who associates with such almost spectral, necessarily unsatisfied beings is to be commiserated with, yet it is precisely they who are able to arouse the desire of the man most strongly: he seeks for her soul – and goes on seeking.

406

Marriage as a long conversation. – When entering into a marriage one ought to ask oneself: do you believe you are going to enjoy talking with this woman up into your old age? Everything else in marriage is transitory, but most of the time you are together will be devoted to conversation.

407

Girlish dreams. – Inexperienced girls flatter themselves with the idea that it stands within their power to make a man happy; later on they learn that to assume that all that is required to make a man happy is a girl is really to despise him. – The vanity of women demands that a man should be more than a happy husband.

408

Faust and Gretchen dying out. – As a very discerning scholar has remarked, the educated men of present-day Germany resemble a cross between Mephistopheles and Wagner, but certainly do not resemble Fausts, whom their grandfathers (in their youth at least) felt rumbling within them.* For two reasons, therefore – to continue this proposition – *Gretchens* are no longer suited to them. And because they are no longer desired they are, it seems, dying out.

409

Girls as grammar-school pupils. – For heaven's sake don't let us transmit our grammar-school education to girls! An education that so often takes spirited, knowledge-thirsty, passionate young people and makes of them – images of their teachers!

410

Without competitors. – Women can easily tell whether or not a man's soul has already been taken possession of; they want to be loved without competitors and resent the objects of his ambition, his political activities, his arts and sciences, if he has a passion for such things. Except, that is, if he shines on account of them – in that case they hope that a love-union with him will increase the amount *they* shine; if this is how things are, they encourage their lover.

411

The female intellect. – The intellect of women reveals itself as complete control and presence of mind and the utilization of every advantage. She bestows it on her children as her fundamental quality, and the father adds the darker background of the will. His influence determines as it were the rhythm and harmony with which the new life is to be played; but its melody comes from the woman. – Expressed for those who know how to interpret: women possess reason, men temperament and passion. This is not contradicted by the fact that men in fact make so much better use of their reason: they possess deeper, more powerful drives; it is these that carry their reason, which is in itself something passive, so far. Women often secretly wonder at the great respect men pay to the female temperament. If, in the choice of their marriage partner, men seek above all a deep nature full of feeling, while women seek a shrewd, lively minded and brilliant nature, it is clear that at bottom the man is seeking an idealized man, the woman an idealized woman – what they are seeking,

* Faust, Gretchen, Mephistopheles, Wagner: characters in Goethe's *Faust*

that is to say, is not a complement but a perfecting of their own best qualities.

412

*A judgement of Hesiod's confirmed.** – It is a sign of the shrewdness of women that almost everywhere they have known how to get themselves fed, like drones in the beehive. One should consider, however, what that fact means originally, and why men do not have themselves fed by women. It is certainly because male vanity and respect are greater than female shrewdness; for women have known how through subordination to secure for themselves the preponderant advantage, even indeed the dominion. Even the tending of children could originally have been employed by the shrewdness of women as a pretext for avoiding work as much as possible. And even now when they are genuinely occupied, for example as housekeepers, they know how to make such a mind-confusing to-do about it that men usually overestimate the value of their activity tenfold.

413

The shortsighted are in love. – Sometimes it requires only a stronger pair of spectacles to cure the lover, and he who had the imagination to picture a face, a figure twenty years older would perhaps pass through life very undisturbed.

414

Women in hate. – In a state of hatred women are more dangerous than men; first and foremost because, once their hostility has been aroused, they are hampered by no considerations of fairness but allow their hatred to grow undisturbed to its ultimate consequences; then because they are practised in discovering the wounded places everyone, every party possesses and striking at them: to which end their dagger-pointed intellect renders them excellent service (whereas at the sight of wounds men become restrained and often inclined to reconciliation and generosity).

415

Love. – The idolization of love practised by women is fundamentally and originally an invention of their shrewdness, inasmuch as it enhances their power and makes them seem ever more desirable in the eyes of men. But through centuries-long habituation to this exaggerated evaluation of love it has come to pass that they have become entangled in their own net and forgotten how it originated. They themselves are now more deceived than men are and consequently suffer more from the disillusionment that is almost certain to come into the life of every woman – insofar as she has sufficient intelligence and imagination to be deceived and disillusioned at all.

416

On the emancipation of women. – Are women able to be just at all, since they

* Hesiod: Greek epic poet of the eighth century BC

are so accustomed to loving, to at once taking sides for or against? That too is why they are less interested in causes, more interested in persons: if they are interested in a cause, however, they at once become its vehement advocates and thereby spoil the purity of its influence. There is thus no little danger in entrusting politics or certain kinds of science (for example history) to them. For what could be rarer than a woman who really knew what science is? The best of them even harbour in their bosom a secret contempt for it, as though they were in some way superior to it. Perhaps all this may change, but for the present that is how things are.

417

Inspiration in female judgement. – Those sudden decisions for or against that women are accustomed to take, the lightning-quick illumination of personal relationships through the inclinations and aversions that break forth from them, in short the demonstrations of female injustice, have been invested with a lustre by enamoured men, as though all women had inspirations of wisdom even without the Delphic cauldron and the band of laurel: and their declarations are interpreted and explained for long afterwards as though they were sibylline oracles. If you reflect, however, that there is something to be said for every person and every cause but also something to be said against them, that all things have not only two sides but three or four, it becomes almost impossible for such sudden decisions to be completely erroneous; one could even go so far as to say that the nature of things is so constructed that women are always in the right.

418

Letting oneself be loved. – Because one party in a loving couple is usually the one who loves and the other the one who is loved, the belief has arisen that in every love affair there exists a fixed quantity of love: the more one party seizes for himself the less is left for the other. In exceptional cases it happens that the vanity of each of the parties persuades him that *he* is the one who must be loved; so that both want to let themselves be loved: a state of things which, especially in marriage, produces many a half-comic, half-absurd situation.

419

Contradictions in female heads. – Because women are so much more personal than objective, tendencies that logically contradict one another are capable of getting on together within their circle of ideas: for they are accustomed to become enthusiastic for the representatives of these tendencies one after the other and to adopt their systems wholesale; but they do so in such a way that there is always an unemployed spot where a new personality later gains ascendancy. It does perhaps happen that all the philosophy in the head of an elderly woman consists of nothing but such unemployed spots.

420

Who suffers more? – After a quarrel between a man and a woman, one suffers most at the idea of having hurt the other, while the other suffers most at the idea of not having hurt the other enough, from which follow the tears, sobs and distracted mien through which the heart of the other is to be made heavy even after the quarrel is over.

421

Opportunity for female generosity. – If one sets aside the demands of custom for a moment, one might very well consider whether nature and reason do not dictate that a man ought to have two marriages, perhaps in the following form. At first, at the age of twenty-two, he would marry a girl older than him who is intellectually and morally his superior and who can lead him through the perils of the twenties (ambition, hatred, self-contempt, passions of all kinds). Later, her love would pass over wholly into the motherly, and she would not merely endure it but actively encourage it if, in his thirties, the man should enter into an alliance with a young girl whose education he would himself take in hand. – For the twenties marriage is a necessary institution, for the thirties a useful but not a necessary one: in later life it is often harmful and promotes the spiritual retrogression of the man.

422

Tragedy of childhood. – It is perhaps no rare occurrence that noble-minded and aspiring people have to undergo their severest trials in their childhood: perhaps through having to assert themselves against a low-minded father absorbed in appearance and deception, or, like Lord Byron, to live in continual conflict with a childish and irritable mother. If one has experienced such a thing one will, one's whole life long, never get over the knowledge of who one's greatest and most dangerous foe has actually been.

423

Parental folly. – When it comes to assessing the quality of a person, the greatest errors are made by his parents: this is a fact, but how shall one explain it? Do the parents have too much experience of the child and are they no longer capable of bringing all these experiences together into a unity? It has been remarked that travellers among strange peoples correctly grasp the general distinguishing features of a people only during the earliest period of their sojourn with them; the better they get to know them, the less capable they are of seeing what is typical and distinguishing in them. As soon as they become near-sighted, their eyes cease to be far-sighted. Do the parents judge the child mistakenly because they have never stood far enough away from him? – A quite different explanation would be the following: men are accustomed to cease to reflect on those things which surround them most closely and simply to accept them. Perhaps the habitual thoughtlessness of parents is the reason why, when they are for once compelled to judge their children, they judge them so badly.

424

From the future of marriage. – Those noble, free-thinking women who set themselves the task of the education and elevation of the female sex ought not to overlook *one* consideration: the higher conception of marriage as the soul-friendship of two people of differing sex – a conception it is hoped the future will realize – contracted for the purpose of begetting and educating a new generation: such a marriage, which employs the sensual as it were only as a rare, occasional means to a greater end, will, it is to be anticipated, probably require a natural assistant, namely *concubinage*. For if, for reasons of the health of the husband, the wife alone is to serve to satisfy his sexual needs, then in the choice of a wife the decisive consideration will be one hostile to the objectives of the marriage just indicated: the nature of its offspring will be left to chance and the likelihood of their being properly educated remote. A good wife who is supposed to be a friend, assistant, mother, family head and housekeeper, and may indeed have to run her own business or job quite apart from that of her husband – such a wife cannot at the same time be a concubine: it would be too much to demand of her. Thus in the future a state of affairs might arise which would be the opposite of that which obtained in Pericles' Athens: the men, to whom in those days wives were little more than concubines, turned in addition to the Aspasias,* because they desired that head- and heart-satisfying companionship such as only the charm and intellectual flexibility of women can create. All human institutions such as marriage permit only a moderate degree of practical idealization, failing which crude remedies have at once to be effected.

425

Storm-and-stress period of women. – In the three or four civilized countries of Europe women can through a few centuries of education be made into anything, even into men: not in the sexual sense, to be sure, but in every other sense. Under such a regimen they will one day have acquired all the male strengths and virtues, though they will also of course have had to accept all their weaknesses and vices into the bargain: thus much can, as aforesaid, be extorted. But how shall we endure the intermediate stage, which may itself last a couple of centuries, during which the primeval properties of women, their follies and injustices, are still asserting themselves over what has been newly learned and acquired? This will be the age in which the actual masculine affect will be anger: anger at the fact that all the arts and sciences have been choked and deluged by an unheard-of dilettantism, philosophy talked to death by mind-bewildering babble, politics more fantastic and partisan than ever, society in full dissolution, because the custodians of ancient morality and custom have become ludicrous to themselves and are striving to stand outside morality and custom in every respect. For if women possessed their greatest power *in* morality and custom, for what will they have to grasp to regain a comparable abundance of power once they have abandoned morality and custom?

* Aspasia: an Athenian courtesan, the mistress of Pericles

426

Marriage and the free spirit. – Will free spirits live with women? In general I believe that, like the prophetic birds of antiquity, as present-day representatives of true thinking and truth-telling they must prefer *to fly alone.*

427

A happy marriage. – Everything habitual draws around us an ever firmer net of spider-webs; and soon we notice that the threads have become cords and that we ourself are sitting in the middle as the spider who has caught himself and has to live on his own blood. That is why the free spirit hates all habituation and rules, everything enduring and definitive, that is why he sorrowfully again and again rends apart the net that surrounds him: even though he will as a consequence suffer numerous great and small wounds – for he has to rend those threads *from himself,* from his own body and soul. He has to learn to love where he formerly hated, and the reverse. Nothing, indeed, may be impossible to him, he must sow dragon's teeth in the same field upon which he formerly poured out the cornucopias of his benevolence. – From all this it may be inferred whether he is created for a happy marriage.

428

Too close. – If we live together with another person too closely, what happens is similar to when we repeatedly handle a good engraving with our bare hands: one day all we have left is a piece of dirty paper. The soul of a human being too can finally become tattered by being handled continually; and that is how it finally *appears* to us – we never see the beauty of its original design again. – One always loses by too familiar association with friends and women; and sometimes what one loses is the pearl of one's life.

429

The golden cradle. – The free spirit will always breathe a sigh of relief when he has finally resolved to shake off that motherly watching and warding with which women govern him. For what harm is there in the raw air that has so anxiously been kept from him, what does one real disadvantage, loss, mischance, sickness, debt, befooling more or less in life mean, compared with the unfreedom of the golden cradle, peacock-tail fan and the oppressive feeling that he must in addition be grateful because he is waited on and spoiled like an infant? That is why the milk offered him by the women who surround him can so easily turn to gall.

430

Voluntary sacrifice. – Women of consequence alleviate the life of their men, when they happen to be great and famous, by nothing so much as by becoming as it were the receptacle of the general disfavour and occasional ill-humour of the rest of mankind. Contemporaries tend to forgive their great men many blunders and follies, indeed many crude acts of injustice, if only they can find someone whom, to relieve their feelings, they may mishandle and slaughter as a sacrificial beast. It is no rare thing for a woman to discover in herself the ambition to offer herself to this sacrifice, and then the man can feel very contented – assuming, that is, that he is enough of an egoist to endure the proximity of such a voluntary lightning-, storm- and rain-conductor.

431
Pleasing adversary. – The natural tendency of women towards a quiet, calm, happily harmonious existence, the way they pour soothing oil on the sea of life, unwittingly works against the heroic impulse in the heart of the free spirit. Without realizing it, women behave as one would do who removed the stones from the path of a wandering mineralogist so that his foot should not strike against them – whereas he has gone forth so that his foot *shall* strike against them.

432
Disharmony of concords. – Women want to serve and in that they discover their happiness: and the free spirit wants not to be served and in that he discovers his happiness.

433
Xantippe. – Socrates found the kind of wife he needed – but even he would not have sought her if he had known her well enough: the heroism of even this free spirit would not have extended to that. For Xantippe in fact propelled him deeper and deeper into his own proper profession, inasmuch as she made his house and home uncomfortable and unhomely to him: she taught him to live in the street and everywhere where one could chatter and be idle, and thus fashioned him into the greatest Athenian street-dialectician: so that in the end he had to compare himself to an importunate gadfly which a god had placed on the neck of the beautiful steed Athens that it might never be allowed any rest.

434
Near-sighted. – Just as mothers can really see and feel only the visible and palpable troubles of their children, so the wives of aspiring men cannot bring themselves to see their husbands suffering, in want or despised – while all this is perhaps not merely a sign they have chosen their life's course truly but actually a guarantee that their great goals *must* at some time or other be attained. Wives always secretly intrigue against the higher being of their husbands; they desire to deprive them of their future for the sake of a quiet, comfortable present.

435
Power and freedom. – However much women may honour their husbands, they nonetheless honour the recognized authorities and conceptions of society even more: for millennia they have been accustomed to stand before everything dominant with head bowed and arms folded across the chest, and they disapprove of all rebellion against the established power. For this reason they attach themselves – without even intending to do so

but rather as though by instinct – to the wheels of a free-spirited, independent endeavour as a brake on them, and sometimes try the patience of their husbands beyond all measure, especially when the latter persuade themselves that what at bottom drives women to this behaviour is love. To disapprove of the methods of women and magnanimously to honour the motivation behind these methods – that is the way of men and often enough their despair.

436

*Ceterum censeo.** – It is laughable when a society of the penniless decrees the abolition of the right of inheritance, and it is no less laughable when the childless participate in a country's practical lawgiving: – for they have insufficient ballast in their ship to be able safely to set sail into the ocean of the future. But it appears equally absurd when he who has chosen for his task the most universal knowledge and the evaluation of the totality of existence burdens himself with personal considerations of family, nutrition, security, care of wife and child, and extends before his telescope that dark veil through which scarcely a ray from the distant firmament is able to penetrate. Thus I too arrive at the proposition that in affairs of the highest philosophical kind all married men are suspect.

437

Finally. – There are many kinds of hemlock, and fate usually finds an opportunity of setting a cup of this poison draught to the lips of the free spirit – so as to 'punish' him, as all the world then says. What will the women around him then do? They will lament and cry out and perhaps disturb the repose of the thinker's sunset hours: as they did in the prison at Athens. 'O Criton, do tell someone to take those women away!', Socrates finally said.

* *Ceterum censeo:* It is my opinion, moreover

8

A GLANCE AT
THE STATE

438

Permission to speak! – The demagogic character and the intention to appeal
to the masses is at present common to all political parties: on account of
this intention they are all compelled to transform their principles into
great *al fresco* stupidities and thus to paint them on the wall. This is no
longer alterable, indeed it would be pointless to raise so much as a finger
against it; for in this domain there apply the words of Voltaire: *quand la
populace se mêle de raisonner, tout est perdu.** Since this has happened one
has to accommodate oneself to the new conditions as one accommodates
oneself when an earthquake has displaced the former boundaries and
contours of the ground and altered the value of one's property. Moreover, if the purpose of all politics really is to make life endurable for as
many as possible, then these as-many-as-possible are entitled to determine what they understand by an endurable life; if they trust to their
intellect also to discover the right means of attaining this goal, what good
is there in doubting it? They *want* for once to forge for themselves their
own fortunes and misfortunes; and if this feeling of self-determination,
pride in the five or six ideas their head contains and brings forth, in fact
renders their life so pleasant to them they are happy to bear the calamitous consequences of their narrow-mindedness, there is little to be objec-
ted to, always presupposing that this narrow-mindedness does not go so
far as to demand that *everything* should become politics in this sense, that
everyone should live and work according to such a standard. For a few
must first of all be allowed, now more than ever, to refrain from politics
and to step a little aside: they too are prompted to this by pleasure in self-
determination; and there may also be a degree of pride attached to staying silent when too many, or even just many, are speaking. Then these
few must be forgiven if they fail to take the happiness of the many,
whether by the many one understands nations or social classes, so very
seriously and are now and then guilty of an ironic posture; for their
seriousness is located elsewhere, their happiness is something quite different, their goal is not to be encompassed by any clumsy hand that has
only five fingers. Finally, from time to time there comes to them – what it
will certainly be hardest to concede to them but must be conceded to
them nonetheless – a moment when they emerge from their silent solitude and again try the power of their lungs: for then they call to one
another like those gone astray in a wood in order to locate and encourage
one another; whereby much becomes audible, to be sure, that sounds ill

* *quand . . . perdu:* when the mob joins in and adds its voice, all is lost.

to ears for which it is not intended. – Soon afterwards, though, it is again still in the wood, so still that the buzzing, humming and fluttering of the countless insects that live in, above and beneath it can again clearly be heard.

439

Culture and caste. – A higher culture can come into existence only where there are two different castes in society: that of the workers and that of the idle, of those capable of true leisure; or, expressed more vigorously: the caste compelled to work and the caste that works if it wants to. Differences in good fortune and happiness are not the essential element when it comes to the production of a higher culture; in any event, however, the caste of the idle is the more capable of suffering and suffers more, its enjoyment of existence is less, its task heavier. If an exchange between these two castes should take place, moreover, so that more obtuse, less spiritual families and individuals are demoted from the higher to the lower caste and the more liberated in the latter obtain entry into the higher, then a state is attained beyond which there can be seen only the open sea of indeterminate desires. – Thus speaks to us the fading voice of ages past; but where are there still ears to hear it?

440

Of the nobility. – That in which men and women of the nobility excel others and which gives them an undoubted right to be rated higher consists in two arts ever more enhanced through inheritance: the art of commanding and the art of proud obedience. – Now wherever commanding is part of the business of the day (as in the great mercantile and industrial world) there arises something similar to those families 'of the nobility', but they lack nobility in obedience, which is in the former an inheritance from the feudal ages and will no longer grow in our present cultural climate.

441

Subordination. – Subordination, which is so highly rated in the military and bureaucratic state, will soon become as unbelievable to us as the closed tactics of the Jesuits already are; and when this subordination is no longer possible a host of the most astonishing operations will no longer be capable of achievement and the world will be the poorer. It is bound to disappear because its foundation is disappearing: belief in unconditional authority, in definitive truth; even in military states it cannot be generated even by physical compulsion, for its origin is the inherited adoration of the princely as of something suprahuman. – In *freer* circumstances people subordinate themselves only under conditions, as the result of a mutual compact, thus without prejudice to their own interests.

442

Conscript armies. – The greatest disadvantage of the conscript armies so much extolled nowadays is the squandering of men of the highest civilization they involve; it is only by the grace of circumstances that they exist at all – how thrifty and cautious we ought therefore to be with them, since it requires a great space of time to create the chance conditions for the production of such delicately organized brains! But as the Greeks once waded in Greek blood, so Europeans now do in European blood: and it is always the most highly cultivated, those who guarantee a good and abundant posterity, who are sacrificed in relatively the largest numbers: for they stand in the van of the battle as the commanders and on account of their superior ambition expose themselves most to danger. – Now, when quite different and higher missions than *patria* and *honor* demand to be done, crude Roman patriotism is either something dishonest or a sign of retardedness.

443
Hope and presumption. – Our social order will slowly melt away, as all previous orders have done, as soon as the suns of novel opinions shine out over mankind with a new heat. One can *desire* this melting away only if one harbours hope: and one may reasonably harbour hope only if one credits oneself and one's kind with more power in head and heart than is possessed by the representatives of what at present exists. Usually, therefore, this hope will be a piece of *presumption* and an *overvaluation*.

444
War. – Against war it can be said: it makes the victor stupid, the defeated malicious. In favour of war: through producing these two effects it barbarizes and therefore makes more natural; it is the winter or hibernation time of culture, mankind emerges from it stronger for good and evil.

445
In the service of the prince. – To be able to act with complete ruthlessness, a statesman will do best to perform his work not on his own behalf but on behalf of a prince. The glitter of this general disinterestedness will dazzle the eye of the beholder, so that he will fail to see the knavery and harshness involved in the work of the statesman.

446
A question of power, not of justice. – To men who with regard to every cause keep in view its higher utility, socialism, assuming it is *really* the rebellion of those who have been oppressed and held down for millennia against their oppressors, represents not a problem of *justice* (with its ludicrous, feeble question: 'how far *ought* one to give in to its demands?') but only a problem of *power* ('how far *can* one exploit its demands?'); the situation is the same as in the case of a force of nature, for example steam, which is either pressed into service by man as god of the machine or, if the machine is faulty, if that is to say human calculation in its construction is faulty, blows the machine and man with it to pieces. To solve this question of power one has to know how strong socialism is, with what modification it can still be employed as a mighty lever within the existing play of political forces; under certain circumstances one would even have to do all one could to strengthen it. Whenever a great force exists – even

though it be the most dangerous – mankind has to consider how to make of it an instrument for the attainment of its objectives. – Socialism will acquire rights only if war appears to be imminent between the two powers, the representatives of the old and the new, but prudent calculation of possible advantage and preservation gives rise to the desire on the part of both parties for a compact. Without a compact no rights. Up to now, however, there has in the said domain been neither war nor compacts, and thus no rights, no 'ought', either.

447
Making use of petty dishonesty. – The power of the press resides in the fact that the individual who works for it feels very little sense of duty or obligation. Usually he expresses *his* opinion, but sometimes, in the service of his party or the policy of his country or in the service of himself, he does *not* express it. Such little lapses into dishonesty, or perhaps merely a dishonest reticence, are not hard for the individual to bear, but their consequences are extraordinary because these little lapses on the part of many are perpetrated simultaneously. Each of them says to himself: 'In exchange for such slight services I shall have a better time of it; if I refuse such little acts of discretion I shall make myself impossible'. Because it seems almost a matter of indifference morally whether one writes one more line or fails to write it, perhaps moreover without one's name being attached to it, anyone possessing money and influence can transform any opinion into public opinion. He who knows that most people are weak in small matters and desires to attain to his goal by means of them is thus always a dangerous man.

448
Complaining too loudly. – When abuses (for example defects in an administration, corruption and arbitrary favouritism in political or learned bodies) are painted in greatly exaggerated colours, the representation may fail in its effect among the knowledgeable but will produce all the stronger an effect upon the unknowledgeable (who would have remained indifferent to a cautious, sober representation). Since these are markedly in the majority, however, and harbour within them stronger willpower and a more impetuous desire for action, that exaggeration will lead to investigations, punishments, undertakings, reorganizations. – To this extent it is useful to paint abuses in exaggerated colours.

449
The apparent weather-makers of politics. – Just as the people secretly assume that he who understands the weather and can forecast it a day ahead actually makes the weather, so, with a display of superstitious faith, even the learned and cultivated attribute to great statesmen all the important changes and turns of events that take place during their term of office as being their own work, provided it is apparent that they knew something about them before others did and calculated accordingly: thus they too

are taken for weather-makers – and this faith is not the least effective instrument of their power.

450

New and old conception of government. – To distinguish between government and people as though there were here two distinct spheres of power, a stronger and higher and a weaker and lower, which treated and came to an understanding with one another, is a piece of inherited political sensibility which even now corresponds exactly to the historical settlement of the power situation in *most* states. When, for example, Bismarck describes the constitutional form as a compromise between government and people, he speaks in accordance with a principle whose rationality lies in history (and for just that reason, to be sure, also an admixture of irrationality, without which nothing human can exist). On the other hand, one is now supposed to learn – in accordance with a principle that has emerged purely from the *head* and is supposed to *make* history – that government is nothing but an organ of the people and not a provident, venerable 'above' in relation to a diffident 'below'. Before one accepts this hitherto unhistorical and arbitrary, if nonetheless more logical assertion of the concept government, one might be advised to consider the consequences: for the relationship between people and government is the most pervasive ideal relationship upon which commerce between teacher and pupil, lord and servants, father and family, general and soldier, master and apprentice have unconsciously been modelled. All these relationships are now, under the influence of the dominant constitutional form of government, altering their shape a little: they are *becoming* compromises. But how greatly they will change and be displaced, exchange their name and nature, when that latest concept has conquered minds everywhere! – for which, however, it may well take another century. In this matter nothing is *more* desirable than caution and slow evolution.

451

Justice as party call-notes. – Noble (if not particularly judicious) representatives of the ruling class can by all means vow: let us treat men as equals, concede to them equal rights. To this extent a socialist mode of thought resting on *justice* is possible; but, as aforesaid, only within the ruling class, which in this case *practises* justice with sacrifices and self-denials. To *demand* equality of rights, on the other hand, as the socialists of the subject caste do, is never an emanation of justice but of greed. – If one holds up bleeding chunks of meat to an animal and takes them away again until it finally roars: do you think this roaring has anything to do with justice?

452

Property and justice. – When the socialists show that the division of property among present-day mankind is the outcome of countless acts of injustice and violence, and *in summa* repudiate any obligation towards something having so unjust a foundation, they are seeing only one aspect of the matter. The entire past of the old culture was erected upon force, slavery, deception, error; but we, the heirs and inheritors of all these past things, cannot decree our own abolition and may not wish away a single part of them. The disposition to injustice inhabits the souls of the non-possessers too, they are no better than the possessers and have no moral prerogative over them, for their own ancestors were at some time or other possessers. What is needed is not a forcible redistribution but a gradual transformation of mind: the sense of justice must grow greater in everyone, the instinct for violence weaker.

453

The steersman of the passions. – The statesman excites public passions so as to profit from the counter-passions thereby aroused. To take an example: any German statesman knows well that the Catholic Church will never form an alliance with Russia, but would indeed rather form one even with the Turks; he likewise knows that an alliance between France and Russia would spell nothing but danger for Germany. If, therefore, he is able to make of France the hearth and home of the Catholic Church he will have abolished this danger for a long time to come. Consequently he has an interest in exhibiting hatred towards the Catholics and, through hostile acts of all kinds, transforming those who acknowledge the authority of the Pope into a passionate political power which, hostile to German policy, will naturally ally itself with France as the opponent of Germany: his goal is just as necessarily the Catholicization of France as Mirabeau's* was its decatholicization. – One state thus desires the darkening of millions of minds of another state so as to derive advantage from this darkening. It is the same disposition as that which favours the republican form of government of the neighbouring state – *le désordre organisé*, as Mérimée calls it – for the sole reason that it assumes this form of government will make the people feebler, more divided and less capable of war.

454

Those who are dangerous among the revolutionary spirits. – Those who are deliberating the revolutionary overthrow of society should be divided into those who want to achieve something for themselves and those who want to achieve something for their children and grandchildren. The latter are the more dangerous; for they believe they are disinterested and possess the good conscience that goes with that belief. The others can be bought off: the ruling orders are still rich and prudent enough for that. The danger begins as soon as the goals become impersonal; the revolutionary from impersonal interests can regard the defenders of the existing system as personally interested and thus feel superior to them.

455

Political value of fatherhood. – If a man has no sons he lacks full right to a voice in discussion of public affairs. One has to have staked, with the others, that which one loves best: that alone ties one firmly to the state; to

---

* Honoré Gabriel de Riqueti, Conte de Mirabeau (1749–91): French statesman

possess a just and natural interest in the fate of institutions one has to have in view the happiness of one's posterity, and thus of course to possess posterity. The evolution of a higher morality in a person depends upon his having sons; the fact makes him unegoistic, or, more correctly, it broadens his egoism in respect of duration and enables him seriously to pursue objectives that transcend his individual lifespan.

456
Pride of ancestry. – One has a right to be proud of a line of *good* ancestors up to one's father – but not of a line as such, for everyone has this. Origin in good ancestors constitutes nobility of birth; a single break in that chain, that is to say *one* bad forefather, annuls nobility of birth. One ought to ask of anyone who boasts of his noblity: have you no violent, covetous, dissolute, wicked, cruel men among your forefathers? If he is able to answer No to that question knowledgeably and with a clear conscience one should sue for his friendship.

457
Slaves and workers. – That we place more value on satisfaction of vanity than on any other form of well-being (security, accommodation, pleasure of all kinds) is demonstrated to a ludicrous degree in the fact that, quite apart from any political reasons, everyone desires the abolition of slavery and abominates the idea of reducing people to this condition: whereas everyone must at the same time realize that slaves live in every respect more happily and in greater security than the modern worker, and that the work done by slaves is very little work compared with that done by the 'worker'. One protests in the name of 'human dignity': but that, expressed more simply, is that precious vanity which feels being unequal, being publicly rated lower, as the hardest lot. – The Cynic thinks differently, because he despises honour: – and thus Diogenes was for a time a slave and private tutor.

458
Leading spirits and their instruments. – We see great statesmen, and in general all those who need to employ many people in the execution of their designs, acting in one of two ways: either they select those who are suited to their designs with great care and subtlety and then leave them relatively great freedom of movement because they know that the nature of these select people will take them where they themselves want them to be; or they select at random, taking indeed what happens to lie at hand, but shape out of this clay something that will serve their purpose. This latter kind is the more violent and desires more easily subjugated instruments; his knowledge of people is much less, his contempt for them greater than in the case of the first-named spirits, but the machine he constructs commonly works better than does the machine from the former's workshop.

459
Arbitrary law necessary. – Jurists dispute as to whether the law that

triumphs in a nation ought to be that which has been most thoroughly thought out or that which is easiest to understand. The former, the supreme model of which is the Roman, seems to the layman incomprehensible and consequently not an expression of his sense of law. Popular codes of law, for example the Germanic, have been crude, superstitious, illogical and in part stupid, but they corresponded to quite definite, inherited and indigenous custom and feelings. – Where, however, law is no longer tradition, as is the case with us, it can only be *commanded*, imposed by constraint; none of us any longer possesses a traditional sense of law, so we have to put up with *arbitrary law*, which is the expression of the necessity of the fact that there *has to be* law. The most logical is in this event the most acceptable, because it is the *most impartial*: even admitting that in every case the smallest unit of measurement in the relationship between crime and punishment is fixed arbitrarily.

460

The great man of the masses. – The recipe for that which the masses call a great man is easy to give. Under all circumstances one must procure for them something they find very pleasant, or first put it into their heads that this or that would be very pleasant and then give it to them. But at no price do it immediately: one has to gain it by the greatest exertion and struggle, or seem to do so. The masses must receive the impression that a mighty, indeed invincible force of will is present; at the least it must seem to be present. Everyone admires strength of will because no one has it and everyone tells himself that if he did have it he and his egoism would no longer know any limitations. If it now appears that such a strong will, instead of listening to the dictates of its own desires, performs something the masses find very pleasant, everyone marvels on two accounts and congratulates himself. For the rest, the great man possesses all the qualities of the masses: thus are they all the less embarrassed in his presence, thus is he all the more popular. He is violent, envious, exploitative, scheming, fawning, cringing, arrogant, all according to circumstances.

461

Prince and god. – Men traffic with their princes in much the same way as they do with their god, as indeed the prince has been to a great degree the representative of the god, or at least his high priest. This almost uncanny mood of reverence and fear and shame has grown and is growing much feebler, but occasionally it flares up and attaches itself to powerful persons in general. The cult of the genius is an echo of this reverence for gods and princes. Wherever there is a striving to exalt individual men into the suprahuman, there also appears the tendency to imagine whole classes of the people as being coarser and lower than they really are.

462

My utopia. – In a better ordering of society the heavy work and exigencies of life will be apportioned to him who suffers least as a consequence of them, that is to say to the most insensible, and thus step by step up to him who is most sensitive to the most highly sublimated species of suffering and who therefore suffers even when life is alleviated to the greatest degree possible.

463

A delusion in the theory of revolution. – There are political and social fantasists who with fiery eloquence invite a revolutionary overturning of all social orders in the belief that the proudest temple of fair humanity will then at once rise up as though of its own accord. In these perilous dreams there is still an echo of Rousseau's superstition, which believes in a miraculous primeval but as it were *buried* goodness of human nature and ascribes all the blame for this burying to the institutions of culture in the form of society, state and education. The experiences of history have taught us, unfortunately, that every such revolution brings about the resurrection of the most savage energies in the shape of the long-buried dreadfulness and excesses of the most distant ages: that a revolution can thus be a source of energy in a mankind grown feeble but never a regulator, architect, artist, perfector of human nature. – It is not *Voltaire*'s moderate nature, inclined as it was to ordering, purifying and reconstructing, but *Rousseau*'s passionate follies and half-lies that called forth the optimistic spirit of the Revolution against which I cry: '*Ecrasez l'infame!*' It is this spirit that has for a long time banished *the spirit of the Enlightenment and of progressive evolution*: let us see – each of us within himself – whether it is possible to call it back!

464

Moderation. – When thought and inquiry have become decisive – when, that is to say, free-spiritedness has become a quality of the character – action tends to moderation: for thought and inquiry weaken covetousness, draw much of the available energy to themselves for the promotion of spiritual objectives, and reveal the merely half-usefulness or the total uselessness and perilousness of all sudden changes.

465

Resurrection of the spirit. – A nation usually rejuvenates itself on the political sickbed and rediscovers its spirit, which it gradually lost in its seeking for and assertion of power. Culture owes this above all to the ages of political weakness.

466

New opinions in an old house. – The overturning of opinions does not immediately follow upon the overturning of institutions: the novel opinions continue, rather, to live on for a long time in the deserted and by now uncomfortable house of their predecessors, and even keep it in good condition because they have nowhere else to live.

467

Schooling. – In great cities the schooling will always be at the best mediocre, for the same reason that in great kitchens the cooking will be at best mediocre.

468

Innocent corruption. – In all institutions that are not open to the biting air of public criticism an innocent corruption flourishes like a fungus (as, for example, in learned bodies and senates).

469

Scholars as politicians. – Scholars who become politicians are usually allotted the comic role of being the good conscience of a party's policy.

470

The wolf behind the sheep. – Almost every politician has at some time or other such need of an honest man that he breaks into a sheepstall like a ravenous wolf: not, however, so as then to eat the ram he has stolen, but so as to hide himself behind its woolly back.

471

Ages of happiness. – An age of happiness is quite impossible, because men want only to desire it but not to have it, and every individual who experiences good times learns to downright pray for misery and disquietude. The destiny of man is designed for *happy moments* – every life has them – but not for happy ages. Nonetheless they will remain fixed in the imagination of man as 'the other side of the hill' because they have been inherited from ages past: for the concept of the age of happiness was no doubt acquired in primeval times from that condition in which, after violent exertion in hunting and warfare, man gives himself up to repose, stretches his limbs and hears the pinions of sleep rustling about him. It is a false conclusion if, in accordance with that ancient familiar experience, man imagines that, *after whole ages* of toil and deprivation, he can then partake of that condition of happiness *correspondingly enhanced and protracted.*

472

Religion and government. – As long as the state, or, more clearly, the government knows itself appointed as guardian for the benefit of the masses not yet of age, and on their behalf considers the question whether religion is to be preserved or abolished, it is very highly probable that it will always decide for the preservation of religion. For religion quietens the heart of the individual in times of loss, deprivation, fear, distrust, in those instances, that is to say, in which the government feels unable to do anything towards alleviating the psychical sufferings of the private person: even in the case of universal, unavoidable and in the immediate prospect inevitable evils (famines, financial crises, wars), indeed, religion guarantees a calm, patient, trusting disposition among the masses. Wherever the chance or inevitable shortcomings of the state government or the perilous consequences of dynastic interests force themselves upon the attention of the knowledgeable man and put him in a refractory mood, the unknowledgeable will think they see the hand of God and patiently submit to instructions from *above* (in which concept divine and human government are usually fused): thus internal civil peace and continuity of development is ensured. The power that lies in unity of popular sentiment, in the fact that everyone holds the same opinions and has the same objectives, is sealed and protected by religion, apart from in those rare cases in which a priesthood cannot agree with the authorities as to the price of its services and enters into conflict with them. As a rule the state will know how to win the priests over to itself because it needs their concealed and intimate education of souls and knows how to value servants who appear outwardly to represent a quite different interest. Without the assistance of the priests even now no power can become 'legitimate': as Napoleon grasped. – Thus absolute tutelary government and the careful preservation of religion necessarily go together. In this it has to be presupposed that the governing persons and classes are enlightened as to the advantages accruing to them from religion and thus feel to a certain extent superior to it, inasmuch as they employ it as an instrument; which is why free-spiritedness has its origin here. – But what if that quite different conception of government such as is taught in *democratic* states begins to prevail? If it is regarded as nothing but the instrument of the popular will, not as an Above in relation to a Below but merely as a function of the sole sovereign power, the people? Here the attitude towards religion adopted by the government can only be the same as that adopted towards it by the people; every dissemination of enlightenment must find its echo in their representatives, and an employment and exploitation of the religious drives and consolations for political ends will no longer be so easy (unless it happens that powerful party leaders for a time exercise an influence similar to that of enlightened despotism). But if the state is no longer free to profit from religion itself or the people come to hold far too diverse opinions on religious matters for the government to be permitted any single unified policy regarding religious measures – then the way out will necessarily be to treat religion as a private affair and to hand it over to the conscience and customs of every individual. The first consequence of this will be an apparent strengthening of religious feeling, inasmuch as suppressed and concealed manifestations of it to which the state involuntarily or deliberately gave no breathing space now break forth and proceed to excesses and extremes; later religion will be overrun with sects, and it will become plain that at the moment religion was made a private affair an abundance of dragon's teeth were sown. The sight of this conflict, the malignant exposure of all the weaknesses of the religious confessions, will finally admit of no other way out than that every better and better gifted man will make irreligion his private affair: which disposition will then come to dominate the minds of those in government and, almost against their will, give to the measures they take a character hostile to religion. As soon as this happens the mood of those still moved by religion, who formerly adored the state as something half or wholly sacred, will be transformed into one decidedly *hostile to the state*; they will lie in wait for the measures taken by the government, seek to obstruct, to cross, to disrupt as much as they can, and through the heat of their opposition drive the counter-party into an almost fanatical enthusiasm *for* the state; in which development they are secretly aided by the fact that, since their sundering from religion, hearts in these circles have felt a sense of emptiness which they are seeking provisionally to fill with a kind of substitute in the form of devotion to the state. After these transitional struggles, which may well last a long time, it will at length be decided whether the religious parties are still strong enough to revive the past and turn back the wheel: in which case the state will unavoidably fall into the hands of enlightened despotism (perhaps less enlightened and more troubled by fear than formerly) – or whether the anti-religious parties will prevail and, perhaps through schooling and education, in the course of generations undermine the propagation of their opponents and finally render it impossible. Then, however, they too will experience a slackening of their enthusiasm for the state: it will grow ever clearer that, together with that religious adoration to which the state is a sacred mystery, a supraterrestrial institution, the attitude of veneration and piety towards it has also been undermined. Henceforth the individual will see only that side of it that promises to be useful or threatens to be harmful to him, and will bend all his efforts to acquiring influence upon it. But this competition will soon become too great, men and parties alternate too quickly, hurl one another too fiercely down from the hill after barely having attained the top. None of the measures effected by a government will be guaranteed continuity; everyone will draw back from undertakings that require quiet tending for decades or centuries if their fruits are to mature. No one will feel towards a law any greater obligation than that of bowing for the moment to the force which backs up the law: one will then at once set to work to subvert it with a new force, the creation of a new majority. Finally – one can say this with certainty – distrust of all government, insight into the uselessness and destructiveness of these short-winded struggles will impel men to a quite novel resolve: the resolve to do away with the concept of the state, to the abolition of the distinction between private and public. Private companies will step by step absorb the business of the state: even the most resistant remainder of what was formerly the work of government (for example its activities designed to protect the private person from the private person) will in the long run be taken care of by private contractors. Disregard for and the decline and *death of the state*, the liberation of the private person (I take care not to say: of the individual), is the consequence of the democratic conception of the state; it is in this that its mission lies. When it has performed its task – which like everything human bears much rationality and irrationality in its womb – when every relapse into the old sickness has been overcome, a new page will be turned in the storybook of humanity in which there will be many strange tales to read and perhaps some of them good ones. – To repeat in brief what has just been said: the interests of tutelary government and the interests of religion go hand in hand together, so that when the latter begins to die out the foundations of the state too are undermined. The belief in a divine order in the realm of politics, in a sacred mystery in the existence of the state, is of religious origin: if religion disappears the state will unavoidably lose its ancient Isis veil and cease to excite reverence. Viewed from close to, the sovereignty of the people serves then to banish the last remnant of magic and superstition from this realm of feeling; modern democracy is the historical form of the *decay of the state*. – The prospect presented by this certain decay is, however, not in every respect an unhappy one: the prudence and self-interest of men are of all their qualities the best developed; if the state is no longer equal to the demands of these forces then the last thing that will ensue is chaos: an invention more suited to their purpose than the state was will gain victory over the state. How many an organizing power has mankind not seen die out: for example that of the racial clan, which was for millennia far mightier than that of the family and indeed ruled and regulated long before the family existed. We ourselves have seen the idea of familial rights and power which once ruled as far as the Roman world extended grow ever paler and more impotent. Thus a later generation will see the state too shrink to insignificance in various parts of the earth – a notion many people of the present can hardly contemplate without fear and revulsion. To *work* for the dissemination and realization of this notion is another thing, to be sure: one has to have a very presumptuous idea of one's own intelligence and scarcely half an understanding of history to set one's hand to the plough already – while no one can yet show what seedcorn is afterwards to be scattered on the riven soil. Let us therefore put our trust in 'the prudence and self-interest of men' to preserve the existence of the state for some time yet and to repulse the destructive experiments of the precipitate and the over-zealous!

473
Socialism with regard to its means. – Socialism is the fanciful younger brother of the almost expired despotism whose heir it wants to be; its endeavours are thus in the profoundest sense reactionary. For it desires an abundance of state power such as only despotism has ever had; indeed it outbids all the despotisms of the past inasmuch as it expressly aspires to the annihilation of the individual, who appears to it like an unauthorized luxury of nature destined to be improved into a useful *organ of the community*. On account of its close relationship to them it always appears in the proximity of all excessive deployments of power, as the typical old socialist Plato did at the court of the Sicilian tyrant; it desires (and sometimes promotes) the Caesarian despotic state of the present century because, as aforesaid, it would like to be its heir. But even this inheritance would be inadequate to its purposes: it requires a more complete subservience of the citizen to the absolute state than has ever existed before; and since it can no longer even count on the ancient religious piety towards the state but has, rather, involuntarily to work ceaselessly for its abolition – because, that is, it works for the abolition of all existing *states* – socialism itself can hope to exist only for brief periods here and

there, and then only through the exercise of the extremest terrorism. For this reason it is secretly preparing itself for rule through fear and is driving the word 'justice' into the heads of the half-educated masses like a nail so as to rob them of their reason (after this said reason has already greatly suffered from exposure to their half-education) and to create in them a good conscience for the evil game they are to play. – Socialism can serve to teach, in a truly brutal and impressive fashion, what danger there lies in all accumulations of state power, and to that extent to implant mistrust of the state itself. When its harsh voice takes up the watchword *as much state as possible* it thereby at first sounds noisier than ever: but soon the opposite cry comes through with all the greater force: *as little state as possible*.

474

The evolution of the spirit feared by the state. – Like every organizing political power, the Greek *polis* was mistrustful of the growth of culture and sought almost exclusively to paralyse and inhibit it. It wanted to admit no history, no development in this realm; the education sanctioned by state law was intended to be imposed upon every generation and to rivet it to *one* stage of development. The same thing was later desired by Plato too for his ideal state. This culture evolved *in spite of* the *polis*: it assisted indirectly and against its will, to be sure, because the individual's thirst for honour was incited to the highest degree in the *polis*, so that, once entered upon the path of spiritual cultivation, he continued along it as far as he could go. On the other hand, one should not invoke the glorificatory speech of Pericles: for it is no more than a grand, optimistic illusion as to the supposedly necessary connection between the *polis* and Athenian culture; immediately before night descends on Athens (the plague and the rupture of tradition), Thucydides makes it rise resplendent once again, like a transfiguring evening glow in whose light the evil day that preceded it could be forgotten.

475

European man and the abolition of nations. – Trade and industry, the post and the book-trade, the possession in common of all higher culture, rapid changing of home and scene, the nomadic life now lived by all who do not own land – these circumstances are necessarily bringing with them a weakening and finally an abolition of nations, at least the European: so that as a consequence of continual crossing a mixed race, that of European man, must come into being out of them. This goal is at present being worked against, consciously or unconsciously, by the separation of nations through the production of *national* hostilities, yet this mixing will nonetheless go slowly forward in spite of that temporary countercurrent: this artificial nationalism is in any case as perilous as artificial Catholicism used to be, for it is in its essence a forcibly imposed state of siege and self-defence inflicted on the many by the few and requires cunning, force and falsehood to maintain a front of respectability. It is not the interests of the many (the peoples), as is no doubt claimed, but above all the interests of certain princely dynasties and of certain classes of business and society, that impel to this nationalism; once one has recognized this fact, one should not be afraid to proclaim oneself simply a *good European* and actively to work for the amalgamation of nations: wherein the Germans are, through their ancient and tested quality of being the *interpreter and mediator between peoples*, able to be of assistance. – Incidentally: the entire problem of the *Jews* exists only within national states, inasmuch as it is here that their energy and higher intelligence, their capital in will and spirit accumulated from generation to generation in a long school of suffering, must come to preponderate to a degree calculated to arouse envy and hatred, so that in almost every nation – and the more so the more nationalist a posture the nation is again adopting – there is gaining ground the literary indecency of leading the Jews to the sacrificial slaughter as scapegoats for every possible public or private misfortune. As soon as it is no longer a question of the conserving of nations but of the production of the strongest possible European mixed race, the Jew will be just as usable and desirable as an ingredient of it as any other national residue. Every nation, every man, possesses unpleasant, indeed dangerous qualities: it is cruel to demand that the Jew should constitute an exception. In him these qualities may even be dangerous and repellent to an exceptional degree; and perhaps the youthful stock-exchange Jew is the most repulsive invention of the entire human race. Nonetheless I should like to know how much must, in a total accounting, be forgiven a people who, not without us all being to blame, have had the most grief-laden history of any people and whom we have to thank for the noblest human being (Christ), the purest sage (Spinoza), the mightiest book and the most efficacious moral code in the world. Moreover: in the darkest periods of the Middle Ages, when the cloudbanks of Asia had settled low over Europe, it was the Jewish freethinkers, scholars and physicians who, under the harshest personal constraint, held firmly to the banner of enlightenment and intellectual independence and defended Europe against Asia; it is thanks not least to their efforts that a more natural, rational and in any event unmythical elucidation of the world could at last again obtain victory and the ring of culture that now unites us with the enlightenment of Graeco-Roman antiquity remain unbroken. If Christianity has done everything to orientalize the occident, Judaism has always played an essential part in occidentalizing it again: which in a certain sense means making of Europe's mission and history a *continuation of the Greek*.

476
Apparent superiority of the Middle Ages. – The Middle Ages exhibit in the church an institution possessing a universal goal embracing all mankind, and one that is supposedly concerned with mankind's highest interests: contrasted with this, the goals of the states and nations exhibited by modern history produce an oppressive impression; they appear petty, mean, materialistic and spatially limited. But these varying impressions

upon the imagination must certainly not be allowed to determine our judgement; for that universal institution was designed to meet artificial needs reposing on fictions which, where they did not yet exist, it was obliged to invent (need of redemption); the modern institutions supply remedies for real states of distress; and the time is coming when institutions will come into being to serve the true needs of all men and to cast their fantastic archetype, the Catholic Church, into shadow and oblivion.

477

War indispensable. – It is vain reverie and beautiful-soulism to expect much more (let alone only then to expect much) of mankind when it has unlearned how to wage war. For the present we know of no other means by which that rude energy that characterizes the camp, that profound impersonal hatred, that murderous coldbloodedness with a good conscience, that common fire in the destruction of the enemy, that proud indifference to great losses, to one's own existence and that of one's friends, that inarticulate, earthquake-like shuddering of the soul, could be communicated more surely or strongly than every great war communicates them: the streams and currents that here break forth, though they carry with them rocks and rubbish of every kind and ruin the pastures of tenderer cultures, will later under favourable circumstances turn the wheels in the workshops of the spirit with newfound energy. Culture can in no way do without passions, vices and acts of wickedness. – When the Romans of the imperial era had grown a little tired of war they tried to gain new energy through animal-baiting, gladiatorial combats and the persecution of Christians. Present-day Englishmen, who seem also on the whole to have renounced war, seize on a different means of again engendering their fading energies: those perilous journeys of discovery, navigations, mountain-climbings, undertaken for scientific ends as they claim, in truth so as to bring home with them superfluous energy acquired through adventures and perils of all kinds. One will be able to discover many other such surrogates for war, but they will perhaps increasingly reveal that so highly cultivated and for that reason necessarily feeble humanity as that of the present-day European requires not merely war but the greatest and most terrible wars – thus a temporary relapse into barbarism – if the means to culture are not to deprive them of their culture and of their existence itself.

478

Industriousness in south and north. – Industriousness originates in two quite different ways. Workmen in the south are industrious, not from a desire for gain, but because others are always in need. Because someone always comes along who wants a horse shod, a cart repaired, the smith is always industrious. If no one came along, he would lounge about in the market-place. To feed himself in a fruitful country requires no great effort: a very moderate amount of work will suffice, in any event he has no need for industriousness; ultimately he would be quite content to beg. – The industriousness of English workers, on the other hand, has behind it the sense for gain: it is aware of itself and of its objectives, and desires with possessions power, with power the greatest possible freedom and individual nobility.

479

Wealth as the origin of a nobility of birth. – Wealth necessarily engenders an aristocracy of race, for it permits one to select the fairest women, pay the best teachers, grants to a man cleanliness, time for physical exercises, and above all freedom from deadening physical labour. To this extent it creates all the conditions for the production over a few generations of a noble and fair demeanour, even noble and fair behaviour, in men: greater freedom of feeling, the absence of the wretched and petty, of abasement before breadgivers, of penny-pinching. – It is precisely these negative qualities that are the richest gifts of happiness for a young man; a very poor man usually destroys himself through nobility of disposition, it takes him nowhere and gains him nothing, his race is not capable of life. – What must also be considered, however, is that wealth exercises almost the same effects whether one has 300 or 30,000 talers a year to spend: there is no essential progression in favouring circumstances. But to have less, as a boy to beg and abase oneself, is dreadful: although for those who seek their happiness in the glitter of the court, in subordination to the powerful and influential, or desire to be heads of the church, it may well be the right starting-point. (– It teaches one to steal stooping into the casements of favour.)

480

Envy and indolence in different directions. – The two opposing parties, the socialist and the nationalist – or whatever their names may be in the various countries of Europe – are worthy of one another: envy and laziness are the moving forces in both of them. In the former camp they want to work as little as possible with their hands, in the latter as little as possible with their heads; in the latter they hate and envy the prominent, self-evolved individuals unwilling to let themselves be enlisted in the ranks for the production of a mass effect, in the former the better, outwardly more favoured caste of society whose real task, the production of the supreme cultural values, makes their inner life so much harder and more painful. If, to be sure, the nationalists should succeed in imposing the spirit of the mass effect upon the higher classes of society, then the socialist hordes would be quite justified in seeking to level them with themselves also outwardly, since they would already be level with one another in head and heart. – Live as higher men and perform perpetually the deeds of higher culture – to this all that lives admits your right, and the order of society whose summit you are will be proof against every evil eye and evil claw!

481

Grand politics and what they cost. – Just as the greatest cost to a people involved in war and preparation for war is not the expense of the war or the interruption to trade and commerce, nor the maintenance of standing armies – however great these expenses may be now that eight states of Europe expend between two and three milliards annually on it – but the cost involved in the removal year in, year out of an extraordinary number of its efficient and industrious men from their proper professions and occupations so that they may become soldiers: so a people which sets about practising grand politics and ensuring to itself a decisive voice among the most powerful states does not incur the highest costs where these are usually thought to lie. It is true that from this moment on a host of the most prominent talents are continually sacrificed on the 'altar of the fatherland' or of the national thirst for honour, whereas previously other spheres of activity were open to these talents now devoured by politics. But aside from these public hecatombs, and at bottom much more horrible, there occurs a spectacle played out continually in a hundred thousand simultaneous acts: every efficient, industrious, intelligent, energetic man belonging to such a people lusting after political laurels is dominated by this lust and no longer belongs wholly to his own domain, as he formerly did: questions and cares of the public weal, renewed every day, devour a daily tribute from the capital in every citizen's head and heart: the sum total of all these sacrifices and costs in individual energy and work is so tremendous that the political emergence of a people almost necessarily draws after it a spiritual impoverishment and enfeeblement and a diminution of the capacity for undertakings demanding great concentration and application. Finally one may ask: is all this inflorescence and pomp of the whole (which is, after all, apparent only in the fear of other states for the new colossus and in the more favourable terms for trade and travel extorted from them) *worth it*, if all the nobler, tenderer, more spiritual plants and growths in which its soil was previously so rich have to be sacrificed to this coarse and gaudy flower of the nation?

482

And to repeat. – Public opinions – private indolence.

MAN
ALONE WITH
HIMSELF

483
Enemies of truth. – Convictions are more dangerous enemies of truth than lies.

484
Upside down world. – One criticizes a thinker more severely when he advances a proposition we find unpleasing; and yet it would be more reasonable to do so when his proposition pleases us.

485
Full of character. – A man appears full of character much more often because he always obeys his temperament than because he always obeys his principles.

486
The one thing needful. – There is one thing one has to have: either a cheerful disposition by nature or a *disposition made cheerful* by art and knowledge.

487
Passion for causes. – He who directs his passion upon causes (the sciences, the common weal, cultural interests, the arts) deprives his passion for people (even when they are advocates of these causes, as statesmen, philosophers, artists are advocates of their creations) of much of its fire.

488
Composure in action. – Just as a waterfall grows slower and more lightly suspended as it plunges down, so the great man of action usually acts with *greater* composure than the fierceness of his desires before he acted had led us to expect.

489
Not too deep. – People who comprehend a thing to its very depths rarely stay faithful to it for ever. For they have brought its depths into the light of day: and in the depths there is always much that is unpleasant to see.

490
Delusion of the idealists. – All idealists imagine that the causes they serve are essentially better than all the other causes in the world and refuse to believe that, if their cause is to prosper at all, it requires precisely the same evil-smelling manure as all other human undertakings have need of.

491
Self-observation. – Man is very well defended against himself, against

179

being reconnoitred and besieged by himself, he is usually able to perceive of himself only his outer walls. The actual fortress is inaccessible, even invisible to him, unless his friends and enemies play the traitor and conduct him in by a secret path.

492
The right profession. – Men can rarely endure a profession of which they do not believe or convince themselves it is at bottom more important than any other. Women adopt a similar attitude towards their lovers.

493
Nobility of mind. – Nobility of mind consists to a great degree in good-naturedness and absence of distrust, and thus contains precisely that which successful and money-hungry people are so fond of looking down on and laughing at.

494
Goal and path. – Many are obstinate with regard to the path once they have entered upon it, few with regard to the goal.

495
What excites indignation in an individual way of life. – All very individual rules of life excite hostility against him who adopts them; other people feel humiliated by the exceptional treatment he accords himself, as though they were being treated as merely commonplace creatures.

496
Privilege of greatness. – It is the privilege of greatness to give great delight with meagre gifts.

497
Involuntarily noble. – Man involuntarily conducts himself nobly when he has become accustomed to desiring nothing of men and always bestowing gifts upon them.

498
Condition for heroism. – If a man wants to become a hero the serpent must first have become a dragon: otherwise he will lack his proper enemy.

499
Friend. – Fellow rejoicing [*Mitfreude*], not fellow suffering [*Mitleiden*], makes the friend.

500
Employing ebb and flow. – To the ends of knowledge one must know how to employ that internal current that draws us to a thing and then that other current that after a time draws us away from it.

501
Pleasure in oneself. – One says 'pleasure in a thing': but in reality it is pleasure in oneself by means of a thing.

502

The modest man. – He who comports himself modestly in relation to people is all the more presumptuous in relation to things (city, state, society, the age, mankind). This constitutes his revenge.

503

Envy and jealousy. – Envy and jealousy are the privy parts of the human soul. The comparison can perhaps be extended.

504

The noblest hypocrite. – Never to speak about oneself is a very noble piece of hypocrisy.

505

Ill-humour. – Ill-humour is a physical illness that is by no means done away with if the occasion for ill-humour is subsequently abolished.

506

Advocates of truth. – Not when it is dangerous to tell the truth does truth lack advocates, but when it is boring to do so.

507

More troublesome than enemies. – People who we are not convinced would be sympathetically inclined towards us under all circumstances but to whom we are for any reason (e.g. gratitude) on our part obligated to maintain the appearance of unconditional sympathy torment our imagination much more than our enemies do.

508

The open countryside. – We enjoy being in the open countryside so much because it has no opinion concerning us.

509

Everyone superior in one thing. – Under civilized conditions everyone feels himself to be superior to everyone else in at any rate *one* thing: it is upon this that the general mutual goodwill that exists depends, inasmuch as everyone is someone who under certain circumstances is able to be helpful and who thus feels free to accept help without a sense of shame.

510

Grounds of consolation. – When somebody dies one needs grounds of consolation most of all not so much to assuage one's grief as to provide an excuse for the fact that one is so easily consoled.

511

Those faithful to their convictions. – He who has much to do preserves his general opinions and points of view almost unaltered. Likewise anyone who works in the service of an idea: he will cease to examine even the idea itself, for he has no time for that; indeed it is against his interests to regard it as so much as discussable.

512

Morality and quantity. – One man's morality is higher compared with another's often only because its goals are quantitavely greater. The latter is drawn down by his narrowly bounded occupation with the petty.

513

Life as the yield of life. – No matter how far a man may extend himself with his knowledge, no matter how objectively he may come to view himself, in the end it can yield to him nothing but his own biography.

514

Iron necessity. – Iron necessity is a thing which in the course of history men come to see as neither iron nor necessary.

515

From experience. – The irrationality of a thing is no argument against its existence, rather a condition of it.

516

Truth. – No one now dies of fatal truths: there are too many antidotes to them.

517

Fundamental insight. – There is no pre-established harmony* between the furtherance of truth and the well-being of mankind.

518

The human lot. – He who considers more deeply knows that, whatever his acts and judgements may be, he is always wrong.

519

Truth as Circe. – Error has transformed animals into men; is truth perhaps capable of changing man back into an animal?

520

Danger facing our culture. – We belong to an age whose culture is in danger of perishing through the means to culture.

521

Greatness means giving direction. – No river is great and abundant of itself: it is the fact that it receives and bears onward so many tributaries that makes it so. Thus it is too with all great men of the spirit. All that matters is that one supplies the direction which many inflowing tributaries then have to follow, not whether one is poorly or richly gifted from the beginning.

522

Feeble conscience. – People who speak of their own significance for humanity possess with regard to common, bourgeois integrity, in the keeping of compacts and promises, a feeble conscience.

---

* pre-established harmony: Leibnitz's conception of the world as composed of monads, individuals whose relations of mutual agreement are predetermined by God.

523
Wanting to be loved. – The demand to be loved is the greatest of all pieces of presumption.

524
Contempt of man. – The most unambiguous sign that one holds men in contempt is this, that one acknowledges them only as a means to *one's own* ends or does not acknowledge them at all.

525
Adherents out of contradictoriness. – He who has raised men up in rage against him has always gained a party in his favour too.

526
Forgetting experiences. – He who thinks a great deal, and thinks objectively, can easily forget his own experiences, but not the thoughts these experiences called forth.

527
Retaining an opinion. – One person retains an opinion because he flatters himself it was his own discovery, another because he acquired it with effort and is proud of having grasped it: thus both do so out of vanity.

528
Shunning the light. – The good deed shuns the light just as fearfully as does the bad deed: the latter fears that detection will bring pain (in the form of punishment), the former fears that detection will bring loss of pleasure (namely that pure pleasure in oneself that ceases immediately vanity is satisfied).

529
The length of the day. – When one has a great deal to put into it a day has a hundred pockets.

530
Genius of tyranny. – When there is alive in the soul an invincible desire for tyrannical rule, and the fire is constantly being fuelled, even a modest talent (in politicians, artists) will gradually become an almost irresistible natural force.

531
The life of one's enemy. – He who lives for the sake of combating an enemy has an interest in seeing that his enemy stays alive.

532
More seriously. – One takes an obscure and inexplicable thing more seriously than a clear and explicable one.

533
Evaluation of services rendered. – We value services anyone renders us according to the worth he places upon them, not according to the value they possess for us.

534

Misfortune. – The distinction bestowed by misfortune (as though to feel lucky were a sign of shallowness, unpretentiousness, commonplaceness) is so great that when anyone is told: 'but how lucky you are!' he usually protests.

535

Chimera of fear. – The chimera of fear is that evil, apish kobold who leaps on to the back of man at precisely the moment he is already bearing the heaviest burden.

536

Value of tasteless opponents. – Sometimes one stays faithful to a cause only because its opponents are unfailingly tasteless.

537

Value of a profession. – A profession makes one thoughtless, therein lies its greatest blessing. For it is a rampart behind which one can lawfully retreat when one is assailed by commonplace cares and scruples.

538

Talent. – The talent of many a man appears less than it is because he has always set himself too great tasks.

539

Youth. – Youth is unpleasant; for in youth it is not possible or not sensible to be productive, in any sense of the word.

540

Too great objectives. – He who has publicly set himself great objectives and afterwards realizes he is too weak for them is usually also too weak publicly to repudiate them, and then he unavoidably becomes a hypocrite.

541

In the stream. – Mighty waters draw much stone and rubble along with them, mighty spirits many stupid and bewildered heads.

542

Perils of spiritual liberation. – When a man is seriously engaged upon liberating himself spiritually his desires and passions as well hope to derive some advantage from it.

543

Embodiment of the spirit. – When we think much and sagaciously not only our face but our body too assumes a sagacious appearance.

544

Seeing badly and listening badly. – He who sees badly sees less and less; he who listens badly hears more than has been said.

545

Self-enjoyment in vanity. – The vain man wants not so much to predomi-nate as to feel himself predominant; that is why he disdains no means of self-deception and self-outwitting. What he treasures is not the opinion of others but his own opinion of their opinion.

546

Vain exceptionally. – He who is usually self-sufficient is vain and receptive to fame and commendation on exceptional occasions, namely when he is physically ill. To the extent that he feels himself diminishing he has to try to recoup himself from outside through the opinion of others.

547

The 'rich in spirit'. – He has no spirit who seeks spirit.

548

Hint for party leaders. – If you can bring people to declare themselves in favour of something publicly you have usually also brought them to declare themselves in favour of it inwardly; they want to be regarded as consistent.

549

Contempt. – Contempt gained through others is more painful to a man than contempt gained through himself.

550

Cord of gratitude. – There are slavish souls who go so far in readiness to acknowledge favours done them that they choke themselves with the cord of gratitude.

551

Trick of the prophet. – To divine in advance how ordinary people will act one has to assume that, when they are in an unpleasant situation, they always seek to get out of it with the smallest expenditure of intelligence.

552

The only human right. – He who deviates from the traditional falls victim to the extraordinary; he who remains in the traditional becomes its slave. In either event he perishes.

553

Lower than the animal. – When man neighs with laughter he excels any animal in his vulgarity.

554

Half-knowledge. – He who speaks little of a foreign language gets more pleasure from it than he who speaks it well. Enjoyment is with the half-knowers.

555

Dangerous readiness to help. – There are people who want to make other people's life harder for no other reason than to be able afterwards to offer them their recipe for alleviating life (for example their Christianity).

556
Industriousness and conscientiousness. – Industriousness and conscientious- ness are often at odds with one another because industriousness wants to pluck the fruit from the tree while it is sour whereas conscientiousness lets it hang too long until it falls and smashes itself to pieces.

557
Casting suspicion. – Upon people one cannot endure one seeks in one's own mind to cast suspicion.

558
No occasion. – Many people wait their whole life long for an opportunity of being good in *their* fashion.

559
Lack of friends. – A lack of friends may be put down to envy or presump- tion. Many owe their friends only to the fortunate circumstance that they have no occasion for envy.

560
Danger in multiplicity. – With one talent more one often stands less se- curely than with one fewer: as a table stands better on three than on four legs.

561
A model for others. – He who wants to give a good example must add a grain of folly to his virtue; then others will imitate and at the same time surpass him they imitate – which men love to do.

562
Being a target. – Unkind remarks about us by others are often not really directed at us but are an expression of an annoyance, of an ill-humour of quite a different origin.

563
Easily resigned. – One suffers little from disappointed wishes if one has trained one's imagination to blacken the past.

564
In danger. – One is most in danger of being run over when one has just avoided a carriage.

565
The role suited to the voice. – He who is compelled to speak louder than he is used to speaking (to a half-deaf person, for instance, or before a great auditorium) usually exaggerates the things he has to say. – Many a person has become a conspirator, a malicious gossip, an intriguer, simply because his voice is best suited to whispering.

566
Love and hatred. – Love and hatred are not blind but dazzled by the fire they themselves bear with them.

567
Advantageous enmity. – People unable to make the world see them at their true worth seek to arouse violent enmity towards themselves. They then have the consolation of thinking that this enmity is standing between their true worth and recognition of it – and that many others suppose the same: which is very advantageous for their reputation.

568
Confession. – One forgets one's sins when one has confessed them to another, but the other does not usually forget them.

569
Self-satisfaction. – The golden fleece of self-satisfaction protects against blows but not against pinpricks.

570
Shadows in the flame. – The flame is not as bright to itself as it is to those it illumines: so too the sage.

571
Our own opinions. – The first opinion that occurs to us when we are suddenly asked about something is usually not our own but only the customary one pertaining to our caste, station, origin; our own opinions rarely swim to the top.

572
Origin of courage. – The ordinary man is as courageous and invulnerable as a hero when he does not perceive the danger and has no eyes for it. Conversely: the hero's only vulnerable spot is on his back, that is to say where he has no eyes.

573
Danger in one's physician. – One must have the physician one was born for, otherwise one will perish by one's physician.

574
Miraculous vanity. – He who has boldly foretold the weather three times and each time successfully believes a little in the depths of his soul that he is prophetically gifted. We accept the existence of the miraculous and irrational when it flatters our self-esteem.

575
Profession. – A profession is the backbone of life.

576
Danger in personal influence. – He who feels he exercises a great inner influence upon another has to allow him entirely free rein, occasionally

indeed be glad to see resistance in him and even induce it: otherwise he will inevitably make for himself an enemy.

577
Acknowledging heirs. – He who has founded something great in a selfless attitude of mind takes pains to rear heirs for himself. To see an opponent in every possible heir of one's work and to live in a state of self-defence against them is a sign of a tyrannical and ignoble nature.

578
Half-knowledge. – Half-knowledge is more victorious than whole knowledge: it understands things as being more simple than they are and this renders its opinions more easily intelligible and more convincing.

579
Not suited to be a party man. – He who thinks a great deal is not suited to be a party man: he thinks his way through the party and out the other side too soon.

580
Bad memory. – The advantage of a bad memory is that one can enjoy the same good things for the first time *several* times.

581
Causing oneself pain. – Ruthlessness in thinking is often the sign of a discordant inner disposition that desires insensitizing.

582
Martyr. – A martyr's disciples suffer more than the martyr.

583
Vanity behind the times. – The vanity of many people who have no need to be vain is a habit, retained and exaggerated, from a time when they did not yet have the right to believe in themselves and had first to beg for this belief from others in small coinage.

584
Punctum saliens *of passion.** – He who is on the point of getting into a rage or a violent attack of love reaches a point at which the soul is as full as a vessel: but one drop of water has still to be added, an assent to passion (which is something one usually dissents from). Only this little drop is needed and then the vessel runs over.

585
Ill-humoured reflections. – It is with men as with the charcoal-kilns in the forest. Only when the young have ceased to glow and are carbonized do they become *useful.* As long as they are smoking and smouldering they may perhaps be more interesting but they are of no use and all too often unmanageable. – Mankind mercilessly employs every individual as material for heating its great machines: but what then is the purpose of the machines if all individuals (that is to say mankind) are of no other use

---

* *punctum saliens*: salient point

than as material for maintaining them? Machines that are an end in them-selves – is that the *umana commedia*?

586

Of the hour-hand of life. – Life consists of rare individual moments of the highest significance and countless intervals in which at best the phantoms of those moments hover about us. Love, spring, a beautiful melody, the mountains, the moon, the sea – they all speak truly to our heart only once: if they ever do in fact truly find speech. For many people never experience these moments at all but are themselves intervals and pauses in the symphony of real life.

587

To attack or to intervene. – We often make the mistake of actively opposing a tendency or party or age because we happen to have seen only its external side, its deliquescence or the 'faults of its virtues' necessarily adhering to it – perhaps because we ourselves have participated in them to a marked degree. Then we turn our back on them and go off in an opposite direction; but it would be better if we sought out their good and strong side instead or evolved and developed it in ourself. It requires, to be sure, a more penetrating eye and a more favourable inclination to advance what is imperfect and evolving than to see through it in its imperfection and deny it.

588

Modesty. – There is true modesty (that is, the recognition that we are not the work of ourselves); and it well becomes the great mind because it is precisely he who can grasp the idea of his complete unaccountability (also for the good he creates). One hates the immodesty of the great man, not to the extent that it comes from a sensation of his own strength, but because through it he evidences a desire to experience this strength by wounding others, treating them in a domineering way and seeing how far they will put up with it. As a rule this behaviour is even a sign that he lacks a calm certainty of his strength and thus leads men to doubt his greatness. To this extent immodesty is from a prudential point of view very inadvisable.

589

The first thought of the day. – The best way of beginning each day well is to think on awakening whether one cannot this day give pleasure to at any rate *one* person. If this could count as a substitute for the religious practice of prayer, then this substitution would be to the benefit of one's fellow men.

590

Presumption as the last means of comfort. – When we interpret a misfortune, our intellectual shortcomings or an illness in such a way that we see in them our prescribed destiny, a testing or a secret punishment for past actions, we make our own being interesting to ourselves and in our own imagination raise ourselves above our fellow men. The proud sinner is a familiar figure in all ecclesiastical sects.

591

Vegetation of happiness. – Close beside the woe of the world, and often upon its volcanic soil, man has laid out his little garden of happiness. Whether one views life with the eye of him who desires of existence only knowledge, or of him who submits and is resigned, or of him who rejoices over difficulties overcome – everywhere one will find a little happiness sprung up beside the misfortune – and the more happiness the more volcanic the soil – only it would be ludicrous to say that with this happiness suffering itself is justified.

592

The road of one's forebears. – It is sensible for anyone to develop further in himself the *talent* upon which his father and grandfather expended effort and not to turn to something completely new, otherwise he will make it impossible for himself to achieve perfection in any trade at all. That is why the proverb says: 'What road should you take? – the road of your forebears.'

593

Vanity and ambition as education. – So long as a man has not yet become an instrument of general human utility let him be plagued by ambition; if that goal has been attained, however, if he is working with the necessity of a machine for the good of all, then let him be visited by vanity; it will humanize him and make him more sociable, endurable and indulgent in small things, now that ambition (to render him useful) has finished roughhewing him.

594

Philosophical novices. – If we have just become the recipient of the wisdom of a philosopher we walk along the street feeling we have been recreated and become a great man; for we encounter only people who are unaware of this wisdom and have therefore to deliver a new, so far unknown verdict on all things: because we acknowledge a code of law we think we are henceforth obliged to bear ourselves like a judge.

595

Pleasing by displeasing. – People who prefer to draw attention to themselves and thereby cause displeasure desire the same thing as those who want not to draw attention to themselves and give pleasure, only they do so to a far greater degree and indirectly, by means of a state through which they appear to be retreating from their goal. They desire power and influence, and therefore demonstrate their superiority even in a way that makes them unpleasing; for they know that he who has finally attained to power pleases in almost all he does and says, and that even when he causes displeasure he still seems to please. – The free spirit too, and likewise the believer, desire power in order to please through it;

when they are threatened by an ill fate, persecution, imprisonment, execution on account of their teaching they rejoice in the thought that in this way their teaching will be cut and burned into mankind; they accept it as a painful but vigorous, if late-acting means of nonetheless attaining to power.

596

*Casus belli and the like.** – The prince who, having resolved on war with his neighbour, discovers a *casus belli*, is like a father who foists upon his child a mother who is henceforth to count as such. And are almost all the publicly declared motives for our actions not such substituted mothers?

597

Passion and rights. – No one talks more passionately about his rights than he who in the depths of his soul doubts whether he has any. By enlisting passion on his side he wants to stifle his reason and its doubts: thus he will acquire a good conscience and with it success among his fellow men.

598

Trick of renouncers. – He who protests against marriage, in the way Catholic priests do, will try to think of it in its lowest and most vulgar form. Likewise he who refuses to be honoured by his contemporaries will understand the concept in a base sense; thus he will render this self-denial and the struggle against it easier for himself. In general he who denies himself much in things of importance will tend to permit himself petty indulgences. It may be possible that he who is raised above the applause of his contemporaries is nonetheless incapable of denying himself the satisfaction of little vanities.

599

Age of presumption. – With gifted people the actual period of presumption lies between their twenty-sixth and thirtieth years; it is the time of their first maturity, with a strong residue of acidulousness. On the basis of what they feel within them they demand honour and humility of men who see little or nothing of it, and when these are at first denied them they revenge themselves with that presumptuous glance and bearing, that tone of voice which a subtle ear and eye can recognize in every product of that age, whether it be poetry, philosophy, pictures or music. Older, more experienced men smile at this, and recall with emotion that fair time of life in which one is angry that it is one's fate to *be* so much and *seem* so little. Later one really does *appear more* – but one has by then lost the belief that one *is* very much: one then remains an incorrigible fool of vanity for the rest of one's life.

600

Deceptive and yet tenable. – Just as in order to walk beside an abyss or cross a deep stream by a plank one needs a railing, not so as to hold on to it – for it would at once collapse if one did that – but to give to the eye a feeling of

* *casus belli*: motive for war

security, so as a youth one has need of people who without knowing it perform for us the service of a railing. It is true that, if we were really in great danger, they would not help us if we sought to rely on them, but they give us the quieting sensation that there is protection close at hand (for example fathers, teachers, friends, as all three usually are).

601

Learning to love. – We have to learn to love, learn to be charitable, and this from our youth up; if education and chance offer us no opportunity to practise these sensations our soul will grow dry and even incapable of understanding them in others. Hatred likewise has to be learned and nourished if one wants to become a good hater: otherwise the germ of that too will gradually wither away.

602

Ruins as ornamentation. – Those who go on many intellectual journeys retain certain outlooks and habits belonging to earlier ages, which then intrude into their modern thoughts and actions like a piece of inexplicable antiquity and grey stonework: often to the embellishment of the whole region.

603

Love and honour. – Love desires, fear shuns. That is why one cannot be loved and honoured by one and the same person, at least not at the same time. For he who honours recognizes power, that is to say he fears it. Love, however, recognizes no power, nothing that separates, contrasts, ranks above and below. Because love does not honour, ambitious men are, secretly or openly, recalcitrant towards being loved.

604

Prejudice in favour of the cold. – People who catch fire quickly, quickly grow cold and are thus on the whole unreliable. That is why all those who are always cold, or pretend to be so, have in their favour the prejudice that they are particularly trustworthy and reliable: people confuse them with those who catch fire slowly and retain it a long time.

605

What is dangerous in independent opinions – Occasional indulgence in independent opinions is stimulating, like a kind of itch; if we proceed further in them we begin to scratch the spot; until in the end we produce an open wound, that is to say until our independent opinions begin to disturb and harass us in our situation in life and our human relationships.

606

Thirst for profound pain. – When it has passed, passion leaves behind an obscure longing for itself and even in departing casts a seductive glance. To be scourged by it must have afforded us a kind of joy. The milder sensations, on the other hand, appear insipid; it seems we always prefer the more vehement displeasure to a feeble pleasure.

607

Ill-humour with others and with the world. – When, as we so often do, we expend our ill-humour on others while it is really against ourselves that we feel it, what we are doing at bottom is endeavouring to befog and deceive our own judgement: we want to motivate this ill-humour *a posteriori* through the blunders and deficiencies of others and thus lose sight of ourselves. – Those rigorously religious people who are inexorable judges of themselves have at the same time been the most vehement accusers of mankind in general: the saint has never lived who reserved sin for himself and virtue for others: just as little as has the man who, following Buddha's prescript, has concealed his good from the people and let his evil alone shine forth.

608

Cause confused with effect. – We unconsciously seek for the principles and dogmas appropriate to our temperament, so that in the end it appears as though these principles and dogmas had created our character and given it firmness and assurance: whereas what has happened is precisely the reverse. Our thinking and judgement are, it seems, to be made the cause of our nature: but in fact it is *our* nature that is the cause of our thinking and judging thus and thus. – And what is it destines us for this almost unconscious comedy? Indolence and love of ease and not least the desire of our vanity to be thought consistent through and through, homogeneous in thought and being: for this procures respect and bestows confidence and power.

609

Age and truth. – Young people love what is strange and interesting, regardless of whether it is true or false. More mature spirits love in truth that which is strange and interesting in it. Heads fully mature, finally, love truth also where it appears plain and simple and is boring to ordinary people: they have noticed that truth is accustomed to impart its highest spiritual possessions with an air of simplicity.

610

Men as bad poets. – Just as in the second half of a stanza bad poets seek the idea that will fit the rhyme, so men are in the second half of life accustomed to become more anxious to seek actions, positions, relationships suited to those of their earlier life, so that externally it all sounds in harmony: but their life is no longer dominated and repeatedly directed by a powerful idea, in place of which there appears the objective of finding a rhyme.

611

Boredom and play. – Need compels us to perform work with the proceeds of which the need is assuaged; need continually recurs and we are thus accustomed to working. In the intervals, however, during which our needs have been assuaged and are as it were sleeping, we are overtaken by boredom. What is this? It is our habituation to work as such, which

now asserts itself as a new, additional need; and the more strongly ha-
bituated we are to working, perhaps even the more we have suffered
need, the stronger this new need will be. To elude boredom man either
works harder than is required to satisfy his other needs or he invents
play, that is to say work designed to assuage no other need than the need
for work as such. He who has become tired of play, and who has no fresh
needs that require him to work, is sometimes overtaken by a longing for a
third condition which stands in the same relation to play as floating does
to dancing and dancing to walking – for a state of serene agitation: it is the
artist's and philosopher's vision of happiness.

612

Instruction from pictures. – When we regard a series of pictures of ourselves from our late childhood to our mature manhood, we are pleasantly
surprised to see that the man resembles the child more closely than he
does the youth: what this process probably indicates is that a temporary
alienation from our basic character occurred during our youth but has
been overcome by the accumulated strength of manhood. This observation is consistent with this other, that all those powerful influences
exerted upon us in our youth by our passions and by theories and political events seem later on to be again reduced back to a firm basis, so that,
although they certainly continue to live on in us and affect our actions,
our fundamental feelings and outlook have come to dominate them and,
while we continue to employ them as sources of energy, they no longer
regulate us as they did in our twenties. Thus the thinking and feelings of
the man are likewise more conformable to those of his childhood – and
this inward fact is expressed in the external one referred to.

613

Age and tone of voice. – The tone in which young people speak, praise,
blame, poetize displeases their elders because it is too loud and yet at the
same time hollow and indistinct, like a sound in a vault that acquires such
volume through the emptiness surrounding it; for most of what young
people think does not proceed from the abundance of their own nature
but is a resonance and echo of what has been thought, said, praised and
blamed in their presence. But because sensations (inclination and aversion) resound in them much more strongly than do the reasons for them,
when they again give vent to these sensations there arises that hollow,
resonant tone through which one can recognize the absence or sparse-
ness of reasons. The tone of more mature years is stern, abrupt, of
moderate loudness but, like everything clearly articulated, very far-
carrying. Old age, finally, often introduces a certain gentleness and forbearance into the voice and as it were sweetens it: in many cases, to be
sure, it also sours it.

614

Retarded and anticipatory men. – The unpleasant character who is full of
mistrust, consumed with envy whenever competitors or neighbours

achieve a success, and violently opposes all opinions not his own, demonstrates that he belongs to an earlier stage of culture and is thus a relic: for the way in which he traffics with men was the apt and right one for conditions obtaining during an age of club-law; he is a *retarded* man. Another character who readily rejoices with his fellow men, wins friends everywhere, welcomes everything new and developing, takes pleasure in the honours and successes of others and makes no claim to be in the sole possession of the truth but is full of a diffident mistrust – he is an anticipatory man striving towards a higher human culture. The unpleasant character derives from ages when the rude foundations of human intercourse had still to be constructed, the other dwells on its highest floor as far removed as possible from the savage beast which, locked in the cellars beneath the foundations of culture, howls and rages.

615

Comfort for hypochondriacs. – Whenever a great thinker is temporarily subject to hypochondriac self-torments he may comfort himself with the words: 'it is your own great strength upon which this parasite is feeding; if it were less you would suffer less'. The statesman may do the same whenever jealousy and feelings of revengefulness, the mood of *bellum omnium contra omnes** in general for which as representative of a nation he must necessarily have a decided gift, intrudes into his private life and makes it hard for him.

616

Estranged from the present. – There is great advantage to be gained in distantly estranging ourselves from our age and for once being driven as it were away from its shores back on to the ocean of the world-outlooks of the past. Looking back at the coast from this distance we command a view, no doubt for the first time, of its total configuration, and when we approach it again we have the advantage of understanding it better as a whole than those who have never left it.

617

Sowing and reaping with one's personal shortcomings. – Men like Rousseau know how to employ their weaknesses, deficiencies and vices as it were as manure for their talents. If he bewails the depravity and degeneration of society as the deplorable consequence of culture, he does so on the basis of a personal experience; it is the bitterness deriving from this that gives to his general condemnation the sharpness of its edge and poisons the arrows with which he shoots; he unburdens himself first of all as an individual and thinks to seek a cure that, operating directly upon society, will indirectly and through society also be of benefit to him himself.

618

Being philosophically minded. – We usually endeavour to acquire a *single* deportment of feeling, a *single* attitude of mind towards all the events and situations of life – that above all is what is called being philosophically

* *bellum . . . omnes*: 'war of all against all'; Hobbes' phrase.

minded. But for the enrichment of knowledge it may be of more value not to reduce oneself to uniformity in this way, but to listen instead to the gentle voice of each of life's different situations; these will suggest the attitude of mind appropriate to them. Through thus ceasing to treat oneself as a *single* rigid and unchanging individuum one takes an intelligent interest in the life and being of many others.

619

In the fire of contempt. – It is a new step towards independence when first we venture to express views regarded as disgraceful in him who harbours them; even our friends and acquaintances then begin to worry. The gifted nature must pass through this fire too; after it has done so it will belong much more to itself.

620

Sacrifice. – When there is a choice in the matter, a great sacrifice will be preferred to a small one: because in the case of the former we can indemnify ourselves through the self-admiration we feel, which we cannot do in the case of the latter.

621

Love as artifice. – He who really wants to get to *know* something new (be it a person, an event, a book) does well to entertain it with all possible love and to avert his eyes quickly from everything in it he finds inimical, repellent, false, indeed to banish it from mind: so that, for example, he allows the author of a book the longest start and then, like one watching a race, desires with beating heart that he may reach his goal. For with this procedure one penetrates to the heart of the new thing, to the point that actually moves it: and precisely this is what is meant by getting to know it. If one has got this far, reason can afterwards make its reservations; that over-estimation, that temporary suspension of the critical pendulum, was only an artifice for luring forth the soul of a thing.

622

Thinking too well and too ill of the world. – Whether one thinks too well or too ill of things one always enjoys the advantage of reaping a greater pleasure: for if our preconceived opinion is too favourable we usually introduce more sweetness into things (experiences) than they actually contain. A preconceived opinion that is too unfavourable causes a pleasant disappointment: what was already pleasant in the thing receives an addition through the pleasantness of the surprise. – A gloomy temperament will in both cases experience the opposite.

623

Deep men. – Those whose strength lies in the depth impressions make on them – they are usually called deep men – are when they encounter the unexpected relatively calm and resolved: for at the first moment the impression was still shallow, only then did it *become* deep. Long foreseen and expected things and people, on the other hand, excite such natures the most, and when such things finally do arrive their presence of mind almost deserts them.

624

Traffic with one's higher self. – Everyone has his good days when he discovers his higher self; and true humanity demands that everyone be evaluated only in the light of this condition and not in that of his working-day unfreedom and servitude. A painter, for example, should be appraised and revered in the light of the highest vision he is capable of seeing and reproducing. But men themselves traffic in very various ways with this higher self of theirs and are often actors of themselves, inasmuch as they afterwards continually imitate that which they are in those moments. Many live in awe of and abasement before their ideal and would like to deny it: they are afraid of their higher self because when it speaks it speaks imperiously. It possesses, moreover, a spectral freedom to come or to stay away as it wishes; on this account it is often called a gift of the gods, whereas in reality it is everything else that is a gift of the gods (of chance): this however is man himself.

625

Solitary men. – Some men are so accustomed to being alone with themselves that they do not compare themselves with others at all but spin out their life of monologue in a calm and cheerful mood, conversing and indeed laughing with themselves alone. If they are nonetheless constrained to compare themselves with others they are inclined to a brooding underestimation of themselves: so that they have to be compelled to *acquire* again a good and just opinion of themselves from others: and even from this acquired opinion they will tend continually to detract and trade away something. – We must therefore allow certain men their solitude and not be so stupid, as we so often are, as to pity them for it.

626

Without melody. – There are people who repose so steadily within themselves and whose capacities are balanced with one another so harmoniously that any activity directed towards a goal is repugnant to them. They are like music that consists of nothing but long drawn out harmonious chords, without even the beginning of a moving, articulated melody making an appearance. Any movement from without serves only to settle the barque into a new equilibrium on the lake of harmonious euphony. Modern men usually grow extremely impatient when confronted by such natures, which *become* nothing without our being able to say that they *are* nothing. But in certain moods the sight of them prompts the unusual question: why melody at all? Why does the quiet reflection of life in a deep lake not suffice us? – The Middle Ages were richer in such natures than our age is. How seldom do we now encounter one able to live thus happily and peaceably with himself even in the turmoil of life, saying to himself with Goethe: 'the best is the profound stillness towards the world in which I live and grow, and win for myself what they cannot take from me with fire and sword'.

627

Living and experiencing. – When we observe how some people know how to manage their experiences – their insignificant, everyday experiences – so that they become an arable soil that bears fruit three times a year, while others – and how many there are! – are driven through surging waves of destiny, the most multifarious currents of the times and the nations, and yet always remain on top, bobbing like a cork: then we are in the end tempted to divide mankind into a minority (a minimality) of those who know how to make much of little, and a majority of those who know how to make little of much; indeed, one does encounter those inverted sorcerers who, instead of creating the world out of nothing, create nothingness out of the world.

628

Seriousness in play. – In Genoa at the time of evening twilight I heard coming from a tower a long peal of bells: it seemed it would never stop, resounding as though it could never have enough of itself over the noise of the streets out into the evening sky and the sea breeze, so chilling and at the same time so childlike, so melancholy. Then I recalled the words of Plato and suddenly they spoke to my heart: *Nothing human is worthy of being taken very seriously; nonetheless** – –

629

Of conviction and justice. – That a man must, in subsequent cold sobriety, continue to adhere to what he has said, promised, resolved in passion – this demand is among the heaviest of the burdens that oppress mankind. To be obliged to recognize the consequences of anger, of a blazing revengefulness, of an enthusiastic devotion, for all future time – that can engender an animosity towards these sensations made the more bitter by their idolization everywhere and especially by the artists. These latter greatly encourage the *high value accorded the passions* and have always done so; they also, to be sure, glorify the fearful amends one must make for these same passions, the death, maiming and voluntary banishment following on outbursts of revenge, the resignation of the broken heart. In any event, they keep awake our curiosity regarding the passions, as though to say: 'experience without passion is nothing at all'. – Because we have sworn to be faithful, perhaps even to a purely fictitious being such as a god, because we have surrenderd our heart to a prince, to a party, to a woman, to a priestly order, to an artist, to a thinker, in a state of deluded infatuation that made that being seem worthy of every kind of sacrifice and reverence – are we now ineluctably committed? Were we not indeed at that time deceiving ourselves? Was it not a hypothetical promise, made under the admittedly silent condition that the beings to which we consecrated ourselves were in reality what they appeared to us to be? Are we obliged to be faithful to our errors, even when we realize that

* *Republic*, X 604c

198

through this faithfulness we are injuring our higher self? – No, there exists no law, no obligation, of this kind; we *have* to become traitors, be unfaithful, again and again abandon our ideals. We cannot advance from one period of our life into the next without passing through these pains of betrayal and then continuing to suffer them. If we were to avoid these pains, would it not be necessary for us to guard ourselves against these ebullitions of our emotions? Would the world not then become too dreary, too spectral for us? Let us ask ourselves, rather, whether these pains are *necessarily* attendant on a change in our convictions, or whether they do not proceed from an *erroneous* evaluation and point of view. – Why do we admire him who is faithful to his convictions and despise him who changes them? I am afraid the answer must be: because everyone assumes that such a change can be motivated only by considerations of vulgar advantage or personal fear. That is to say, we believe at bottom that no one would change his convictions so long as they are advantageous to him, or at least so long as they do not do him any harm. If this is so, however, it is an ill witness as to the *intellectual* significance of all convictions. Let us for once examine how convictions originate, and let us see whether they are not greatly overestimated: what will emerge too is that a *change* in convictions has also invariably been assessed by a false criterion and that we have hitherto been accustomed to suffer too much when such a change has occurred.

630

Conviction is the belief that on some particular point of knowledge one is in possession of the unqualified truth. This belief thus presupposes that unqualified truths exist; likewise that perfect methods of attaining to them have been discovered; finally, that everyone who possesses convictions avails himself of these perfect methods. All three assertions demonstrate at once that the man of convictions is not the man of scientific thought; he stands before us in the age of theoretical innocence and is a child, however grown up he may be in other respects. But whole millennia have lived in these childish presuppositions and it is from them that mankind's mightiest sources of energy have flowed. Those countless numbers who have sacrificed themselves for their convictions thought they were doing so for unqualified truth. In this they were all wrong: probably a man has never yet sacrificed himself for truth; at least the dogmatic expression of his belief will have been unscientific or half-scientific. In reality one wanted to be in the right because one thought one *had* to be. To allow oneself to be deprived of one's belief perhaps meant calling one's eternal salvation into question. In a matter of such extreme importance as this the 'will' was only too audibly the prompter of the intellect. The presupposition of every believer of every kind was that he *could* not be refuted; if the counter-arguments proved very strong it was always left to him to defame reason itself and perhaps even to set up the '*credo quia absurdum est*'* as the banner of the extremest fanaticism. It is not conflict

* '*credo quia absurdum est*': I believe it because it is absurd

of opinions that has made history so violent but conflict of belief in opinions, that is to say conflict of convictions. But if all those who have
thought so highly of their convictions, brought to them sacrifices of every
kind, and have not spared honour, body or life in their service, had devoted only half their energy to investigating with what right they
adhered to this or that conviction, by what path they had arrived at it,
how peaceable a picture the history of mankind would present! How
much more knowledge there would be! We should have been spared all
the cruel scenes attending the persecution of heretics of every kind, and
for two reasons: firstly because the inquisitors would have conducted
their inquisition above all within themselves and emerged out of the presumptuousness of being the defenders of unqualified truth; then because
the heretics themselves would, after they had investigated them, have
ceased to accord any further credence to such ill-founded propositions as
the propositions of all religious sectarians and 'right believers' are.

631
From the ages in which men were accustomed to believe in possession of
unqualified truth there has come a profound *displeasure* with all sceptical
and relativistic positions in regard to any question of knowledge whatever; one usually prefers to surrender unconditionally to a conviction
harboured by people in authority (fathers, friends, teachers, princes) and
feels a kind of pang of conscience if one fails to do so. This tendency is
quite comprehensible, and its consequences give us no right to any violent reproaches against the way human reason has evolved. But gradually
the scientific spirit in men has to bring to maturity that virtue of *cautious
reserve*, that wise moderation which is more familiar in the domain of the
practical life than in the domain of the theoretical life and which, for
example, Goethe has depicted in Antonio as an object of animosity for all
Tassos,* that is to say for unscientific and at the same time inactive
natures. The man of conviction has in himself the right to fail to comprehend the man of cautious thinking, the theoretical Antonio; the scientific
man, on the other hand, has no right to blame him for that: he makes al-
lowances for him, and knows moreover that in the end the latter will
come to cleave to him, as Tasso finally does to Antonio.

632
He who has not passed through different convictions, but remains in the
belief in whose net he was first captured, is on account of this unchange-
ability under all circumstances a representative of *retarded* cultures; in
accordance with this lack of cultivation (which always presupposes culti-
vatability) he is a man hard, uncomprehending, unteachable, ungener-
ous, everlastingly suspicious and unheeding, who neglects no means of
constantly asserting his own point of view because he is quite incapable
of grasping that there are bound to be other points of view; on this
account he is perhaps a source of strength, and in cultures grown too
slack and flabby even salutary, but only because he arouses vigorous op-

* Antonio . . . Tassos: characters in Goethe's play *Torquato Tasso*

position: for in being compelled to struggle against him the more fragile structure of the new culture itself grows strong.

633

We are essentially the same men as those of the age of the Reformation: and how could it be otherwise? But that we no longer permit ourselves certain means of assisting our opinion to victory distinguishes us from that age and demonstrates that we belong to a higher culture. He who still, in the manner of the Reformation man, combats and crushes other opinions with defamations and outbursts of rage betrays clearly that he would have burned his opponents if he had lived in another age, and that he would have had recourse to all the methods of the Inquisition if he had been an opponent of the Reformation. This Inquisition was at that time reasonable, for it signified nothing other than the state of siege that had to be decreed for the whole domain of the Church and which, like every state of siege, justified the extremest measures, always under the presupposition (which we now no longer share with the men of those days) that in the Church one *possessed* the truth and was *obliged* to preserve it at the cost of any sacrifice for the salvation of mankind. Nowadays, however, we no longer so easily concede to anyone that he is in possession of the truth: the rigorous procedures of inquiry have propagated distrust and caution, so that anyone who advocates opinions with violent word and deed is felt to be an enemy of our present-day culture, or at least as one retarded. And the pathos of *possessing* truth does now in fact count for very little in comparison with that other, admittedly gentler and less noisy pathos of seeking truth that never wearies of learning and examining anew.

634

The methodical search for truth is, moreover, itself a product of those ages in which convictions were at war with one another. If the individual had not been concerned with *his* 'truth', that is to say with his being in the right, there would have been no methods of inquiry at all; but with the claims of different individuals to unqualified truth everlastingly in conflict with one another, men went on step by step to discover incontestable principles by which these claims could be tested and the contest decided. At first they appealed to authorities, later they criticized the ways and means through which the other's supposed truths had been discovered; in between there was a period when they drew the consequences of their opponent's proposition and perhaps found it harmful and productive of unhappiness: from which everyone was supposed to see that the opponent's conviction contained an error. *The personal strife of thinkers* at last rendered their procedures so acute that truths really could be discovered and the aberrations of earlier procedures exposed for all to see.

635

On the whole, the procedures of science are at least as important a product of inquiry as any other outcome: for the scientific spirit rests upon an insight into the procedures, and if these were lost all the other products of science together would not suffice to prevent a restoration of superstition and folly. There are people of intelligence who can *learn* as many of the facts of science as they like, but from their conversation, and especially from the hypotheses they put forward, you can tell that they lack the spirit of science: they have not that instinctive mistrust of devious thinking which, as a consequence of long practice, has put its roots down in the soul of every scientific man. For them it is enough to have discovered any hypothesis at all concerning any matter, then they are at once on fire for it and believe the whole thing is accomplished. To possess an opinion is to them the same thing as to become a fanatical adherent of it and henceforth to lay it to their heart as a conviction. When something is in need of explanation they grow impassioned for the first idea to enter their head that looks in any way like an explanation of it: a procedure productive of the evilest consequences, especially in the domain of politics. – It is for this reason that everyone now should have acquired a thorough knowledge of at least *one* science: then he would know what is meant by method and procedure and how vital it is to exercise the greatest circumspection. Women are especially in need of this advice: for they are at present the helpless victims of every hypothesis that appears, especially when it produces the impression of being intelligent, thrilling, animating, invigorating. On closer examination, indeed, one sees that by far the greater part of all educated people even now still desire from a thinker convictions and nothing but convictions, and that only a small minority want *certainty*. The former want to be violently carried away, so as themselves to experience an increase in strength; the latter few possess that objective interest that ignores personal advantage, even the increase in strength referred to. The former, vastly preponderant class is what the thinker has in view when he takes himself for a *genius*, and presents himself as a higher being possessing authority. Insofar as genius of every kind maintains the fire of convictions and awakens distrust of the modesty and circumspection of science, it is an enemy of truth, no matter how much it may believe itself to be truth's suitor.

636
There is, to be sure, a quite different species of genius, that of justice; and I cannot in any way persuade myself to regard it as lower than any kind of philosophical, political or artistic genius. It is the way of this kind of genius to avoid with hearty indignation everything that confuses and deceives us in our judgement of things; it is consequently an *opponent of convictions*, for it wants to give to each his own, whether the thing be dead or living, real or imaginary – and to that end it must have a clear knowledge of it; it therefore sets every thing in the best light and observes it carefully from all sides. In the end it will give to its opponent, blind or shortsighted 'conviction' (as men call it: – women call it 'faith'), what is due to conviction – for the sake of truth.

637

Opinions grow out of *passions; inertia of the spirit* lets them stiffen into *convictions*. – He, however, whose spirit is *free* and restlessly alive can prevent this stiffening through continual change, and even if he should be altogether a thinking snowball, he will have in his head, not opinions, but only certainties and precisely calculated probabilities. – But let us, who are compound creatures, now heated up by fire, now cooled down by the spirit, kneel down before justice as the only goddess we recognize over us. *The fire* in us usually makes us unjust and, from the viewpoint of that goddess, impure; in this condition we may never grasp her hand, never will the smile of her pleasure light upon us. We revere her as the veiled Isis of our lives; abashed, we offer up to her our pain as penance and sacrifice whenever the fire seeks to burn and consume us. It is *the spirit* that rescues us, so that we are not wholly reduced to ashes; it tears us away from the sacrificial altar of justice or encloses us in a coat of asbestos. Redeemed from the fire, driven now by the spirit, we advance from opinion to opinion, through one party after another, as noble *traitors* to all things that can in any way be betrayed – and yet we feel no sense of guilt.

638

The Wanderer. – He who has attained to only some degree of freedom of mind cannot feel other than a wanderer on the earth – though not as a traveller *to* a final destination: for this destination does not exist. But he will watch and observe and keep his eyes open to see what is really going on in the world; for this reason he may not let his heart adhere too firmly to any individual thing; within him too there must be something wandering that takes pleasure in change and transience. Such a man will, to be sure, experience bad nights, when he is tired and finds the gate of the town that should offer him rest closed against him; perhaps in addition the desert will, as in the Orient, reach right up to the gate, beasts of prey howl now farther off, now closer to, a strong wind arise, robbers depart with his beasts of burden. Then dreadful night may sink down upon the desert like a second desert, and his heart grow weary of wandering. When the morning sun then rises, burning like a god of wrath, and the gate of the town opens to him, perhaps he will behold in the faces of those who dwell there even more desert, dirt, deception, insecurity than lie outside the gate – and the day will be almost worse than the night. Thus it may be that the wanderer shall fare; but then, as recompense, there will come the joyful mornings of other days and climes, when he shall see, even before the light has broken, the Muses come dancing by him in the mist of the mountains, when afterwards, if he relaxes quietly beneath the trees in the equanimity of his soul at morning, good and bright things will be thrown down to him from their tops and leafy hiding-places, the gifts of all those free spirits who are at home in mountain, wood and solitude and who, like him, are, in their now joyful, now thoughtful way, wanderers and philosophers. Born out of the mysteries of dawn, they ponder on how, between the tenth and the twelfth stroke of the clock, the day could present a face so pure, so light-filled, so cheerful and transfigured: – they seek the *philosophy of the morning*.

AMONG FRIENDS

AN EPILOGUE

1

Fine to lie in quiet together,
Finer still to join in laughing –
Underneath a silken heaven
Lying back amid the grasses
Join with friends in cheerful laughing,
Showing our white teeth together.

Am I right? let's lie in quiet;
Am I wrong? let's join in laughing
And in being aggravating,
Aggravating, loudly laughing,
Till we reach the grave together.

Shall we do this, friends, again?
Amen! and *auf Wiedersehn*!

2

No excuses! No forgiving!
You who laugh and joy in living
Grant this book, with all its follies,
Ear and heart and open door!
Friends, believe me, all my folly's
Been a blessing heretofore!

What *I* seek, what *I* discover –
Has a book contained it ever?
Hail in me the guild of fools!
Learn what this fools-book's offence is:
Reason coming to its senses!

Shall we, friends, do this again?
Amen! and *auf Wiedersehn*!

VOLUME TWO

PREFACE

1

One should speak only when one may not stay silent; and then only of that which one has *overcome* – everything else is chatter, 'literature', lack of breeding. My writings speak *only* of my overcomings: 'I' am in them, together with everything that was inimical to me, *ego ipsissimus*, indeed, if a yet prouder expression be permitted, *ego ipsissimum*.* One will divine that I already have a great deal – beneath me . . . But it has always required time, recovery, distancing, before the desire awoke within me to skin, exploit, expose, 'exhibit' (or whatever one wants to call it) for the sake of knowledge something I had experienced and survived, some fact or fate of my life. To this extent, all my writings, with a single though admittedly substantial exception, are to be *dated back* – they always speak of something 'behind me' – : some, as with the first three *Untimely Meditations*, even to a period earlier than that in which I experienced and produced a book published before them (the *Birth of Tragedy* in the case mentioned: as a more subtle observer and comparer will be able to tell for himself). That angry outburst against the inflated Germanism, complacency and beggarly language of the aged David Strauss, the content of the first *Meditation*,† gave vent to feelings engendered long before when I had sat as a student in the midst of German culture and cultural philistinism (I make claim to be the father of the nowadays so much used and misused expression 'cultural philistine' –); and what I had to say against the 'historical sickness' I said as one who had slowly and toilsomely learned to recover from it and was in no way prepared to give up 'history' thereafter because he had once suffered from it. When, in the third *Untimely Meditation*, I then went on to give expression to my reverence for my first and only educator, the *great* Arthur Schopenhauer – I would now express it much more strongly, also more personally – I was, so far as my own development was concerned, already deep in the midst of moral scepticism and destructive analysis, *that is to say in the critique and likewise the intensifying of pessimism as understood hitherto*, and already 'believed in nothing any more', as the people puts it, not even in Schopenhauer: just at that time I produced an essay I have refrained from publishing, 'On Truth and Falsehood in an Extra-Moral Sense'. Even my festive victory address in honour of Richard Wagner on the occasion of his celebration of victory at Bayreuth in 1876 – Bayreuth signifies the greatest victory an artist has ever

---

* *ego ipsissimus*: my very own self; *ego ipsissimum*: my innermost self
† David Strauss (1800–74): German theologian an attack on whom forms the substance of the first of the *Untimely Meditations*

achieved – a work wearing the strongest *appearance* of being 'up to the minute', was in its background an act of homage and gratitude to a piece of my own past, to the fairest but also most perilous period of dead calm of my whole voyage . . . and in fact a liberation, a farewell. (Was Richard Wagner himself deceived as to this? I do not believe so. As long as one still loves one does not paint pictures like this; one does not yet 'meditate' on one's subject, one does not set oneself at a distance in the way a 'meditator' must. 'Even contemplation involves a secret *antagonism*, the antagonism involved in comparison' – it says on page forty-six* of the said essay itself, in a revealing and melancholy phrase perhaps intended for but few ears.) The composure needed to be *able* to speak of an inner solitude and self-denial extending over long intervening years first came to me with the book *Human, All Too Human*, to which this second foreword and intercession too is to be dedicated. As a book 'for free spirits', there reposes upon it something of the almost cheerful and inquisitive coldness of the psychologist who takes a host of painful things that lie *beneath* and *behind* him and identifies and as it were *impales* them with the point of a needle: – is it any wonder if, with such sharp-pointed and ticklish work, a certain amount of blood occasionally flows, if the psychologist engaged on it has blood on his fingers and not always only – on his fingers? . . .

2

The 'Assorted opinions and maxims' were, like 'The wanderer and his shadow', first published *singly* as continuations and appendices of the above-named human-all-too-human 'Book for free spirits': at the same time as a continuation and redoubling of a spiritual cure, namely of the *anti-romantic* self-treatment that my still healthy instinct had itself discovered and prescribed for me against a temporary attack of the most dangerous form of romanticism. May these same writings now, after six years of convalescence, prove acceptable *united* as the second volume of *Human, All Too Human*: perhaps taken together they will teach their precepts more powerfully and clearly – they are *precepts of health* that may be recommended to the more spiritual natures of the generation just coming up as a *disciplina voluntatis*. There speaks out of them a pessimist whose insights have often made him jump out of his skin but who has always known how to get back into it again, a pessimist, that is to say, well disposed *towards* pessimism – and thus in any event no longer a romantic: what? should a spirit who understands the serpent's prudent art of *changing his skin* not be permitted to read a lecture to our pessimists of today, who are one and all still in danger of romanticism? And at the very least to demonstrate to them how it is – *done*? . . .

3

– At that time it was indeed high time *to say farewell*: and I immediately received a confirmation of the fact. Richard Wagner, seemingly the all-conquering, actually a decaying, despairing romantic, suddenly sank

---

* p.223 of the Cambridge University Press edition of *Untimely Meditations*.

down helpless and shattered before the Christian cross...* Was there no German with eyes in his head, empathy in his conscience, for this dreadful spectacle? Was I the only one who – suffered from it? Enough, this unexpected event illumined for me like a flash of lightning the place I had left – and likewise gave me those subsequent horrors that he feels who he has passed through a terrible peril unawares. As I went on alone, I trembled; not long afterwards I was sick, more than sick, I was weary of the unending disappointment with everything we modern men have left to inspire us, of the energy, labour, hope, youth, love everywhere *dissipated*; weary with disgust at the femininity and ill-bred rapturousness of this romanticism, weary of the whole idealist pack of lies and softening of conscience that had here once again carried off the victory over one of the bravest; weary, last but not least, with the bitterness of a suspicion – that, after this disappointment, I was condemned to mistrust more profoundly, despise more profoundly, to be more profoundly alone than ever before. My *task* – where had it gone? What? was it now not as if my task had withdrawn from me, as though I would for a long time to come cease to have any right to it? How was I going to be able to endure this *greatest* of privations? – I began by *forbidding* myself, totally and on principle, all romantic music, that ambiguous, inflated, oppressive art that deprives the spirit of its severity and cheerfulness and lets rampant every kind of vague longing and greedy, spongy desire. '*Cave musicam*'† is to this day my advice to all who are man enough to insist on cleanliness in things of the spirit; such music unnerves, softens, feminizes, its 'eternal womanly' draws *us* – downwards! ... At that time I was first and foremost suspicious of and circumspect towards romantic music; and if I continued to harbour any hope at all for music it lay in the expectation that a musician might come who was sufficiently bold, subtle, malicious, southerly, superhealthy to confront that music and in an immortal fashion *take revenge* on it. –

4

Henceforth alone and sorely mistrustful of myself, I thus, and not without a sullen wrathfulness, took sides *against* myself and *for* everything painful and difficult precisely for *me*: – thus I again found my way to that courageous pessimism that is the antithesis of all romantic mendacity, and also, as it seems to me today, the way to 'myself', to *my* task. That concealed and imperious something for which we for long have no name until it finally proves to be our *task* – this tyrant in us takes a terrible retribution for every attempt we make to avoid or elude it, for every premature decision, for every association on equal terms with those with whom we do not belong, for every activity, however respectable, if it distracts us from our chief undertaking, even indeed for every virtue that would like to shield us from the severity of our own most personal

---

* Richard Wagner ... Christian cross: alludes to Wagner's last work, *Parsifal* (produced at Bayreuth in 1882).
† '*Cave musicam*': Beware music

responsibility. Illness is the answer every time we begin to doubt our right to *our* task – every time we begin to make things easier for ourselves. Strange and at the same time terrible! It is our *alleviations* for which we have to atone the most! And if we afterwards want to return to health, we have no choice: we have to burden ourselves *more heavily* than we have ever been burdened before . . .

5

– It was only then that I learned that solitary's speech that only the most silent and the most suffering understand: I spoke without witnesses, or rather in indifference to witnesses, so as not to suffer from staying silent, I spoke only of things that had nothing to do with me but did so as though they had something to do with me. It was then I learned the art of *appearing* cheerful, objective, inquisitive, above all healthy and malicious – and this, it seems to me, constitutes 'good taste' on the part of an invalid. A subtler eye and empathy will nonetheless not fail to see what perhaps constitutes the charm of this writing – that here a sufferer and self-denier speaks as though he were *not* a sufferer and self-denier. Here there is a *determination* to preserve an equilibrium and composure in the face of life and even a sense of gratitude towards it, here there rules a vigorous, proud, constantly watchful and sensitive will that has set itself the task of defending life *against* pain and of striking down all those inferences that pain, disappointment, ill-humour, solitude, and other swampgrounds usually cause to flourish like poisonous fungi. This perhaps offers to precisely our pessimists a signpost to their own self-testing? – for it was then that I acquired for myself the proposition: 'a sufferer has *no right* to pessimism because he suffers!', it was then that I conducted with myself a patient and tedious campaign against the unscientific basic tendency of that romantic pessimism to interpret and inflate individual personal experiences into universal judgements and, indeed, into condemnations of the world . . . in short, it was then that I turned my perspective *around*. Optimism, for the purpose of restoration, so that at some future time I could again have the *right* to be a pessimist – do you understand that? Just as a physician places his patient in a wholly strange environment so that he may be removed from his entire 'hitherto', from his cares, friends, letters, duties, stupidities and torments of memory and learn to reach out his hands and senses to new nourishment, a new sun, a new future, so I, as physician and patient in one, compelled myself to an opposite and unexplored *clime of the soul*, and especially to a curative journey into strange parts, into *strangeness* itself, to an inquisitiveness regarding every kind of strange thing . . . A protracted wandering around, seeking, changing followed from this, a repugnance towards all staying still, towards every blunt affirmation and denial; likewise a dietetic and discipline designed to make it as easy as possible for the spirit to run long distances, to fly to great heights, above all again and again to fly away. A *minimum* of life, in fact, an unchaining from all coarser desires, an independence in the midst of all kinds of unfavourable outward circumstances together with pride in being *able* to live surrounded by these unfavourable circumstances; a certain amount of cynicism, perhaps, a certain amount of 'barrel',* but just as surely a great deal of capricious happiness, capricious cheerfulness, a great deal of stillness, light, subtler folly, concealed enthusiasm – all this finally resulted in a great spiritual strengthening, an increasing joy and abundance of health. Life itself *rewards* us for our tough will to live, for the long war such as I then waged with myself against the pessimism of weariness with life, even for every attentive glance our gratitude accords to even the smallest, tenderest, most fleeting gift life gives us. Finally our reward is the *greatest* of life's gifts, perhaps the greatest thing it is able to give of any kind – we are given our *task* back. – –

6

– Shall my experience – the history of an illness and recovery, for a recovery was what eventuated – have been my personal experience alone? And only *my* 'human, all-too-human'? Today I would like to believe the reverse; again and again I feel sure that my travel books were not written solely for myself, as sometimes seems to be the case – . May I now, after six years of growing confidence, venture to send them off again? May I venture to commend them especially to the hearts and ears of those burdened with any kind of 'past' and have sufficient spirit left still to suffer from the *spirit* of their past too? Above all, however, to *you*, who have the hardest fate, you rare, most imperilled, most spiritual, most courageous men who have to be the *conscience* of the modern soul and as such have to possess its *knowledge*, and in whom all that exists today of sickness, poison and danger comes together – whose lot it is to have to be sicker than any other kind of individual because you are not *'only* individuals' ... whose comfort it is to know the way to a *new* health, and alas! to go along it, a health of tomorrow and the day after, you predestined and victorious men, you overcomers of your age, you healthiest and strongest men, you *good Europeans*! – –

7

– Finally, to reduce my opposition to *romantic pessimism*,† that is to say the pessimism of the renunciators, the failed and defeated, to a formula: there is a will to the tragic and to pessimism that is as much a sign of severity and of strength of intellect (taste, feeling, conscience). With this will in one's heart one has no fear of the fearful and questionable that characterizes all existence; one even seeks it out. Behind such a will there stands courage, pride, the longing for a *great* enemy. – This has been *my* pessimistic perspective from the beginning – a novel perspective, is it not? a perspective that even today is still novel and strange? To this very

---

* 'barrel': reference to Diogenes the Cynic (c. 400 to c. 325 BC), reputed to have lived in a barrel.

† Nietzsche's term 'romantic pessimism' circumscribes Schopenhauer's philosophy of the will as well as Wagner's music. In *The Gay Science*, section 370, it is set against Dionysian pessimism.

moment I continue to adhere to it and, if you will believe me, just as much *for* myself as, occasionally at least, *against* myself . . . Do you want me to prove this to you? But what else does this long preface – prove?

Sils-Maria, Oberengadin
September 1886

PART ONE

ASSORTED OPINIONS
AND MAXIMS

1

To the disappointed of philosophy – If you have hitherto believed that life was one of the highest value and now see yourselves disappointed, do you at once have to reduce it to the lowest possible price?

2

Spoiled. – It is possible to be spoiled even in regard to clarity of concepts: how repulsive one then finds it to traffic with the half-obscure, hazy, aspiring, portentous! How ludicrous and yet not at all cheering an effect is produced by their everlasting fluttering and snatching while being unable to fly or to capture!

3

The wooer of reality. – He who finally sees how long and how greatly he has been made a fool of embraces in defiance even the ugliest reality: so that, viewing the way of the world as a whole, the latter has at all times had the best of all wooers – for it is the best who have always been most thoroughly deceived.

4

Progress of free-spiritedness. – The difference between free-spiritedness as it used to be and as it is now cannot be made clearer than by recalling that proposition for the recognition and expression of which the previous century had to summon up all its intrepidity but which, judged from the present posture of knowledge, nonetheless sinks to being a piece of involuntary naivety – I mean Voltaire's proposition: *'croyez moi, mon ami, l'erreur aussi a son mérite'*.*

5

An original sin of philosophers. – Philosophers have at all times appropriated the propositions of the examiners of men (moralists) and *ruined* them, inasmuch as they have taken them for unqualified propositions and sought to demonstrate the absolute validity of what these moralists intended merely as approximate signposts or even as no more than truths possessing tenancy only for a decade – and through doing so thought to elevate themselves above the latter. Thus we find pieces of popular wisdom originating with the moralists employed to buttress Schopenhauer's celebrated doctrines of the primacy of the will over the intellect, of the unalterability of the character and of the negativity of pleasure – all of which are, in the sense in which he understands them, errors. Even

* *'croyez . . . mérite'*: believe me, my friend, error also has its merits.

215

the word 'will', which Schopenhauer remoulded as a common desig-
nation for many different human states and inserted into a gap in the
language – greatly to his own advantage insofar as he was a moralist,
since he was now at liberty to speak of the 'will' as Pascal had spoken of it
– even Schopenhauer's 'will' has, in the hands of its originator through
the philosopher's rage for generalization turned out to be a disaster for
science: for this will has been turned into a metaphor when it is asserted
that all things in nature possess will; finally, so that it can be pressed into
the service of all kinds of mystical mischief it has been misemployed
towards a false reification – and all the modish philosophers speak of it
and seem to know for certain that all things possess *one* will and, indeed,
are this one will (which, from the description they give of this all-one-will,
is as good as wanting to make God out to be the *stupid Devil*).

6
Against fantasists. – The fantasist denies reality to himself, the liar does so
only to others.

7
Hostile to light. – If we make it clear to someone that strictly speaking he is
never able to speak of truth but only of probability and degrees of probability, we usually discover from the unconcealed joy of one so instructed
how much men prefer the spiritual horizon to be fluctuating and how in
the depths of their soul they *hate* truth on account of its certainty. – Is the
reason that they are all secretly afraid that one day the light of truth will
be directed too brightly upon them? They want to signify something,
consequently no one must know too exactly what they *are*? Or is it merely
dread of a light brighter than their twilight, easily dazzled bat-souls are
unaccustomed to and which they must therefore hate?

8
Christian scepticism. – Christians today like to set up Pilate, with his
question 'What is truth?', as an advocate of Christ, so as to cast suspicion
on everything known or knowable and to erect the Cross against the
dreadful background of the impossibility of knowing.

9
'Law of nature' a superstition. – When you speak so rapturously of a conformity to law in nature you must either assume that all natural things
freely obey laws they themselves have imposed upon themselves – in
which case you are admiring the morality of nature – or you are entranced
by the idea of a creative mechanic who has made the most ingenious
clock, with living creatures upon it as decorations. – Necessity in nature
becomes more human and a last refuge of mythological dreaming
through the expression 'conformity to law'.

10
For〕... *to history*. – The veil-philosophers and world-obscurers, that is to
say all metaphysicians of finer or coarser grain, are seized with eye-, ear-

and toothache when they begin to suspect that the proposition 'The whole of philosophy is henceforth forfeit to history' is quite true. On account of the *pain* they feel they must be forgiven for throwing stones and dirt at him who speaks thus: the proposition itself, however, can thereby become dirty and unsightly for a time, and its effectiveness be diminished.

11

The pessimist of the intellect. – The truly free in spirit will also think freely regarding the spirit itself and will not dissemble over certain dreadful elements in its origin and tendency. On that account others will perhaps designate him the worst of the opponents of free-spiritedness and inflict on him the abusive title of 'pessimist of the intellect': which they will do because they are accustomed to call everyone, not by those strengths and virtues that distinguish him, but by that in him in which he most differs from them.

12

Knapsack of the metaphysicians. – Those who boast so mightily of the scientificality of their metaphysics should receive no answer; it is enough to pluck at the bundle which, with a certain degree of embarrassment, they keep concealed behind their back; if one succeeds in opening it, the products of that scientificality come to light, attended by their blushes: a dear little Lord God, a nice little immortality, perhaps a certain quantity of spiritualism, and in any event a whole tangled heap of 'wretched poor sinner' and Pharisee arrogance.

13

Knowledge occasionally harmful. – The utility of the unconditional search for the true is continually being demonstrated in so many ways that we are obliged to accept unconditionally the subtler and rarer harm the individual has to suffer as a consequence of it. We cannot prevent the chemist from occasionally poisoning or burning himself in the course of his experiments. – What applies to the chemist also applies to our entire culture: from which, by the way, it clearly emerges how much attention the latter has to pay to the provision of ointments to counter burning and to the constant availability of antidotes to poison.

14

Philistine's necessity. – The Philistine believes that what he needs most is a purple drape or turban of metaphysics, and will in no way allow these to be taken from him: and yet he would look less ludicrous without this finery.

15

Fanatics. – However much fanatics may bear themselves as judges (and not as the accused), all they have to say in favour of their gospel or their master is in fact said in their own self-defence: for it reminds them, involuntarily and at almost every moment, that they are exceptions that have to legitimise themselves.

16

Good things seduce one to life. – All good things are powerful stimulants to life, even a good book written against life.

17

Happiness of the historian. – 'When we hear ingenious metaphysicians and backworldsmen talk, we others may feel that we are the "poor in spirit", but we also feel that ours is the kingdom of Heaven of change, with spring and autumn, winter and summer, and that theirs is the backworld – with its gray, frosty, unending mist and shadow.' – Thus a man spoke to himself while walking in the morning sun: one in whom history again and again transforms not only his spirit but also his heart, and who, in contrast to the metaphysicians, is happy to harbour in himself, not 'an immortal soul', but *many mortal souls.*

18

Three kinds of thinker. – There are mineral springs that gush, those that flow, and those that trickle; and correspondingly three kinds of thinker. The laity evaluates them according to the volume of water, the true judge according to the content of the water, that is to say according to precisely that in them that is *not* water.

19

The picture of life. – The task of painting *the* picture of life, however often poets and philosophers may pose it, is nonetheless senseless: even under the hands of the greatest of painter-thinkers all that has ever eventuated is pictures and miniatures *out of one* life, namely their own – and nothing else is even possible. Something in course of becoming cannot be reflected as a firm and lasting image, as a 'the', in something else in course of becoming.

20

Truth will have no other gods beside it. – Belief in truth begins with doubt as to all truths believed in hitherto.

21

Where silence is demanded. – When one speaks of free-spiritedness as of a highly perilous wandering on glaciers and polar seas, those who do not wish to make this journey are offended, as though they had been reproached with timorousness and weak knees. A difficult thing we do not feel up to is not supposed even to be spoken of in our presence.

22

*Historia in nuce.** – The most serious parody I have ever heard is the following: 'in the beginning was the madness, and the madness *was*, by God!, and God (divine) was the madness'.

23

Incurable. – An idealist is incorrigible: if he is ejected from his Heaven he

---

* *Historia in nuce:* History in a nutshell

makes an ideal out of Hell. Let him be disillusioned and behold! – he will embrace this disillusionment just as fervently as a little while before he embraced his hopes. Insofar as his tendency is among the great incurable tendencies of human nature he is able to give rise to tragic destinies and afterwards become the subject of tragedies: for tragedies have to do with precisely what is incurable, ineluctable, inescapable in the fate and character of man.

24

Applause itself as a continuation of the play. – Radiant eyes and a benevolent smile is the kind of applause rendered to the whole great universal comedy of existence – but at the same time a comedy within the comedy aimed at seducing the other spectators to a *'plaudite amici'.**

25

Courage to be boring. – Whoever lacks the courage to allow himself and his work to be found boring is certainly not a spirit of the first rank, whether in the arts or the sciences. – A scoffer who was also, exceptionally, a thinker, might take a glance at the world and its history and add: 'God lacked this courage; he wanted to make all things too interesting, and he did so.'

26

From the thinker's innermost experience. – Nothing is more difficult for man than to apprehend a thing impersonally: I mean to see it as a thing, *not as a person*: one might question, indeed, whether it is at all possible for him to suspend the clockwork of his person-constructing, person-inventing drive even for a moment. He traffics even with *ideas*, though they be the most abstract, as if they were individuals with whom one has to struggle, to whom one was to ally oneself, whom one has to tend, protect and nourish. We have only to spy on ourselves at that moment when we hear or discover a proposition new to us. Perhaps it displeases us because of its defiant and autocratic bearing; we unconsciously ask ourselves whether we shall not set a counter-proposition as an enemy beside it, whether we can append to it a 'perhaps', a 'sometimes'; even the little word 'probably' does us good, because it breaks the personally burdensome tyranny of the unconditional. If, on the other hand, this new proposition approaches us in a milder shape, nice and tolerant, humble, and sinking as it were into the arms of contradiction, we try another way of testing our autocracy: what, can we not come to the assistance of this weak creature, stroke and feed it, give it strength and fullness, indeed truth and even unconditionality? Can we possibly be parental or knightly or pitying towards it? – Then again, we behold a judgement here and a judgement there, separated from one another, not regarding one another, making no impression one upon the other: and we are tickled by the thought of whether here a marriage might not be arranged, a *conclusion*

---

* *plaudite amici*: applaud, friends!

drawn, in the presentiment that, if a consequence should proceed from this conclusion, the honour of it will fall not only to the two married judgements but also to those who arranged the marriage. If, however, one can get hold of that idea neither by means of defiance and ill-will nor by means of good-will (if one holds it for *true* –), then one yields and pays it homage as a prince and leader, accords it a seat of honour and speaks of it with pomp and pride: for in *its* glitter one glitters too. Woe to him who seeks to darken it; unless it itself should one day become suspicious to us: – then, unwearying king-makers in the history of the spirit that we are, we hurl it from the throne and immediately raise its opponent in its place. Let one ponder this and then think on a little further: certainly no one will then speak of a 'drive to knowledge in and for itself'! – Why then does man prefer the true to the untrue in this *secret* struggle with idea-persons, in this usually hidden idea-marrying, idea-state-founding, idea-pedagogy, idea-tending of the sick and poor? For the same reason as he practises justice in traffic with real persons: now out of habit, heredity and training, *originally* because the true – as also the fair and just – is *more useful* and *more productive of honour* than the untrue. For in the realm of thought, *power* and *fame* are hard to maintain if erected on the basis of error or lies: the feeling that such a building could at some time or other fall down is *humiliating* to the self-conceit of its architect; he is ashamed of the fragility of his material and, because he takes *himself more seriously* than he does the rest of the world, wants to do nothing that is not *more enduring* than the rest of the world. It is as a consequence of his demand for truth that he embraces belief in personal immortality, that is to say the most arrogant and defiant idea that exists, united as it is with the hidden thought *'pereat mundus, dum ego salvus sim!'** His work has become for him his *ego*, he transforms himself into the intransitory, the all-defiant. It is his immeasurable pride which wants to employ only the finest, hardest stones for its work, that is to say truths or what it takes for truths. At all times *arrogance* has rightly been designated the 'vice of the intellectual' – yet without the motive power of this vice truth and the respect accorded it would be miserably accommodated on this earth. That we are *afraid* of our own ideas, concepts, words, but also *honour* ourselves in them and involuntarily ascribe to them the capacity to instruct, despise, praise and censure us, that we thus traffic with them as with free intelligent persons, with independent powers, as equals with equals – it is in this that the strange phenomenon I have called 'intellectual conscience' has its roots. – Thus here too something moral of the highest sort has blossomed out of a black root.

27
Obscurantists. – The essential element in the black art of obscurantism is not that it wants to darken individual understanding but that it wants to blacken our picture of the world, and *darken our idea of existence*. Darkening of the understanding is, to be sure, often the means that serves it to

* *'pereat . . . sim'*: let the world perish so long as I am safe.

thwart the enlightenment of the mind: sometimes, however, it employs the opposite means and seeks through the highest refinement of the intellect to induce a *satiation* with its fruits. Ingenious metaphysicians who prepare the way for scepticism, and through their excessive acuteness invite mistrust of acuteness, are excellent instruments in the hands of a more refined obscurantism. – Is it possible that even Kant can be used to this end? that he himself, indeed, according to his own notorious declaration, desired something of the kind, at any rate for a time: to open a path for *faith* by showing *knowledge* its limitations? – which, to be sure, he failed to do, just as little as did his successors on the wolf- and fox-paths of this most refined and dangerous obscurantism: the most dangerous of all, indeed, for here the black art appears in a veil of light.

28
By what kind of philosophy art is corrupted. – When the mists of a metaphysical-mystical philosophy succeed in rendering all aesthetic phenomena *opaque*, it follows that they are also *incapable of being evaluated* one against another, because each of them has become inexplicable. If, however, they are never again compared with one another for the purpose of evaluation, there at last arises a completely *uncritical frame of mind*, a blind toleration, but likewise a steady decline in the *enjoyment* of art (which is distinguished from the crude appeasement of a need only by a highly acute tasting and distinguishing). The more this enjoyment declines, however, the more the desire for art is transformed back to a vulgar hunger which the artist then seeks to satisfy with ever coarser fare.

29
In Gethsemane. – The most grievous thing the thinker can say to the artists is: 'What, could ye not *watch with me* one hour?'

30
At the loom. – The few who take pleasure in untying the knot of things and unravelling its threads are actively opposed by those many (for example all artists and women) who repeatedly try to tie it again, to entangle it and thus transform what is comprehended into the uncomprehended and, where possible, incomprehensible. Whatever else may eventuate from this – the resulting knots and ravelled threads are always bound to look a trifle dirty, because too many hands have been working and tugging at them.

31
In the desert of science. – To the man of science on his unassuming and laborious travels, which must often enough be journeys through the desert, there appear those glittering mirages called 'philosophical systems': with bewitching, deceptive power they show the solution of all enigmas and the freshest draught of the true water of life to be near at hand; his heart rejoices, and it seems to the weary traveller that his lips already touch the goal of all the perseverance and sorrows of the scientific

life, so that he involuntarily presses forward. There are other natures, to be sure, which stand still, as if bewildered by the fair illusion: the desert swallows them up and they are dead to science. Other natures again, which have often before experienced this subjective solace, may well grow exceedingly ill-humoured and curse the salty taste which these apparitions leave behind in the mouth and from which arises a raging thirst – without one's having been brought so much as a single step nearer to any kind of spring.

32

Alleged 'real reality'. – When he describes the various professions – e.g. that of the general, the silk-weaver, the seaman – the poet poses as *knowing* of these things to the very bottom; indeed, when it comes to the conflict of human actions and destinies he acts as though he had been present at the weaving of the whole nexus of the world; to this extent he is a deceiver. And he practises his deception only before those who *do not know* – and that is why his deception is successful: the latter commend him for his profound and genuine knowledge and in the end induce in him the delusion that he really does know these things as well as do the individuals he is describing, indeed as well as the great world-spider itself. Thus at last the deceiver becomes honest and believes in his own veracity. People of sensibility, indeed, even tell him to his face that he possesses a *higher* truth and veracity – for they are for a time tired of reality and accept the poetic dream as a beneficent relaxation and night for head and heart. What this dream shows them now seems to them more *valuable*, because, as remarked, they find it more beneficent: and men have always believed that that which seems more valuable is the truer and more real. Poets *conscious* of possessing this power deliberately set out to discredit that which is usually called reality and transform it into the uncertain, apparent, spurious, sinful, suffering, deceptive; they employ all the doubts that exist as to the limitations of knowledge, all the extravagances of scepticism, to spread a wrinkled veil of uncertainty over things: in order that after this darkening their sorcery and soul-magic shall be unhesitatingly taken for the path to 'true truth', to 'real reality'.

33

The desire to be just and the desire to be a judge. – Schopenhauer, whose great knowledgeability about the human and all-too-human, whose native sense of reality was not a little dimmed by the motley leopard-skin of his metaphysics (which one must first remove from him if one is to discover the real moralist genius beneath it) – Schopenhauer makes that striking distinction which is very much more justified than he really dared to admit to himself: 'the insight into the strict necessity of human actions is the boundary line which divides *philosophical* heads from *the others*'. This mighty insight, which from time to time he publicly avowed, he nonetheless counteracted in his own mind with that prejudice which he still had in common with moral men (*not* with the moralists) and which, quite innocuously and credulously, he expressed as: 'the ultimate and true elucidation of the inner nature of the whole of things must necessarily hang closely together with that of the ethical significance of human behaviour' – which is absolutely not 'necessary' but, on the contrary, has been rejected by precisely that proposition of the strict necessity of human actions, that is to say, the unconditional unfreedom and unaccountability of the will. Philosophical heads will thus distinguish themselves from the others through their unbelief in the metaphysical significance of morality: and that may establish a gulf between them of whose depth and unbridgeability the so much lamented gulf between the 'cultured' and the 'uncultured', as it now exists, gives hardly any idea. Many more back-doors, to be sure, which 'philosophical heads' have, like Schopenhauer himself, left open must be recognised as useless: *none* leads outside, into the air of free will: *every one* which has hitherto been slipped through reveals behind it every time a brazen wall of fate: we *are* in prison, we can only *dream* ourselves free, not make ourselves free. That this knowledge cannot for very much longer be resisted is indicated by the despairing and incredible postures and contortions of those who assail it, who still continue to wrestle with it. – This, approximately, is how they go on: 'What, is no man accountable? And is everything full of guilt and feeling of guilt? But someone or other has to be the sinner, if it is impossible and no longer permissible to accuse and to judge the individual, the poor wave in the necessary wave-play of becoming – very well: then let the wave-play itself, becoming, be the sinner: here is free will, here there can be accusing, condemning, atonement and expiation: then let *God be the sinner and man his redeemer*: then let world history be guilt, self-condemnation and suicide; thus will the offender become his own judge, the judge his own executioner.' – This *Christianity stood on its head* – for what else is it? – is the final lunge in the struggle of the theory of uncon-ditional morality with that of unconditional freedom – a horrible thing if it were anything *more* than a *logical grimace*, more than an ugly gesture on the part of the defeated idea – perhaps the death-throes of the despairing and salvation-thirsty heart to which madness whispers: 'Behold, thou art the lamb that beareth the sins of God.' – The error lies not only in the feel-ing 'I am accountable', but equally in that antithesis 'I am not, but some-body has to be.' – This is, in fact, not true: the philosopher thus has to say, as Christ did, 'judge not!' and the ultimate distinction between philo-sophical heads and the others would be that the former desire *to be just*, the others *to be a judge*.

34
Sacrifice. – Do you think that the mark of the moral action is sacrifice? – But reflect whether sacrifice is not present in *every* action that is done with deliberation, in the worst as in the best.

35
Against the examiners of morality. – To know the strength of a man's moral nature one has to know the best and the worst he is capable of in thought and deed. But to learn that is impossible.

36

Serpent's tooth. – We do not know whether or not we have a serpent's tooth until someone has set his heel on us. A woman or mother would say: until someone has set his heel on our darling, our child. – Our character is determined even more by the lack of certain experiences than by that which we experience.

37

Deception in love. – We forget a great deal of our own past and deliberately banish it from our minds: that is to say, we want the image of ourself that shines upon us out of the past to deceive us and flatter our self-conceit – we are engaged continually on this self-deception. – And do you think, you who speak so much of 'self-forgetfulness in love', of 'the merging of the ego in the other person', and laud it so highly, do you think this is anything essentially different? We shatter the mirror, impose ourself upon someone we admire, and then enjoy our ego's new image, even though we may call it by that other person's name – and this whole proceding is supposed *not* to be self-deception, *not* egoism! A strange delusion! – Those who conceal something of themselves *from themselves* and those who conceal themselves from themselves as a whole are, I think, alike in this, that they perpetrate a *robbery* in the treasure-house of knowledge: from which we can see against which transgression the injunction 'know thyself' is a warning.

38

To him who denies his vanity. – He who denies he possesses vanity usually possesses it in so brutal a form he instinctively shuts his eyes to it so as not to be obliged to despise himself.

39

Why the stupid are so often malicious. – When our head feels too weak to answer the objections of our opponent our heart answers by casting suspicion on the motives behind his objections.

40

The art of the moral exceptions. – An art that exhibits and glorifies the exceptional cases of morality – in which good becomes bad and the unjust just – should be listened to only rarely: just as we now and then buy something from the gipsies but do so in trepidation lest they should obtain much more from us than the purchase is worth.

41

Enjoyment and non-enjoyment of poisons. – The only decisive argument that has at all times prevented men from drinking a poison is not that it would kill them but that it tasted nasty.

42

The world without feeling of sin. – If only those deeds were done which engendered no bad conscience the human world would still look bad and villainous enough: but not as sickly and wretched as it does now. – There have at all times been sufficient bad men *without* a conscience: and many good and fine men lack the pleasurable sensation of the good conscience.

43
The conscientious. – It is more comfortable to follow one's conscience than one's reason: for it offers an excuse and alleviation if what we undertake miscarries – which is why there are always so many conscientious people and so few reasonable ones.

44
Opposite ways of avoiding embitterment. – To one kind of temperament it is useful to be able to expel its ill-humour in words: in speech it sweetens itself. Another temperament, however, attains to the height of its bitterness only through articulation: to this kind it is more advisable to have to swallow something down: compulsion to constrain themselves before enemies or superiors improves the character of such people and prevents them from growing too acrid and sour.

45
Not too seriously. – To get bed-sores is unpleasant, but it is not evidence against the validity of the cure that consigned one to bed. – Men who lived for long outside themselves and finally turned to the philosophical inner life know that the heart and the spirit can also get bed-sores. This is likewise no argument against the mode of life they have chosen as a whole, but it makes a few little exceptions and apparent relapses necessary.

46
The human 'thing in itself'. – The thing most vulnerable and yet the most unconquerable is human vanity: indeed, its strength increases, and can in the end become gigantic, through being wounded.

47
Farce of many of the industrious. – Through an excess of exertion they gain for themselves free time, and afterwards have no idea what to do with it except to count the hours until it has expired.

48
Having much joy. – He who has much joy in his life must be a good man: but he is perhaps not the cleverest, even though he has attained precisely that which the cleverest man strives after with all his cleverness.

49
In the mirror of nature. – Has a man not been fairly exactly described when one hears that he likes to wander between fields of tall yellow corn, that he prefers the colours of the woods and flowers in glowing and golden autumn because they intimate greater beauty than ever nature achieved, that he feels quite at home among great thick-leaved nut-trees as though among his blood relations, that in the mountains his greatest joy is to encounter those remote little lakes out of which solitude itself seems to gaze

up at him, that he loves that gray reposefulness of twilight mist that creeps up to the windows on autumn and early winter evenings and shuts out every soulless sound as though with velvet curtains, that he feels the unhewn rocks to be unwillingly mute witnesses to times primeval and has revered them from a child, and finally that the sea, with its rippling snake-skin and beast-of-prey beauty, is and remains alien to him? – Yes, *something* of this man has therewith been described, to be sure, but the mirror of nature says nothing of the fact that the same man, with all his idyllic sensibility (and not even 'in spite of it'), could be somewhat loveless, niggardly and conceited. Horace, who understood such things as this, placed the tenderest feeling for country life in the mouth and soul of a Roman *usurer*, in the celebrated *'beatus ille qui procul negotiis'.**

50

Power without victories. – The strongest knowledge (that of the total unfreedom of the human will) is nonetheless the poorest in successes: for it always has the strongest opponent, human vanity.

51

Joy and error. – One person has a beneficent effect on his friends involuntarily through his nature, another does so voluntarily through individual actions. Although the former *counts* as the higher, yet only the latter is associated with joy and a good conscience – the joy, that is, attending the performance of good works, which rests on belief in the voluntary nature of our good or wicked acts, that is to say on an error.

52

It is foolish to act unjustly. – An injustice we have perpetrated is much harder to bear than an injustice perpetrated against us (not precisely on moral grounds, *nota bene* –); the actor is always the actual sufferer, *if*, that is to say, he is accessible to pangs of conscience or has the insight to see that through his action he has armed society against him and isolated himself. That is why we ought, purely for the sake of our inner happiness, that is to say so as not to lose our ease and quite apart from the commandments of religion and morality, to guard ourselves against committing injustice even more than against experiencing injustice: for the latter carries with it the consolation of the good conscience and hope of revenge and of the sympathy and applause of the just, indeed of the whole of society, who live in fear of the evil-doer. – There are not a few who understand the unclean art of self-duping by means of which every unjust act they perform is reminted into an injustice done to them by others and the exceptional right of self-defence reserved to what they themselves have done: the purpose being greatly to ease the weight of their own burden.

53

Envy with or without mouthpiece. – Commonplace envy is accustomed to cackle as soon as the envied hen has laid an egg: it thereby relieves itself

* *'beatus . . . negotiis'*: happy the man who, far from business cares . . . (Horace: *Epodes* II).

and grows gentler. But there exists a yet deeper envy: in such a case it becomes deathly silent and, wishing that every mouth would now become sealed, grows ever angrier that precisely this is what is not happening. Silent envy grows in silence.

54
Anger as spy. – Anger empties out the soul and brings even its dregs to light. That is why, if we know no other way of discovering the truth of the matter, we must know how to put our acquaintances, our adherents and opponents, into a rage, so as to learn all that is really being thought and undertaken against us.

55
Defence presents greater moral difficulty than attack. – The real heroic deed and masterpiece of the good man lies not in his attacking the cause and continuing to love the person but in the much more difficult feat of *defending* his *own* cause without inflicting and desiring to inflict with bitter anguish the person attacked. The sword of attack is broad and honest, that of defence usually comes to a needle-point.

56
Honest about honesty. – He who is publicly honest about himself ends by priding himself a little on this honesty: for he knows only too well why he is honest – for the same reason another prefers appearance and dissimulation.

57
Hot coals. – Heaping hot coals on another's head is usually misunderstood and miscarries, because the other likewise knows he is in possession of the right and for his part has also thought of heaping coals.

58
Dangerous books. – Somebody remarked: 'I can tell by my own reaction to it that this book is harmful.' But let him only wait and perhaps one day he will admit to himself that this same book has done him a great service by bringing out the hidden sickness of his heart and making it visible. – Altered opinions do not alter a man's character (or do so very little); but they do illuminate individual aspects of the constellation of his personality which with a different constellation of opinions had hitherto remained dark and unrecognizable.

59
Feigned sympathy. – We feign sympathy when we want to *demonstrate* our superiority to feelings of hostility: but usually in vain. When we notice this we experience a sharp rise in those hostile sensations.

60
Open contradiction often reconciliatory. – When someone publicly declares that he differs from a celebrated party leader or teacher in a matter of dogma all the world believes that at that moment he must harbour a

dislike of him. But sometimes it is at precisely that moment that he ceases to dislike him: he ventures to set himself up beside him and is free of the torment of unspoken jealousy.

61

Seeing one's light shine. – In dark states of distress, sickness or debt we are glad when we perceive others still shining and they perceive in us the bright disk of the moon. In this indirect way we participate in our own capacity to illumine.

62

Joying with. – The serpent that stings us means to hurt us and rejoices as it does so; the lowest animal can imagine the *pain* of others. But to imagine the joy of others and to rejoice at it is the highest privilege of the highest animals, and among them it is accessible only to the choicest exemplars – thus a rare *humanum*:* so that there have been philosophers who have denied the existence of joying with.

63

Pregnancy after birth. – Those who have arrived at their works and deeds they know not how usually go about afterwards all the more pregnant with them: as though later to prove that these children are theirs and not those of chance.

64

Hard-hearted out of vanity. – Just as justice is so often a cloak for weakness, so fair thinking but weak men are sometimes led by ambition to dissimulation and deliberately behave unjustly and harshly so as to leave behind them an impression of strength.

65

Humiliation. – If anyone given a whole sack of advantages finds in it even one grain of humiliation he cannot help making the worst of a good bargain.

66

Extreme of Herostratism. – There could be Herostratuses who burned down their own temple where their images were venerated.

67

The diminutive world. – The circumstance that everything weak and in need of assistance speaks to our heart has produced in us the habit of characterizing everything that speaks to our heart with diminishing and enfeebling words – so as to *make* it seem weak and in need of assistance.

68

Pity's bad qualities. – Pity has a singular piece of impudence for its companion: for, because it is absolutely determined to render assistance, it experiences no perplexity as to either the means of cure or the nature and

---

* *humanum*: human quality

cause of the illness, but gaily sets about quackdoctoring at the health and reputation of its patient.

69

Importunity. – There also exists an importunate attitude towards works; and to associate oneself imitatively on a *Du* and *Du* basis with the most illustrious works of all time while still no more than a youth reveals a complete lack of shame. – Others are importunate only through ignorance: they do not know whom they are dealing with – as, for instance, is often the case with philologists old and young in regard to the works of the Greeks.

70

The will is ashamed of the intellect. – We draw up rational plans in all coldness to counter our emotions: then, however, we commit the crudest blunders with respect to these plans, because at the moment we are supposed to act we are often overcome with shame at the coldness and circumspection with which we conceived them. And what we then do is precisely the irrational – out of that species of defiant magnanimity that every emotion brings with it.

71

Why sceptics dislike morality. – He who takes his morality with high seriousness is angry with the sceptics in the domain of morals: for here where he is expending all his strength others are supposed to *stand astonished*, not inquire and express doubts. – Then there are natures in whom belief in morality is the last remnant of morality remaining to them; they likewise oppose the sceptics, if possible even more passionately.

72

Bashfulness. – All moralists are bashful, because they know that as soon as people notice their inclinations they will be taken for spies and traitors. Then they are in general aware of being feeble in action; for in the midst of what they are doing their attention is largely distracted from it by the motives behind it.

73

A danger to general morality. – People who are at the same time noble and honest accomplish the feat of deifying every piece of devilry their honesty concocts and for a time making the scales of moral judgement stand still.

74

Bitterest error. – It offends us beyond forgiving when we discover that where we were convinced we were loved we were in fact regarded only as a piece of household furniture and room decoration for the master of the house to exercise his vanity upon before his guests.

75

Love and duality. – What is love but understanding and rejoicing at the fact that another lives, feels and acts in a way different from and opposite to ours? If love is to bridge these antitheses through joy it may not deny or seek to abolish them. – Even self-love presupposes an unblendable duality (or multiplicity) in one person.

76
Interpreting by dreams. – That which we sometimes do not know or feel precisely while awake – whether we have a good or a bad conscience towards a particular person – the dream informs us of without any ambiguity.

77
Excess. – The mother of excess is not joy but joylessness.

78
Reward and punishment. – No one utters an accusation without there being present in his mind the thought of revenge and punishment – even when he accuses his fate, or indeed himself. – All complaining is accusation, all rejoicing is praise: whether we do the one or the other we are always making somebody responsible.

79
Twice unjust. – We sometimes promote truth through a twofold injustice, namely when, being unable to see both sides of a thing at the same time, we see and represent them one after the other, but in such a way that we always misjudge or deny the other side in the delusion that what we are seeing is the whole truth.

80
Mistrust. – Mistrust of oneself does not always go about shy and uncertain but sometimes as though mad with rage: it has got drunk so as not to tremble.

81
Philosophy of the parvenu. – If you want to become a person of standing you must hold your shadow too in honour.

82
Knowing how to wash oneself clean. – You must learn how to emerge out of unclean situations cleaner, and if necessary to wash yourself with dirty water.

83
Indulging oneself. – The more a person indulges himself the less others are willing to indulge him.

84
The innocent knave. – The path to every kind of vice and knavishness is a slow one proceeded along step by step. He who walks it is, by the time he reaches its end, wholly free of the insect-swarms of the bad conscience, and, although wholly infamous, he nonetheless goes in innocence.

85

Making plans. – To make plans and project designs brings with it many good sensations; and whoever had the strength to be nothing but a forger of plans his whole life long would be a very happy man: but he would occasionally have to take a rest from this activity by carrying out a plan – and then comes the vexation and the sobering up.

86

The eyes with which we behold the ideal. – Every proficient man is stuck in his proficiency and cannot see freely beyond it. If he were not very imperfect in other respects his virtue would prevent him from attaining to any spiritual and moral freedom at all. Our deficiencies are the eyes with which we behold the ideal.

87

False praise. – We afterwards feel far more pangs of conscience over false praise than we do over false blame, probably merely because with too great praise we have compromised our judgement far worse than with too great, even unjust blame.

88

How one dies is a matter of indifference. – The whole way in which a person thinks of death during the high tide of his life and strength bears, to be sure, very eloquent witness as to that which is called his character; but the hour of death itself, his bearing on the deathbed, hardly does so at all. The exhaustion of expiring existence, especially when old people die, the irregular or insignificant nourishment of the brain during this last period, the occasional very bad attacks of pain, the new and untried nature of the whole condition and all too often the coming and going of superstitious impressions and fears, as if dying were a very important thing and bridges of the most terrible description were here being crossed – all this does not *permit* us to employ dying as evidence as to the living. It is, moreover, not true that the dying are in general more *honest* than the living: almost everyone is, rather, tempted by the solemn bearing of the bystanders, the streams of tears and feeling held back or let flow, into a now conscious, now unconscious comedy of vanity. The seriousness with which every dying person is treated has certainly been for many a poor despised devil the most exquisite pleasure of his entire life and a kind of indemnification and part-payment for many deprivations.

89

Custom and its sacrifices. – The origin of custom lies in two ideas: 'the community is worth more than the individual' and 'an enduring advantage is to be preferred to a transient one'; from which it follows that the enduring advantage of the community is to take unconditional precedence over the advantage of the individual, especially over his momentary wellbeing but also over his enduring advantage and even over his survival. Even if the individual suffers from an arrangement which benefits the whole, even if he languishes under it, perishes by it – the custom must be maintained the sacrifice offered up. Such an attitude *originates*, however, only in those who are *not* the sacrifice – for the latter urges that, in his own case, the individual could be worth more than the many, likewise that present enjoyment, the moment in paradise, is perhaps to be rated higher than an insipid living-on in a painless condition of comfort. The philosophy of the sacrificial beast, however, is always noised abroad too late: and so we continue on with custom and *morality* [*Sittlichkeit*]: which latter is nothing other than simply a feeling for the whole content of those customs under which we live and have been raised – and raised, indeed, not as an individual, but as a member of the whole, as a cipher in a majority. – So it comes about that through his morality the individual *outvotes* himself.

90

The good and the good conscience. – Do you think that every good thing has always had a good conscience? – Science, which is certainly something good, entered the world without one, and quite destitute of pathos, but did so rather in secret, by crooked and indirect paths, hooded or masked like a criminal and at least always with the *feeling* of dealing in contraband. The good conscience has as a preliminary stage the bad conscience – the latter is not its opposite: for everything good was once new, consequently unfamiliar, contrary to custom, *immoral*, and gnawed at the heart of its fortunate inventor like a worm.

91

Success sanctifies the ends. – We do not hesitate to take the path to a virtue even when we are clearly aware that the motives which impel us – utility, personal comfort, fear, considerations of health, of fame or reputation – are nothing but egoism. These motives are called selfish and ignoble: very well, but when they incite us to a virtue – to, for example, renunciation, dutifulness, orderliness, thrift, measure and moderation – we pay heed to them, whatever they may be called! For if we attain what they summon us to, *achieved* virtue *ennobles* the remoter motives for our action through the pure air it lets us breathe and the psychical pleasure it communicates, and when we later perform these same actions it is no longer from the same coarse motives that led us to perform them before. – That is why education ought to *compel* to virtue, as well as it can and according to the nature of the pupil: virtue itself, as the sunshine and summer air of the soul, may then perform its own work on the soul and bestow maturity and sweetness upon it.

92

Affecters of Christianity, not Christians. – Just look at your Christianity! – To *irritate* men you praise 'God and his saints'; and when, conversely, you desire to *praise* men you go to such lengths that you must irritate God and his saints. – I wish you would at least learn Christian manners, since you are so greatly wanting in the politeness of the Christian heart.

93

Natural features of the pious and the impious. – A wholly pious man must be an object of reverence to us: but so must a man wholly permeated with a sincere impiety. If with men of the latter sort we are as though in the proximity of high mountains where the mightiest streams have their origin, with the pious we are as though among succulent, wide-shadowed, restful trees.

94

Judicial murders. – The two greatest judicial murders in world history are, not to mince words, disguised and well disguised suicides. In both cases the victim *wanted* to die; in both cases he employed the hand of human injustice to drive the sword into his own breast.

95

'Love' – The subtlest artifice which Christianity has over the other religions is a word: it spoke of *love*. Thus it became the *lyrical* religion (whereas in their two other creations the Semites have given the world heroic-epic religions). There is in the word love something so ambiguous and suggestive, something which speaks to the memory and to future hope, that even the meanest intelligence and the coldest heart still feels something of the lustre of this word. The shrewdest woman and the commonest man think when they hear it of the relatively least selfish moments of their whole life, even if Eros has paid them only a passing visit; and those countless numbers who *never experience* love, of parents, or children, or lovers, especially however the men and women of sublimated sexuality, have made their find in Christianity.

96

Realized Christianity. – Even within Christianity there exists an Epicurean point-of-view: it proceeds from the idea that God could demand of man, his creature and likeness, only that which it is *possible* for the latter to accomplish, and that Christian virtue and perfection must therefore be achievable and frequently achieved. Now, the *belief* that we *love* our enemy, for example – even when it is only belief, fancy, and in no way a psychological reality (is not love, that is to say) – undoubtedly makes us *happy* so long as it really is believed (why? as to that the psychologist and the Christian will, to be sure, think differently). And thus *earthly life* may, through the belief, I mean the fancy, that one has fulfilled not only the demand to love one's enemy but all other Christian demands as well, and has really appropriated and incorporated divine perfection according to the commandment 'be ye perfect, as your Father in Heaven is perfect', in fact become a *life of bliss.* Error is thus able to make Christ's *promise* come true.

97

On the future of Christianity. – As to the disappearance of Christianity, and as to which regions it will fade most slowly in, one can allow oneself a conjecture when one considers on what *grounds* and *where* Protestantism took root so impetuously. As is well known, it promised to do the same things as the old church did but to do them much cheaper: no expensive masses for the soul, pilgrimages, priestly pomp and luxury; it spread especially among the northerly nations, which were not so deeply rooted in the symbolism and love of forms of the old church as were those of the south: for with the latter a much stronger religious paganism continued to live on in Christianity, while in the north Christianity signified a breach with and antithesis of the old native religion and was from the beginning a matter more for the head than for the senses, though for precisely that reason also more fanatical and defiant in times of peril. If the uprooting of Christianity begins in the *head* then it is obvious where it will first start to disappear: in precisely the place, that is to say, where it will also defend itself most strenuously. Elsewhere it will bend but not break, be stripped of its leaves but put forth new leaves in their place – because there it is the *senses* and not the head that have taken its side. It is the senses, however, that entertain the belief that even meeting the cost of the church, high though it is, is nonetheless a cheaper and more comfortable arrangement than existing under a strict regime of work and payment would be: for what price does one not place upon leisure (or lazing about half the time) once one has become accustomed to it! The senses raise against a dechristianized world the objection that too much work would have to be done in it, and the yield of leisure would be too small: they take the side of the occult, that is to say – they prefer to let God work for them (*oremus nos, deus laboret!*).*

98

Honesty and play-acting among unbelievers. – There exists no book that expresses so candidly or contains such an abundance of that which does everybody good once in a while – the joyful enthusiasm, ready for any sacrifice, which we feel when we believe in and behold *our* 'truth' – than does the book that speaks of Christ: a perspicacious man can learn from it all the expedients by which a book can be made into a universal book, a friend of everyone, and especially that master expedient of representing everything as having already been discovered, with nothing still on the way and as yet uncertain. All influential books try to leave behind this kind of impression: the impression that the widest spiritual and psychical horizon has here been circumscribed and that every star visible now or in the future will have to revolve around the sun that shines here. – Must it therefore not be the case that the causes that make such books as this influential will render every *purely scientific* book poor in influence? Is the latter not condemned to live a lowly existence among the lowly, and finally to be crucified, never to rise again? Are all honest men of science not 'poor in spirit' by comparison with that which religious men proclaim of their 'knowledge', of their 'holy' spirit? Can any religion demand more renunciation, draw the egoistic more inexorably out of themselves, than science does? – – Thus and in similar ways, and in any event with a cer-

---

* *oremus ... laboret!*: let *us* pray, let God labour!

tain amount of play-acting, may *we* speak if we have to defend ourselves before believers; for it is hardly possible to conduct a defence without employing some degree of play-acting. Among ourselves, however, we must speak more honestly: here we may employ a freedom which, in their own interests, everyone is not permitted even to understand. Away, therefore, with the monk's cowl of renunciation! with the humble mien! Much more and much better: that is how our truth sounds! If science were not united with the *joy* of knowledge and the *utility* of what is known, what interest would we have in science? If a little faith, hope and charity did not lead our soul towards knowledge, what else would draw us to science? And if the ego does indeed have no place in science, the happy, inventive ego, even that honest and industrious ego already mentioned, has a very considerable place in the republic of scientific men. Respect, the pleasure of those we wish well or revere, sometimes fame and a modest personal immortality are the achievable rewards of this depersonalization, not to speak of lesser objectives and remunerations, even though it is on their account that most have sworn and continue to swear allegiance to the laws of that republic and of science in general. If we had not remained to some extent *unscientific* men what meaning could science possibly have for us? Taken as a whole and expressed without qualification: *to a purely cognitive being knowledge would be a matter of indifference.* – What distinguishes us from the pious and the believers is not the quality but the quantity of belief and piety; we are contented with less. But if the former should challenge us: then be contented and appear to be contented! – then we might easily reply: 'We are, indeed, not among the least contented. You, however, if your belief makes you blessed then appear to be blessed! Your faces have always been more injurious to your belief than our objections have! If those glad tidings of your Bible were written in your faces you would not need to insist so obstinately on the authority of that book: your works, your actions ought continually to render the Bible superfluous, through you a new Bible ought to be continually in course of creation! As things are, however, all your apologies for Christianity have their roots in your lack of Christianity; with your defence plea you inscribe your own bill of indictment. But if you should wish to emerge out of this insufficiency of Christianity, then ponder the experience of two millennia: which, clothed in the modesty of a question, speaks thus: "if Christ really intended to redeem the world, must he not be said to have failed?"'

99
The poet as signpost to the future. – That poetic power available to men of today which is not used up in the depiction of life ought to be dedicated, not so much to the representation of the contemporary world or to the re-animation and imaginative reconstruction of the past, but to signposting the future: – not, though, as if the poet could, like a fabulous economist, figuratively anticipate the kind of conditions nations and societies would prosper better under and how they could then be brought about. What

he will do, rather, is emulate the artists of earlier times who imaginatively developed the existing images of the gods and *imaginatively develop* a fair image of man; he will scent out those cases in which, in the *midst* of our modern world and reality and without any artificial withdrawal from or warding off of this world, the great and beautiful soul is still possible, still able to embody itself in the harmonious and well-proportioned and thus acquire visibility, duration and the status of a model, and in so doing through the excitation of envy and emulation help to create the future. The poems of such poets will be distinguished by the fact that they appear to be secluded and secured against the fire and breath of the *passions*: the incorrigible error, the shattering of the entire human instrument, mocking laughter and gnashing of teeth, and everything tragic and comic in the old customary sense will be experienced as a tedious, archaisizing coarsening of the human image when confronted with his new art. Strength, goodness, mildness, purity and an involuntary inborn moderation in the characters and their actions: a level ground which it is repose and joy to the feet to walk upon: countenances and events mirroring a luminous sky: knowledge and art blended to a new unity: the spirit dwelling together with its sister, the soul, without presumptuousness or jealousy and evoking from what divides them not impatience and contention but a graceful seriousness: – all this would make up the general and all-embracing golden ground upon which alone the tender *distinctions* between the different embodied ideals would then constitute the actual *painting* – that of the ever increasing elevation of man. – Many a path to this poetry of the future starts out from *Goethe*: but it requires good pathfinders and above all a much greater power than present-day poets – that is to say the innocuous depicters of the semi-animal and of immaturity and abnormality confused with force and naturalness – possess.

100

The muse as Penthesilea.* – 'Rather perish than be a woman who does not *charm.*' When once the Muse thinks like that the end of her art is again in sight. But its termination can be tragic as well as comic.

101

Detour to the beautiful. – If the beautiful is at the same time the gladdening – and the Muses once sang that it is – then the utilitarian is the frequently necessary *detour to the beautiful*: it can rightly repulse the shortsighted censure of those men who cleave to the moment, are unwilling to wait and think to attain to every good thing without a detour.

102

An excuse for many a fault. – The ceaseless desire to create on the part of the artist, together with his ceaseless observation of the world outside him, prevent him from becoming better and more beautiful as a person, that is to say from creating *himself* – except, that is, if his self-respect is suf-

* Penthesilea: in Greek mythology, an Amazonian queen killed by Achilles in the Trojan war.

ficiently great to compel him to exhibit himself before others as being as great and beautiful as his works increasingly are. In any event, he possesses only a fixed quantity of strength: that of it which he expends upon *himself* – how could he at the same time expend it on his *work*? – and the reverse.

103

Satisfying the best. – If one has 'satisfied the best of one's age' with one's art, this is an indication that one *will not satisfy* the best of the next age with it: one will 'live to all future ages', to be sure – the applause of the best will ensure one's fame.

104

Of one substance. – If we are of one substance with a book or a work of art we are quite convinced it must be excellent, and we are offended if others find it ugly, over-spiced or inflated.

105

Language and feeling. – That language is not given us for the communication of *feeling* is demonstrated by the fact that all simple men are ashamed to seek words for their profounder excitations: these find expression only in actions, and even here the man blushes if the other appears to divine their motives. Among poets, to whom the gods have in general denied this sense of shame, the nobler are nonetheless inclined to be monosyllabic in the language of feeling and give evidence of acting under constraint: while the actual poets of feeling are in practical life mostly quite shameless.

106

Error regarding privation. – He who has not long disaccustomed himself to an art but is still at home in it has not the remotest notion *how little* one is deprived of when one lives without this art.

107

Three-quarter strength. – If a work is to make an impression of health its originator must expend at most three-quarters of his strength on it. If, on the contrary, he has gone to the limit of his capacity, the tension in the work produces in its audience a feeling of agitation and distress. All good things have something easygoing about them and lie like cows in the meadow.

108

Turning away hunger. – To the hungry man delicate food is as good as but no better than coarse: thus the more pretentious artist will never think of inviting the hungry to his repast.

109

Living without art and wine. – Works of art are like wine: it is better if one has need of neither, keeps to water and, through one's own inner fire and sweetness of soul, again and again transforms the water into wine on one's own account.

110

The robber-genius. – The robber-genius in the arts, who knows how to deceive even discriminating spirits, originates when anyone has from his youth on naively regarded every good thing not expressly the legal property of some particular person as free for all to plunder. Now, all the good things of past ages and masters lie freely about, hedged round and guarded by the reverential awe of the few who know them: by virtue of the lack of this feeling in him, the robber-genius is able to bid these few defiance and to accumulate for himself an abundance of riches that itself evokes reverence and awe in its turn.

111

To the poets of the great cities. – In the gardens of contemporary poetry one notices that they stand too close to the sewers of the great cities: the scent of flowers is blended with something that betrays nausea and putridity. – I ask in sorrow: when you want to baptise some fair and innocent sensation, do you, you poets, always have to call on dirt and witticisms to be the godfathers? Do you absolutely need to set a comical devils-cap on the head of your noble goddess? But why do you feel this need, this compulsion? – Precisely because you dwell too close to the sewers.

112

Of the salt of speech. – No one has yet explained why the Greek writers made so thrifty a use of the means of expression available to them in such unheard-of strength and abundance that every book that comes after them seems by comparison lurid, glaring and exaggerated. – One understands that the use of salt is more sparing both in the icy regions near the North Pole and in the hottest countries, but that the dwellers of the coasts and plains in the more temperate zones use it most liberally. Is it not likely that, since their intellect was colder and clearer but their passions very much more tropical than ours, the Greeks would have had less need of salt and spices than we have?

113

The most liberated writer. – How, in a book for free spirits, should there be no mention of Laurence Sterne,* whom Goethe honoured as the most liberated spirit of his century! Let us content ourselves here simply with calling him the most liberated spirit of all time, in comparison with whom all others seem stiff, square, intolerant and boorishly direct. What is to be praised in him is not the closed and transparent but the 'endless melody': if with this expression we may designate an artistic style in which the fixed form is constantly being broken up, displaced, transposed back into indefiniteness, so that it signifies one thing and at the same time another. Sterne is the great master of *ambiguity* – this word taken in a far wider sense than is usually done when it is accorded only a sexual signification. The reader who demands to know exactly what Sterne really thinks of a thing, whether he is making a serious or a laughing face, must be given

* Laurence Sterne (1713–68): English writer, the author of *Tristram Shandy.*

up for lost: for he knows how to encompass both in a *single* facial expression; he likewise knows how, and even wants to be in the right and in the wrong at the same time, to knot together profundity and farce. His digressions are at the same time continuations and further developments of the story; his aphorisms are at the same time an expression of an attitude of irony towards all sententiousness, his antipathy to seriousness is united with a tendency to be unable to regard anything merely superficially. Thus he produces in the right reader a feeling of uncertainty as to whether one is walking, standing or lying: a feeling, that is, closely related to floating. He, the supplest of authors, communicates something of this suppleness to his reader. Indeed, Sterne unintentionally reverses these roles, and is sometimes as much reader as author; his book resembles a play within a play, an audience observed by another audience. One has to surrender unconditionally to Sterne's caprices – always in the expectation, however, that one will not regret doing so. – It is strange and instructive to see how as great a writer as Diderot* adopted this universal ambiguity of Sterne's: though he did so, of course, ambiguously – and thus truly in accord with the Sternean humour. Was he, in his *Jacques le fataliste*, imitating Sterne, or was he mocking and parodying him? – it is impossible finally to decide: and perhaps precisely this was Diderot's intention. It is precisely this dubiety that makes the French *unjust* to one of their greatest masters (who can challenge comparison with any other of any time): for the French are too serious for humour, and especially for this taking of humour humorously. – Is it necessary to add that, of all great writers, Sterne is the worst model, the author who ought least to be imitated, or that even Diderot had to pay for the risk he took? That which good French writers, and before them certain Greeks and Romans, wanted and were able to do in prose is precisely the opposite of what Sterne wants and is able to do: for, as the masterly exception, he raises himself above that which all artists in writing demand of themselves: discipline, compactness, simplicity, restraint in motion and deportment. – Unhappily, Sterne the man seems to have been only too closely related to Sterne the writer: his squirrel-soul leaped restlessly from branch to branch; he was familiar with everything from the sublime to the rascally; he had sat everywhere, and always with the same shamelessly watering eyes and play of sensibility on his features. If language does not start back at such a juxtaposition, he possessed a hard-hearted good-naturedness; and in the enjoyment of a baroque, indeed depraved imagination he almost exhibited the bashful charm of innocence. Such an ambiguousness become flesh and soul, such a free-spiritedness in every fibre and muscle of the body, have as he possessed these qualities perhaps been possessed by no other man.

114

Select reality. – Just as the good prose-writer employs only words that

---

* Denis Diderot (1713–84): French essayist and dramatist; a leading spirit of the Enlightenment.

belong to common speech, but by no means all the words that belong to it
– this is precisely how select or high style originates – so the good poet of
the future will depict *only reality* and completely ignore all those fantastic,
superstitious, half-mendacious, faded subjects upon which earlier poets
demonstrated their powers. Only reality, but by no means every reality! –
he will depict a select reality!

115

Degenerate varieties of art. – Beside the genuine species of art, those of great
repose and those of great motion, there exist degenerate varieties – art in
search of repose and excited and agitated art: both would like their weakness to be taken for strength and that they themselves should be mistaken for the genuine species.

116

No colours for painting the hero. – Poets and artists who really belong to the
present love to lay their colours on to a background flickering in red,
green, grey and gold, on to the background of *nervous sensuality*: in this
the children of this century are skilled. The disadvantage of it – if one
beholds these paintings with eyes other than those of this century – is
that when they paint their grandest figures they seem to have something
flickering, trembling, giddy about them: so that one simply cannot credit
them with heroic deeds, but at the most with boastful misdeeds posing as
heroism.

117

Overladen. – The florid style in art is the consequence of a poverty of
organizing power in the face of a superabundance of means and ends. –
In the earliest stages of art we sometimes find the exact opposite.

118

*Pulchrum est paucorum hominum.** – History and experience tell us that the
monstrosity which secretly rouses the imagination and bears it beyond
actuality and the everyday is *older* and of more abundant growth than the
beautiful and the cult of beauty in art – and that if the sense for the beautiful grows dim it at once breaks exuberantly out again. It seems that the
great majority of men have greater need of it than they do of the beautiful:
no doubt because it contains a stronger narcotic.

119

Origins of the taste for works of art. – If we think of the original germs of the
artistic sense and ask ourselves what different kinds of pleasure are
evoked by the firstlings of art, for example among savage peoples, we discover first of all the pleasure of *understanding* what another *means*; here art
is a kind of solving of a riddle that procures for the solver enjoyment of
his own quick perspecuity. – Then, the rudest work of art calls to mind
that which *has been* pleasurable in actual experience and to this extent produces present pleasure, for example whenever the artist has depicted a

* *Pulchrum . . . hominum*: Beauty is for the few.

hunt, a victory, a wedding. – Again, what is represented can arouse, move, enflame the auditor, for example through the glorification of revenge or danger. Here the pleasure lies in the arousal as such, in the victory over boredom. – Even recollection of the unpleasurable, insofar as it has been overcome, or insofar as it makes us ourselves interesting to the auditor as a subject of art (as when a minstrel describes the misfortunes of an intrepid seafarer), can produce great pleasure, which pleasure is then attributed to art. – That pleasure which arises at the sight of anything regular and symmetrical in lines, points, rhythms, is already of a more refined sort; for a certain similarity in appearance evokes the feeling for everything orderly and regular in life which alone we have, after all, to thank for all our wellbeing: in the cult of symmetry we thus unconsciously honour regularity and proportion as the source of our happiness hitherto; pleasure is a kind of prayer of thanksgiving. Only when we have become to some extent satiated with this last-mentioned pleasure does there arise the even subtler feeling that enjoyment might also lie in breaking through the orderly and symmetrical; when, for example, it seems enticing to seek the rational in the apparently irrational: whereby this feeling is then, as a kind of reading of aesthetic riddles, revealed as a higher species of the pleasure in art referred to first of all. – Whoever continues on in this train of thought will realize what *kind of hypotheses* for the explanation of aesthetic phenomena are here being avoided on principle.

120

Not too close. – It is a disadvantage for good ideas if they follow upon one another too quickly; they get in one another's way. – That is why the greatest artists and writers have always made abundant use of the mediocre.

121

Coarseness and weakness. – Artists of all ages have made the discovery that a certain strength lies in *coarseness*, and that many who would no doubt like to be coarse are unable to be so; they have likewise discovered that many kinds of *weakness* make a strong impression on the feelings. From these discoveries there have been derived not a few artifices and surrogates which even the greatest and most conscientious artists have found it hard wholly to abstain from.

122

Good memory. – Many a man fails to become a thinker only because his memory is too good.

123

Making hungry instead of stilling hunger. – Great artists believe that through their art they have taken a soul entirely into their possession and filled it utterly: in truth, and often to their painful disappointment, this soul has only been rendered all the more spacious and unfillable, so that now ten greater artists could plunge into its depths without satisfying it.

124

Artist's fear. – The fear that the figures they create will not produce the appearance of *being alive* can mislead artists of declining taste into constructing them in such a way that they behave as though *mad*: just as, on the other hand, the same fear induced the Greek artists of the first dawn to bestow even on the dying and the gravely injured that smile which they knew to be the liveliest indication of life – quite unconcerned at what such people on the edge of life would look like in reality.

125

The circle must be closed. – He who has followed a philosophy or a species of art to the end of its course and then around the end will grasp from his inner experience why the masters and teachers who came afterwards turned away from it, often with an expression of deprecation. For, though the circle has to be circumscribed, the individual, even the greatest, sits firmly on his point of the periphery with an inexorable expression of obstinacy, as though the circle ought never to be closed.

126

Art of the past and the soul of the present. – Because every art becomes capable of expressing states of soul with ever increasing suppleness and refinement, with greater and greater passion and intensity, later masters spoiled by these means of expression feel a sense of discomfort in the presence of works of art of earlier ages, as though what was wrong with the ancients was merely that they lacked these means of expressing their souls clearly, or perhaps even were missing only a few technical accomplishments; and they think they have to put things right here – for they believe in the equality, indeed in the complete unity of souls. In truth, however, the soul of this master himself was a different soul, *greater* perhaps, but in any case colder and still averse to what we find stimulating and lively: moderation, symmetry, contempt for the joyful and pleasing, an unconscious astringency and morning chilliness, an avoidance of passion as though it will prove the ruin of art – this is what constituted the mind and morality of the older masters, and they selected and breathed life into their means of expression, not by chance but of necessity, in accordance with the same morality. – But does this insight mean we have to deny those who come later the right to reanimate the works of earlier times with their own souls? No, for it is only if we bestow upon them our soul that they can continue to live: it is only *our* blood that constrains them to speak to *us*. A truly 'historical' rendition would be ghostly speech before ghosts. – We honour the great artists of the past less through that unfruitful awe which allows every word, every note, to lie where it has been put than we do through active endeavours to help them to come repeatedly to life again. – To be sure, if we were to imagine Beethoven suddenly returning and hearing one of his works rendered in the animated and nervous manner for which our masters of performance are celebrated, he would probably for a long time stay dumb, undecided whether to raise his hand in a blessing or a curse, but at length say perhaps: 'Well, yes! That is neither I nor not-I but some third thing – and if it is not exactly *right*, it is nonetheless right in its own way. But you had better take care what you're doing, since it's you who have to listen to it – and, as our Schiller says, the living are always in the right. So *be* in the right and let me depart again.'

127

Against the censurers of brevity. – Something said briefly can be the fruit of much long thought: but the reader who is a novice in this field, and has as yet reflected on it not at all, sees in everything said briefly something embryonic, not without censuring the author for having served him up such immature and unripened fare.

128

Against the shortsighted. – Do you think this work must be fragmentary because I give it to you (and have to give it to you) in fragments?

129

Readers of maxims. – The worst readers of maxims are the friends of their author when they are exercised to trace the general observation back to the particular event to which the maxim owes its origin: for through this prying they render all the author's efforts null and void, so that, instead of philosophical instruction, all they receive (and all they deserve to receive) is the satisfaction of a vulgar curiosity.

130

Reader's ill breeding. – Two kinds of ill breeding exhibited by the reader towards the author are to praise his second book at the expense of his first (or the reverse) and at the same time to demand that the author should be grateful to him.

131

The seditious in the history of art. – If we follow the history of an art, that of Greek rhetoric for instance, as we proceed from master to master and behold the ever increasing care expended on obedience to all the ancient rules and self-limitations and to those added subsequently, we are aware of a painful tension in ourselves: we grasp that the bow *has* to break and that the so-called inorganic composition bedecked and masked with the most marvellous means of expression – the baroque style of Asia, that is to say – was sooner or later a necessity and almost an *act of charity.*

132

To the great men of art. – That enthusiasm for a cause which you, great men, bear into the world *cripples* the reason of many others. To know this is humbling. But the enthusiast wears his hump with pride and joy: to this extent you have the consolation of knowing that through you the amount of happiness in the world is *increased.*

133

Those with no aesthetic conscience. – The actual fanatics of an artistic faction are those completely inartistic natures who have not penetrated even the elements of artistic theory or practice but are moved in the strongest way by all the *elemental* effects of an art. For them there is no such thing as an aesthetic conscience – and therefore nothing to hold them back from fanaticism.

134

How modern music is supposed to make the soul move. – The artistic objective pursued by modern music in what is now, in a strong but nonetheless obscure phrase, designated 'endless melody' can be made clear by imagining one is going into the sea, gradually relinquishing a firm tread on the bottom and finally surrendering unconditionally to the watery element: one is supposed to *swim*. Earlier music constrained one – with a delicate or solemn or fiery movement back and forth, faster and slower – to *dance*: in pursuit of which the needful preservation of orderly measure compelled the soul of the listener to a continual *self-possession*: it was upon the reflection of the cooler air produced by this self-possession and the warm breath of musical enthusiasm that the charm of this music rested. – Richard Wagner desired a different kind of *movement of the soul*: one related, as aforesaid, to swimming and floating. Perhaps this is the most essential of his innovations. The celebrated means he employs, appropriate to this desire and sprung from it – 'endless melody' – endeavours to break up all mathematical symmetry of tempo and force and sometimes even to mock it; and he is abundantly inventive in the production of effects which to the ear of earlier times sound like rhythmic paradoxes and blasphemies. What he fears is petrifaction, crystallization, the transition of music into the architectonic – and thus with a two-four rhythm he will juxtapose a three-four rhythm, often introduce bars in five-four and seven-four rhythm, immediately repeat a phrase but expanded to two or three times its original length. A complacent imitation of such an art as this can be a great danger to music: close beside such an over-ripeness of the feeling for rhythm there has always lain in wait the brutalization and decay of rhythm itself. This danger is especially great when such music leans more and more on a wholly naturalistic art of acting and language of gesture uninfluenced and uncontrolled by any higher plastic art: for such an art and language possesses in itself no limit or proportion, and is thus unable to communicate limit and proportion to that element that adheres to it, the *all too feminine* nature of music.

135

Poet and reality. – When a poet is not *in love with* reality his muse will consequently not be reality, and she will then bear him hollow-eyed and fragile-limbed children.

136

Means and ends. – In art the end does not sanctify the means: but sacred means can here sanctify the end.

137

The worst readers. – The worst readers are those who behave like plundering troops: they take away a few things they can use, dirty and confound the remainder, and revile the whole.

138

Marks of the good writer. – Good writers have two things in common: they prefer to be understood rather than admired; and they do not write for knowing and over-acute readers.

139

The mixed genres. – The mixed genres in art bear witness to the mistrust their originators felt towards their own powers; they sought assistants, advocates, hiding-places – for example, the poet who calls on philosophy for aid, the composer who calls on the drama, the thinker who calls on rhetoric.

140

Shutting his mouth. – When his work opens its mouth, the author has to shut his.

141

Insignia of rank. – All poets and writers enamoured of the superlative want to do more than they can.

142

Cold books. – The good thinker counts on readers who appreciate the happiness that lies in good thinking: so that a book distinguished by coldness and sobriety can, when viewed through the right eyes, appear as though played about by the sunshine of spiritual cheerfulness and as a true comfort for the soul.

143

Artifices of the ponderous. – The ponderous thinker usually chooses garrulousness or pomposity for his allies: through the former he thinks to appropriate to himself flexibility and fleetness of foot, through the latter he makes it appear as though his quality were a product of free will, of artistic intention, with the object of achieving the dignity that slowness of movement promotes.

144

On the baroque style. – He who knows that, as a thinker or writer, he was not born or educated for dialectics and the analysis of ideas will involuntarily reach for the *rhetorical* and *dramatic*: for in the long run what he is concerned with is to make himself *understood* and thereby to acquire force, its being a matter of indifference to him whether he conducts sensibilities towards him along a level path or overtakes them unawares – either as a shepherd or a brigand. This applies to the plastic as much as to the poetic arts; where the feeling of a lack of dialectics or inadequacy in expressive or narrative ability, combined with an over-abundant, pressing formal impulsion, gives rise to that stylistic genre called the *baroque*. – Only the ill-instructed and presumptuous, by the way, will at once feel a sense of contempt at the sound of this word. The baroque style originates whenever any great art starts to fade, whenever the demands in the art of classic expression grow too great, as a natural event which one may well behold with sorrow – for it means night is coming – but at the same time with admiration for the substitute arts of expression and narration peculiar to it. To these belong the choice of material and themes of the highest dramatic tension of a kind that make the heart tremble even without the assistance of art because they bring Heaven and Hell all too close: then the eloquence of strong emotions and gestures, of the sublime and ugly, of great masses, of quantity as such – as was already proclaimed in the case of Michelangelo, the father or grandfather of the artists of the Italian baroque – : the glow of twilight, transfiguration or conflagration upon such strongly constructed forms: in addition a continual daring experimentation in new methods and objectives, strongly underlined by the artist for other artists, while the laity are obliged to think they behold a constant involuntary overflowing of all the cornucopias of a primeval art born of nature: all these qualities in which this style possesses its greatness are not possible, not permitted, in the earlier, preclassical and classical epochs of a species of art: such delicacies hang long on the tree as forbidden fruit. – It is precisely now, when *music* is entering this last epoch, that we can get to know the phenomenon of the baroque style in a particularly splendid form and learn a great deal about earlier ages through comparison with it: for a baroque style has already existed many times from the age of the Greeks onwards – in poetry, rhetoric, in prose style, in sculpture, as well as in architecture – and, although this style has always lacked the highest nobility and an innocent, unconscious, victorious perfection, it has nonetheless satisfied many of the best and most serious of its age: which is why I called it presumptuous straightaway to judge it with contempt; even though he whose receptivity for the purer and greater style is not blunted by it may count himself lucky.

145
Value of honest books. – Honest books make the reader honest, at least to the extent that they lure out his antipathy and hatred, which cunning prudence otherwise knows best how to conceal. Against a book, however, we may let ourselves go, however much we may restrain ourselves when it comes to men.

146
How art creates a faction. – Individual beautiful passages, an exciting overall effect and a rapturous mood at the end – *this much* in a work of art is accessible even to most of the laity: and in an artistic period in which it is desired to *draw over* the great mass of the laity to the side of the artist – to create a faction, that is to say, perhaps for the purpose of preserving art

as such – the creator will do well to give no *more* than this: otherwise he will squander his strength in areas where no one will thank him for it. For to do what remains undone – to imitate nature in its *organic* growth and shaping – would in any case be to scatter seed on water.

147

Growing great to the prejudice of history. – Every later master who leads the taste of those who appreciate art on to *his* path involuntarily gives rise to a reordering and new assessment of the earlier masters and their works: that in them which is attuned and related to *him*, which constitutes a fore-taste and annunciation of *him*, henceforth counts as that which is really *significant* in them and in their works – a fruit in which there is usually concealed a great worm of *error*.

148

How an age is lured to art. – If, with the aid of all the magical tricks of artist and thinker, one teaches men to feel reverence for their deficiencies, their spiritual poverty, their senseless infatuations and passions – and this can be done – if one exhibits only the sublime aspect of crime and madness, only what is moving and heart-touching in the weakness of the will-less and blindly devoted – this too has happened often enough – : then one has acquired the means of imbuing even a wholly inartistic and unphilo-sophical age with a *love* of philosophy and art (and especially of artists and philosophers as persons) and, under unfavourable circumstances, perhaps the sole means of preserving the existence of such delicate and imperilled creatures.

149

Joy and criticism. – Criticism, onesided and unjust criticism just as much as judicious, gives him who practises it so much pleasure that the world owes a debt of gratitude to every work, every action that invites a great deal of criticism from a great many people: for behind it it drags a glitter-ing tail of joy, wit, self-admiration, pride, instruction and intention to do better. – The god of joy created the bad and mediocre for the same reason he created the good.

150

Beyond his limits. – When an artist wants to be more than an artist, for example the moral awakener of his nation, the retribution is that he ends up enamoured of a moral monster – and the muse laughs at him: for this goddess, otherwise so good-hearted, can grow malicious out of jealousy. Consider Milton and Klopstock.*

151

Glass eye. – A gift for *moral* subjects, characters, motives directed upon the beautiful soul of a work of art is sometimes only the glass eye which the artist who *lacks* a beautiful soul inserts into himself: the consequence can

* Friedrich Gottlieb Klopstock (1724–1803): German poet, often alluded to in his lifetime as the 'German Milton'.

be, though rarely is, that this eye at length becomes living nature, even if somewhat jaundiced nature – the usual consequence, however, is that all the world thinks it sees nature where there is only glass.

152
Writing and the desire for victory. – Writing ought always to advertise a victory – an overcoming of *oneself* which has to be communicated for the benefit of others; but there are dyspeptic authors who write only when they cannot digest something, indeed when it is still stuck in their teeth: they involuntarily seek to transfer their own annoyance to the reader and in this way exercise power over him: that is to say, they too desire victory, but over others.

153
'A good book takes its time.' – Every good book tastes astringent when it appears: it possesses the fault of newness. In addition it is harmed by its living author if he is celebrated and much is known about him: for all the world is accustomed to confound the author with his work. What there is of spirit, sweetness and goodness in the latter can evolve only over the years, under the care of growing, then established, finally traditional reverence. Many hours must pass over it, many a spider have spun her web on it. Good readers continually improve a book and good opponents clarify it.

154
Extravagance as an artistic method. – Artists well understand what it means to employ extravagance as an artistic method so as to produce an impression of wealth. It is among the innocent subterfuges for seducing the soul which artists have to be skilled in: for in their world, in which what is aimed at is appearance, the methods by which appearance is produced do not necessarily have to be genuine.

155
The hidden barrel-organ. – Geniuses know better than the talented how to hide the barrel-organ, by virtue of their more abundant drapery; but at bottom they too can do no more than repeat their same old tunes.

156
The name on the title-page. – That the name of the author should be inscribed on the book is now customary and almost a duty; yet it is one of the main reasons books produce so little effect. For if they are good, then, as the quintessence of the personality of their authors, they are worth more than these; but as soon as the author announces himself on the title-page, the reader at once dilutes the quintessence again with the personality, indeed with what is most personal, and thus thwarts the object of the book. It is the intellect's ambition to seem no longer to belong to an individual.

157
Sharpest criticism. – We criticize a man or a book most sharply when we sketch out their ideal.

158

Few and without love. – Every good book is written for a definite reader and those like him, and for just this reason will be viewed unfavourably by all other readers, the great majority: which is why its reputation rests on a narrow basis and can be erected only slowly. – The mediocre and bad book is so because it tries to please many and does please them.

159

Music and sickness. – The danger inherent in modern music lies in the fact that it sets the chalice of joy and grandeur so seductively to our lips and with such a show of moral ecstasy that even the noble and self-controlled always drink from it a drop too much. This minimal intemperance, continually repeated, can however eventuate in a profounder convulsion and undermining of spiritual health than any coarser excess is able to bring about: so that there is in the end nothing for it but one day to flee the nymph's grotto* and to make one's way through the perils of the sea to foggy Ithaca and to the arms of a simpler and more human wife.

160

Advantage for the opponent. – A book full of spirit communicates some of it to its opponents too.

161

Youth and criticism. – To criticize a book means to a young person no more than to repulse every single productive idea it contains and to defend oneself against it tooth and claw. A youth lives in a condition of perpetual self-defence against everything new that he cannot love wholesale, and in this condition perpetrates a superfluous crime against it as often as ever he can.

162

Effect of quantity. – The greatest paradox in the history of poetry lies in the fact that in everything in which the old poets possess their greatness one can be a barbarian, that is to say erroneous and deformed from head to toe, and yet still be the greatest of poets. For such is the case with Shakespeare, who, when compared with Sophocles, resembles a mine full of an immeasurable quantity of gold, lead and rubble, while the latter is not merely gold but gold in so noble a form its value as metal almost comes to be forgotten. But quantity raised to the highest pitch *has the effect* of quality. That fact benefits Shakespeare.

163

All beginnings are dangerous. – The poet has the choice of either raising the feelings from one step to the next and thus eventually raising them very high – or attempting an assault on them and pulling on the bellrope with all his force from the very beginning. Both courses have their dangers: in the former instance his listeners may perhaps desert him out of boredom, in the latter out of fear.

* Nymph's grotto: reference to Odysseus' seduction by and stay with the nymph Calypso.

164

In favour of critics. – Insects sting, not out of malice, but because they too want to live: likewise our critics; they want, not to hurt us, but to take our blood.

165

Maxims and their outcome. – When a maxim straightaway impresses them with its simple truth, the inexperienced always believe it to be old and familiar, and they look askance at its author as though he has desired to steal for himself what is common property: whereas they take pleasure in spiced-up half-truths and make this fact known to the author. The latter knows how to evaluate such a hint and has no difficulty in divining from it where he has succeeded and where failed.

166

Desire for victory. – An artist who in all he undertakes exceeds his powers will nonetheless at last draw the crowd along with him through the spectacle of a mighty struggle he affords: for success is accorded not only to victory but sometimes to the desire for victory too.

167

Sibi scribere.* – The sensible author writes for no other posterity than his own, that is to say for his old age, so that then too he will be able to take pleasure in himself.

168

In praise of the maxim. – A good maxim is too hard for the teeth of time and whole millennia cannot consume it, even though it serves to nourish every age: it is thus the great paradox of literature, the imperishable in the midst of change, the food that is always in season, like salt – though, unlike salt, it never loses its savour.

169

Artistic need of the second rank. – The people no doubt possesses something that might be called an artistic need, but it is small and cheap to satisfy. The refuse of art is at bottom all that is required: we should honestly admit that to ourselves. Just consider, for instance, the kind of songs and tunes the most vigorous, soundest and most naive strata of our populace nowadays take true delight in, dwell among shepherds, cowherds, farmers, huntsmen, soldiers, seamen, and then supply yourself with an answer. And in the small town, in precisely the homes that are the seat of those civic virtues inherited from of old, do they not love, indeed dote on, the very worst music in any way produced today? Whoever talks of a profound need for art, of an unfulfilled desire for art, on the part of the people *as it is*, is either raving or lying. Be honest! Nowadays it is only in *exceptional men* that there exists an artistic need of an *exalted kind* – because art as such is again in decline and the powers and expectations of men

---

* *Sibi scribere*: To write for oneself.

have for a time been directed at other things. – In addition, that is to say apart from the people, there does indeed still exist a broader, more extensive artistic need in the higher and highest strata of society, but it is of the *second rank*. Here something like a seriously intentioned artistic community is possible: but just look at what elements it consists of! They are, generally speaking, the more refined discontented unable to take any real pleasure in themselves: the cultivated who have not become sufficiently free to do without the consolations of religion and yet find its oil insufficiently sweet-scented: the half-noble who are too weak to correct the one fundamental mistake of their life or the harmful inclinations of their character through a heroic conversion or abstinence: the richly gifted who think themselves too fine for modest useful activities and are too indolent for a serious, self-sacrificing labour: the girl who does not know how to create for herself a satisfying circle of duties: the woman who has tied herself to a frivolous or mischievous marriage and knows she is not tied to it tightly enough: the scholar, physician, merchant, official who became one too soon and whose nature has as a whole never been given free rein, and who pays for this by performing his duties efficiently but with a worm in his heart: finally, all the imperfect and defective artists – it is these who *now* still possess a true artistic need! And what is it they really desire of art? That it shall scare away their discontent, boredom and uneasy conscience for moments or hours at a time and if possible magnify the errors of their life and character into errors of world-destiny – being in this very different from the Greeks, to whom their art was an outflowing and overflowing of their own healthiness and wellbeing and who loved to view their perfection *repeated* outside themselves: – self-enjoyment was what led them to art, whereas what leads our contemporaries to it is – self-disgust.

170

The Germans in the theatre. – The real theatrical talent among the Germans has been Kotzebue;* he and his Germans, those of the higher as well as those of middle-class society, necessarily belonged together, and his contemporaries could have said of him in all seriousness: 'in him we live and move and have our being'. Here there was nothing forced, imaginary, only half enjoyed: what he desired and could do was comprehended; to the present day, indeed, *genuine* theatrical success on the German stage is in the possession of the admitted or unadmitted inheritors of Kotzebue's methods and effects, especially wherever comedy is still to some extent flourishing; from which it appears that much of the German character of that time still lives on, particularly away from the great cities. Good-natured, intemperate in small pleasures, eager for tears, with the desire to be allowed to throw off an inborn, dutiful sobriety at least in the theatre and here to practise a smiling, indeed laughing tolerance, confusing goodness with pity and mingling them together – for such is the

---

* Kotzebue: August Friedrich von Kotzebue (1761–1819), the most prolific and popular German dramatist of his time.

essence of German sentimentality – delighted with a fair, magnanimous action, for the rest subservient towards those above, envious towards one another, and yet in the depths of them self-satisfied – that is how they were, that is how he was. – The second theatrical talent was Schiller: he discovered a class of auditors who had previously not come into consideration; he found them among the immature, in German youths and girls. With his works he came out to meet their higher, nobler, stormier, even if vague impulses, their pleasure in the jangle of moral expressions (which tends to fade in the thirties), and by virtue of the passionateness and thirst for taking sides that characterizes this age-group achieved a success that gradually produced a favourable impression on those of maturer age too: in general, Schiller *rejuvenated* the Germans. – Goethe stood above the Germans in every respect and still stands above them: he will never belong to them. How could a people ever be equal to Goethean *spirituality* in *wellbeing and well-wishing*! Just as Beethoven composed music above the heads of the Germans, just as Schopenhauer philosophized above the heads of the Germans, so Goethe wrote his *Tasso*, his *Iphigenie*, above the heads of the Germans. His following was composed of a *very small* band of the most highly cultivated people, educated by antiquity, life and travels, and grown beyond the confines of the merely German: – he himself did not desire it otherwise. – When the romantics then established their cult of Goethe, whose aim they were well aware of; when their astonishing accomplishment in tasting everything passed over to the pupils of Hegel, the actual educators of the Germans of this century; when awakening national ambition also came to benefit the fame of German poets, and the actual standard applied by the people, which is whether they can *honestly* say they *enjoy* something, was inexorably subordinated to the judgement of individuals and to that national ambition – that is to say, when one began to feel *compelled* to enjoy – then there arose that mendaciousness and spuriousness in German culture which felt ashamed of Kotzebue, which put Sophocles, Calderón and even Goethe's continuation of *Faust* on the stage, and which on account of its furred tongue and congested stomach in the end no longer knows what it likes and what it finds boring. – Blessed are those who possess taste, even though it be bad taste! – And not only blessed: one can be wise, too, only by virtue of this quality; which is why the Greeks, who were very subtle in such things, designated the wise man with a word that signifies the *man of taste*, and called wisdom, artistic and practical as well as theoretical and intellectual, simply 'taste' (*sophia*).

171
Music as the late fruit of every culture. – Of all the arts that grow up on a particular cultural soil under particular social and political conditions, music makes its appearance *last*, in the autumn and deliquescence of the culture to which it belongs: at a time when the first signs and harbingers of a new spring are as a rule already perceptible; sometimes, indeed, music resounds into a new and astonished world like the language of an age that

has vanished and arrives too late. It was only in the art of the musicians of the Netherlands that the soul of the Christian Middle Ages found its full resonance: their tonal architecture is the posthumous but genuine and equal sister of the Gothic. It was only in the music of Handel that there sounded the best that the soul of Luther and his like contained, the mighty Jewish-heroic impulse that created the whole Reformation movement. It was only Mozart who gave forth the age of Louis the Fourteenth and the art of Racine and Claude Lorraine* in *ringing* gold. It was only in the music of Beethoven and Rossini that the eighteenth century sang itself out: the century of enthusiasm, of shattered ideals and of fleeting happiness. So that a friend of delicate metaphors might say that all truly meaningful music is swan-song. – Music is thus *not* a universal language for all ages, as has so often been claimed for it, but accords precisely with a measure of time, warmth and sensibility that a quite distinct individual culture, limited as to area and duration, bears within it as an inner law: the music of Palestrina would be wholly inaccessible to a Greek, and conversely – what would Palestrina hear in the music of Rossini? – Perhaps our latest German music too, dominant and thirsting for dominance though it is, will in a short time cease to be understood: for it arose from a culture that is going speedily downhill; its soil is that period of reaction and recuperation in which a certain *catholicity of feeling* together with a joy in everything *primevally national* came into flower and exuded a mingled odour over Europe: both of which directions of sensibility, comprehended in their greatest intensity and pursued to their farthest limits, finally became audible in the art of Wagner. Wagner's appropriation of the old Germanic sagas, his ennobling disposing of the strange gods and heroes contained in them – who are actually sovereign beasts of prey with occasional impulses to thoughtfulness, magnanimity and world-weariness – the reanimation of these figures, to whom he added the Christian-medieval thirst for ecstatic sensuality and asceticism, this entire Wagnerian giving and taking in regard to subject-matter, souls, forms and words, would also be clearly expressed in the *spirit of his music* if, in common with all music, it were able to speak of itself with complete unambiguity: this spirit wages the *ultimate* war of reaction against the spirit of the Enlightenment wafted across from the preceding century into this, likewise against the supra-national ideas of French revolutionary enthusiasm and English-American sobriety in the reconstruction of state and society. – But is it not evident that these spheres of ideas and feelings – here seemingly still repressed by Wagner himself and by his adherents – have long since regained the upper hand, and that this late musical protest against them sounds mostly into ears that prefer to hear other and antithetical tones? So that this wonderful and elevated art will one day quite suddenly become incomprehensible and covered in forgetfulness and cobwebs. – One must not allow oneself to be misled as to this state of affairs by the fleeting fluctuations that appear as a reaction within reaction, as a temporary sinking of the wave-crest in the midst of the total

* Claude Lorraine: adoptive name of Claude Gellée (1600–82): French landscape painter

movement; thus it may be that the subtler after-effects of this decade of national wars, ultramontane martyrdom* and socialist uneasiness may assist the above-named art to a sudden radiance of glory – without, however, therewith supplying it with a guarantee of 'having a future', let alone of possessing *the future*. – It lies in the nature of music that the fruits of its great cultural vintages grow unpalatable more quickly and are more speedily ruined than the fruits of the plastic arts, let alone those that have ripened on the tree of knowledge: for of all the products of the human artistic sense *ideas* are the most enduring and durable.

172

Poets no longer teachers. – Strange though it may sound to our age, there were once poets and artists whose souls were beyond the passions and their raptures and convulsions and who therefore took pleasure in purer materials, worthier men, more delicate combinations and resolutions. If today's great artists are mostly unchainers of the will and for that reason under certain circumstances liberators of life, those earlier artists were tamers of the will, transformers of animals, creators of men, and in general sculptors and remodellers of life: whereas the fame of those of today may lie in unharnessing, unfettering, destroying. – The older Greeks demanded of the poet that he should be a teacher of adults: but how embarrassed a poet would be now if this was demanded of him – he who was no good teacher of himself and thus himself failed to become a fine poem, a fair statue, but at best as it were the modest, attractive ruins of a temple, though at the same time a cave of desires, overgrown with flowers, thistles and poisonous weeds, and dwelt in or haunted by snakes, reptiles, birds and spiders – an object inspiring sad reflections on why the noblest and most precious must nowadays grow up straightway as a ruin without any past or future perfection.

173

Looking before and after. – An art such as *issues forth* from Homer, Sophocles, Theocritus,† Calderón, Racine, Goethe, as the *surplus* of a wise and harmonious conduct of life – this is the art we finally learn to reach out for when we ourselves have grown wiser and more harmonious: not that barbaric if enthralling spluttering out of hot and motley things from a chaotic, unruly soul which as youths we in earlier years understood to be art. It goes without saying, however, that during certain periods of life an art of high tension, excitation, repugnance for the regulated, monotonous, simple and logical, is a necessary requirement that artists *have* to meet if the soul is during this period not to discharge itself in other directions through mischief and improprieties of all kinds. Thus youth, as it usually is, full, fermenting, plagued by nothing *more* than by boredom, needs this art of thrilling disorder – women who lack a soul-fulfilling

---

* Ultramontane martyrdom: ultramontanism was a term used to refer to the Catholic movements that upheld papal supremacy, in France, Germany and the Netherlands in the seventeenth and eighteenth centuries
† Theocritus (c. 310 to 250 BC): Greek poet.

occupation also need it. Their longing for a contentment that knows no change, a happiness without delirium and stupefaction, will be kindled all the more vehemently.

174
Against the art of works of art. – Art is above and before all supposed to *beautify* life, thus make *us* ourselves endurable, if possible pleasing to others: with this task in view it restrains us and keeps us within bounds, creates social forms, imposes on the unmannerly rules of decency, cleanliness, politeness, of speaking and staying silent at the proper time. Then, art is supposed to *conceal* or *reinterpret* everything ugly, those painful, dreadful, disgusting things which, all efforts notwithstanding, in accord with the origin of human nature again and again insist on breaking forth: it is supposed to do so especially in regard to the passions and psychical fears and torments, and in the case of what is ineluctably or invincibly ugly to let the *meaning* of the thing shine through. After this great, indeed immense task of art, what is usually termed art, *that of the work of art*, is merely an *appendage*. A man who feels within himself an excess of such beautifying, concealing and reinterpreting powers will in the end seek to discharge this excess in works of art as well; so, under the right circumstances, will an entire people. – Now, however, we usually start with art where we should end with it, cling hold of it by its tail and believe that the art of the work of art is true art out of which life is to be improved and transformed – fools that we are! If we begin the meal with the dessert and cram ourselves with sweet things, is it any wonder if we spoil our stomach, and even our appetite, for the good, strengthening, nourishing meals to which art invites us!

175
Endurance of art. – Why, at bottom, is it that an art of works of art continues to endure? It is because most of those who possess leisure – and it is only for them that such an art exists – believe that without music, attendance at the theatre and picture-galleries, without reading novels and poems, they will never get through the day. Supposing one were able to *deprive* them of these satisfactions, they would either cease to strive after leisure so eagerly and the envy-inspiring sight of the rich would become *rarer* – a great gain for the stability of society; or, still possessing leisure, they could learn how to *reflect* – which can be learned and also unlearned – upon their work, for example, their relationships, upon pleasures they might bestow: in both cases all the world, the artists alone excepted, would derive advantage from it. – There are many fine and sensible readers who at this point would certainly raise a valid objection. For the sake of the dull and malevolent, however, it should for once be said that, here as so often in this book, the author is alive to this objection, and that there is much in it that does not appear on the printed page.

176
The mouthpiece of the gods. – The poet expresses the general higher

opinions possessed by a people, he is their flute and mouthpiece – but, by virtue of metric and all the other methods of art, he expresses them in such a way that the people receive them as something quite new and marvellous and believe in all seriousness that the poet is the mouthpiece of the gods. Indeed, in the clouds of creation the poet himself forgets whence he has acquired all his spiritual wisdom – from his father and mother, from teachers and books of all kinds, from the street and especially from the priests; he is deceived by his own art and, in naive ages, really does believe that *a god* is speaking through him, that he is creating in a state of religious illumination – whereas he is repeating only what he has learned, popular wisdom mixed up with popular folly. Thus, insofar as the poet really *is vox populi* he *counts* as *vox dei.**

177

What all art wants to do but cannot. – The hardest and ultimate task of the artist is the representation of the unchanging, of that which reposes in itself, the exalted and simple; that is why the highest forms of moral perfection are rejected by the weaker artists themselves as inartistic sketches, because the sight of this fruit is all too painful to their ambition: it glitters down upon these artists from the highest branches of art, but they lack the ladder, the courage and the skill to dare to venture so high. In itself, a Phidias† *as poet* is perfectly possible, but, considering what modern capacities are like, almost only in the sense that with God all things are possible. The desire even for a poetic Claude Lorrain is, indeed, at the present time a piece of immodesty, however much the heart may crave it. – To the representation of the *ultimate* man, *that is to say the simplest and at the same time the most whole,* no artist has so far been equal; perhaps, however, in the *ideal of Athene* the Greeks cast their eyes farther than any other men have done hitherto.

178

Art and recuperation. – The retrogressive movements in history, the so-called periods of recuperation, which seek to restore life to a spiritual and social condition preceding them and do actually seem to achieve a brief awakening of the dead, possess the charm of an agreeable recollection, a yearning desire for what has almost been lost, a hurried embracing of a happiness that lasts for but a few minutes. On account of this strange deepening of mood it is in precisely such fleeting, almost dreamlike ages that art and poetry find a natural soil: just as the rarest and most delicate plants flourish on steep mountainsides. – Thus many a fine artist is driven unawares to a recuperative disposition in politics and society for which he prepares for himself on his own account a quiet corner and little garden: where he then assembles around him the human remains of this historical era he finds so comfortable and lets his lyre resound before no one but the dead, the half-dead and the weary unto death, perhaps with the outcome referred to above of a brief awakening of the dead.

* *vox populi*: voice of the people; *vox dei*: voice of God
† *Phidias* (fifth century BC): Greek sculptor.

179

Our age's good fortune. – There are two respects in which our age may be called fortunate. With respect to the *past* we have enjoyment of all the cultures there have ever been and of their productions, and nourish ourselves with the noblest blood of every age; we still stand sufficiently close to the magical forces of the power out of whose womb they were born to be able to subject ourselves to them in passing with joy and awe: whereas earlier cultures were capable of enjoying only themselves, with no view of what lay outside – it was as though they lay beneath a vaulted dome, of greater or less extent, which, though light streamed down upon them from it, was itself impenetrable to their gaze. In respect to the *future* there opens out before us, for the first time in history, the tremendous far-flung prospect of human-ecumenical goals embracing the entire inhabited earth. At the same time we feel conscious of possessing the strength to be allowed without presumption to take this new task in hand ourselves without requiring supernatural assistance; indeed, let our undertaking eventuate as it may, even if we have overestimated our strength, there is in any case no one to whom we owe a reckoning except ourselves: henceforth mankind can do with itself whatever it wishes. – There are, to be sure, singular human bees who know how to extract from the flower-cup of all things only what is bitterest and most vexatious; – and all things do in fact contain in them something of this non-honey. Let these feel as they must about the good fortune of our age just described and carry on with the construction of their beehive of discontent.

180

A vision. – Lectures and hours of meditation for adults, for the mature and maturest, and these daily, without compulsion but attended by everyone as a command of custom: the churches as the worthiest venues for them because richest in memories: every day as it were a festival of attained and attainable dignity of human reason: a new and fuller efflorescence of the ideal of the teacher, in which the priest, the artist and the physician, the man of knowledge and the man of wisdom, are fused with one another, with a resultant fusion of their separate virtues into a single total virtue which would also be expressed in their teaching itself, in their delivery and their methods – this is my vision: it returns to me again and again, and I firmly believe that it lifts a corner of the veil of the future.

181

Educational contortion. – The reason for the extraordinary precariousness of all institutions of instruction, which gives every adult the feeling his only educator has been chance – for the fact that educational methods and objectives are like a weather-vane – is that today the *oldest* and the *newest* cultural powers want, as in a noisy popular assembly, to be heard rather than understood and through their shrill cries to demonstrate at any price that they *still exist* or *already exist*. In the midst of this senseless hubbub the poor teachers and educators have at first been deafened, then grown silent and finally apathetic, and they now bear all patiently and merely pass it on to their pupils. They themselves are not educated: how should they be able to educate? They themselves are not trees grown straight, strong and full of sap: whoever wants to attach himself to them will have to bend and twist himself, and will in the end appear contorted and deformed.

182

Philosophers and artists of our time. – Dissoluteness and indifference, burning desires, cooling of the heart – this repulsive juxtaposition is to be found in the higher society of Europe of the present day. The artist believes he has done a great deal if through his art he has for once set the heart aflame *beside* these burning desires: and likewise the philosopher if, given the coolness of the heart he has in common with his age, he succeeds through his world-denying judgements in cooling the heat of the desires in himself and in this society.

183

Do not be a warrior of culture if you do not need to be. – At long last we learn that of which our ignorance in our youth caused us so much harm: that we have first to *do* what is excellent, then *seek out* what is excellent, wherever and under whatever name it is to be found, but avoid all that is bad and mediocre *without combatting it,* and that to doubt the goodness of a thing – as can easily happen to a more practised taste – may already count as an argument against it and a reason for ignoring it completely: though this must be at the risk of sometimes blundering and confusing goodness accessible only with difficulty with the bad and imperfect. Only he who can do nothing better should assault the basenesses of the world as a warrior of culture. But the teachers and promoters of culture destroy themselves when they desire to go about in arms and through precautions, night watches and evil dreams transform the tranquillity of their house and calling into an uncanny lack of tranquillity.

184

How natural history should be narrated. – Natural history, as the history of the war of the spiritual-moral forces against fear, imaginings, inertia, superstition, folly, and their victory over them, ought to be narrated in such a way that everyone who hears it is irresistibly inspired to strive after spiritual and bodily health and vigour, to the glad feeling of being the heir and continuator of mankind, and to an ever nobler need for practical activity. Up to now it has not yet discovered its proper language, because artists inventive in language and eloquence – for these are what is needed – refuse to relinquish an obstinate mistrust of it and above all refuse to learn from it. Nonetheless, it must be allowed that the English have taken admirable steps in the direction of that ideal with their natural science textbooks for the lower strata of the people: the reason is that they are written by their most distinguished scholars – whole, complete and fulfilling natures – and not, as is the case with us, by mediocrities.

185

Genius of humanity. – If genius consists, according to Schopenhauer's observation, in the connected and lively recollection of experience, then in the striving for knowledge of the entire historical past – which ever more mightily distinguishes the modern age from all others and has for the first time demolished the ancient walls between nature and spirit, man and animal, morality and the physical world – it may be possible to recognize a striving for the genius of humanity as a whole. History perfect and complete would be cosmic self-consciousness.

186

Cult of culture. – To great spirits there has been joined the repellent all-too-human aspects of their nature, their blindnesses, deformities, extravagances, so that their mighty influence, that can easily grow all too mighty, shall be kept within bounds by the mistrust these qualities inspire. For the system of all that which humanity has need of for its continued existence is so comprehensive, and lays claim to so many and such varying forces, that humanity as a whole would have to pay heavily for any *onesided* preference, whether it be science or the state or art or trade, to which these individuals would entice it. It has always been the greatest fatality for culture when men have been worshipped: in which sense one may even feel in accord with the Mosaic law which forbids us to have other gods beside God. – Next to the cult of the genius and his force there must always be placed, as its complement and palliative, the cult of culture: which knows how to accord to the material, humble, base, misunderstood, weak, imperfect, onesided, incomplete, untrue, merely apparent, indeed to the evil and dreadful, a proper degree of understanding and the admission *that all this is necessary;* for the harmonious endurance of all that is human, attained through astonishing labours and lucky accidents and as much the work of ants and cyclops as of genius, must not be lost to us again: how, then, could we dispense with the common, deep and often uncanny groundbass without which melody cannot be melody?

187

Joy in the ancient world. – The men of the world of antiquity knew better how to *rejoice:* we how *to suffer less;* the former employed all their abundance of ingenuity and capacity to reflect for the continual creation of new occasions for happiness and celebration: whereas we employ our minds rather towards the amelioration of suffering and the removal of sources of pain. In regard to an existence of suffering the ancients sought forgetfulness or some way or other of converting their feelings into pleasurable ones: so that in this matter they sought palliatives, while we attack the cause of suffering and on the whole prefer prophylactic measures. – Perhaps we are only constructing the foundations upon which men of the future will again erect the temple of joy.

188

The muses as liars. – 'We are capable of telling many lies' – thus the muses once sang when they revealed themselves to Hesiod. – Many vital discoveries can be made if we for once apprehend the artist as a deceiver.

189

How paradoxical Homer can be. – Is there anything more audacious, uncanny or unbelievable shining down on the destiny of man like a winter sun than that idea we find in Homer:

> then did the gods make resolve and ordain unto men
> *destruction, that in after times too there might be matter for song.*

Thus we suffer and perish so that the poets shall not lack *material* – and this according to the decree of the gods of Homer, who seem to be very much concerned about the pleasures of coming generations but very indifferent to us, the men of the present. – That such ideas should ever have entered the head of a Greek!

190

Subsequent justification of existence. – Many ideas have entered the world as errors and fantasies but have become truths, because men have afterwards foisted upon them a substratum of reality.

191

Need for pro and contra. – Whoever has not grasped that every great man has not only to be supported but, for the good of the general wellbeing, also *opposed*, is certainly still a great child – or himself a great man.

192

Injustice on the part of genius. – Genius is most unjust towards geniuses, when they happen to be its contemporaries: in the first place it believes it has no need of them and thus regards them as superfluous – for it is what it is without them – then their influence clashes with the effect of *its* electric current: on which account it even calls them *harmful*.

193

The worst fate that can befall a prophet. – He laboured for twenty years at persuading his contemporaries to believe in him – finally he succeeded; but in the meantime his adversaries had also succeeded: he no longer believed in himself.

194

Three thinkers equal a spider. – In every philosophical sect three thinkers follow one after the other in the following way: the first produces out of himself the seed and sap, the second draws it out into threads and spins an artificial web, the third lurks in this web for victims who get caught in it – and tries to live off philosophy.

195

Trafficking with authors. – To seize an author by the nose is as bad mannered as to take him by the horns – and every author has his horns.

196

Two-horse team. – Unclear thinking and sentimental emotionalism are as frequently united with a ruthless will to self-assertion, to ascendancy at all cost, as is a warm benevolence and desire to help with the drive to clean and clear thinking, to moderation and restraint of feeling.

197

That which unites and that which divides. – Does that which unites men – their understanding of what constitutes their common advantage and disadvantage – not lie in the head, and that which divides them – their blind groping and selectivity in love and hatred, their preference for one at the expense of all others and the contempt for the general wellbeing that arises from it – not lie in the heart?

198

Marksmen and thinkers. – There are curious marksmen who, though they miss the target, depart from the range complacently proud of the fact that their bullet did at any rate fly a great distance (well beyond the target in any event), or that, though they did not hit the target, they did at any rate hit something. And there are thinkers like this.

199

From two sides. – We are hostile to an intellectual tendency and movement if we are superior to it and disapprove of its objectives, or if its objectives are too remote and we cannot understand them, that is to say when they are superior to us. Thus a party can be opposed from two sides, from above and below; and it is no rare thing for both opponents to form an alliance grounded in their common hatred that is more repulsive than anything they join in hating.

200

Originality. – Not that a man sees something new as the first one to do so, but that he sees something old, familiar, seen but overlooked by everyone, *as though it were new*, is what distinguishes true originality. The first discoverer is usually that quite commonplace and mindless fantasist – chance.

201

Error of philosophers. – The philosopher believes that the value of his philosophy lies in the whole, in the building: posterity discovers it in the bricks with which he built and which are then often used again for better building: in the fact, that is to say, that that building can be destroyed and *nonetheless* possess value as material.

202

Witticism. – A witticism is an epigram on the death of a feeling.

203

The moment before the solution. – In the realm of science it happens every hour that someone stands immediately before the solution of a problem convinced that all his efforts have been in vain – like one untying a bow who, at just the moment before it is about to come apart, hesitates: for it is precisely then that it looks most like a knot.

204

Going among fanatics. – The thoughtful man who is sure of his reason can profit by going among fantasists for a decade and, within this torrid zone, surrendering himself to a modest degree of folly. By doing so he has gone a good stretch of the way towards that cosmopolitanism of the spirit which can say without presumption: 'nothing of the spirit is any longer alien to me'.

205

Keen air. – The finest and healthiest element in science is, as in the mountains, the keen air that wafts through it. – The spiritually delicate (such as the artists) avoid and slander science on account of this air.

206

Why scholars are nobler than artists. – Science requires *nobler* natures than does poetry: they have to be simpler, less ambitious, more abstemious, quieter, less concerned with posthumous fame, and able to lose themselves in contemplation of things few would consider worthy of such a sacrifice of the personality. In addition they are conscious of another deprivation: the nature of their occupation, its constant demand for the greatest sobriety, enfeebles their *will*, the fire is not maintained at such heat as it is in the hearth of the poetic nature: and that is why they often lose the best of their energy and efflorescence earlier in life than do the latter – and, as aforesaid, they *know* of this danger. Under all circumstances they *seem* less gifted because they glitter less, and will be accounted less than they are.

207

To what extent piety obscures. – In later centuries, the great man is made a present of all the great qualities and virtues of his own century – and thus all that is best is continually *obscured* by piety, which sees it as a sacred image to which votive offerings are brought and before which they are set up, until in the end it is completely covered and concealed by them and is henceforth an object of faith rather than of observation.

208

Standing on one's head. – When we set truth on its head we usually fail to notice that our head too is not standing where it ought to stand.

209

Origin and utility of fashion. – The obvious self-contentment of the *individual* with his form excites imitation and gradually produces the form of the *many*, that is to say fashion: the many want through fashion to attain to precisely that pleasing self-contentment with one's form and they do attain it. – If one considers how much reason every person has for anxiety and timid self-concealment, and how three-quarters of his energy and goodwill can be paralysed and made unfruitful by it, one has to be very grateful to fashion, insofar as it sets that three-quarters free and communicates self-confidence and mutual cheerful agreeableness to those who know they are all bound by its law. Even foolish laws bestow freedom and quietness of heart provided many have agreed to be subject to them.

210

Tongue-loosener. – The value of many books and people lies solely in their ability to constrain everyone to express what is most concealed and deeply buried within them: they are tongue-looseners and crowbars for even the most clenched teeth. Many events and ill-deeds, too, which seem to exist merely to be the curse of mankind, possess a similar value and utility.

211

Free-ranging spirits. – Which of us would dare to call himself a free spirit if he would not wish to pay homage in his own way to those men to whom this name has been applied as an *insult* by taking on to his own shoulders some of this burden of public disapprobation and revilement? What, however, we may call ourselves in all seriousness (and without being in any way defiant) is 'free-ranging spirits', because we feel the tug towards freedom as the strongest drive of our spirit and, in antithesis to the fettered and firm-rooted intellects, see our ideal almost in a spiritual nomadism – to employ a modest and almost contemptuous expression.

212

Yes, the favour of the muses! – What Homer says of it is so true and so terrible it pierces us through: 'the muse loved him dearly and gave to him good and evil; for she took from him his eyes and bestowed upon him sweet song'. – This is a text without end for the thinker: she gives good *and* evil, that is *her* way of loving dearly! And everyone will interpret for himself why it is we thinkers and poets *have* to give our *eyes* in exchange.

213

Against the cultivation of music. – The artistic education of the eye from childhood on through drawing and painting, and the sketching of landscapes, people and events, brings with it in later life the invaluable attendant benefit of rendering the eye *sharp, tranquil and persevering* in the observation of men and situations. No similar attendant advantage is to be derived from the artistic cultivation of the ear: for which reason schools would in general do well to give the art of the eye preference over that of the ear.

214

The discoverers of trivialities. – Subtle spirits to whom nothing could be more alien than a triviality often discover one after all kinds of roving about and mountain-climbing, and take great pleasure in it – much to the amazement of the non-subtle.

215

Morality of the learned. – Regular and rapid progress in the sciences is possible only when the individual is *not* obliged to be *too mistrustful* in the testing of every account and assertion made by others in domains in which
he is a relative stranger: the condition for this, however, is that in his own
field everyone must have rivals who are *extremely mistrustful* and are
accustomed to observe him very closely. It is out of this juxtaposition of
'not too mistrustful' and 'extremely mistrustful' that the integrity of the
republic of the learned originates.

216

Ground of unfruitfulness. – There are highly gifted spirits who are always
unfruitful simply because, from a weakness in their temperament, they
are too impatient to wait out the term of their pregnancy.

217

Upside-down world of tears. – The manifold discomforts imposed upon men
by the claims of higher culture at last distort nature so far that they
usually bear themselves stiffly and stoically and have tears only for rare
attacks of good fortune, so that many, indeed, are constrained to weep
merely because they have ceased to feel pain: – only when they are happy
do their hearts beat again.

218

The Greeks as interpreters. – When we speak of the Greeks we involuntarily
speak of today and yesterday: their familiar history is a polished mirror
that always radiates something that is not in the mirror itself. We employ
our freedom to speak of them so as to be allowed to remain silent about
others – so that the latter may now say something into the thoughtful
.reader's ear. Thus the Greeks make it easier for modern man to communicate much that is delicate and hard to communicate.

219

On the acquired character of the Greeks. – The celebrated clarity, transpar-
ency, simplicity and orderliness of the Greeks, the crystalline naturalness
and at the same time crystalline artisticality of their works, can easily mislead us into believing that all this was simply handed to the Greeks: that,
for example, they were incapable of not writing well, as Lichtenberg* did
in fact say. But nothing could be more untenable or hasty. The history of
prose from Gorgias† to Demosthenes shows a labouring and struggling
to emerge out of obscurity, floridity and tastelessness into the light that
recalls the efforts of heroes breaking a first pathway through forest and
swamp. The dialogue of tragedy is the actual *achievement* of the dramatists, on account of its uncommon definiteness and clarity against a background of a people who revelled in symbolism and allusions and who

---

* Georg Christoph Lichtenberg (1742–94): German writer and aphorist.
† Gorgias (fl. 430 BC): Greek philosopher and teacher of rhetoric.

were educated away from this especially by the great choral lyrics of the tragedy: just as it is the achievement of Homer to have liberated the Greeks from Asiatic pomp, vagueness and obscurity and to have attained to architectural clarity on a large scale and a small. It was, moreover, by no means accounted easy to say something with true distinctness and lucidity; how else would there have been such great admiration for the epigram of Simonides, which presents itself so plainly, without gilded figures or witty arabesques but saying what it has to say clearly, with the reposefulness of the sunlight, not the snatching at effects of a flash of lightning. It is because striving towards the light out of an as it were inborn twilight characterizes the Greeks that a cry of rejoicing goes through the people when they hear a laconic maxim, the language of the elegy, the sayings of the Seven Wise Men. That is why the promulgation of laws in verse, which we find offensive, was so well loved: it represented the actual Apollonian task for the Hellenic spirit of triumphing over the perils of metre, over the darkness and obscurity that otherwise characterizes the poetic. Simplicity, suppleness, sobriety were *extorted* from the people, they were not inherent in them – the danger of a relapse into the Asiatic hovered over the Greeks at all times, and now and then they were in fact as though inundated by a stream of mysticism and elemental savagery and darkness. We see them sink, we see Europe as it were flushed away and drowned – for Europe was very small in those days – but always they come to the surface again, excellent swimmers and divers that they are, the nation of Odysseus.

220

The real paganism. – Perhaps nothing astonishes the observer of the Greek world more than when he discovers that from time to time the Greeks made as it were a festival of all their passions and evil natural inclinations and even instituted a kind of official order of proceedings in the celebration of what was all-too-human in them: this constitutes the real paganism of their world, uncomprehended by and incomprehensible to Christianity, which has always despised and combatted it with the greatest severity. – They took this all-too-human to be inescapable and, instead of reviling it, preferred to accord it a kind of right of the second rank through regulating it within the usages of society and religion: indeed, everything in man possessing *power* they called divine and inscribed it on the walls of their Heaven. They do not repudiate the natural drive that finds expression in the evil qualities but regulate it and, as soon as they have discovered sufficient prescriptive measures to provide these wild waters with the least harmful means of channeling and outflow, confine them to definite cults and days. This is the root of all the moral free-mindedness of antiquity. One granted to the evil and suspicious, to the animal and backward, likewise to the barbarian, the pre-Greek and Asiatic, that still lived on in the foundations of the Hellenic nature, a moderate discharge, and did not strive after their total annihilation. The entire system of such procedures was comprehended in the state, which was constituted to accommodate, not individual people or castes, but the ordinary qualities of mankind. In its construction the Greeks demonstrated that wonderful sense for the factual and typical that later qualified them to become natural scientists, historians, geographers and philosophers. The constitution of the state and of the state religion was determined, not by a circumscribed priestly or caste-dominated moral code, but by the most comprehensive regard for *all human actuality*. – Where did the Greeks acquire this freedom, this sense for the actual? Perhaps from Homer and the poets before him; for it is precisely the poets, whose natures are not commonly the most sagacious or judicious, who possess by way of compensation a joy in the actual and active *of every kind* and have no desire to deny even evil altogether: they are satisfied if it keeps itself within bounds and refrains from wholesale slaughter or inner subversion – that is to say, they think in much the same way as the creators of the Greek states, and were their instructors and pathfinders.

221

Exceptions among the Greeks. – In Greece the profound, thorough, serious spirits were the exceptions: the instinct of the people was inclined, rather, to regard seriousness and thoroughness as a kind of distortion. Not to create forms but to borrow them from abroad and transform them into the fairest appearance of beauty – that is Greek: imitation, not for use but for the end of artistic deception, the repeated defeating of an imposed seriousness, ordering, beautifying, making shallow and superficial – that is the course they pursued, from Homer to the sophists of the third and fourth centuries of the Christian era, who are wholly surface, pompous phrases, animated gestures, and address themselves to hollowed-out souls thirsting for mere noise, effect and appearance. – And now try to assess the greatness of those exceptional Greeks who created *science*! He who tells of them, tells the most heroic story in the history of the human spirit!

222

The simple comes neither first nor last in time. – In the history of the religious conceptions, much false evolution and graduality has been invented in the case of things which in truth grew up, not out of and after one another, but side by side and separately; the simple, especially, is still much too much reputed to be the oldest and primary. Not a little that is human originates through subtraction and division, not through duplication, addition, growing together. – One still believes, for example, in a gradual evolution of *representations of gods* from clumsy stones and blocks of wood up to complete humanization: and yet the fact of the matter is that, *so long as* the divinity was introduced into trees, pieces of wood, stones, animals, and felt to reside there, one shrank from a humanization of their form as from an act of godlessness. It required the poets, existing outside the religious cult and the spell of religious *awe*, to accustom the imagination of men to acceding to such a thing: overweighed again by more pious moods and moments, however, this liberating influence of the poets again withdrew and the sacred remained, as before, in the realm of the monstrous, uncanny and quite specifically non-human. But even much of that which the imagination dares to construct for itself would, translated into outward, bodily representation, nonetheless produce a painful effect: the inward eye is very much bolder and less bashful than the outward (which is why it is difficult, and in part impossible, to convert epic material into dramatic). The religious imagination for a long time *refuses* absolutely to believe in the identity of the god and an image: the image is supposed to be the visible evidence that the *numen* of the divinity is, in some mysterious, not fully comprehensible way, active in this place and bound to it. The oldest image of the god is supposed to *harbour and at the same time conceal* the god – to intimate his presence but not expose it to view. No Greek ever truly *beheld* his Apollo as a wooden obelisk, his Eros as a lump of stone; they were symbols whose purpose was precisely to excite fear *of* beholding him. The same applies to those wooden idols furnished with paltry carvings of individual limbs, sometimes an excess of them: such as a Spartan Apollo with four hands and four ears. In the incompleteness, allusiveness or overladenness of these figures there lies a dreadful holiness which is supposed to *fend off* any association of them with anything human. It is not at an embryonic stage of art at which such things are fashioned: as though in the ages when such figures were revered men were *incapable* of speaking more clearly, representing more accurately. What was the case, rather, was that one thing was specifically avoided: direct statement. As the cella contains the holy of holies, the actual *numen* of the divinity, and conceals it in mysterious semi-darkness, *but does not wholly conceal it*; as the peripteral temple in turn contains the cella and as though with a canopy and veil shelters it from prying eyes, *but does not wholly shelter it*: so the image is the divinity and at the same time the divinity's place of concealment. – Only when, in the secular world of competition outside the religious cult, joy in the victory in the contest had risen so high that the waves here produced flooded over into the lake of the religious sensations; only when the statue of the victor was set up in the courts of the temples and the eye and the soul of the pious frequenter of the temple had, willingly or unwillingly, to accustom itself to this inescapable sight of *human* strength and beauty, so that, standing thus close to one another, spatially and in the soul, reverence for man and reverence for god came to blend together: only then was the fear of an actual humanization of the divine image also overcome and the great arena for plastic art in the grand style opened up: yet still with the restriction that wherever *worship* was to be conducted the ancient forms and ugliness were preserved and scrupulously imitated. But the *sanctifying and bestowing* Hellene might now pursue to his heart's content his desire to let god become man.

223

Whither we have to travel. – Direct self-observation is not nearly sufficient for us to know ourselves: we require history, for the past continues to flow within us in a hundred waves; we ourselves are, indeed, nothing but that which at every moment we experience of this continued flowing. It may even be said that here too, when we desire to descend into the river of what seems to be our own most intimate and personal being, there applies the dictum of Heraclitus: we cannot step into the same river twice. – This is, to be sure, a piece of wisdom that has gradually grown stale, but it has nonetheless remained as true and valid as it ever was: just as has this other piece of wisdom, that to understand history we have to go in quest of the living remnants of historical epochs – we have to *travel*, as the father of history, Herodotus, travelled, to other nations – for these are only earlier *stages of culture* grown firm upon which we can *take a stand* – to the so-called savage and semi-savage peoples, and especially to where man has taken off the garb of Europe or has not yet put it on. But there exists a *subtler* art and object of travel which does not always require us to move from place to place or to traverse thousands of miles. The last three centuries very probably still continue to live on, in all their cultural colours and cultural refractions, *close beside us*: they want only to be *discovered*. In many families, indeed in individual men, the strata still lie neatly and clearly one on top of the other: elsewhere there are dislocations and faults which make understanding more difficult. A venerable specimen of very much older sensibility could certainly have been more easily preserved in remoter regions, in less travelled mountain valleys, in more self-enclosed communities: while it is improbable that such discoveries would be made in, for example, Berlin, where people come into the world washed and scalded clean. He who, after long practice in this art of travel, has become a hundred-eyed Argos, will in the end be attended everywhere by his *Io** – I mean his *ego* – and will rediscover the adventurous travels of this *ego* in process of becoming and transformation in Egypt and Greece, Byzantium and Rome, France and Germany, in the age of the nomadic or of the settled nations, in the Renaissance and the Reformation, at home and abroad, indeed in the sea, the forests, in the plants and in the mountains. – Thus self-knowledge will become universal knowledge with regard to all that is past: just as, merely to allude to another chain of reflections, self-determination and self-education could, in the freest and most far-sighted spirits, one day become universal determination with regard to all future humanity.

224

Balm and poison. – This fact can never be sufficiently pondered: Christianity is the religion of antiquity grown old, its presupposition is degenerated ancient cultures; on these it could and can act as a balm. In ages in which ears and eyes are 'filled with mud', so that they are no longer capable of hearing the voice of reason and philosophy, or of seeing wisdom in bodily form, whether it bear the name of Epictetus or of Epi-

* *Io*: in Greek mythology, daughter of King Inachos and lover of Zeus turned into a cow by Hera and given to the giant Argos.

curus: in such ages the cross of martyrdom and the 'trumpet of the last judgement' may perhaps still move the peoples to live a *decent* life. If one thinks of the Rome of Juvenal,* that poison-toad with the eyes of Venus, one learns what it means to confront the 'world' with a Cross, one comes to respect the quiet Christian community and is grateful that it overran the Graeco-Roman world. When most people were born as though with the souls of slaves and the sensuality of old men, what a blessing it must have been to encounter beings who were more soul than body and seemed to be an actualisation of the Greek conception of the shades of Hades: modest, elusive, benevolent figures living in expectation of a 'better life' and thereby become so undemanding, so silently contempt-uous, so proudly patient! – This Christianity as the evening-bell of *good* antiquity, a bell broken and weary yet still sweet-sounding, is a balm to the ears even for him who now wanders through these centuries only as a historian: what must it have been for the men of these centuries them-selves! – On the other hand, for youthful, vigorous barbarians Christi-anity is *poison;* to implant the teaching of sinfulness and damnation into the heroic, childish and animal soul of the ancient German, for example, is nothing other than to poison it; a quite tremendous chemical fermen-tation and decomposition, a confusion of feelings and judgements, a rank exuberance of every kind of fantasy must have been the outcome, and thus in the longer run a fundamental enfeeblement of such bar-barians. – One must, to be sure, ask what, without this enfeeblement, there would have been left to us of Greek culture! of the entire cultural past of the human race! – for the barbarian races *untouched* by Christianity were capable of doing away with ancient cultures altogether: as, for example, was demonstrated with fearful clarity by the pagan conquerors of Romanized Britain. Christianity was obliged against its will to assist in making the 'world' of antiquity immortal. – Here too there still remains another counter-question and the possibility of a counter-reckoning: if it had not been enfeebled by the poison referred to, would one or other of these vigorous peoples, the German possibly, have perhaps been capable of gradually finding a higher culture for themselves, one of their own, a new one? – of which, as things are, mankind has not now the remotest conception? – Thus it is the same here as everywhere: one does not know, to speak the language of Christianity, whether God owes more gratitude to the Devil or the Devil more gratitude to God for everything having turned out as it has.

225
Belief makes blessed and damns. – A Christian who ventured upon forbidden pathways of thought might well ask himself one day: is it really *necessary* that there should actually *be* a God, and a deputizing Lamb of God, if *belief* in the *existence* of these beings suffices to produce the same effects? Are they not *superfluous* beings, even supposing they do exist? For all the benefits, consolations and moral improvements, as likewise all the

* Juvenal (60 to 140 AD): Roman satirical poet

darkenings and prostrations, bestowed by the Christian religion upon the human soul proceed from this belief and not from the objects of this belief. The case here is no different from that other celebrated case: there were, to be sure, no witches, but the terrible effects of the belief in witches were the same as they would have been if there really had been witches. For all those occasions on which the Christian expects the direct intervention of a God but does so in vain – because there is no God – his religion is sufficiently inventive in reasons and excuses to pacify him: in this it is certainly an ingenious religion. – Faith has hitherto been unable to move any real mountains, to be sure, even though I know not who asserted it could; but it is able to place mountains where there were none before.

226

Tragi-comedy of Regensburg.* – Now and then we have a frighteningly clear view of Fortuna's farcical comedy: how she takes a few days, a single place, the condition and opinions of one head, and attaches to them the rope along which she intends the coming centuries to dance. Thus the destiny of modern Germany lies in the days of disputation of Regensburg: a peaceful outcome of ecclesiastical and moral contentions, without religious wars or Counter-reformation, seemed guaranteed, as did the unity of the German nation; the conciliatory spirit of Contarini† hovered for a moment over the theological wrangling, victorious as the representative of a more mature Italian piety upon whose pinions was reflected the daybreak of spiritual freedom. But Luther's bony head, full of suspicions and uncanny fears, bristled up: because justification through grace seemed to him *his* great discovery and motto, he did not credit this proposition when it was uttered by Italians: whereas, as is well known, the latter had discovered it much earlier and, in profound quietness, had propagated it throughout all Italy. Luther saw in this apparent accord a trick of the Devil and hindered the work of peace as well as he could: thereby considerably furthering the aims of the enemies of the Reich. – And now, to get the full flavour of the horrible farcicality of these proceedings, consider in addition that none of the propositions over which they were then contending in Regensburg – neither that of original sin, nor that of redemption by proxy, nor that of justification by faith – is in any way true or has anything whatever to do with truth, that they are now all recognized as undiscussable: – and yet on their account the world was set in flames, that is to say on account of opinions to which nothing real corresponds; whereas contention is permitted least regarding purely philological questions, for example the declaration of the sacramental words of the Eucharist, because here it is possible to speak the truth. But where there is nothing, truth too has lost its rights. – Finally, however, nothing remains to be said but that these days saw the appearance of

---

* Regensburg: theological and political conference of 1541.

† Cardinal Gasparo Contarini (1483–1542): a reformer in the Catholic Church who was sent to Regensburg to achieve reconciliation with the Lutherans; despite his celebrated diplomacy, the conference failed.

sources of energy by which the mills of the modern world were driven more powerfully than they otherwise would have been. And energy comes first, and only then, and a long way after, truth – isn't that true, my dear contemporaries?

227

Goethe's errors. – Goethe is the great exception among the great artists in that he did not live within the *narrow-mindedness of his actual ability*, as though it were, for himself and for all the world, the essence and excellence, the be-all and end-all of everything. Twice he thought he possessed something higher than he actually did possess – and in the *second* half of his life went astray in apparently being overwhelmingly convinced he was one of the greatest *scientific* discoverers and illuminators. And likewise in the *first* half of his life too: he *wanted* of himself something higher than poetry appeared to him to be – and in this he was already in error. Nature had wanted to make of him a *plastic* artist – that was the glowing and burning secret that finally drove him to Italy so that he might truly revel in this illusion and bring to it every sacrifice. At last, reflective man that he was and one genuinely hostile to all creations of illusion, he realized what a deceitful little demon of desire it was that had enticed him to believe this was his calling, and how he had to liberate himself from the greatest passion of his will and say *farewell* to it. The agonizing conviction that it was necessary *to say farewell* is finally exhausted in the mood of *Tasso*: over him, the 'intensified Werther',* there lies the presentiment of something that is worse than death, as when one says to himself: 'now all is over – after this farewell; how can I go on living without going mad!' – It was these two fundamental errors of his life that, in the face of a purely literary posture towards poetry such as was at that time the only attitude towards it, bestowed on Goethe a demeanour apparently so independent and almost capricious. Except for the time in which Schiller – poor Schiller, who had no time and wasted no time – drew him out of his abstemious coyness towards poetry, his fear of all literary activity and professionalism, Goethe seems like a Greek who now and then visits a mistress but does so wondering whether she may not be a goddess he is not quite able to name. In all his poetry there is perceptible the breath of the plastic arts and of nature: the lineaments of these forms as they hovered before him – and he perhaps always believed that he was only tracing the transformations of a goddess – became, without his knowing or desiring it, the lineaments of all the children of his art. Without this *digression through error* he would not have become Goethe: that is to say, the only German literary artist who has not yet become antiquated – because he desired to be a writer by profession just as little as he desired to be a German by profession.

228

Grades of traveller. – We can distinguish five grades of traveller: those of

* Goethe's epistolary novel *The Sorrows of Young Werther*, a tale of disappointed love, appeared in 1774; *Torquato Tasso* (final version 1789) represents the Italian poet drawing comfort from the company of a pure woman.

the first and lowest grade are those who travel and, instead of seeing, are themselves seen – they are as though blind; next come those who actually see the world; the third experience something as a consequence of what they have seen; the fourth absorb into themselves what they have experienced and bear it away with them; lastly there are a few men of the highest energy who, after they have experienced and absorbed all they have seen, necessarily have to body it forth again out of themselves in works and actions as soon as they have returned home. – It is like these five species of traveller that all men travel through the whole journey of life, the lowest purely passive, the highest those who transform into action and exhaust everything they experience.

229
Climbing higher. – As soon as we climb higher than those who have hitherto admired us we appear to them to have sunk and fallen lower: for they thought they had hitherto been standing *with* us (even if through us) *on the heights.*

230
Measure and moderation. – Of two very exalted things – measure and moderation – it is best never to speak. Some few know their significance and power through inner sacred paths of experience and conversion: they revere in them something divine and refuse to speak of them aloud. All the rest hardly listen when they are spoken of, and confuse them with boredom and mediocrity: except perhaps for those who did once hear a premonitory echo from that domain but closed their ears to it. The recollection of it now makes them agitated and angry.

231
Humanity in friendship and mastery. – 'If you are going towards the morning I shall draw towards evening' – to feel thus is a high sign of humanity in closer association with others: in the absence of this feeling every friendship, every discipleship and pupilage, becomes sooner or later a piece of hypocrisy.

232
The profound. – Men who think deeply appear as comedians when they traffic with others, because in order to be understood they always have first to simulate a surface.

233
For the despisers of 'herd humanity'. – He who regards men as a herd and flees from them as fast as he can will certainly be overtaken by them and gored by their horns.

234
Capital sin against the vain. – He who gives another an opportunity to display to society his knowledge, feelings or experiences, sets himself above him and thus, in the event that the latter does not regard him as definitely

his superior, commits an assault on his vanity – whereas what he thought he was doing was gratifying it.

235
Disappointment. – When a long and active life has, together with speeches and writings, borne public witness to the nature of a person, association with him is usually disappointing, and this for two reasons: firstly because one expects too much from a brief period of acquaintanceship – namely all that which only the thousand occasions of a lifetime could make visible – and then because a person who has won general recognition makes no effort to solicit recognition anew from every separate individual. He is too indolent – and we are too eager.

236
Two sources of goodness. – To treat all men with equal benevolence and to be kind to everyone irrespective of who he is can be just as much an emanation of a profound cynicism as of a thorough philanthropy.

237
The wanderer in the mountains addresses himself. – There exist definite signs to show that you have advanced forwards and climbed higher: the view around you is more open and extensive than it was, the air that wafts upon you is cooler but also more gentle – you have unlearned the folly of confusing gentleness with warmth – your step has grown firmer and more lively, courage and thoughtfulness have grown together: – for all these reasons your path may now be more solitary, and in any event more perilous, than the one you trod before, though certainly not to the extent those who watch you from the misty valley below believe it to be.

238
Except for my neighbour. – It is obvious that my head does not stand properly on my shoulders; for it is well known that everyone else knows better than I what I should do and not do: only I, poor rogue, do not know what I should be at. Are we not *all* like statues with the wrong heads on them? Isn't that so, my dear neighbour? – But no, you, precisely you, are the exception.

239
Caution. – With people who lack respect for what is private and personal one should not associate or, if one does associate with them, first pitilessly snap on them the handcuffs of propriety.

240
The desire to appear vain. – To express only thoughts of a choice and distinguished nature when conversing with people one does not know, or does not know very well, to talk to them of one's celebrated acquaintances and interesting travels and experiences, is a sign one is not proud, or at least that one does not desire to appear so. Vanity is the proud man's mask of politeness.

241

A good friendship. – A good friendship originates when one party has a great respect for the other, more indeed than for himself, when one party likewise loves the other, though not so much as he does himself, and when, finally, one party knows how to facilitate the association by adding to it a delicate *tinge* of intimacy while at the same time prudently withholding actual and genuine intimacy and the confounding of I and Thou.

242

Friends as ghosts. – If we greatly transform ourselves, those friends of ours who have not been transformed become ghosts of our past: their voice comes across to us like the voice of a shade – as though we were hearing ourself, only younger, more severe, less mature.

243

One eye and two glances. – Those people in whose eye there is the pleading glance asking for charity and favours are, because of their frequent humiliation and consequent feeling of revengefulness, also capable of the impudent glance.

244

In the blue distance. – A child all his life – that sounds very moving, but is only a judgement from a distance; seen and experienced close to, it always means: boyish all his life.

245

Advantage and disadvantage in the same misunderstanding. – When a subtle head is struck dumb with embarrassment the unsubtle usually interpret it as silent superiority and greatly fear it: whereas if they perceived it was embarrassment they would feel well disposed towards him.

246

The wise man pretending to be a fool. – The wise man's philanthropy sometimes leads him to *pose* as excited, angry, delighted, so that the coldness and reflectiveness of his *true* nature shall not harm those around him.

247

Compelling oneself to pay attention. – As soon as we notice that anyone has to *compel* himself to pay attention when associating and talking with us, we have a valid proof that he does not love us or loves us no longer.

248

Path to a Christian virtue. – To learn from one's enemies is the best path to loving them: for it puts us in a grateful mood towards them.

249

Stratagem of the importunate. – The importunate give gold coins in exchange for our conventional coins, their object being to compel us afterwards to treat our conventions as a mistake and them as exceptions.

250
Ground of aversion. – We grow hostile to many an artist or writer, not because we finally come to see he has deceived us, but because he thought no subtler means were required to ensnare us.

251
In parting. – It is not in how one soul approaches another but in how it distances itself from it that I recognize their affinity and relatedness.

252
Silentium. – One should not talk about one's friends: otherwise one will talk away the feeling of friendship.

253
Impoliteness. – Impoliteness is frequently the sign of a clumsy diffidence which loses its head when surprized and tries to conceal the fact through rudeness.

254
Miscalculation in honesty. – What we have previously kept silent about we sometimes first reveal to our most recent acquaintances: we foolishly believe that this demonstration of our trust is the strongest chain by which we could fetter them to us – but they do not know enough of us to appreciate the sacrifice we are making, and, without any thought of betrayal, betray our secrets to others: so that as a consequence we perhaps lose our old acquaintances.

255
In the antechamber of favour. – People whom we keep standing a long time in the antechamber of our favour start to ferment and turn sour.

256
Warning to the despised. – If you have unmistakably sunk in the estimation of men you should hold on like grim death to decorum in society with others: otherwise you will betray to them that you have sunk in your own estimation too. When a man is cynical in society it is a sign that he treats himself like a dog when he is alone.

257
Ennobling ignorance. – In regard to one's standing in the estimation of those who accord estimation it is more advantageous clearly *not* to understand certain things. Ignorance too bestows privileges.

258
Opponents of gracefulness. – The arrogant and impatient do not like gracefulness and sense in it a bodily visible reproach; for gracefulness is tolerance of the heart as movement and gesture.

259
On meeting again. – When old friends meet again after a long separation it often happens that they feign an interest in things mentioned to which

they have in fact grown quite indifferent: and sometimes both of them notice this but dare not lift the veil – from a sad apprehension of what they might see. Thus conversations arise like those in the realm of the dead.

260

Make friends only with the industrious. – The idle man is a danger to his friends: for, because he does not have enough to do, he talks about what his friends do and do not do, finally involves himself in it and makes a nuisance of himself: for which reason it is prudent to form friendships only with the industrious.

261

One weapon twice as good as two. – It is an unequal contest when one urges his cause with head *and* heart, the other only with his head: the former has as it were both sun and wind against him and his two weapons get in the way of one another: he forfeits the prize – in the eyes of *truth*. On the other hand, the victory of the latter with his one weapon is seldom a victory of the kind admired by all *other* spectators and it loses him their sympathy.

262

Deep waters and troubled waters. – The public easily confuses him who fishes in troubled waters with him who plumbs the depths.

263

Demonstrating one's vanity on friend and foe alike. – Many people mistreat even their friends out of vanity when there are witnesses present to whom they want to demonstrate their superiority: and others exaggerate the worth of their foes so as to be able to show with pride that they are worthy of such foes.

264

Cooling. – The heating up of the heart is commonly associated with a sickness of the head and the judgement. He who is for a time concerned with the health of the latter must therefore know what it is he has to cool down: unconcerned about the future of his heart! For if one is capable of warming up at all, one will surely grow warm again and have one's summer season.

265

Mixed feelings. – Women and selfish children feel against science something compounded of envy and sentimentality.

266

When danger is greatest. – It is rare to break one's leg when in the course of life one is toiling upwards – it happens much more often when one starts to take things easy and to choose the easy paths.

267

Not too early. – One must take care not to become sharp too early – because one will at the same time become thinly honed too early.

268

Joy in recalcitrance. – A good educator knows cases in which he is proud of the fact that his pupil remains true to himself *in opposition to him*: in those cases, that is to say, in which the youth ought not to understand the man or would be harmed if he did understand him.

269

Experiment with honour and honesty. – Youths who aspire to increase their reputation for honour and honesty first seek out a man recognized as a man of honour and attack him, their purpose being to be considered his equal by scolding and abusing him – and all the time with the thought that this first experiment at any rate presents no danger, inasmuch as this man of honour would be the last to censure or punish effrontery in pursuit of honesty and honour.

270

The eternal child. – We think that play and fairy tales belong to childhood: how shortsighted that is! As though we would want at any time of life to live without play and fairy tales! We give these things other names, to be sure, and feel differently about them, but precisely this is the evidence that they are the same things – for the child too regards play as his work and fairy tales as his truth. The brevity of life ought to preserve us from a pedantic division of life into different stages – as though each brought something new – and a poet ought for once to present a man of two hundred: one, that is, who really does live without play and fairy tales.

271

Every philosophy is a philosophy of a certain stage of life. – The stage of life at which a philosopher discovered his teaching is audible within it: he cannot prevent it, however exalted above time and the hour he may feel himself to be. Thus Schopenhauer's philosophy remains the reflected image of passionate and dejected *youth* – it is not a mode of thinking proper to men of older years; thus Plato's philosophy recalls the mid-thirties, when a cold and hot current are accustomed to buffet against one another, so that spray and delicate little clouds are thrown up and, under favouring circumstances and sunlight, the enchanting image of a rainbow.

272

Of the spirit of women. – The spiritual power of a woman is best demonstrated by her sacrificing her own spirit to that of a man out of love of him and of his spirit but then, despite this sacrifice, immediately evolving *a new spirit* within the new domain, originally alien to her nature, to which the man's disposition impels her.

273

Sexual elevation and degradation. – The tempest of the desires sometimes draws a man up to a height where all desire ceases: to that height where he truly *loves* and dwells in a better state of being even more than in a better state of volition. And, again, a good woman will often descend from true love down to desire and thereby *degrade* herself in her own eyes. The latter especially is among the most heart-moving things that can accompany the idea of a good marriage.

274

Woman fulfils, man promises. – Through the woman nature shows the point it has by now reached in its work on the image of mankind; through the man it shows what it had to overcome in attaining to this point, but also what its *intentions* are with respect to mankind. – The complete woman of every era is the idleness of the creator on that seventh day in the creation of culture, the repose of the artist in his work.

275

Transplantation. – If we have employed our spirit to master the intemperance of the affects, we have perhaps achieved this at the expense of transferring such intemperance to the spirit and are henceforth dissolute in thinking and the desire for knowledge.

276

Laughter as treason. – How and when a woman laughs is a mark of her culture: but in the sound of her laughter there is disclosed her nature, in the case of very cultured women perhaps even the last inextinguishable remnant of her nature. – That is why the psychologist will say with Horace, though for a different reason: *ridete puellae.**

277

From the souls of youths. – In their attitude towards one and the same person, youths alternate between devotion and impudence: the reason is that at bottom it is only themselves they are revering and despising and until experience has taught them the measure of their own will and ability they cannot help reeling from one of these sensations to the other in their attitude towards themselves.

278

For the improvement of the world. – If we prevented the discontented, atrabilious and sullen from propagating themselves we could magically transform the earth into a garden of happiness. – This proposition belongs in a practical philosophy for the female sex.

279

Trusting one's feelings. – The female expression that one ought to trust one's feelings means hardly more than that one ought to eat what one likes the taste of. This may be a good everyday rule, especially for sober natures. Other natures, however, have to live according to a different principle: 'you must eat, not only with your mouth, but also with your head, so that you shall not perish by the mouth's love of sweetmeats'.

---

* *ridete puellae*: laugh, maidens.

280

Love's cruel notion. – Every great love brings with it the cruel idea of killing the object of that love, so that he may be removed once and for all from the wicked game of change: for love dreads change more than it does destruction.

281

Doors. – The child sees, just as the man does, in everything he learns and experiences *doors*: but to the former they are *entrances*, to the latter only *through-ways*.

282

Sympathizing women. – The sympathy of women, which is garrulous, bears the sick man's bed into the public market-place.

283

Precocious merit. – He who acquires merit while still young usually thereby forgets how to be respectful to age and to what is older and thus to his profound disadvantage excludes himself from the society of the mature and that which bestows maturity: so that in spite of his precocious merit he remains green, importunate and boyish longer than others do.

284

Wholesale souls. – Women and artists think that when one does not contradict them one could not contradict them; reverence on ten points and silent disapprobation on ten others seems to them impossible at the same time, because they possess wholesale souls.

285

Youthful talents. – In regard to youthful talents one must act strictly in accordance with Goethe's maxim that it is often necessary to refrain from attacking error so as not to attack truth. Their condition resembles the sicknesses of pregnancy and is attended by strange appetites: these one must satisfy and look after as far as one can for the sake of the fruit one hopes they will produce. As sick-nurse to these curious invalids one must, to be sure, understand the difficult art of self-abasement.

286

Disgust at truth. – Women are so constituted that all truth regarding men, love, children, society, the aim of life, disgusts them – and that they seek to revenge themselves upon anyone who opens their eyes.

287

The source of great love. – Whence is the origin of the sudden passion – the passion of the profound and inward kind – that a man feels for a woman? Least of all from sensuality alone: but when a man encounters weakness and need of assistance and at the same time high spirits together in the same being, then something takes place in him like the sensation of his soul wanting to gush over: he is at the same moment moved and offended. At this point there arises the source of great love.

288

Cleanliness. – The sense for cleanliness should be kindled in a child to the point of passion: later it will flame up in ever new transformations almost to the height of every virtue and at last appear, as an attendant to all talents, like an aureole of purity, moderation, gentleness, character – bearing happiness within it, spreading happiness around it.

289

Of vain old men. – Deep thought pertains to youth, clear thought to age: when old men nonetheless sometimes speak and write in the manner of deep thinkers they do so out of vanity, in the belief that they will thereby assume the charm of enthusiastic youth, evolving and full of hope and presentiment.

290

Employment of novelties. – Men employ something newly learned or experienced henceforth as a ploughshare, perhaps also as a weapon: but women straightway turn it into an ornament for themselves.

291

How the two sexes act when they are in the right. – If you admit to a woman that she is in the right, she cannot refrain from setting her heel triumphantly on the neck of the defeated – she has to enjoy victory to the full; while between men in such a case being in the right usually produces a feeling of embarrassment. As a consequence the man is accustomed to victory, while to the woman it comes as an exception.

292

Renunciation in the will to beauty. – If she is to become beautiful a woman must not want to be considered pretty: that is to say, in ninety-nine cases when she could please she must disdain to please so as on the hundredth occasion to harvest as a reward the ravishment of him the portal of whose soul is great enough to admit greatness.

293

Inexplicable, insupportable. – A youth cannot grasp that an older man has already lived through his raptures, daybreaks of feeling, turns and flights of thought, once before: it even offends him to think they could have existed twice – but he grows altogether hostile when he hears that, if he is to become *fruitful*, he will have to lose these blossoms and do without their fragrance.

294

Party with the air of the sufferer. – Every party that knows how to give itself the air of the sufferer draws the hearts of the goodnatured over to it and thereby itself acquires an air of goodnaturedness – to its profound advantage.

295

Assertion safer than proof. – An assertion produces a stronger effect than an argument, at least among the majority of mankind: for argument arouses mistrust. That is why public speakers seek to hammer home their party's arguments with assertions.

296

The best concealers. – All those who regularly enjoy success possess a profound skill in always exposing their errors and weaknesses only as apparent strengths; for which reason they have to know these errors and weaknesses uncommonly well and with uncommon clarity.

297

From time to time. – He sat himself at the city gate and said to one who passed through it that this was the city gate. The latter responded that this was true, but that one should not want to be too much in the right if one wanted to be thanked for it. Oh, the former replied, I desire no thanks; but from time to time it is nonetheless very pleasant not only to be in the right but to be acknowledged to be right as well.

298

Virtue was not invented by the Germans. – Goethe's nobility and freedom from envy, Beethoven's noble hermit's resignation, Mozart's charm and graciousness of the heart, Handel's inflexible manliness and freedom under the law, Bach's confident and transfigured inner life which did not even need to renounce fame and success – are these supposed to be *German* qualities? – If not, however, it at least shows what Germans should strive after and what they can attain to.

299

*Pia fraus or something else.** – I may be wrong, but it seems to me that in contemporary Germany a twofold kind of hypocrisy has been made the duty of the moment for everyone: what is demanded is a Germanism out of care for the political interests of the Reich and a Christianity out of fear for the interests of society, both however only in words and demeanour and especially in the ability to keep silent. It is the *gloss and varnish* that now costs so much, is paid for at such a rate: it is the *spectators* on whose account the nation's face is assuming a German- and Christian-looking expression.

300

To what extent the half can be more than the whole even in the realm of the good. – In the case of all things intended to endure and demanding the service of many people much that is *less good* has to be made the *rule*, even though the organizer is very well aware of what is better and more difficult: but he will calculate on there never being any lack of people *able* to be adequate to the rule – and he knows that a middling degree of strength is the rule. – A youth is seldom able to comprehend this, and then, as a newcomer, he is amazed at how much in the right he is and how strangely blind others are.

* *Pia fraus*: pious fraud

301

The party man. – The genuine party man no longer learns, he only experiences things and judges them: whereas Solon, who was never a party man but pursued his aims beside and above the parties or in opposition to them, is significantly the father of that simple saying in which there lies enclosed the health and inexhaustibility of Athens: 'I grow old and still I go on learning.'

302

What, according to Goethe, is German. – The truly unendurable, from whom one does not like to receive even what is good, are those who, possessing *freedom of mind,* fail to notice they lack *freedom of taste and spirit.* But precisely this is, according to Goethe's well-considered opinion, *German.* – His voice and his example indicate that a German has to *be more* than a German if he wants to be useful, indeed even endurable, to other nations – and *in what direction* he ought to strive in order to emerge above and beyond himself.

303

When it is necessary to stand still. – When the masses begin to rage and reason grows dark, one does well, if one is not quite sure of the health of one's soul, to step into a doorway and take stock of the weather.

304

Possessors and revolutionaries. – The only weapon against socialism you still have at your command is not to challenge it: that is to say, yourselves to live modestly and moderately, as far as you can prevent the public display of extravagance and assist the state when it imposes heavy taxes on all superfluities and things that resemble luxuries. Do you feel disinclined to employ this weapon? In that case, you wealthy bourgeois who call yourselves 'liberal', admit to yourselves that it is the desires of your own heart that you find so fearful and threatening in the socialists, though in yourselves you consider them inevitable, as though there they were something quite different. If, as you are now, you did not have your *property* and your worries about preserving it, these desires of yours would make of you socialists: possession of property is the only thing that distinguishes you from them. You must first of all conquer yourselves if you want any kind of victory over the enemies of your wealth and comfort. – And if only this wealth and comfort were true wellbeing! It would be less external and less of an incitement to envy, it would be shared more, be more benevolent, more minded of the demands of equity, more willing to lend a helping hand. But what is ungenuine and histrionic in your pleasures, which derive more from a sense of contrast (that others do not have them and envy you) than from a sense of a fulfilment and enhancement of your powers – your houses, clothes, carriages, shop-windows, gustatory demands, your noisy enthusiasm for music and opera, finally your women, patterned and moulded but out of base metal, gilded but without the ring of gold, chosen by you as showpieces, offering themselves as showpieces: – these are the poison-bearing propagators of that sickness of the people which, as socialist scabies of the heart, is now spreading faster and faster among the masses but has its primary seat and incubator *in you*. And who is there now who can arrest this pestilence?

305
Party tactics. – When a party notices that a member has changed from being an unconditional adherent to a conditional one, it is so little capable of enduring this that it tries, through incitements and insults of all kinds, to bring him to the point of outright defection and turn him into an opponent: for it has the suspicion that the intention of seeing in their faith something of *relative* value that admits of a For and Against, a weighing and distinguishing, is more dangerous to it than a wholesale opposition.

306
Strengthening a party. – If you want to strengthen the inner constitution of a party you should give it the opportunity of being treated with obvious *injustice*; it will thereby accumulate a capital of good conscience that it perhaps previously lacked.

307
Taking care of one's past. – Because men really respect only that which was founded of old and has developed slowly, he who wants to live on after his death must take care not only of his posterity but even more of his *past*: which is why tyrants of every kind (including tyrannical artists and politicians) like to do violence to history, so that it may appear as preparation for and step-ladder to them.

308
Party writers. – The drumbeat from which young writers in the service of a party derive such satisfaction sounds to him who does not belong to the party like the rattling of chains and inspires pity rather than admiration.

309
Taking sides against ourself. – Our adherents never forgive us if we take sides against ourself: for in their eyes this means, not only to repulse their love, but also to compromise their intelligence.

310
Danger in riches. – Only he who has *spirit* ought to have *possessions*: otherwise possessions are a *public danger*. For the possessor who does not know how to make use of the free time which his possessions could purchase him will always *continue* to strive after possessions: this striving will constitute his entertainment, his strategy in his war against boredom. Thus in the end the moderate possessions that would suffice the man of spirit are transformed into actual riches – riches which are in fact the glittering product of spiritual dependence and poverty. They only *appear* quite different from what their wretched origin would lead one to expect because they are able to mask themselves with art and culture: for they

are, of course, able to *purchase* masks. By this means they arouse envy in the poorer and the uncultivated – who at bottom are envying culture and fail to recognize the masks as masks – and gradually prepare a social revolution: for gilded vulgarity and histrionic self-inflation in a supposed 'enjoyment of culture' instil into the latter the idea 'it is only a matter of money' – whereas, while it is to *some* extent a matter of money, it is *much more a matter of spirit.*

311

Pleasure in commanding and obeying. – Commanding and obeying both give pleasure: the former when it has not yet become a habit, the latter however when it has become a habit. Old servants under new masters promote pleasure in one another.

312

Ambition for the advanced post. – There is an ambition to occupy the advanced post which impels a party to venture into extreme danger.

313

When asses are needed. – You will never get the crowd to cry Hosanna until you ride into town on an ass.

314

Party custom. – Every party tries to represent everything significant that has evolved outside itself as being insignificant; if it fails in this endeavour, however, its animosity towards it is the more virulent the more excellent it is.

315

Becoming empty. – Of him who surrenders himself to events there remains less and less. Great politicians can thus become completely empty men and yet once have been rich and full.

316

Wished-for enemies. – The socialist movements are now more welcome than fear-inspiring to the dynastic governments, because through them the latter can get into their hands *the right and the weapons* for taking the exceptional measures with which they are able to strike at the figures that really fill them with terror, the democrats and anti-dynasts. – For all that such governments publicly hate they now have a secret inclination and affinity: they are obliged to veil their soul.

317

Possessions possess. – It is only up to a certain point that possessions make men more independent and free; one step further – and the possessions become master, the possessor becomes a slave: as which he must sacrifice to them his time and his thoughts and henceforth feel himself obligated to a society, nailed to a place and incorporated into a state none of which perhaps meets his inner and essential needs.

318

On the hegemony of men of knowledge. – It is easy, ridiculously easy, to erect a model for the election of a lawgiving body. First of all the honest and trustworthy men of a country who are at the same time masters and experts in one or another subject have to select one another through a process of mutual scenting out and recognition: in a narrower election those experts and men of knowledge of the first rank in each department of life must again choose one another, likewise through mutual recognition and guaranteeing. If these constituted the lawgiving body, then finally in each individual case only the voices and judgements of those expert in this specific matter would be decisive and all the rest would, as a matter of honour and simple decency, leave the vote to them alone: so that in the strictest sense the law would proceed out of the understanding of those who understand best. – Now it is parties who vote: and at every vote there must be hundreds of abashed consciences – those of the ill-informed and incapable of judgement, of those who merely repeat what they have heard, are drawn along and borne away. Nothing debases the dignity of every new law so much as this clinging blush of dishonesty to which every party vote constrains. But, as aforesaid, it is easy, ridiculously easy, to erect such a thing: no power in the world is at present strong enough to bring anything better – unless, that is, a belief in the supreme *utility of science and the man of knowledge* finally dawns even upon the most malevolent and comes to be preferred to the now dominant belief in numbers. In the sense of this future let our watchword be: 'More respect for the man of knowledge! And down with all parties!'

319

On the 'nation of thinkers' (or of bad thinking). – The obscure, undecided, ominous, elemental, intuitive elements – to employ unclear expressions for unclear things – that are attributed to the German nature, would, if they in fact existed, be a proof that its culture was many steps retarded and still enclosed within the spell and atmosphere of the Middle Ages. – There are, to be sure, certain advantages too to be found in such a retardedness: with these qualities – if, to repeat, they should still possess them – the Germans would be qualified for certain things, and especially to understand certain things, for which other nations have lost all capacity. And much is lost, certainly, if *lack of rationality* – and that is what these qualities have in common – is lost: but here, however, there is no loss without the highest compensatory gain, so that no ground at all exists for grief, presupposing one does not, like children and dainty eaters, want to enjoy the fruits of every season at the same time.

320

Owls to Athens. – The governments of the great states have in their hands two means of keeping the people subject to them in fear and obedience: a cruder one, the army, and a more refined one, the school. With the aid of the former they enlist on their side the *ambition* of the higher and the *energy* of the lower strata, insofar as both are usually composed of active and vigorous men of moderate and inferior gifts; with the aid of the other means they win for themselves the *gifted* poor, and especially the intellectually ambitious semi-poor of the middle classes. Above all, they make of the teachers of every grade a spiritual princely household that involuntarily looks 'upwards': by placing obstacle after obstacle in the way of the private school, not to speak of education at home, which they greatly disfavour, they secure to themselves the disposal of a very significant number of teaching posts upon which there are certainly directed five times the number of hungry and obsequious eyes than can ever be satisfied. These posts, however, must offer their occupants only *meagre* nourishment: thus there will be maintained in them a feverish thirst for *advancement* and they will become even more closely attached to the aims of the government. For it is always more advantageous to cultivate a moderate discontent than to encourage contentedness, which is the mother of courage and the grandmother of freethinking and presumption. Through the agency of this teaching body thus physically and spiritually curbed all the youth of the land are, as far as can be, raised to a certain level of culture graded according to the needs and objectives of the state: above all, however, the immature and ambitious spirits of all classes are almost imperceptibly imbued with the idea that only a life-course recognized and authorized by the state can bring immediate *social* distinction. The effect of this belief in state examinations and state titles is so extensive that even those who have remained independent, men who have risen through trade or craft, are still plagued by a thorn of discontent until their position too has been noted and recognized from above through the gracious bestowal of ranks and orders – until they 'have no need to be ashamed'. Finally the state attaches to all those countless official posts and positions of profit in its possession the *obligation* to be educated and certificated by the state schools if one wishes to pass through these portals: the respect of society, bread for oneself, the possibility of a family, protection from above, the feeling of solidarity shared by those with a common upbringing – all this constitutes a net of expectations within which every young man is caught: who is there to warn him against it! If, after all this, the obligation upon everyone to be a *soldier* for some years has during the course of generations become an unthinking habit and natural event in accordance with which one tailors the programme of one's life, then the state can go on to venture the masterstroke of weaving *together* school *and* army, giftedness, ambition and energy through the offering of advantages: that is to say, by enticing the *more highly gifted* and *cultivated* into the army with more favourable conditions and imbuing them with the soldierly spirit of cheerful obedience, so that they will perhaps join the colours for an extended period and with their talents create for them a new and ever more glittering reputation. – Nothing is then lacking but opportunities for great wars: and this will be taken care of, as a professional matter and thus in all *innocence*, by the diplomats, together with the newspapers and stock exchanges: for the 'nation', as a nation of soldiers, always has a good conscience when it comes to wars, there is no need to worry about that.

321

The press. – If we consider how even now all great political occurrences creep on to the stage silent and shrouded, how they are concealed by insignificant events and seem small in proximity to them, how it is not until long after they have happened that their profound effects are felt and the ground trembles – what significance can we then accord the press as it is now, with its daily expenditure of lungpower on exclaiming, deafening, inciting, shocking – is it anything more than the *permanent false alarm* that leads ears and senses off in the wrong direction?

322

After a great event. – A man or a nation whose soul has come to light on the occasion of a great event usually feels afterwards the need for a piece of *childishness* or *coarseness*, as much out of embarrassment as for the purpose of recovery.

323

To be a good German means to degermanize oneself. – That in which national differences are seen to consist is to a far greater degree than has yet been realized only a difference between varying *stages of culture* and to a very small extent something permanent (and even this not in a strict sense). That is why all argumentation on the basis of national character is so little incumbent upon him who labours at the *transformation* of convictions, that is to say at culture. If we consider, for example, all that *has been* German, we shall at once improve the theoretical question 'what *is* German?' into the counter-question 'what is *now* German?' – and every *good* German will give it a practical answer precisely by overcoming his German qualities. For whenever a people goes forward and grows it bursts the girdle that has hitherto given it its *national* appearance; if it remains stationary, if it languishes, a new girdle fastens itself about its soul, the crust forming ever more firmly around it constructs as it were a prison whose walls grow higher and higher. If, therefore, a people possesses a great deal that is firm, this is a proof that it wants to become petrified and would like to turn itself into a *monument*: as from a certain point of time onwards happened with Egypt. He therefore who has the interests of the Germans at heart should for his part see how he can grow more and more beyond what is German. That is why a *change into the ungermanic* has always been the mark of the most able of our people.

324

What a foreigner said. – A foreigner travelling in Germany gave offence and pleasure through certain things he said according to where he was when he said them. All Swabians with intelligence – he used to say – are coquettish. – The other Swabians, however, still thought that Uhland had been a poet and Goethe had been immoral. – The best thing about the German novels now so highly praised was that you did not need to read them: you knew them already. – The Berliner seemed more goodnatured than the South German, for he was very fond of a joke and could therefore take one against himself: which was not so with the South German. – The minds of the Germans were being kept down by their beer and news-papers: he recommended to them tea and pamphlets, though only as a cure of course. – He advised taking a look at how the various nations of aged Europe each had a special knack of displaying some particular qual-ity of old age, to the enjoyment of those sitting before this great stage: how well the French represented the prudence and amiability of old age, the English its experience and restraint, the Italians its innocence and ingenuousness. Was it likely that the other masks of old age would not be represented? Where was arrogant old age? Where tyrannical old age? Where avaricious old age? – The most dangerous region of Germany was Saxony and Thuringia: nowhere else was there more intellectual activity and knowledge of human nature, together with free-spiritedness, and yet it was all so modestly concealed by the ugly dialect of the populace and their eagerness to be of service that you hardly noticed that what you were dealing with was the intellectual sergeant-majors of Germany and its instructors in good and evil. – The arrogance of the North Germans was kept within bounds by their inclination to obedience, that of the South Germans by their inclination to indolence. – It seemed to him that German men had in their women inept but very self-confident house-wives: they persistently spoke so well of themselves they had convinced almost all the world, and in any event their men, of the existence of a peculiarly German housewifely virtue. – When conversation then turned to Germany's internal and external politics, he was accustomed to say – or, as he put it, to disclose – that Germany's greatest statesman did not believe in great statesmen. – The future of the Germans he found threat-ened and threatening: for they had forgotten how to *enjoy* themselves (which the Italians understand so well) but through the great game of chance of wars and dynastic revolutions became *accustomed to emotion*, consequently they would one day have an uprising. For this was the strongest emotion a people could procure for itself. – The reason the German socialist was the most dangerous was that he was driven by no *definite* need; he suffered from not knowing what he wanted; thus, even if he achieved a great deal, he would languish from desire even in the midst of plenty just like Faust, though presumably like a very plebeian Faust. 'For Bismarck has driven out of the cultivated Germans the *Faust Devil* that plagued them so', he cried in conclusion: 'but now the Devil has entered into the swine and is worse than ever he was!'

325

Opinions. – Most people are nothing and count for nothing until they have clad themselves in general convictions and public opinions – in accordance with the tailor's philosophy: clothes make the man. In regard to exceptional men, however, the saying should read: *only the wearer creates the costume*; here opinions cease from being public and become something other than masks, finery and camouflage.

326
Two kinds of sobriety. – So as not to confuse sobriety out of exhaustion with sobriety out of moderation one has to observe that the former is ill-tempered, the latter cheerful.

327
Adulteration of joy. – Not to call something good a day longer than it seems to us good, and above all: *not a day sooner* – that is the only way of preserving the genuiness of *joy*: which otherwise all too easily grows pale and insipid to the palate and is now among the adulterated provisions of life for whole strata of the people.

328
The scapegoat of virtue. – When a man does the best he can, those who wish him well but are not adequate to his deed promptly seek out a goat so as to slaughter it, believing it to be the scapegoat – but it is in fact the scapegoat, not of sin, but of virtue.

329
Sovereignty. – To revere the bad, too, and to embrace it, if it *pleases* us, and to have no idea that we might be ashamed of being thus pleased, is the mark of sovereignty, in great things and small.

330
Effect a phantom, not reality. – The significant man gradually learns that *insofar as he produces an effect* he is a *phantom* in the heads of others, and perhaps his soul begins to torment him with the subtle question whether he is not obliged to preserve and maintain this phantom of himself for the *benefit* of his fellow men.

331
Giving and taking. – If we have taken from someone the slightest thing (or prevented him from having it), he is blind to the fact that we have given him much greater, indeed even the greatest things.

332
The fruitful field. – All rejection and negation points to a lack of fruitfulness: if only we were fruitful fields, we would at bottom let nothing perish unused and see in every event, thing and man welcome manure, rain or sunshine.

333
Society as enjoyment. – If a man deliberately renounces others and keeps himself in solitude, he can thereby make of the society of men, enjoyed rarely, a rare delicacy.

334
Knowing how to suffer publicly. – We must display our unhappiness and from time to time be heard to sigh, be seen to be impatient: for if we let others see how happy and secure in ourselves we are in spite of suffering

and deprivation, how malicious and envious we would make them! – We have to take care not to corrupt our fellow men; moreover, they would in the instance referred to impose upon us a heavy impost, and our *public suffering* is in any event also our *private advantage*.

335
Warmth in the heights. – It is warmer in the heights than people in the valleys think, especially in winter. The thinker will know what is meant by this metaphor.

336
Willing the good, achieving the beautiful. -- It is not enough to practise the *good*, one must have willed it and, in the words of the poet, receive the divinity into one's *will*. But one may not will the *beautiful*, one must be *able to achieve* it, in blindness and innocence, without anything of the in-quisitiveness of Psyche. He who lights his lantern to seek out perfect men should take note of this sign: they are those who always act for the sake of the good and in doing so always attain to the beautiful without giving thought to it. For many of the better and nobler sort present, for all their good will and good works, an unpleasant and ugly aspect for lack of a beautiful soul and its capacities; we recoil from them, and even virtue is done harm to by the repellent garb in which their bad taste dresses it.

337
Danger in renunciation. – We must take care not to establish our life on too narrow an area of desires: for if we renounce the joys that position, hon-ours, companionship, sensual pleasures, comforts, the arts afford, the day may come when we discover that through doing without these things we have acquired for a neighbour, not *wisdom*, but *boredom with life*.

338
Final opinion about opinions. – One should either conceal one's opinions or conceal oneself behind one's opinions. He who does otherwise does not know the ways of the world or belongs to the order of holy foolhardiness.

339
*'Gaudeamus igitur'.** – Joy must contain edifying and healing powers for the moral nature of man too: how otherwise could it happen that, as soon as it reposes in the sunlight of joy, our soul involuntarily promises itself 'to be good', 'to become perfect', and that as it does so it is seized as though by a blissful shudder with a presentiment of perfection?

340
To one who is praised. – So long as you are praised think only that you are not yet on your own path but on that of another.

341
Loving the master. – The apprentice loves the master differently from the way the master loves him.

*'*Gaudeamus igitur'*: Let us then rejoice.

342

All too beautiful and human. – 'Nature is too beautiful for you, poor mortal' – this feeling is by no means rare: yet once or twice, when I have intimately observed all that is human, all its abundance, strength, tenderness, complicatedness, it has seemed to me as though I had to say in all humility: '*man* too is too beautiful for the man who reflects on him!' – and I do not mean some particular kind of man, moral man for instance, but every man.

343

Movable goods and landed property. – If life has treated a man like a brigand, and has taken from him all it could in the way of honours, friends, adherents, health, possessions of all kinds, he may perhaps, after the first shock, discover that he is *richer* than before. For it is only now that he knows what is truly his, what no brigand is able to get his hands on; so that he perhaps emerges out of all this plundering and confusion wearing the noble aspect of a great landed proprietor.

344

Involuntarily an ideal. – The most painful feeling there is, is to discover that one is always taken for something higher than one is. For one is then obliged to admit to oneself: something in you is lies and deception, your words, the impression you make, your glance, your actions – and this deceptive something is as necessary as your honesty in other matters but continually undermines the effect of this honesty and devalues it.

345

Idealist and liar. – We should not let ourselves be tyrannized over by our fairest ability – that of elevating things into the ideal: otherwise one day truth will depart from us with the angry words: 'you liar from the very heart, what have I to do with you?'

346

Being misunderstood. – If we are misunderstood as a whole, it is impossible completely to eradicate misunderstanding on any one individual point. We have to realize this if we are not to squander superfluous energy on our own defence.

347

The water-drinker speaks. – Go on drinking the wine that has refreshed you all your life – what is it to you that I have to be a water-drinker? Are wine and water not peaceable, fraternal elements which dwell side by side in harmony?

348

From the land of the cannibals. – In solitude the solitary man consumes himself, in the crowd the crowd consumes him. Now choose.

349

At the freezing-point of the will. – 'It will come, one day, that hour that will envelope you in a golden cloud where there is no pain: where the soul has the enjoyment of its own weariness and, happy in a patient game with its own patience, is like the waves of a lake which, reflecting the colours of an evening sky on a quiet summer's day, lap and lap against the bank and then are still again – without end, without aim, without satiation, without desire – all repose that rejoices in change, all ebbing back and flooding forward with the pulsebeat of nature.' This is how all invalids feel and speak: but if they do attain to that hour there arrives, after brief enjoyment, boredom. This, however, is a thawing wind for the frozen will: it awakens, stirs itself, and again engenders wish upon wish. – To wish is a sign of recovery or improvement.

350

The disavowed ideal. – It happens exceptionally that a man achieves his highest flight only when he disavows his ideal: for this ideal has hitherto driven him too impetuously, so that he has got out of breath half way along every path he has taken and has had to come to a standstill.

351

Revealing propensity. – It should be regarded as a sign that a man suffers from envy but is striving for higher things when he feels drawn by the idea that in face of the man of excellence there is only one way of escape: love.

352

*Bonheur de l'escalier.** – Just as many people's wit fails to keep pace with the opportunity for it, so that the opportunity has already gone out of the door while the wit is still standing on the stairs: so others experience a kind of *bonheur de l'escalier* which runs too slowly always to stay by the side of fleet-footed time: the best they get to enjoy of an event, or of an entire period of their life, falls to them only a long time afterwards, and then often only as a feeble, spicy fragrance that awakens sorrow and longing – as though it had once been possible to imbibe this element to the full, though now it is too late.

353

Worms. – It says nothing against the ripeness of a spirit that it has a few worms.

354

The seat of victory. – A good posture on a horse robs your opponent of his courage and your audience of their hearts – why do you need to attack? Sit like one who has conquered!

355

Danger in admiration. – Through too great admiration for the virtues of others it is possible to lose interest in one's own and from lack of practice finally lose them altogether without acquiring those of others in return.

* *Bonheur de l'escalier*: Nietzsche's play on '*l'esprit de l'escalier*', the disposition to react only late after the event.

356

Usefulness of sickliness. – He who is often sick does not only have a much greater enjoyment of health on account of the frequency with which he gets well: he also has a greatly enhanced sense of what is healthy and what sick in works and actions, his own and those of others: so that it is precisely the sickliest writers, for example – and almost all the great writers are, unfortunately, among them – who usually evidence in their writings a much steadier and more certain tone of health, because they understand the philosophy of psychical health and recovery better and are better acquainted with its teachers – morning, sunshine, forests and springs – than the physically robust.

357

Disloyalty, condition of mastership. – There is nothing to be done about it: every master has only one pupil – and he becomes disloyal to him – for he too is destined for mastership.

358

Never in vain. – In the mountains of truth you will never climb in vain: either you will get up higher today or you will exercise your strength so as to be able to get up higher tomorrow.

359

Before an ancient window. – Is what you see of the world through this window so beautiful, then, that you have lost all desire to look through any other – and even try to prevent others from doing so?

360

Indication of violent changes. – If we dream of people we have long since forgotten or who have for long been dead, it is a sign that we have gone through a violent change within ourself and that the ground upon which we live has been completely turned over: so that the dead rise up and our antiquity becomes our modernity.

361

Medicine of the soul. – Lying still and thinking little is the cheapest medicine for all sicknesses of the soul and, if persisted with, grows more pleasant hour by hour.

362

On spiritual order of rank. – It ranks you far beneath him that you seek to establish the exceptions while he seeks to establish the rule.

363

The fatalist. – You *have* to believe in fate – science can compel you to. What then grows out of this belief in your case – cowardice, resignation or frankness and magnanimity – bears witness to the soil upon which that seedcorn has been scattered but not, however, to the seedcorn itself – for out of this anything and everything can grow.

364

Ground of much ill-humour. – He who prefers the beautiful in life to the useful will, like a child who prefers sweets to bread, certainly end by ruining his digestion and will look out on the world very ill-humouredly.

365

Excess as cure. – One can reacquire a taste for one's own talents by revering and enjoying antithetical talents for a long time to excess. – The employment of excess as a cure is one of the more refined artifices in the art of living.

366

'Will a self'. – Active, successful natures act, not according to the dictum 'know thyself', but as if there hovered before them the commandment: *will* a self and thou shalt *become* a self. – Fate seems to have left the choice still up to them; whereas the inactive and contemplative cogitate on what they *have* already chosen, on *one* occasion, when they entered into life.

367

Living without followers. – We grasp how little adherents are worth only when we have ceased to be an adherent of our adherents.

368

Darkening ourselves. – If we are to get free of the troublesome gnat-swarms of our admirers we have to know how to darken ourselves.

369

Boredom. – There is a boredom known to the most refined and cultivated heads to whom the best the earth has to offer has become stale: accustomed to eating choice and ever choicer food and to disgust with the coarser, they are in danger of starving to death – for of the very best there is very little, and sometimes it has become inaccessible or rock-hard, so that even good teeth cannot bite into it.

370

Danger in admiration. – Admiration for a quality or an art can be so great it can hinder us from striving to possess it.

371

What we desire of art. – One man wants to enjoy his own nature by means of art, another wants with its aid to get above and away from his nature for a time. In accordance with both needs there exists a twofold species of art and artist.

372

Apostasy. – He who reneges on us perhaps does not thereby offend us but he certainly offends our adherents.

373

After death. – Usually it is only long after a man's death that we find it incomprehensible that he is no longer here: in the case of very great men often only after decades. He who is honest usually feels when someone dies that he has really been deprived of very little and that the solemn funeral orator is a hypocrite. Only when we need him do we learn the necessity of an individual, and his true epitaph is a late sigh.

374
Leaving in Hades. – There are many things we must leave in the Hades of half-conscious feeling, and not desire to redeem them out of their shadow existence, otherwise they will, as thoughts and words, become our demonic masters and cruelly demand our blood of us.

375
Closeness of beggary. – Even the richest spirit occasionally loses the key to the chamber where his hoarded treasure lies, and is then no different from the poorest, who has to beg merely to stay alive.

376
Chain-thinkers. – To him who has thought a great deal every new thought he hears or reads at once appears in the form of a link in a chain.

377
Pity. – In the gilded sheath of pity there is sometimes stuck the dagger of envy.

378
What is genius? – To will an exalted end *and* the means to it.

379
Fighter's vanity. – He who has no hope of winning a fight, or has plainly lost it, is all the more anxious to secure admiration for the way in which he has fought it.

380
The philosophical life is misinterpreted. – At the moment when anyone begins to take philosophy seriously all the world believes the opposite.

381
Imitation. – The bad acquires esteem by being imitated, the good loses it – especially in art.

382
Ultimate lesson of history. – 'Ah, if only I had lived in those days!' – that is the speech of foolish and trifling men. Every piece of history one has studied *seriously*, though it be that of the most lauded land of the past, will rather lead one to exclaim at last: 'Anything rather than back to that! The spirit of that age would press upon you with the weight of a hundred atmospheres, the good and beautiful in it you would not enjoy, the bad in it you would not be able to digest.' – Posterity can be relied on to pass the same judgement on our own age: it will have been intolerable, life in it unliveable. – And yet does not everyone endure it in his own age? – Yes,

and the reason is that the spirit of his age does not only lie *upon* him but is also *within* him. The spirit of the age offers resistance to itself, bears up against itself.

383

Nobility as mask. – With nobility of bearing we provoke our enemies, with unconcealed envy we almost reconcile them with us: for envy compares, equates, it is an involuntary and groaning kind of modesty. – Has, on account of this advantage, envy ever been assumed as a mask by those who were in fact not envious? Perhaps; it is certain, however, that nobility of bearing is often employed as a mask for envy by ambitious people who would rather suffer disadvantages and provoke their enemies than let it be seen that inwardly they equate themselves with them.

384

Unforgivable. – You gave him an opportunity of showing greatness of character and he did not seize it. He will never forgive you for that.

385

Anti-theses. – The most senile thing ever thought about man is contained in the celebrated saying 'the ego is always hateful'; the most childish in the even more celebrated 'love thy neighbour as thyself'. – In the former knowledge of human nature has ceased, in the latter it has not yet even begun.

386

The missing ear. – 'So long as one always lays the blame on others one still belongs to the mob, when one always assumes responsibility oneself one is on the path of wisdom; but the wise man blames no one, neither himself nor others.' – Who says this? – Epictetus, eighteen hundred years ago. – It was heard but forgotten. – No, it was not heard and forgotten: not everything gets forgotten. But there was lacking an ear for it, the ear of Epictetus. – So did he say it into his own ear? – Yes, that is how it is: wisdom is the whispering of the solitary to himself in the crowded marketplace.

387

Error of standpoint, not of eye. – We always stand a few paces too close to ourselves, and always a few paces too distant from our neighbour. So it happens that we judge him too much wholesale and ourselves too much by individual, occasional, insignificant traits and occurrences.

388

Ignorance in arms. – How little we mind whether another knows or does not know something – whereas he perhaps sweats blood at the very idea of being thought ignorant in the matter. There are, indeed, egregious fools who go about armed with a quiver full of anathemas and peremptory decrees, ready to shoot down anyone who exposes the fact that there are things in which his judgement does not count.

389

At the inn-table of experience. – People who, out of inborn moderation, leave every glass standing only half-emptied refuse to admit that everything in the world has its dregs and sediment.

390

Singing birds. – The adherents of a great man are accustomed to blind themselves the better to sing his praises.

391

Not up to it. – The good displeases us when we are not up to it.

392

The rule as mother or as child. – The condition that gives birth to the rule is different from the condition the rule gives birth to.

393

Comedy. – We sometimes harvest love and honour for deeds or works which we have long since cast from us like a skin: and then we are easily tempted to play the comedians of our own past and throw our old hide back over our shoulders – and not only out of vanity but also from goodwill towards our admirers.

394

Biographers' error. – The small amount of force required to push a boat into the river should not be confused with the force of this river that thereafter bears it along: but this confusion exists in almost all biographies.

395

Do not buy too dear. – What we buy too dear we usually make bad use of, because we do so without love and with painful recollections – and thus we suffer a twofold disadvantage from it.

396

Which philosophy society is always in need of. – The pillars of the social order rest on this foundation: that everyone cheerfully regards that which he is, does and strives after, his health or sickness, his poverty or prosperity, his honour or insignificance, and feels as he does so *'I would not change places with anyone.'* – He who wants to influence the order of society has only to implant into people's hearts this philosophy of cheerful rejection of changing places and absence of envy.

397

Mark of the noble soul. – A noble soul is not that which is capable of the highest flights but that which rises little and falls little but dwells *permanently* in a free, translucent atmosphere and elevation.

398

Greatness and those who see it. – The finest effect of greatness is that it bestows on those who see it a magnificatory and discriminating eye.

399

Being satisfied. – That maturity of understanding has been attained is manifested in the fact that one no longer repairs to where rare flowers stand among the thorniest hedgerows of knowledge but is satisfied with garden, forest, field and meadow, in the knowledge that life is too short for the rare and extraordinary.

400

Advantage in privation. – He who dwells always in warmth and fullness of heart and as it were in the summer air of the soul can have no idea of that shuddery rapture which seizes on wintery natures who are by way of exception touched by rays of love and the cool breath of a sunny February day.

401

Recipe for the sufferer. – Is the burden of living becoming too heavy for you? – Then you must increase the burden of your life. When the sufferer at last thirsts for the river of Lethe and seeks it – he must become a *hero* if he is to be sure of finding it.

402

The judge. – He who has beheld anyone's ideal is his inexorable judge and as it were his bad conscience.

403

Utility of great renunciation. – The most useful thing about a great renunciation is that it communicates to us that pride in virtue through which we are from then on able easily to demand of ourselves many petty renunciations.

404

How duty acquires lustre. – The means of transforming your iron duty into gold in everyone's eyes is: always to perform a little more than you promise.

405

Prayer to men. – 'Forgive us our virtues' – that is how one should pray to men.

406

Those who create and those who enjoy. – Everyone who enjoys believes the tree was concerned about the fruit; but it was, in fact, concerned about the seed. – It is in this that there lies the difference between all who create and all who enjoy.

407

The glory of the great. – Of what account is genius if it does not communicate to him who contemplates and reveres it such freedom and elevation of feeling that he no longer has need of genius! – *Rendering themselves superfluous* – that is the glory of all great men.

408

Descent into Hades. – I too have been in the underworld, like Odysseus, and will often be there again; and I have not sacrificed only rams to be able to talk with the dead, but have not spared my own blood as well. There have been four pairs who did not refuse themselves to me, the sacrificer: Epicurus and Montaigne, Goethe and Spinoza, Plato and Rousseau, Pascal and Schopenhauer. With these I have had to come to terms when I have wandered long alone, from them will I accept judgement, to them will I listen when in doing so they judge one another. Whatever I say, resolve, cogitate for myself and others: upon these eight I fix my eyes and see theirs fixed upon me. – May the living forgive me if *they* sometimes appear to me as shades, so pale and ill-humoured, so restless and, alas! so lusting for life: whereas those others then seem to me so alive, as though now, *after* death, they could never again grow weary of life. *Eternal liveliness*, however, is what counts: what do 'eternal life', or life at all, matter to us!

PART TWO

THE WANDERER
AND
HIS SHADOW

The Shadow: As it is so long since I heard your voice, I would like to give you an opportunity of speaking.

The Wanderer: Someone said something: – where? and who? It almost seems as though it were I myself speaking, though in an even weaker voice than mine.

The Shadow (after a pause): Are you not glad to have an opportunity of speaking?

The Wanderer: By God and all the things I do not believe in, it is my shadow speaking; I hear it but I do not believe it.

The Shadow: Let us accept it and think no more about it: in an hour it will all be over.

The Wanderer: That is just what I thought when, in a wood near Pisa, I saw first two and then five camels.

The Shadow: It is well we are both indulgent if our understanding for once comes to a stop: thus we shall converse together without recriminations and not press one another too hard if we fail to understand something the other has said. If we know not what to reply, it will be enough to say something: it is under this reasonable condition that I agree to converse with anyone. In a long discussion even the wisest of us is once a fool and three times a simpleton.

The Wanderer: Your modesty is not flattering to him you confess it to.

The Shadow: Ought I, then, to flatter?

The Wanderer: I thought a man's shadow was his vanity: but his vanity would never ask: 'ought I, then, to flatter?'

The Shadow: Neither does a man's vanity, insofar as I know it, ask, as I have asked twice already, *whether* it may speak; it never ceases from speaking.

The Wanderer: Only now do I notice how impolite I am towards you, my beloved shadow: I have not yet said a word of how very much I *rejoice* to hear you and not merely to see you. You will know that I love shadow as much as I love light. For there to be beauty of face, clarity of speech, benevolence and firmness of character, shadow is as needful as light. They are not opponents: they stand, rather, lovingly hand in hand, and when light disappears, shadow slips away after it.

The Shadow: And I hate the same thing you hate: night. I love mankind because they are disciples of light, and I rejoice in the gleam that burns in their eyes when they discover and acquire knowledge, indefatigable knowers and discoverers that they are. That shadow all things cast whenever the sunlight of knowledge falls upon them – that shadow too am I.

The Wanderer: I believe I understand you, even though your expressions are somewhat shadowy. But you were right: good friends now and then exchange an obscure word as a sign of agreement which to any third party is intended for an enigma. And we are good friends. And so enough preamble! There are a couple of hundred questions pressing upon my soul, and the time you have in which to answer them is perhaps only brief. Let us hasten to see what there is we can peaceably agree upon.

The Shadow: But shadows are more bashful than men: promise you will tell no one how we talked together!

The Wanderer: *How* we talked together? Heaven defend me from long-spun-out literary conversations! If Plato had taken less pleasure in spinning-out his readers would take more pleasure in Plato. A conversation that gives delight in reality is, if transformed into writing and read, a painting with nothing but false perspectives: everything is too long or too short. – But shall I perhaps be permitted to tell *what* it was we were in accord over?

The Shadow: That I am content with; for they will all recognize in it only your opinions: no one will think of the shadow.

The Wanderer: Perhaps you are wrong, my friend! Up to now people have perceived in my opinions more shadow than me.

The Shadow: More shadow than light! Is it possible?

The Wanderer: Be serious, dear fool! My very first question demands seriousness. –

1

Of the tree of knowledge. – Probability but no truth: appearance of freedom but no freedom – it is on account of these two fruits that the tree of knowledge cannot be confounded with the tree of life.

2

The rationality of the world. – That the world is *not* the epitome of an eternal rationality can be conclusively proved by the fact that that *piece of the world* which we know – I mean our own human rationality – is not so very rational. And if *it* is not always perfectly wise and rational, then the rest of the world will not be so either; here the conclusion *a minori ad majus, a parte ad totum,** applies, and does so with decisive force.

3

'In the beginning'. – To glorify the origin – that is the metaphysical after-shoot that breaks out when we meditate on history and makes us believe that what stands at the beginning of all things is also what is most valuable and essential.

4

Standard for the value of truth. – The effort required to climb a mountain is certainly not the standard by which to assess its height. And are things supposed to be different in the case of science! – do some who would like

* *'a minori . . . ad totum'*: from the less to the greater, from the part to the whole.

to be accounted initiates tell us that the effort required to attain to truth is to decide the value of truth! This mad morality derives from the idea that 'truths' are really nothing more than gymnastic apparatus upon which we are supposed bravely to work ourselves to exhaustion – a morality for athletes and gymnasts of the spirit.

5

Linguistic usage and reality. – There exists a feigned disrespect for all the things which men in fact take most seriously, *for all the things closest to them.* One says, for example, 'one eats only in order to live' – which is a damned *lie,* as is that which speaks of the begetting of children as the real objective of all voluptuousness. Conversely, the high esteem in which the 'most serious things' are held is almost never quite genuine: the priests and metaphysicians, to be sure, have in these domains altogether accustomed us to a feignedly exaggerated *linguistic usage,* but they have not converted the feeling which refuses to take these most serious things as seriously as those despised closest things. – An unfortunate consequence of this twofold hypocrisy, however, is always that the closest things, for example eating, housing, clothing, social intercourse, are not made the object of constant impartial and *general* reflection and reform: because these things are accounted degrading, they are deprived of serious intellectual and artistic consideration; so that here habit and frivolity easily carry off the victory over the unthinking, especially over inexperienced youth: while on the other hand our continual offences against the most elementary laws of the body and the spirit reduce us all, young and old, to a disgraceful dependence and bondage – I mean to that, at bottom wholly unnecessary dependence on physicians, teachers and curers of souls who still lie like a burden on the whole of society.

6

Earthly frailty and its chief cause. – When we look around us we can always encounter people who have eaten eggs all their lives and have never noticed that the longer ones are the best tasting, who do not know that a thunderstorm is beneficial to the bowels, that pleasant odours smell stronger in cold clear air, that our sense of taste differs with differing phases of the moon, that speaking well or listening intently at mealtimes is harmful to the stomach. Even if these examples of a lack of the power of observation may seem inadequate, one is bound to admit that most people see the *closest things of all* very badly and very rarely pay heed to them. And is this a matter of indifference? – One should consider that *almost all the physical and psychical frailties* of the individual derive from this lack: not knowing what is beneficial to us and what harmful in the institution of our mode of life, in the division of the day, in for how long and with whom we enjoy social intercourse, in profession and leisure, commanding and obeying, feeling for art and nature, eating, sleeping and reflecting; being *unknowledgeable in the smallest and most everyday things* and failing to keep an eye on them – this it is that transforms the earth for so many into a 'vale of tears'. Let it not be said that, here as everywhere, it is a question of human *lack of understanding*: on the contrary – there exists enough, and more than enough understanding, only it is *employed in the wrong direction* and *artificially diverted* away from these smallest and closest things. Priests and teachers, and the sublime lust for power of idealists of every description, the cruder and the more refined, hammer even into children that what matters is something quite different: the salvation of the soul, the service of the state, the advancement of science, or the accumulation of reputation and possessions, all as the means of doing service to mankind as a whole; while the requirements of the individual, his great and small needs within the twenty-four hours of the day, are to be regarded as something contemptible or a matter of indifference. – Already in ancient Greece Socrates was defending himself with all his might against this arrogant neglect of the human for the benefit of the human race, and loved to indicate the true compass and content of all reflection and concern with an expression of Homer's: it comprises, he said, nothing other than 'that which I encounter of good and ill in my own house'.

7
Two means of consolation. – Epicurus, the soul-soother of later antiquity, had that wonderful insight, which is still today so rarely to be discovered, that to quieten the heart it is absolutely not necessary to have solved the ultimate and outermost theoretical questions. Thus to those tormented by 'fear of the gods' it sufficed him to say: 'if the gods exist they do not concern themselves with us' – instead of indulging in fruitless and distant disputation over the ultimate question whether the gods do in fact exist. This position is much more favourable and much stronger: one gives the other a few steps advantage and thus makes him more willing to listen and ponder. As soon, however, as he sets about demonstrating the opposite – that the gods do concern themselves with us – into what wrong paths and thorny thickets the poor fellow must stray, entirely of his own volition and not through any cunning of his interlocutor, who needs only to possess sufficient humanity and subtlety to conceal the pity he feels at this spectacle. At last this other will arrive at a feeling of disgust, the strongest argument against any proposition, disgust at his own assertion; he will cool down and depart in the same mood as that which characterizes the pure atheist: 'what do the gods matter to me anyway! The devil take them!' – In other instances, especially when some hypothesis belonging half to physics and half to morals had cast gloom over someone's spirits, he refrained from refuting this hypothesis and admitted it might well be true: but he added that there was *yet another* hypothesis to explain the same phenomenon; perhaps this second hypothesis represented the truth. A *multiplicity* of hypotheses, for example as to the origin of the bad conscience, suffices still in our own time to lift from the soul that shadow that so easily arises from a laborious pondering over a single hypothesis which, being the only one visible, is a hundredfold overrated. – Thus he who wishes to offer consolation – to the unfortunate,

ill-doers, hypochondriacs, the dying – should call to mind the two pacifying formulae of Epicurus, which are capable of being applied to very
many questions. Reduced to their simplest form they would perhaps
become: firstly, if that is how things are they do not concern us; secondly,
things may be thus but they may also be otherwise.

8

In the night. – As soon as night falls our perception of the most immediate
things changes. The wind goes along as though on forbidden pathways,
whispering as though seeking something, ill-humoured because it does
not find it. The lamplight shines with a dull ruddy glow, gazing wearily,
unwillingly struggling against the night, an impatient slave of wakeful
man. The sleeper lies breathing fitfully, a shuddery beat to which ever-
recurring care seems to play the melody – we cannot hear it, but when the
sleeper's breast rises we feel our heart tighten, and when his breath sinks
down and almost dies away into deathly silence we say to ourself 'rest,
rest, poor perturbed spirit!' – we desire for all that lives, because it lives so
oppressed, an eternal rest; night lures us over to death. – If men had to do
without the sun, and waged war against the night with moonlight and
oil, what philosophy would envelop them in its veil! One can see only
too well, as things are, how the darkness and deprivation of sun that
enshrouds half his life has rendered the spiritual and psychical nature
of man on the whole dark and gloomy.

9

Where the theory of freedom of will originated. – Over one man *necessity* stands
in the shape of his passions, over another as the habit of hearing and
obeying, over a third as a logical conscience, over a fourth as caprice and a
mischievous pleasure in escapades. These four will, however, seek the
freedom of their will precisely where each of them is most firmly fettered: it
is as if the silkworm sought the freedom of its will in spinning. How does
this happen? Evidently because each considers himself most free where
his *feeling of living* is greatest; thus, as we have said, in passion, in duty, in
knowledge, in mischievousness respectively. That through which the individual human being is strong, wherein he feels himself animated, he
involuntarily thinks must also always be the element of his freedom: he
accounts dependence and dullness, independence and the feeling of
living as necessarily coupled. – Here an experience in the social-political
domain has been falsely transferred to the farthest metaphysical domain:
in the former the strong man is also the free man; the lively feeling of joy
and sorrow, high hope, boldness in desire, powerfulness in hatred is the
property of the rulers and the independent, while the subjected man, the
slave, lives dull and oppressed. – The theory of freedom of will is an
invention of *ruling* classes.

10

Feeling no new chains. – So long as we do not *feel* that we are dependent on
anything we regard ourselves as independent: a false conclusion that

demonstrates how proud and lusting for power man is. For he here assumes that as soon as he experiences dependence he must under all circumstances notice and recognize it, under the presupposition that he is *accustomed* to living in independence and if, exceptionally, he lost it, he would at once perceive a sensation antithetical to the one he is accustomed to. – But what if the opposite were true: that he is *always* living in manifold dependence but regards himself *as free* when, out of long habituation, he *no longer perceives* the weight of the chains? It is only from *new* chains that he now suffers: – 'freedom of will' really means nothing more than feeling no new chains.

11

Freedom of will and isolation of facts. – Our usual imprecise mode of observation takes a group of phenomena as one and calls it a fact: between this fact and another fact it imagines in addition an empty space, it *isolates* every fact. In reality, however, all our doing and knowing is not a succession of facts and empty spaces but a continuous flux. Now, belief in freedom of will is incompatible precisely with the idea of a continuous, homogeneous, undivided, indivisible flowing: it presupposes that *every individual action is isolate and indivisible*; it is an *atomism* in the domain of willing and knowing. – Just as we understand characters only imprecisely, so do we also facts: we speak of identical characters, identical facts: *neither exists.* Now, we praise and censure, however, only under this false presupposition that there are *identical* facts, that there exists a graduated order of *classes* of facts which corresponds to a graduated world-order: thus we *isolate*, not only the individual fact, but also again groups of supposedly identical facts (good, evil, sympathetic, envious actions, etc.) – in both cases erroneously. – The word and the concept are the most manifest ground for our belief in this isolation of groups of actions: we do not only *designate* things with them, we think originally that through them we grasp the *true* in things. Through words and concepts we are still continually misled into imagining things as being simpler than they are, separate from one another, indivisible, each existing in and for itself. A philosophical mythology lies concealed in *language* which breaks out again every moment, however careful one may be otherwise. Belief in freedom of will – that is to say in *identical* facts and in *isolated* facts – has in language its constant evangelist and advocate.

12

The fundamental errors. – For man to feel any sort of psychical pleasure or displeasure he must be in the grip of one of these two illusions: *either* he believes in the *identity* of certain facts, certain sensations: in which case he experiences psychical pleasure or displeasure through comparing his present states with past ones and declaring them identical or not identical (as happens in all recollection); *or* he believes in *freedom of will*, for instance when he thinks 'I did not have to do this', 'this could have happened differently', and likewise gains pleasure or displeasure. Without the errors which are active in every psychical pleasure and displeasure a humanity would never have come into existence – whose fundamental feeling is and remains that man is the free being in a world of unfreedom, the eternal *miracle worker* whether he does good or ill, the astonishing exception, the superbeast and almost-god, the meaning of creation which cannot be thought away, the solution of the cosmic riddle, the mighty ruler over nature and the despiser of it, the creature which calls *its* history *world history! – Vanitas vanitatum homo.**

13

Saying a thing twice. – It is good to repeat oneself and thus bestow on a thing a right and a left foot. Truth may be able to stand on one leg; but with two it can walk and get around.

14

Man, the comedian of the world. – Let us hope there really are more spiritual beings than men are, so that all the humour shall not go to waste that lies in the fact that man regards himself as the goal and purpose of the existence of the whole universe and that mankind will not seriously rest satisfied with itself as anything less than the accomplisher of a universal mission. If a god created the world then he created men as the *apes of god*, so as always to have on hand something to cheer him up in his all-too-protracted eternities. The music of the spheres encompassing the earth would then no doubt be the mocking laughter of all other creatures encompassing man. That bored immortal tickles his favourite animal with *pain*, so as to take pleasure in the proud and tragic way this vainest of all creatures displays and interprets his sufferings and in his spiritual inventiveness in general – as the inventor of this inventor. For he who devised man for his amusement possessed more spirit than man, and more enjoyment of spirit. Yet even here, where we are for once willing to see our humanity humiliated, our vanity is playing a trick on us, inasmuch as we men would like to be something quite incomparable and miraculous at least in *possessing* this vanity. Our uniqueness in the universe! alas, it is all too improbable an idea! The astronomers, to whom there is sometimes given a horizon that really is free of the earth, give us to understand that the drop of *life* in the universe is without significance for the total character of the tremendous ocean of becoming and passing away: that uncounted stars possess similar conditions for the production of life as the earth does – very many thus do, though they constitute only a handful compared with the limitless number which have never experienced the eruption of life or have long since recovered from it; that measured against the duration of their existence life on each of these stars has been a moment, a sudden flickering up, with long, long spaces of time afterwards – and thus in no sense the goal and ultimate objective of their existence. Perhaps the ant in the forest imagines it is the goal and objective of the forest just as firmly as we do when in our imagination we almost involuntarily associate the destruction of mankind with the destruction of the earth: indeed, we are being modest if we halt at that

* *Vanitas vanitatum homo*: man is the vanity of vanities

and do not organize a general twilight of the gods and the universe for the funeral rites of the last man. Even the most unprejudiced astronomer himself can hardly imagine the earth without life other than as the luminous and floating grave-mound of mankind.

15

Modesty of man. – How little pleasure most people need to make them find life good, how modest man is!

16

Where indifference is needed. – Nothing could be more wrongheaded than to want to wait and see what science will one day determine once and for all concerning the first and last things and until then continue to think (and especially to believe!) in the *customary* fashion – as we are so often advised to do. The impulse to desire in this domain *nothing but certainties* is a *religious after-shoot*, no more – a hidden and only apparently sceptical species of the 'metaphysical need', coupled with the consideration that there is no prospect of these ultimate certainties being to hand for a long time to come and that until then the 'believer' is right not to trouble his head about anything in this domain. We have absolutely no *need* of these certainties regarding the furthest horizon to live a full and excellent human life: just as the ant has no need of them to be a good ant. What we need, rather, is to become clear in our minds as to the origin of that calamitous weightiness we have for so long accorded these things, and for that we require a *history* of the ethical and religious sensations. For it is only under the influence of these sensations that those finest of all questions of knowledge have acquired for us such consequence and dreadfulness: into the outermost regions *to which* the spiritual eye is strained but *into which* it is unable to penetrate we have displaced such concepts as guilt and punishment (and everlasting punishment moreover!): and this the more incautiously the darker these regions have been. Where we could establish nothing for a certainty it has been our practice from of old boldly to fantasize, and we have persuaded our posterity to take these fantasies seriously and for truth, when all else has failed by resorting to the detestable assertion that faith is worth more than knowledge. What is now needed in regard to these last things is not knowledge against faith but *indifference against faith and supposed knowledge* in those domains! – *Everything* else must be of more concern to us than that which has hitherto been preached to us as the most important of all things – I mean the questions: what is the purpose of man? What is his fate after death? How can he be reconciled with God? – and all the rest of these *curiosa*. Just as little as with these questions of the religious are we concerned with the questions of the philosophical dogmatists, whether they be idealists or materialists or realists. Their object, one and all, is to compel us to a decision in domains where neither faith nor knowledge is needed; it is more useful, even for the greatest lovers of knowledge, if around everything accessible to reason and investigation there lies a misty and deceptive girdle of quagmire, a band of the impenetrable, indefinable, and eternally fluid. It is precisely through the contrast it presents to the realm of darkness at the edge of the world of knowledge that the bright world of knowledge close to us is continually enhanced in value. – We must again become *good neighbours to the closest things* and cease from gazing so contemptuously past them at clouds and monsters of the night. In forests and caves, in swampy regions and under cloudy skies – this is where man has lived all too long, and lived poorly, as on the cultural steps of whole millennia. There he has *learned to despise* the present and neighbourhood and life and himself – and we, who dwell in the *brighter* fields of nature and the spirit, we too have inherited in our blood something of this poison of contempt for what is closest.

17
Deep explanations. – He who explains a passage in an author 'more deeply' than the passage was meant has not explained the author but *obscured* him. This is how our metaphysicians stand in regard to the text of nature; indeed, they stand much worse. For in order to apply their deep explanations they frequently first adjust the text in a way that will facilitate it: in other words, they *spoil* it. As a curious example of the spoiling of a text and the obscuring of its author let us here consider Schopenhauer's thoughts on the pregnancy of women. The sign of the continued existence in time of the will to live is, he says, coitus; the sign that there has again been allied to this will the possibility of redemption held open by the light of knowledge, and knowledge indeed of the highest degree of clarity, is the renewed incarnation of the will to live. The mark of this latter is pregnancy, which thus goes about freely and openly, indeed proudly, while coitus crawls away and hides like a criminal. He asserts that *every woman* if surprised in the act of procreation would like to die of shame, but *'displays her pregnancy without a trace of shame, indeed with a kind of pride'*. The first thing to remark is that this condition could hardly be displayed *more* than it displays itself; but inasmuch as Schopenhauer emphasizes *only* the intentionality of this displaying he is preparing the text for himself so as to harmonize it with the 'explanation' he is about to bring forward. Then we must add that what he says as to the universality of the phenomenon to be explained is untrue: he speaks of 'every woman': but many, especially younger women, often evidence a painful embarrassment, even before their closest relations, when in this condition; and if women of more mature or the maturest years, in particular those of the lower orders, do in fact pride themselves on being in such a condition, then it is no doubt because it provides evidence that they are *still* desired by their men. That at the sight of it her neighbour or his wife or a passing stranger should say or think: 'can it be possible – ': female vanity is, at a low level of intelligence, always happy to receive this alms. On the other hand, it would have to follow from Schopenhauer's propositions that precisely the cleverest and most intelligent women would openly rejoice the most at their condition: for they have the greatest prospect of bearing a prodigy of intellect in whom 'the will' can, to the general

wellbeing, again 'deny' itself; stupid women, on the contrary, would have every reason to conceal their pregnancy more bashfully than anything else they conceal. It cannot be said that these things derive from reality. Supposing, however, that Schopenhauer were in a quite general sense right to say that in a condition of pregnancy women evidence a greater self-contentment than they otherwise do, there is an explanation lying closer to hand than his does. One can imagine a hen cackling *before* she has laid an egg, the content of the cackling being: 'Look! Look! I am going to lay an egg! I am going to lay an egg!'

18

The modern Diogenes. – Before one seeks men one must have found the lantern. Will it have to be the lantern of the cynic?

19

Immoralists. – Because they dissect morality, moralists must now be content to be upbraided as immoralists. But he who wants to dissect has to kill; yet only for the sake of better knowledge, better judgement, better living; not so that all the world shall start dissecting. Unhappily, however, people still believe that every moralist has to be a model and ideal in all he does and that others are supposed to imitate him: they confuse him with the preacher of morals. The older moralists dissected too little and preached too much: which is why the moralists of today experience this confusion and its unpleasant consequences.

20

Not to be confused. – Moralists who treat the grandiose, mighty, self-sacrificing disposition such as is evidenced by Plutarch's heroes, or the pure, enlightened, heat-conducting state of soul of truly good men and women, as weighty problems and seek to discover their origin by exhibiting the complexity in the apparent simplicity and directing the eye to the interlacing of motives, to the delicate conceptual illusions woven into it, and to the individual and groups of sensations inherited from of old and slowly intensified – these moralists are most *different* from precisely those moralists with whom they are most *confused*: from the trivial spirits who have no belief at all in these dispositions and states of soul and suppose that greatness and purity are only an outward show concealing behind them a paltriness similar to their own. The moralists say: 'here there are problems', and these wretches say: 'here there are deceivers and deceptions'; they thus *deny* the *existence* of that which the former are intent upon *explaining*.

21

Man as the measurer. – Perhaps all the morality of mankind has its origin in the tremendous inner excitement which seized on primeval men when they discovered measure and measuring, scales and weighing (the word *'Mensch'*, indeed, means the measurer, he desired to name himself after his greatest discovery!). With these conceptions they climbed into realms that are quite unmeasurable and unweighable but originally did not seem to be.

22

Principle of equilibrium. – The brigand and the man of power who promises to defend a community against the brigand are probably at bottom very similar beings, except that the latter obtains what he wants in a different way from the former: namely through regular tributes paid to him by the community and not by imposts levied by force. (It is the same relationship as that between merchant and pirate, who are for a long time one and the same person: where one function does not seem to him advisable he practises the other. Even now, indeed, merchant's morality is really only a *more prudent* form of pirate's morality: to buy as cheap as possible – where possible for no more than the operational costs – to sell as dear as possible). The essential thing is: this man of power promises to maintain an *equilibrium* with the brigand; in this the weaker perceive a possibility of living. For they must either combine together to produce an *equivalent* power or subject themselves to one already possessing this equivalent power (perform services for him in exchange for his protection). The latter proceeding is easily the preferred one, because at bottom it holds *two* dangerous beings in check: the former through the latter, the latter through considerations of advantage; for the latter derives benefit from treating the subject community with kindness or restraint so that they may feed not only themselves but their master too. In reality the people can still have a hard enough time of it even under this arrangement, but when they compare it with the perpetual possibility of complete *destruction* that preceded it they find even this condition endurable. – The community is originally the organization of the weak for the production of an *equilibrium* with powers that threaten it with danger. An organization to produce preponderance would be more advisable if the community could thereby become strong enough to *destroy* the threatening power once and for all: and if it were a matter of a single powerful depredator this would certainly be *attempted*. If, however, he is the head of a clan or has a large following his speedy and decisive destruction is unlikely to be accomplished and what is to be expected is a long-drawn-out *feud*: but this state of things is the least desirable one for the community, since it must deprive them of the time they need for the provision of their subsistence with the regularity it requires and be attended by the ever-present threat that they will be deprived of all the products of their labours. That is why the community prefers to bring its power of defence and attack up to precisely the point at which the power possessed by its dangerous neighbour stands and then to give him to understand that the scales are now evenly balanced: why, in that event, should they not be good friends with one another? – *Equilibrium* is thus a very important concept for the oldest theory of law and morality; equilibrium is the basis of justice. When in ruder ages justice says: 'An eye for an eye, a tooth for a tooth', it presupposes that equilibrium has been attained and seeks through this retribution to *preserve* it: so that when one man now transgresses against another, the other no longer takes on him the revenge of blind animosity. On the contrary, by virtue of the *jus talionis** the equilibrium of the disturbed power relationship is *restored*: for in such primeval conditions one eye, one arm *more* is one piece of power more, one weight more in the scales. – Within a community in which all regard themselves as equivalent there exist *disgrace* and *punishment* as measures against transgressions, that is to say against disruptions of the principle of equilibrium: disgrace as a weight placed in the scales against the encroaching individual who has procured advantages for himself through his encroachment and now through the disgrace he incurs experiences disadvantages which abolish these earlier advantages and *outweigh* them. The same applies to punishment: against the preponderance which every criminal promises himself it imposes a far greater counter-weight, enforced imprisonment for acts of violence, restitution and punitive fines for theft. In this way the transgressor is *reminded* that through his act he has *excluded* himself from the community and its moral *advantages*: the community treats him as one who is not equivalent, as one of the weak standing outside it; that is why punishment is not only retribution but contains something *more*, something of the *harshness of the state of nature*; it is precisely *this* that it wants to *recall*.

23

Have the adherents of the theory of free-will the right to punish? – People who judge and punish as a profession try to establish in each case whether an ill-doer is at all accountable for his deed, whether he was *able* to employ his intelligence, whether he acted for *reasons* and not unconsciously or under compulsion. If he is punished, he is punished for having preferred the worse reasons to the better: which he must therefore have *known*. Where this knowledge is lacking a man is, according to the prevailing view, unfree and not responsible: except if his lack of knowledge, his *ignorantia legis*† for example, is a result of an intentional neglect to learn; in which case, when he failed to learn what he should have learned he had already preferred the worse reasons to the better and must now suffer the consequences of his bad choice. If, on the other hand, he did not see the better reasons, perhaps from dull-wittedness or weakness of mind, it is not usual to punish him: he lacked, one says, the capacity to choose, he acted as an animal would. For an offence to be punishable presupposes that its perpetrator intentionally acted contrary to the better dictates of his intelligence. But how can anyone intentionally be less intelligent than he has to be? Whence comes the decision when the scales are weighted with good and bad motives? Not from error, from blindness, not from an external nor from an internal compulsion? (Consider, moreover, that every so-called 'external compulsion' is nothing more than the internal compulsion of fear and pain.) Whence? one asks again and

---

* *jus talionis*: right of retribution
† *ignorantia legis*: ignorance of the law

again. The *intelligence* is not the cause, because it could not decide against the better reasons? And here one calls 'free-will' to one's aid: it is *pure wilfulness* which is supposed to decide, an impulse is supposed to enter within which motive plays no part, in which the deed, arising out of nothing, occurs as a miracle. It is this supposed *wilfulness*, in a case in which wilfulness ought not to reign, which is punished: the rational intelligence, which knows law, prohibition and command, ought to have permitted no choice, and to have had the effect of compulsion and a higher power. Thus the offender is punished because he employs 'free-will', that is to say, because he acted without a reason where he ought to have acted in accordance with reasons. Why did he do this? But it is precisely this question that can no longer even be *asked*: it was a deed without a 'for that reason', without motive, without origin, something purposeless and non-rational. – *But such a deed too ought*, in accordance with the first condition of all punishability laid down above, *not to be punished*! It is not as if something had *not* been done here, something omitted, the intelligence had *not* been employed: for the omission is under all circumstances *unintentional*! and only the intentional omission to perform what the law commands counts as punishable. The offender certainly preferred the worse reasons to the better, but *without* reason or intention: he certainly failed to employ his intelligence, but not *for the purpose* of not employing it. The presupposition that for an offence to be punishable its perpetrator must have intentionally acted contrary to his intelligence – it is precisely this presupposition which is annulled by the assumption of 'free-will'. You adherents of the theory of 'free-will' *have no right* to punish, your own principles deny you that right! – But these are at bottom nothing but a very peculiar conceptual mythology; and the hen that hatched it sat on her eggs in a place far removed from reality.

24

Towards an assessment of the criminal and his judge. – The criminal, who is aware of all the circumstances attending his case, fails to find his deed as extraordinary and incomprehensible as his judges and censurers do; his punishment, however, is meted out in accordance with precisely the degree of *astonishment* the latter feel when they regard the incomprehensible nature of his deed. – If the knowledge the criminal's defending counsel possesses of the case and its antecedents is sufficiently extensive, then the so-called extenuating circumstances he presents one by one *must* end by extenuating away his client's entire guilt. Or, more clearly: the defending counsel will step by step *ameliorate* that *astonishment* which condemns his client and metes out his punishment, and finally expunge it altogether, by compelling every honest auditor to confess to himself: 'he had to act as he did; if we were to punish, what we would be punishing would be eternal necessity'. – To determine the degree of punishment according to the *degree of knowledge* one possesses, *or can in any way acquire,* of the history of a crime – does this not conflict with every idea of fairness?

25

A fair exchange. – An exchange is honest and just only when each of those participating demands as much as his own object seems worth to him, including the effort it cost to acquire it, its rarity, the time expended, etc., together with its sentimental value. As soon as he sets the price *with reference to the need of the other* he is a subtler brigand and extortioner. – If money is the exchange object it must be considered that a shilling in the hand of a rich heir, a day-labourer, a shop-keeper, a student are quite different things: according to whether he did almost nothing or a great deal to get it, each ought to receive little or a great deal in exchange for it: in reality it is, of course, the other way round. In the great world of money the shilling of the laziest rich man is more lucrative than that of the poor and industrious.

26

Rule of law as a means. – Law, reposing on compacts between *equals*, continues to exist for so long as the power of those who have concluded these compacts remains equal or similar; prudence created law to put an end to feuding and to *useless* squandering between forces of similar strength. But *just as definitive* an end is put to them if one party has *become* decisively *weaker* than the other: then subjection enters in and law *ceases*, but the consequence is the same as that previously attained through the rule of law. For now it is the *prudence* of the dominant party which advises that the strength of the subjected should be *economized* and not uselessly squandered: and often the subjected find themselves in more favourable circumstances than they did when they were equals. – The rule of law is thus a temporary means advised by prudence, not an end.

27

Explanation of Schadenfreude. – *Schadenfreude* originates in the fact that, in certain respects of which he is well aware, everyone feels unwell, is oppressed by care or envy or sorrow: the harm that befalls another makes him our *equal*, it appeases our envy. – If, on the other hand, he happens to feel perfectly well, he nonetheless gathers up his neighbour's misfortune in his consciousness as a capital upon which to draw when he himself faces misfortune: thus he too experiences 'Schadenfreude'. The disposition bent upon equality thus extends its demands to the domain of happiness and chance as well: *Schadenfreude* is the commonest expression of the victory and restoration of equality within the higher world-order too. It is only since man has learned to see in other men beings like and equal to himself, that is to say only since the establishment of society, that *Schadenfreude* has existed.

28

Capriciousness in the apportionment of punishment. – Most criminals acquire punishment in the way women acquire children. They have done the same thing hundreds of times without noticing any ill consequences: suddenly there is a disclosure, and at its heels punishment. Habituation, however, ought to make the guiltiness of the deed on account of which the criminal is punished seem less culpable: for it happened as the result of a tendency the criminal has acquired and which he would have found it hard to resist. Instead of that, a suspicion of habitual crime procures him severer punishment; habituation is seen as a ground for refusing any amelioration of his sentence. A previously exemplary life in contrast with which the crime stands out all the more fearsomely ought to make its guiltiness seem all the greater! But its customary effect is to ameliorate the punishment. Thus everything is meted out, not with an eye to the criminal, but with an eye to society and the harm and danger it has incurred: the previous serviceability of a man is weighed against his single harmful act, his previous harmfulness added to that at present disclosed and his punishment intensified accordingly. But if one in this way punishes or rewards a man's past as well (in the case of a serviceable past a lighter punishment is a reward), one ought to go back even further and reward or punish the causes of such or such a past, I mean parents, educators, society, etc.: in many cases the *judges* will then be found to be in some way involved in the guilt. It is capricious to halt at the criminal if what one is punishing is the past: if one is not willing to accede to the absolute guilt-lessness of all guilt, one should at least halt at each individual case and look no further back: that is to say, *isolate* the guilt and refrain from con-necting it in any way with the past – otherwise one will come to sin against logic. Draw the necessary conclusion from your doctrine of 'free-dom of the will', you free-willers, and boldly decree: '*no deed possesses a past*'.

29
Envy and its nobler brother. – Where equality really has prevailed and been permanently established there arises that tendency which is on the whole accounted immoral and can hardly be conceived of in a state of nature: *envy*. The envious man is conscious of every respect in which the man he envies exceeds the common measure and desires to push him down to it – or to raise himself up to the height of the other: out of which there arise two different modes of action which Hesiod designated as the evil and the good Eris. There likewise arises in a state of equality a sense of indig-nation that one man should fare badly *beneath* his dignity and equal rights, while another fares well *above* his equal rights: these affects are felt by *nobler* natures. They suffer from the absence of justice and equity in those things that are independent of the despotism of man: that is to say, they demand that that equality recognized by man shall now also be recognized by nature and chance; it angers them that the equal are not ac-corded an equal fate.

30
Envy of the gods. – The 'envy of the gods' arises when he who is accounted lower equates himself with him who is accounted higher (as Ajax does) or who is *made* equal to him by the favour of fortune (as Niobe is as a mother too abundantly blessed). Within the *social* order of rank this envy imposes the demand that no one shall enjoy rewards that *exceed* his station, and

that his happiness too shall accord with his station, and especially that his self-conceit shall not grow beyond these bounds. The victorious general often experiences the 'envy of the gods', as does the pupil who produces a masterly piece of work.

31

Vanity as an offshoot of the antisocial. – For the sake of their security, men have founded the community on the basis of positing themselves as being *equal* to one another; but this conception is at bottom repugnant to the nature of the individual and something imposed upon him; and so it happens that, the more the general security is guaranteed, the more do new shoots of the ancient drive to domination assert themselves: in the division of classes, in the claim to special dignities and privileges, and in vanity in general (in mannerisms, costume, modes of speech, etc.). As soon as the communality comes to feel itself in danger again, the majority, who were unable to assert their domination when a state of general calm obtained, reimpose a condition of equality: the absurd special privileges and vanities disappear for a time. If, however, the communality collapses completely and everything dissolves into anarchy, then there at once breaks through that condition of unreflecting, ruthless inequality that constitutes the state of nature: as, according to the report of Thucydides, happened on Corcyra.* There exists neither a natural right nor a natural wrong.

32

Fairness. – A further development of justice is fairness, arising among those who do not offend against the community's principle of equality: to cases upon which the law does not touch there is applied that subtler regard for equilibrium which looks before and behind and whose motto is 'as thou to me, so I to thee'. *Aequum*† means precisely 'it is *in conformity with our equality*; this ameliorates our little differences too down to an appearance of equality and desires that we overlook many things we do not *have* to'.

33

Elements of revenge. – The word 'revenge' is said so quickly it almost seems as if it could contain no more than one conceptual and perceptional root. And so one continues to strive to discover it: just as our economists have not yet wearied of scenting a similar unity in the word 'value' and of searching after the original root-concept of the word. As if every word were not a pocket into which now this, now that, now several things at once have been put! Thus 'revenge', too, is now this, now that, now something more combined. Distinguish first of all that defensive return blow which one delivers even against lifeless objects (moving machinery, for example) which have hurt us: the sense of our counter-action is to put a stop to the injury by putting a stop to the machine. To achieve this the

---

* Corcyra: the most northern of the Ionian islands, suffered from savage civil war in the fifth century BC
† *Aequum*: equitable

violence of the counter-blow sometimes has to be so great as to shatter the machine; if, however, it is in fact too strong to be instantly destroyed by a single individual, the latter will nonetheless still deliver the most vigorous blow of which he is capable – as a last-ditch effort, so to speak. One behaves in a similar way towards people who have harmed us when we feel the injury directly; if one wants to call this an act of revenge, all well and good; only let it be considered that *self-preservation* alone has here set its clockwork of reason in motion, and that one has fundamentally been thinking, not of the person who caused the injury, but only of oneself: we act thus *without* wanting to do harm in return, but only so as *to get out* with life and limb. – One needs *time* if one is to transfer one's thoughts from oneself to one's opponent and to ask oneself how he can be hit at most grievously. This happens in the second species of revenge: its presupposition is a reflection over the other's vulnerability and capacity for suffering: one wants to hurt. To secure himself against further harm is here so far from the mind of the revenger that he almost always brings further harm upon himself and very often cold-bloodedly anticipates it. If in the case of the first species of revenge it was fear of a second blow which made the counter-blow as vigorous as possible, here there is almost complete indifference to what the opponent *will* do; the vigour of the counter-blow is determined only by that which he *has* done to us. What, then, has he done? And of what use is it to us if our opponent now suffers after we have suffered through him? It is a question of *restitution*: while the act of revenge of the first species serves only *self-preservation*. Perhaps we lost property, rank, friends, children through our opponent – these losses are not made good by revenge, the restitution applies only to an *attendant loss* occasioned by the other losses referred to. Restitutional revenge does not protect one from further harm, it does not make good the harm one has suffered – except in one case. If our *honour* has suffered through our opponent revenge is capable of *restoring* it. But our honour has suffered harm in every case in which someone has done us a deliberate injury: for our opponent proved thereby that he did not *fear* us. By revenging ourself on him we prove that we do not fear him either: it is in this that the compensation, the restitution lies. (The objective of demonstrating the complete absence of *fear* goes so far in the case of some people that the danger to themselves involved in the revenge – loss of health or life or other deprivations – counts as an indispensable condition of the revenge. That is why they choose the path of the duel even when the courts offer them a means of acquiring compensation for the offence they have sustained: they refuse to regard as sufficient a restitution of their honour that involves no risk because it cannot serve to demonstrate their lack of fear.) – In the first species of revenge it is precisely fear which directs the counter-blow: here, on the contrary, it is the absence of fear which, as stated, *wants to prove itself* through the counter-blow. – Nothing, therefore, could appear more different than the inner motives of these two modes of action which are called by the common word 'revenge': and yet it very often happens that the revenger is unclear as to what has really determined his action; perhaps he delivered the counter-blow out of fear and to preserve himself but afterwards, when he has had time to reflect on the motive of wounded honour, convinces himself he has exacted revenge on account of his honour: – this motive is, after all, *nobler* than the other. An essential element in this is whether he sees his honour as having been injured in the eyes of others (the world) or only in the eyes of him who injured it: in the latter case he will prefer secret revenge, in the former public. His revenge will be the more incensed or the more moderate according to how deeply or weakly he can think his way into the soul of the perpetrator and the witnesses of his injury; if he is wholly lacking in this kind of imagination he will not think of revenge at all, since the feeling of 'honour' will not be present in him and thus cannot be wounded. He will likewise not think of revenge if he *despises* the perpetrator and the witnesses: because, as people he despises, they cannot accord him any honour and consequently cannot take any honour from him either. Finally, he will refrain from revenge in the not uncommon case that he loves the perpetrator: he will thus lose honour in the perpetrator's eyes, to be sure, and will perhaps become less worthy of being loved in return. But to renounce even all claim to love in return is a sacrifice which love is prepared to make if only it does not *have to hurt* the beloved being: this would mean hurting oneself more than any sacrifice hurts. – Thus: everyone will revenge himself, except if he is without honour or full of contempt or full of love for the person who has harmed and offended him. Even when he turns to the courts he desires revenge as a private person: *additionally*, however, as a forethoughtful man of society, he desires the revenge of society on one who does not *honour* it. Through judicial punishment, private honour as well as the honour of society is thus *restored*: that is to say – punishment is revenge. – Undoubtedly there is also in it those other elements of revenge already described, insofar as through punishment society serves its own *self-preservation* and delivers a counter-blow in *self-defence*. Punishment serves to prevent *further* injury, it wishes to *deter*. Two such various elements of revenge are thus actually *united* in punishment, and the main effect of this may be to sustain the confusion of concepts referred to by virtue of which the individual who takes revenge usually does not know what he really wants.

34

The virtues that incur loss. – As members of society we believe we ought not to practise certain virtues from which as private persons we acquire the highest honour and a certain satisfaction, for example mercy and consideration for transgressors of all kinds – in general any action by which the interests of society would suffer through our virtue. No bench of judges may conscientiously practise mercy: this privilege is reserved to the king *as an individual*; one rejoices when he makes use of it, as proof that one would like to be merciful, even though as a society one absolutely cannot be. Society thus recognizes only those virtues that are advantageous, or at least not harmful to it (those that can be practised without its incurring loss, for example justice). Those virtues that incur loss cannot, consequently, have come into existence *within society*, since even now there is opposition to them within every society, however circumscribed. They are thus virtues belonging among non-equals, devised by the superior, the individual; they are the virtues of *rulers* bearing the sense: 'I am sufficiently powerful to put up with a palpable loss, this is a proof of my power' – and are thus virtues related to *pride*.

35
Casuistry of advantage. – There would be no casuistry of morality if there were no casuistry of advantage. The freest and subtlest reason is often inadequate to choosing between two things in such a way that its choice must necessarily fall on the one offering the greatest advantage. In such cases we choose because we have to choose and afterwards suffer from a kind of seasickness of the feelings.

36
Becoming a hypocrite. – Every beggar becomes a hypocrite; as does anyone who makes a profession of displaying a lack, a state of distress (whether it be of a personal or a public kind). – The begger does not feel his lack nearly as acutely as he must *make* it felt if he wants to live by begging.

37
A kind of cult of the passions. – In order to raise an accusation against the whole nature of the world, you dismal philosophical blindworms speak of the *terrible character* of human passions. As if wherever there have been passions there had also been terribleness! As if this kind of terribleness was bound to persist in the world! – Through a neglect of the *small* facts, through lack of self-observation and observation of those who are to be brought up, it is you yourselves who first allowed the passions to develop into such monsters that you are overcome by fear at the word 'passion'! It was up to you, and is up to us, to *take from* the passions their terrible character and thus prevent their becoming devastating torrents. – One should not inflate one's oversights into eternal fatalities; let us rather work honestly together on the task of transforming the passions [*Leidenschaften*] of mankind one and all into joys [*Freudenschaften*].

38
Sting of conscience. – The sting of conscience is, like a snake stinging a stone, a piece of stupidity.

39
Origin of rights. – Rights can in the first instance be traced back to *tradition*, tradition to some *agreement*. At some time in the past men were mutually content with the consequences of the agreement they had come to, and at the same time too indolent formally to renew it; thus they lived on as though it were continually being renewed and, as forgetfulness spread its veil over its origin, gradually came to believe they were in possession of a sacred, immutable state of affairs upon which every generation *had* to

continue to build. Tradition was now a *compulsion*, even when it no longer served the purpose for which the agreement had originally been concluded. – The *weak* have at all times found here their sure stronghold: they tend to regard that single act of agreement, that single act of grace, as *valid eternally*.

40

The significance of forgetting for the moral sensation. – The same actions as within primitive society appear to have been performed first with a view to common *utility* have been performed by later generations for other motives: out of fear of or reverence for those who demanded and recommended them, or out of habit because one had seen them done all around one from childhood on, or from benevolence because their performance everywhere produced joy and concurring faces, or from vanity because they were commended. Such actions, whose basic motive, that of utility, has been *forgotten*, are then called *moral* actions: not because, for instance, they are performed out of those *other* motives, but because they are *not* performed from any conscious reason of utility. – Where does it come from, this *hatred* of utility which becomes visible *here*, where all praiseworthy behaviour formally excludes behaviour with a view to utility? – It is plain that society, the hearth of all morality and all eulogy of moral behaviour, has had to struggle too long and too hard against the self-interest and self-will of the individual not at last to rate *any other* motive morally higher than utility. Thus it comes to appear that morality has *not* grown out of utility; while it is originally social utility, which had great difficulty in asserting itself against all the individual private utilities and making itself more highly respected.

41

The heritage of morality. – In the domain of morality too there is a rich heritage: it is possessed by the gentle, the good-natured, the sympathizing and charitable, who have all inherited from their forefathers the good *mode of action* but not the reasons for it (its source). The pleasant thing about this wealth is that it has to be continually expended and spread abroad if it is to be felt to exist at all, and that it thus involuntarily works to reduce the distance between the morally rich and the morally poor: and, what is best and most remarkable, it does so not for the sake of producing some future mean and average between poor and rich, but for the sake of a *universal* enrichment and over-enrichment. – The foregoing is perhaps an adequate summary of the dominant view of what constitutes the moral heritage: but it seems to me that this view is maintained more *in majorem gloriam** of morality than out of respect for truth. Experience at least advances a proposition which, if it does not contradict that universal opinion, at any rate imposes upon it significant limitations. Without the most refined understanding (so says experience), without the capacity for the most delicate choice and a *strong inclination to moderation*, the inheritors of morality become squanderers of morality: by surrendering

* *in majorem gloriam*: to the greater glory

themselves unrestrainedly to their sympathetic, charitable, reconciliatory, ameliorating drives they render all the world around them more indolent, covetous and sentimental. That is why the children of such highly moral squanderers can easily – and, sad to say, at best – become pleasant, feeble good-for-nothings.

42

The judge and extenuating circumstances. – 'You should play fair even with the Devil and pay him what you owe him', said an old soldier after they had told him the story of Faust in a little more detail. 'Faust belongs in Hell!' – 'Oh, you frightful man!' exclaimed his wife. 'How can that be? All he did was to have no ink in his inkwell! To write with blood is a sin, I know, but is that any reason why such a handsome man should burn?'

43

Problem of duty towards truth. – Duty is a compulsive feeling which impels us to some action and which we call good and regard as undiscussable (– we refuse to speak of its origin, limitation and justification or to hear them spoken of). The thinker, however, regards everything as having evolved and everything that has evolved as discussable, and is thus a man without a sense of duty – as long, that is, as he is functioning as a thinker. As such he will thus fail to feel a sense of duty with respect to seeing and telling the truth and will not recognize any such duty; he asks: whence does it come? what is its purpose? – but these questions themselves he will regard as questionable. But is the consequence of this not that the thinker's machine will no longer work properly if, in the act of knowing, he really is able to *feel free of a sense of duty*? Insofar as here the element required to *heat* the machine seems to be the same element as is to be investigated by means of the machine. – The formula would perhaps be: *assuming* there existed a duty to know the truth, in what relation would truth then stand to any other species of duty? – But is a hypothetical sense of duty not a contradiction? –

44

Stages of morality. – Morality is first of all a means of preserving the community and warding off its destruction; then it is a means of preserving the community at a certain height and in a certain quality of existence. Its motive forces are *fear* and *hope*: and they are applied the more severely, powerfully and coarsely the stronger the inclination to perversity, one-sidedness and the purely personal remains. The most dreadful means of inspiring fear have to be pressed into service here for as long as milder ones fail to produce any effect and that twofold species of preservation cannot be achieved in any other way (one of the very strongest is the invention of a Beyond with an everlasting Hell). Further stages of morality, and thus of means of attaining the objectives described, are the commands of a god (such as the Mosaic law); further and higher still the commands of the concept of unconditional duty with its 'thou shalt' – all still somewhat coarsely hewn but *broad* stages and steps, because men do not yet know how to place their feet on narrower, more delicate steps. Then comes a morality of *inclination*, of *taste*, finally that of *insight* – which is above and beyond all illusionary motive forces of morality but has a clear realization of why for long ages mankind could possess no other.

45
Morality of pity in the mouth of the intemperate. – All those who do not have themselves sufficiently under their own control and do not know morality as a continual self-command and self-overcoming practised in great things and in the smallest, involuntarily become glorifiers of the good, pitying, benevolent impulses, of that instinctive morality which has no head but seems to consist solely of heart and helping hands. It is, indeed, in their interest to cast suspicion on a morality of rationality and to make of that other morality the only one.

46
Cloaca of the soul. – The soul too has to have its definite cloaca into which it allows its sewage to flow out: what can serve as these includes people, relationships, classes, or the Fatherland or the world or finally – for the truly fastidious (I mean our dear modern 'pessimists') – God.

47
A kind of repose and contemplativeness. – Take care that your repose and contemplativeness does not resemble that of a dog in front of a butcher's shop, whom fear will not permit to go forward and desire not permit to go back and who stands with his eyes gaping like mouths.

48
Prohibition without reasons. – A prohibition whose reason we do not understand or admit is not only for the obstinate man but also for the man thirsty for knowledge almost the injunction: let us put it to the test, so as to learn *why* this prohibition exists. Moral prohibitions such as those of the Decalogue are suitable only for ages when reason is subjugated: nowadays a prohibition 'thou shalt not kill', 'thou shalt not commit adultery', presented without reasons, would produce a harmful rather than a beneficial effect.

49
Portrait from life. – What kind of a man is he who can say of himself: 'I find it very easy to despise, but I never hate. In everyone I meet I immediately discover something that can be respected and on account of which I respect him: the so-called amiable qualities possess little attraction for me.'

50
Pity and contempt. – To show pity is felt as a sign of contempt because one has clearly ceased to be an object of *fear* as soon as one is pitied. One has sunk below the level of equilibrium, whereas human vanity is not satisfied even with that, the sensation most desired being one of predominance and the inspiration of fear. That is why the *high value* pity has come

to be accorded presents a problem, just as the praise now accorded self-less disinterestedness needs to be explained: originally it was *despised*, or *feared* as a deception.

51

The ability to be small. – One has still to be as close to the flowers, the grass and the butterflies as is a child, who is not so very much bigger than they are. We adults, on the other hand, have grown up high above them and have to condescend to them; I believe the grass *hates* us when we confess our love for it. – He who wants to partake of *all* good things must know how to be small at times.

52

Content of the conscience. – The content of our conscience is everything that was during the years of our childhood regularly *demanded* of us without reason by people we honoured or feared. It is thus the conscience that excites that feeling of compulsion ('I must do this, not do that') which does not ask: *why* must I? – In every case in which a thing is done with 'because' and 'why' man acts *without* conscience; but not yet for that reason against it. – The belief in authorities is the source of the conscience: it is therefore not the voice of God in the heart of man but the voice of some men in man.

53

Overcoming of the passions. – The man who has overcome his passions has entered into possession of the most fertile ground; like the colonist who has mastered the forests and swamps. To *sow* the seeds of good spiritual works in the soil of the subdued passions is then the immediate urgent task. The overcoming itself is only a *means*, not a goal; if it is not so viewed, all kinds of weeds and devilish nonsense will quickly spring up in this rich soil now unoccupied, and soon there will be more rank confusion than there ever was before.

54

Aptitude for serving. – All so-called practical people possess an aptitude for serving: it is this that makes them practical, indeed, whether on their own behalf or that of others. Robinson possessed an even better servant than Friday was: and that was Crusoe.

55

Linguistic danger to spiritual freedom. – Every word is a prejudice.

56

Spirit and boredom. – The saying 'The Magyar is much too lazy to feel bored' is thought-provoking. Only the most acute and active animals are capable of boredom. – A theme for a great poet would be *God's boredom* on the seventh day of creation.

57

Our traffic with animals. – The origination of morality can also be observed in our behaviour towards animals. Where utility or harm do *not* come into consideration we have a feeling of complete irresponsibility; we kill and injure insects, for example, or let them live, usually without giving the slightest thought to the matter. We are so clumsy that even our acts of kindness towards flowers and small creatures are almost always murderous: which in no way diminishes the pleasure we take in them. – Today is the festival of the small creatures, the sultriest day of the year: all around us there is swarming and creeping, and we crush to death now a little worm, now a little winged beetle; we do it without wanting to, *but also* without care or concern. – If an animal harms us we seek any means of *destroying* it, and the means are often sufficiently cruel without our really wanting them to be: it is the cruelty of thoughtlessness. If it is useful we *exploit* it: until a subtler prudence teaches us that certain animals richly repay a different kind of treatment, namely being cared for and disciplined. It is only here that a sense of responsibility comes into being. Tormenting is not practised against domestic animals; one man is indignant if another is merciless towards his cow, quite in accordance with the primitive communal morality which sees the *common* welfare imperilled whenever an individual transgresses. Whoever in the community perceives a transgression fears that harm will come to him indirectly: and we fear for the quality of our meat, our husbandry and our currency when we see domestic animals mistreated. In addition to this, he who is cruel towards animals arouses the suspicion that he is also cruel towards weak, subordinate people incapable of revenge; he counts as ignoble, as lacking refinement in pride. Thus there come about the beginnings of moral sensation and judgement: the best is then added by superstition. Many animals, through the way they look, sound and comport themselves, inspire men *imaginatively to transport* themselves into them, and many religions teach that, under certain circumstances, the souls of men and gods may dwell in animals: for which reason they recommend a noble caution, indeed a reverential awe, in traffic with animals in general. Even after this superstition has vanished, the sentiments it has given rise to continue to operate, mature and flourish. – As is well known, on this point Christianity has proved to be a barren and regressive religion.

58
New actors. – There is among men no greater banality than death; second in line stands birth, since all are not born who nonetheless die; then follows marriage. But these worn-out little tragi-comedies are at each of their uncounted and uncountable performances played by ever new actors and thus do not cease to have interested spectators: whereas one would have thought that the entire audience at the world-theatre would have long since hanged itself from the trees out of satiety with them – which goes to show how much depends on new actors, how little on the play.

59
What does 'obstinate' mean? – The shortest route is not the most direct but

that upon which the most favourable winds swell our sails: thus do sea-farers teach us. Not to follow this teaching is to be *obstinate*: firmness of character is here polluted by stupidity.

60

The word 'vanity'. – It is troublesome that certain words which we moral-ists cannot avoid using bear within them a kind of moral censure deriving from those ages in which the most immediate and natural impulses in man were made heretical. Thus that fundamental conviction that we make good headway or suffer shipwreck on the ocean of society much more through what we *count* as than through what we *are* – a conviction that has to be our rudder in all we do that has a bearing on society – is branded with the most general word 'vanity', 'vanitas', one of the most abundantly content-full of all things with an expression that designates it as emptiness and nullity, something large with a diminutive, indeed with the penstrokes of caricature. There is no help for it, we are obliged to use such words, but when we do so we must close our ears to the whisper-ings of ancient habits.

61

Mohammedan fatalism. – Mohammedan fatalism embodies the fundamen-tal error of setting man and fate over against one another as two separate things: man, it says, can resist fate and seek to frustrate it, but in the end it always carries off the victory; so that the most reasonable thing to do is to resign oneself or to live just as one pleases. In reality every man is him-self a piece of fate; when he thinks to resist fate in the way suggested, it is precisely fate that is here fulfilling itself; the struggle is imaginary, but so is the proposed resignation to fate; all these imaginings are enclosed within fate. – The fear most people feel in face of the theory of the unfree-dom of the will is fear in face of Mohammedan fatalism: they think that man will stand before the future feeble, resigned and with hands clasped because he is incapable of effecting any change in it: or that he will give free rein to all his impulses and caprices because these too cannot make any worse what has already been determined. The follies of mankind are just as much a piece of fate as are its acts of intelligence: that fear in face of a belief in fate is also fate. You yourself, poor fearful man, are the implac-able *moira* enthroned even above the gods that governs all that happens; you are the blessing or the curse and in any event the fetters in which the strongest lies captive; in you the whole future of the world of man is pre-determined: it is of no use for you to shudder when you look upon your-self.

62

Devil's advocate. – 'Only when we are hurt ourselves do we become *wise*, only when others are hurt do we become *good*' – so goes that curious phil-osophy which derives all morality from pity and all intellectuality from the isolation of man: it thereby unconsciously becomes the advocate of all the hurt and injury on earth. For pity has need of suffering and isolation has need of the contempt of others.

63

Moral fancy-dress. – In those ages when the fancy-dress worn by the different classes is considered as firmly fixed as the classes themselves are, moralists are tempted to regard *moral* fancy-dress too as absolute and to depict it as such. Thus Molière is comprehensible as a contemporary of the society of Louis XIV; in our society, which is characterized by transitional forms and halfway stages, he would seem, though still a man of genius, a pedant.

64

The noblest virtue. – In the first era of higher humanity bravery is accounted the noblest of the virtues, in the second justice, in the third moderation, in the fourth wisdom. In which era do we live? In which do you live?

65

What is needed first. – A man who refuses to become master over his wrath, his choler and revengefulness, and his lusts, and attempts to become a master in anything else, is as stupid as the farmer who stakes out his field beside a torrential stream without protecting himself against it.

66

What is truth? – *Schwarzert* (Melanchthon):* 'One often preaches one's faith precisely when one has lost it and is looking for it everywhere – and at such a time one does not preach it worst!' – *Luther*: Thou speak'st true today like an angel, brother! – *Schwarzert*: 'But it is thy enemies who think this thought and they apply it to thee.' – *Luther*: Then it's a lie from the Devil's behind.

67

Habit of seeing opposites. – The general imprecise way of observing sees everywhere in nature opposites (as, e.g., 'warm and cold') where there are, not opposites, but differences of degree. This bad habit has led us into wanting to comprehend and analyse the inner world, too, the spiritual-moral world, in terms of such opposites. An unspeakable amount of painfulness, arrogance, harshness, estrangement, frigidity has entered into human feelings because we think we see opposites instead of transitions.

68

Whether we are able to forgive. – How *can* one forgive them at all, if they know not what they do! One has nothing whatever *to* forgive. – But does a man ever *know completely* what he does? And if this must always remain at least *questionable*, then men never do have anything to forgive one

---

* Philipp Melanchthon (Greek rendition of the German name 'Schwarzert'); a professor of classical philosophy who made contact with Luther at Wittenberg and identified with his cause. He wrote the first major work of protestant theology and represented the Lutherans at Regensburg

another and pardoning is to the most rational man a thing impossible. Finally: *if* the ill-doers really did know what they did – we would have a right to *forgive* them only if we had a right to accuse and to punish them. But this we do not have.

69

Habitual shame. – Why do we feel shame when we are rendered something good and distinguishing which, as we put it, we 'have not deserved'? It seems to us that we have forced our way into a domain where we do not belong, from which we ought to be excluded, into a sanctuary or holy of holies, as it were, where our feet are forbidden to tread. Yet it is through the error of others that we have arrived there: and now we are overcome partly by fear, partly by reverence, partly by surprise; we know not whether we ought to flee or to enjoy the blessed moment and its undeserved advantages. Whenever we feel shame there exists a mystery which seems to have been desecrated, or to be in danger of desecration, through us; all *undeserved grace* engenders shame. – If we consider, however, that we have never 'deserved' anything at all, then if one acquiesces to this proposition within the Christian total view of things the feeling of *shame* will become *habitual*: because such a god seems to be *continually* blessing and bestowing undeserved grace. But, quite apart from this Christian interpretation, to a completely godless being who firmly adhered to the total unaccountability and undeservingness of all behaviour and being this condition of *habitual shame* would be possible: if he was treated *as though* he had deserved this or that, it would seem to him that he had forced his way into a higher order of beings who *are* able to deserve something, who are free and really capable of bearing responsibility for their own desires and actions. He who says to him 'you deserved it' seems to exclaim to him 'you are not a man, but a god'.

70

The ineptest educator. – In the case of one man all his real virtues have been cultivated in the soil of his spirit of contradiction, in the case of another in his inability to say no, that is in his spirit of assent; a third has developed all his morality out of his lonely pride, a fourth his out of his strong drive to sociability. Suppose, now, that in each of these four cases the seeds of virtue had, through the ineptitude of teachers and the vagaries of chance, not been sown in that region of his nature where the topsoil was richest and most plentiful, then they would be without morality and weak and joyless men. And who would have been the ineptest of all educators and the evil fatality of these four men? The moral fanatic, who believes that the good can grow only out of the good and upon the basis of the good.

71

Stylistic caution. – A: But if *everyone* knew this *most* would be harmed by it. You yourself call these opinions dangerous for those exposed to danger, and yet you express them in public? B: I write in such a way that neither the mob, nor the *populi*, nor the parties of any kind want to read me.

Consequently these opinions of mine will never become public. A: But how do you write, then? B: Neither usefully nor pleasantly – to the trio I have named.

72

Divine missionaries. – Socrates too feels himself to be a divine missionary: but even here there is perceptible I know not what touch of Attic irony and sense of humour through which that unfortunate and presumptuous concept is ameliorated. He speaks of it without unction: his images, of the brake and the horse, are simple and unpriestly, and the actual religious task to which he feels himself called, that of *putting the god to the test in a hundred ways* to see *whether* he has told the truth, permits us to imagine that here the missionary steps up to his god with a bold and candid deportment. This putting of the god to the test is one of the subtlest compromises between piety and freedom of spirit that has ever been devised. – Nowadays we no longer have need even of this compromise.

73

Honest painter. – Raphael, who was much concerned with the church (when it was capable of paying) but, like the best men of his age, little concerned with the objects of the church's faith, did not compromise by so much as an inch with the pretentious, ecstatic piety of many of his patrons: he preserved his honesty even in that exceptional picture, originally intended for a processional banner, the Sistine Madonna. He wanted for once to paint a vision: but it was to be such a one as noble young men without 'faith' *too* might and would have, the vision of a future wife, of a clever, noble-souled, silent and very beautiful woman bearing her first-born in her arms. Let the old, who are accustomed to prayer and worship, here revere something suprahuman, like the venerable greybeard to the left of the picture: we younger men, so Raphael seems to cry to us, shall go along with the lovely girl on the right, who with her challenging and in no way devout expression says to the viewer of the picture: 'This mother and her child – a pleasant, inviting sight, isn't it?' This face and this expression reflects the joy in the faces of the viewers; the artist who invented it all in this way has the enjoyment of his own joy and adds it to the joy of the recipients of his art. – With regard to the 'saviour-like' expression in the head of a child Raphael, the honest painter who had no wish to paint a state of soul in whose existence he did not believe, has outwitted his *believing* viewers in a very cunning fashion; he has painted that natural phenomenon which is not all that rare an occurrence, the eyes of a man in the head of a child, and in this instance the eyes of a valiant man ready to assist in some emergency or difficulty. To these eyes there belongs a beard; that it is missing, and that two different ages of life here speak out of one face, is the pleasing paradox which the faithful have interpreted in the sense of their belief in miracles: which the artist was entitled to anticipate from their art of interpretation and imposition of what they wish to see.

74

Prayer. – Only under two presuppositions does prayer – that custom of earlier ages which has not yet completely died out – make any sense: it would have to be possible to induce or convert the divinity to a certain course of action, and the person praying would himself have to know best what he needed, what was truly desirable for him. Both presuppositions, assumed true and established by custom in all other religions, are however denied precisely by Christianity; if it nonetheless adheres to prayer in face of its belief in an omniscient and all-provident rationality in God which renders prayer at bottom senseless and, indeed, blasphemous – in this it once again demonstrates its admirable serpent cunning; for a clear commandment 'thou shalt not pray' would have led Christians into unchristianity through *boredom*. For in the Christian *ora et labora*,* the *ora* occupies the place of *pleasure*: and what would those unfortunates who had renounced *labora*, the saints, have found to do if deprived of *ora*! – but to converse with God, to demand of him all kinds of nice things, to laugh at oneself a little for being so foolish as still to harbour desires in spite of having so excellent a father – this was for the saints a very fine invention.

75

A holy lie. – The lie which Arria† died with on her lips (*Paete, non dolet*)‡ darkens all the truths that have ever been spoken by the dying. It is the only holy *lie* that has become famous; whereas the odour of sanctity has otherwise adhered only to *errors*.

76

The most necessary apostle. – Among twelve apostles there must always be one as hard as a rock, so that the new church may be erected upon him.

77

What is the more perishable, the spirit or the body? – In matters of law, morality and religion, the most external aspect, that which can be seen, has, as usage, deportment, ceremony, the most *durability*: it is the *body* to which a *new soul* is always being added. The cult is, like a fixed word-text, always being subjected to new interpretations; concepts and sensations are the liquid element, customs the solid.

78

Belief in the sickness as sickness. – It was Christianity which first painted the Devil on the world's wall; it was Christianity which first brought sin into the world. Belief in the cure which it offered has now been shaken to its deepest roots: but *belief in the sickness* which it taught and propagated continues to exist.

79

Speech and writing of the religious. – If the style and total manner of

---

* *ora et labora*: prayer and work
† Arria: the wife of Caecina Peatus (see Martial: *Epigrams* I 13)
‡ *Paete . . . dolet*: It hardly hurts at all

expression of the priest, in both speech and writing, do not already proclaim the *religious* man, then one no longer needs to take his opinions on religion and in favour of religion seriously. They have become *invalid* for their possessor himself if, as his style betrays, he is given to irony, presumption, malice, hatred and all the confusions and changes the feelings are subject to, just like the most irreligious man; – how much more invalid they must be for his auditors and readers! In short, he will serve to make them more irreligious.

80

Danger in personality. – The more God has counted as a discrete person, the less faithful one has been to him. Men are far more attached to their ideas than they are to their most beloved beloved: that is why they sacrifice themselves for the state, the church, and also for God – so long as he remains *their own* production, *their idea*, and is not taken all too much for a person. In the latter case they almost always wrangle with him: even the most devout of men gave vent, indeed, to the bitter exclamation: 'my God, why hast thou forsaken me!'

81

Secular justice. – It is possible to lift secular justice off its hinges – with the doctrine that everyone is wholly unaccountable and innocent: and an attempt has already been made to do something of the sort, though on the basis of the antithetical doctrine that everyone is wholly accountable and culpable. It was the founder of Christianity who wanted to abolish secular justice and remove judging and punishing from the world. For he understood all guilt as 'sin', that is to say as an offence against *God* and *not* as an offence against the world; on the other hand, he regarded everyone as being in the greatest measure and in almost every respect a sinner. The guilty, however, ought not be the judges of their own kind: thus his sense of equity dictated. *All* judges of the realm of secular justice were thus in his eyes as guilty as those they condemned, and the air of innocence they assumed seemed to him hypocritical and pharisaical. He had eyes, moreover, only for the motives of an action and not for its consequences, and considered there was only one sole person sufficiently sharpsighted to adjudicate on motives: he himself (or, as he himself put it, God).

82

An affectation on departing. – He who wants to desert a party or a religion believes it is incumbent upon him to refute it. But this is a very arrogant notion. All that is needed is that he should be clear as to the nature of the bonds that formerly tied him to this party or religion and to the fact that they no longer do so; that he should understand what kind of outlook impelled him to them and that it now impels him elsewhere. We did *not* attach ourself to this party or religion on *strictly rational grounds*: we ought not to *affect* to have done so when we leave it.

83

Saviour and physician. – The founder of Christianity was, as goes without saying, not without the gravest shortcomings and prejudices in his knowledge of the human soul, and as a physician of the soul devoted to that infamous and untutored faith in a universal medicine. At times his methods seem like those of a dentist whose sole cure for pain is to pull out the teeth; as, for example, when he combats sensuality with the advice: 'If thy eye offend thee, pluck it out.' – But there is this difference, that the dentist at least attains his object, the cessation of pain in his patient; in so clumsy a way, to be sure, as to be ludicrous: while the Christian who follows that advice and believes he has killed his sensuality is deceiving himself: it lives on in an uncanny vampire form and torments him in repulsive disguises.

84

The prisoners. – One morning the prisoners entered the workyard: the warder was missing. Some of them started working straightaway, as was their nature, others stood idle and looked around defiantly. Then one stepped forward and said loudly: 'Work as much as you like, or do nothing: it is all one. Your secret designs have come to light, the prison warder has been eavesdropping on you and in the next few days intends to pass a fearful judgement upon you. You know him, he is harsh and vindictive. But now pay heed: you have hitherto mistaken me: I am not what I seem but much more: I am the son of the prison warder and I mean everything to him. I can save you, I will save you: but, note well, only those of you who *believe* me that I am the son of the prison warder; the rest may enjoy the fruit of their unbelief.' – 'Well now', said one of the older prisoners after a brief silence, 'what can it matter to you if we believe you or do not believe you? If you really are his son and can do what you say, then put in a good word for all of us: it would be really good of you if you did so. But leave aside this talk of belief and unbelief!' – 'And', a younger man interposed, 'I *don't* believe him: it's only an idea he's got into his head. I bet that in a week's time we shall find ourselves here just like today, and that the prison warder knows *nothing*'. – 'And if he did know something he knows it no longer', said the last of the prisoners, who had only just come into the yard; 'the prison warder has just suddenly died'. – 'Holla!' cried several together; 'holla! Son! Son! What does the will say? Are we perhaps now *your* prisoners?' – 'I have told you', he whom they addressed responded quietly, 'I will set free everyone who believes in me, as surely as my father still lives'. – The prisoners did not laugh, but shrugged their shoulders and left him standing.

85

The persecutor of God. – Paul conceived the idea, and Calvin appropriated the idea, that countless numbers have from all eternity been condemned to damnation and that this lovely universal plan was thus instituted so that the glory of God might be revealed in it; Heaven and Hell and humanity are thus supposed to exist so as to – gratify the vanity of God! What a cruel and insatiable vanity must have flickered in the soul of him who first conceived or first appropriated such a thing! – Paul thus remained Saul after all – *the persecutor of God*.

86

Socrates. – If all goes well, the time will come when one will take up the memorabilia of Socrates rather than the Bible as a guide to morals and reason, and when Montaigne and Horace will be employed as forerunners and signposts to an understanding of this simplest and most imperishable of intercessors. The pathways of the most various philosophical modes of life lead back to him; at bottom they are the modes of life of the various temperaments confirmed and established by reason and habit and all of them directed towards joy in living and in one's own self; from which one might conclude that Socrates' most personal characteristic was a participation in every temperament. – Socrates excels the founder of Christianity in being able to be serious cheerfully and in possessing that *wisdom full of roguishness* that constitutes the finest state of the human soul. And he also possessed the finer intellect.

87

Learning to write well. – The age of speaking well is past, because the age of the city cultures is past. The extreme limit Aristotle allowed for the size of a city – it must be possible for the herald to make himself audible to the whole assembled community – this limit is of as little concern to us as is the city community itself: we want to make ourself understood, not merely beyond the city, but out over the nations. That is why everyone who is a good European now has to learn *to write well and ever better*: this is still so even if he happens to have been born in Germany, where writing badly is regarded as a national privilege. To write better, however, means at the same time also to think better; continually to invent things more worth communicating and to be able actually to communicate them; to become translatable into the language of one's neighbour; to make ourselves accessible to the understanding of those foreigners who learn our language; to assist towards making all good things common property and freely available to the free-minded; finally, to *prepare the way* for that still distant state of things in which the good Europeans will come into possession of their great task: the direction and supervision of the total culture of the earth. – Whoever preaches the opposite and sets no store by writing well and reading well – both virtues grow together and decline together – is in fact showing the peoples a way of becoming more and more *national*: he is augmenting the sickness of this century and is an enemy of all good Europeans, an enemy of all free spirits.

88

Teaching of the best style. – The teaching of style can on the one hand be the teaching that one ought to discover the means of expression by virtue of which every state of mind can be conveyed to the reader or auditor; on the other hand, it can be the teaching that one ought to discover the means of expression for the most desirable state of mind, the state, that is to say, which it is most desirable should be communicated and conveyed: that of the spiritually joyful, luminous and honest man who has overcome his passions. This will be the teaching that there exists a best style: the style corresponding to the good man.

89

Paying attention to pace. – The pace of his sentences shows whether the author is tired; the individual phrase can still be good and strong notwithstanding, because it was discovered earlier and independently when the idea first dawned on the author. This is frequently so in the case of Goethe, who too often dictated when he was tired.

90

Already and still. – A: German prose is still very young: Goethe says that Wieland was its father. B: So young and already so ugly! C: But I believe it is true that Bishop Ulfilas* was already writing German prose; it is therefore getting on for 1500 years old. B: So old and still so ugly!

91

Original German. – German prose, which is in fact not based on some foreign model and ought no doubt to be accounted an original product of German taste, might offer a signpost to the zealous advocates of a future original German culture as to how, without imitation of foreign models, a truly German costume, for instance, a German social gathering, a German furnishing of a room, a German luncheon, would look. – Someone who had reflected long on this prospect finally cried out in horror: 'But, for heaven's sake, perhaps we already *have* this original culture – only we don't like to talk about it!'

92

Forbidden books. – Never to read anything written by those arrogant knowalls and muddle-heads who indulge in that most revolting form of illbreeding, that of logical paradox: they employ the forms of *logic* in precisely those places where at bottom everything is impudently improvised and constructed in air. ('Thus' should in their case mean 'you ass of a reader, for you there is no "thus" – though there is for me' – to which the answer is: 'you ass of a writer, whatever do you write for then?')

93

Demonstrating spirit. – Anyone who wants to demonstrate his spirit makes sure everyone notices that he is abundantly supplied with its reverse. That ill-breeding on the part of gifted Frenchmen with which they add to their finest notions a touch of *dédain*† has its origin in the intention of seeming richer than they are: they want to bestow languidly, as though wearied by constant dispensing from overfull treasure-houses.

94

German and French literature. – The misfortune for the German and French

---

* Bishop Ulfilas: Gothic apostle (c. 311 to 383), who translated the Bible into Gothic, sometimes referred to as 'the father of Teutonic literature'.
† *dédain*: disdain

literature of the past hundred years lies in the fact that the Germans *left* the French school too soon – and that later the French *entered* the German school too soon.

95

Our prose. – None of the present-day cultural nations has such bad prose as the German; and if gifted and pampered Frenchmen say there *is* no German prose – then we ought not really to be angry, for it is meant more politely than we deserve. When we look for reasons we arrive at last at the curious conclusion that *the German knows only improvised prose* and has no idea at all that there is any other. It sounds to him simply incomprehensible if an Italian says that writing prose is as much harder than writing poetry as the representation of naked beauty is harder to the sculptor than that of beauty draped. One has to toil honestly at verse, image, rhythm and rhyme – even the German knows that, and is not inclined to accord improvisatory composition an especially high value. But to work on a page of prose as on a statue? – it sounds to him like something from the land of fable.

96

Grand style. – Grand style originates when the beautiful carries off the victory over the monstrous.

97

Avoidance. – One does not know in what the refinement of a turn of phrase or an expression employed by a distinguished spirit consists until one can say what word every mediocre writer would unavoidably have hit upon to express the same thing. All great artists display when driving their vehicle a tendency to avoidance, to running off the road – without thereby having an accident.

98

Something like bread. – Bread neutralizes the taste of other foods, expunges it; that is why it is part of every more extended meal. In all works of art there has to be something like bread, so that they can contain varying effects: if the latter followed directly one upon the other undivided by any rest or pause they would soon exhaust the spectator and arouse in him repugnance, so that a *more extended* artistic meal would be an impossibility.

99

*Jean Paul.** – Jean Paul knew a great deal but had no science, was skilled in all kinds of artistic artifices but had no art, found almost nothing unenjoyable but had no taste, possessed feeling and seriousness but when he offered a taste of them poured over them a repulsive broth of tears, he had indeed wit – but unhappily far too little to satisfy his ravenous

---

* Jean Paul: pen-name of Jean Paul Freidrich Richter (1763–1825): German novelist and man of letters.

hunger for it: which is why it is precisely through his lack of wit that he drives the reader to despair. On the whole he was a motley, strong-smelling weed that shot up overnight in the delicate fruitfields of Schiller and Goethe; he was a complacent, good man, and yet a fatality – a fatality in a dressing-gown.

100

Knowing how to taste the opposite too. – To enjoy a work of the past in the way its contemporaries enjoyed it one has to have on one's tongue the taste prevailing at that time against which it was *contrasted*.

101

Spirits-of-wine authors. – Many writers are neither spirit nor wine but spirits-of-wine: they can catch fire and then they give off heat.

102

The mediating sense. – The sense of taste has, as the true mediating sense, often persuaded the other senses over to its own view of things and imposed upon them its laws and habits. One can obtain information about the subtlest mysteries of the arts at a mealtable: one has only to notice what tastes good, when it tastes good, what it tastes good after and for how long it tastes good.

103

Lessing. – Lessing possessed a genuine French virtue and was in general as a writer the most diligent pupil of the French: he knows how to arrange and exhibit his things well in the shop-window. Without this *art* his ideas would, like the objects of them, have remained somewhat in darkness, and without this having been any very great loss. But many (especially the last generation of German scholars) have learned much from his *art* and countless numbers have taken pleasure in it. These learners, to be sure, did not also have to learn from him, as so many of them did, his un-pleasant tone of voice, with its mixture of quarrelsomeness and honest probity. – As to Lessing the 'lyricist' everyone is now unanimous: as to the 'dramatist' everyone will be.

104

Unwanted readers. – How an author is tormented by those gallant readers with thick, clumsy souls who, whenever they knock against anything, fall over and hurt themselves!

105

Poets' thoughts. – The real thoughts of real poets all go about veiled, like the women in Egypt: only the deep *eyes* of the thought gaze out over the veil. – Poets' thoughts are on average not worth as much as they are accepted as being: for one is also paying for the veil and for one's own curiosity.

106

Write simply and serviceably. – Transitions, amplifications, colourful emotions – all these we will allow the author and his book provided he lets us have something solid in return.

107

*Wieland.** – Wieland wrote German better than anyone (his translations of Cicero's letters and of Lucian are the best German translations), but for all that his thoughts no longer offer us material for thought. We can endure his cheerful moralities as little as his cheerful immoralities: both belong so well together. The people who took pleasure in them were no doubt at bottom better people than we are – but also a good deal slower and more ponderous people of the kind such a writer *had need of.* – *Goethe* had no need of the Germans, which is why they in turn have no idea what use to make of him. Look at even the best of our statesmen and artists: none of them had Goethe for his educator – or can have.

108

Rare feasts. – Pithy compactness, reposefulness and maturity – where you find these qualities in an author stop and celebrate a long feast in the midst of the wilderness: it will be a long time before you experience such a sense of wellbeing again.

109

The treasury of German prose. – Apart from Goethe's writings, and in particular Goethe's conversations with Eckermann,† the best German book there is, what is there really of German prose literature that it would be worthwhile to read over and over again? Lichtenberg's aphorisms, the first book of Jung-Stilling's autobiography,‡ Adalbert Stifter's *Nachsommer*§ and Gottfried Keller's *Leute von Seldwyla*§§ – and that for the present is all.

110

Written style and oral style. – The art of writing demands above all *substitutes* for the modes of expression available only to the speaker: that is to say, for gestures, emphases, tones of voice, glances. That is why written style is quite different from oral style and something much more difficult: – it wants to make itself just as comprehensible as the latter but with fewer means. Demosthenes delivered his orations differently from the way in which we read them: he revised them for reading. – Cicero's orations ought to be demosthenized for the same purpose: at present there is much more Roman forum in them than the reader can take.

111

Caution in quoting. – Young authors do not know that a fine expression, a

---

* Wieland: Christoph Martin Wieland (1733–1813): German novelist, poet and man of letters.
  † Goethe's conversations with Eckermann: Johann Peter Eckermann's *Conversations with Goethe* was published 1837–48.
  ‡ Jung-Stilling: Heinrich Jung-Stilling (1740–1817) published his autobiography in six volumes between 1777 and the year of his death.
  § Adalbert Stifter (1805–68) published his novel *Nachsommer* in 1857.
  §§ Gottfried Keller (1819–90): Swiss poet and story-writer; his collection of novellas, *Die Leute von Seldwyla*, appeared in two volumes in 1856 and 1874.

fine idea, looks fine only among its like and equals, that an excellent quotation can annihilate entire pages, indeed an entire book, in that it warns the reader and seems to cry out to him: 'Beware, I am the jewel and around me there is lead, pallid, ignominious lead!' Every word, every idea, wants to dwell only *in its own company*: that is the moral of high style.

112

How should errors be spoken? – One may dispute whether it is more harmful when errors are spoken badly or as well as the finest truths. What is certain is that in the former case they injure the head twofold and are harder to remove from it; on the other hand, their effect is not as certain as in the latter case: they are not so infectious.

113

Circumscribing and enlarging. – Homer circumscribed the compass of his material and reduced it, but let the individual scenes expand and enlarged them – and so, later on, do the tragedians: each takes the material in *smaller* portions than his predecessors, but each obtains a *richer* abundance of blooms within this hedged-off garden enclosure.

114

Literature and morality casting light on one another. – Greek literature can be employed to demonstrate through what forces the Greek spirit developed and expanded, how it divided on to different paths and what it was that made it grow weak. All this provides a picture of what at bottom happened to Greek *morality* too, and of what must happen to every morality: how it was at first compulsion and enforced with harshness, then gradually grew gentler; how at last men came to take pleasure in certain actions, in certain forms and conventions, and how there grew out of that a tendency to appropriate the practice and possession of these things to oneself; how the course becomes filled and overfilled with competitors, how satiety supervenes, new objects of contest and ambition are sought and old ones recalled to life, how the spectacle is repeated and the spectators grow weary of watching because the entire circle now seems to have been run through – – and then comes a stop, a last breath: the streams lose themselves in the sand. The end has come, at least *an* end.

115

Which regions give lasting pleasure. – This region would be well suited to a painting, yet I cannot find the formula for it, I cannot seize it as a whole. I have noticed that all landscapes that make a lasting appeal to me possess beneath all their multiplicity a simple geometrical shape. No region can give artistic pleasure if it lacks such a mathematical substratum. And perhaps this rule may also be applied metaphorically to men.

116

Reading aloud. – The ability to read aloud presupposes the ability to *present*: one has only pale colours to employ, but has to determine the exact proportions in which they shall appear before the full and deep colours of the ever-present and determining background, that is to say to determine their *presentation*. One therefore has to be capable of this art.

117

The dramatic sense. – He who lacks the four more refined senses of art seeks to understand everything with the coarsest, the fifth: this is the dramatic sense.

118

Herder. * – Herder is none of the things he induced others to suppose he was (and which he himself wished to suppose he was): no great poet and inventor, no new fruitful soil full of fresh primeval energy as yet unemployed. He did possess, however, and in the highest degree, the ability to scent the wind; he perceived and plucked the firstlings of the season earlier than anyone else, so that others could believe it was he who made them grow: his spirit lay in wait like a hunter between light and dark, old and young, and wherever there were bridges, hollows, landslips, signs of hidden springs and new growth: the restlessness of spring drove him hither and thither, but he himself was not spring! – No doubt he was aware of this at times but certainly did not want to believe it, ambitious priest that he was who would have so liked to have been the intellectual pope of his age! This is what he suffers from: he seems to have lived for a long time as the pretender to several kingdoms, indeed to a universal empire, and he had adherents who believed in him: the youthful Goethe was among them. But whenever crowns were in the last resort conferred he went away empty: Kant, Goethe, then the first real German historians and philologists took away from him what he supposed had been reserved for him – yet often secretly and silently did *not* suppose had been. It was precisely when he doubted himself that he liked to drape himself in dignity and enthusiasm: these were all too often a cloak designed to conceal many things and to deceive and console him himself. He really did possess fire and enthusiasm, but his ambition was much greater! This last blew impatiently on the flame and made it flicker, crackle and smoke – his *style* flickers, crackles and smokes – but he desired a *great* flame, and this never broke forth! He never sat at the table of the actual creators: and his ambition did not allow him to seat himself modestly among the actual partakers. Thus he was a restless guest, tasting in advance every spiritual dish the Germans raked together over a half-century from all the realms of space and time. Never truly happy and satisfied, Herder was moreover all too frequently ill: then envy sometimes came and sat on his bed, and hypocrisy too paid him a visit. Something injured and unfree continued to adhere to him: and he lacks simple sturdy manliness more than any other of our so-called 'classics'.

* Herder: Johann Gottfried Herder (1744–1803): German critic and aesthetician.

119

Odour of words. – Every word has its odour: there exists a harmony and disharmony of odours and thus of words.

120

Fine style. – The invented style is an offence to the friend of fine style.

121

Vow. – I intend never again to read an author of whom it is apparent that he wanted to produce a book: but only those whose thoughts unintentionally became a book.

122

Artistic convention. – Three-quarters of Homer is convention; and the same is true of all Greek artists, who had no reason to fall prey to the modern rage for originality. They lacked all fear of convention; it was through this, indeed, that they were united with their public. For conventions are the *achieved* artistic means, the toilsomely acquired common language, through which the artist can truly *communicate* himself to the understanding of his audience. Especially when, like the Greek poets and musicians, he wants to conquer *immediately* with each of his works – since he is accustomed to contend publicly with one or two rivals – the first condition is that he shall also be *understood immediately*: which is possible, however, only through convention. That which the artist invents that goes beyond convention he adds of his own volition and puts himself at risk with it, the most favourable outcome being that he *creates* a new convention. As a rule what is original is admired, sometimes idolized, but rarely understood; obstinately to avoid convention means wanting not to be understood. To what, then, does the modern rage for originality point?

123

Affectation of scientificality on the part of artists. – Schiller believed, like other German artists, that if one possesses spirit one is free to *improvize with the pen* on all kinds of difficult subjects. And now his prose essays lie there – in every respect a model of how *not* to tackle scientific questions of aesthetics and morals – and a danger to young readers who in their admiration for Schiller the poet lack the courage to think ill of Schiller the thinker and essayist. – The temptation to which the artist so readily and so comprehensively succumbs for once to enter fields barred expressly to *him* and to put a word in with regard to *science* – for even the best worker sometimes finds his trade and his workplace unendurable – this temptation draws the artist so far as to show all the world what it has no reason to see at all, namely that his thinking-room looks narrow and in disorder – and why not? he doesn't live in it! – that the storecupboards of his knowledge are in part empty, in part filled with a medley of junk – and why not? this state of things is at bottom not at all ill-suited to the artist-child – but especially that even for the simplest tools and tricks of scientific method with which the merest beginners are familiar his wrists are too thick and unpractised – and of this too he truly has no cause to be ashamed! – On the other hand, he often displays no little art in *imitating* all the blunders, bad habits and bogus scholarliness to be found in the scientific guild, in the belief that those things belong, if not to the heart of the matter, at any rate to its outward appearance; and this, precisely, is what is comical about such artists' writings: without wishing to, the artist here nonetheless does what it is his office to do – to *parody* the scientific and inartistic nature. For a parodistic posture is the only posture he ought to adopt towards science, insofar, that is, as he remains an artist and only an artist.

124

The Faust idea. – A little seamstress is seduced and dishonoured; a great scholar of all the four faculties is the miscreant. But that surely cannot happen in the right nature of things? No, by no means! Without the assistance of the Devil in person the great scholar could not have brought it about. – Is this really supposed to be the greatest German 'tragic idea', as Germans say it is? – But even this idea was still too dreadful for Goethe; after the little seamstress, 'the good soul who erred but once', had suf-fered an involuntary death, his gentle heart could not refrain from trans-porting her into the proximity of the saints; indeed, in due course he even sent to Heaven the great scholar, the 'good man' with the 'impulse obscure', through a trick played on the Devil at the decisive moment: – up in Heaven the lovers find one another again. – Goethe once said that his nature was too conciliatory for real tragedy.

125

Is there such a thing as a 'German classic'? – Sainte-Beuve* once remarked that the word 'classic' altogether refused to sound right when applied to certain literatures: who, for example, would find it easy to speak of a 'German classic'! – What is the view of our German booksellers, who are on their way to augmenting the fifty German classics in whom we are already supposed to believe with a further fifty? Does it not seem that an author needs only to have been dead thirty years and to lie there in public as permitted prey for him suddenly to hear the trumpet of the resurrec-tion summoning him to rise as a classic? And this in an age and among a nation where even of the six great ancestors of its literature five are un-mistakably becoming or have already become antiquated – *without* this age or this nation needing to be ashamed on precisely *that* account! For it is in face of the *strong* of this age that they have receded – this much must in all fairness be admitted! – Goethe, as already indicated, I except; he belongs in a higher order of literatures than 'national literatures': that is why he stands towards his *nation* in the relationship neither of the living nor of the novel nor of the antiquated. Only for a few was he alive and does he live still: for most he is nothing but a fanfare of vanity blown from time to time across the German frontier. Goethe, not only a good and great human being but a *culture*, Goethe is in the history of the Germans an episode without consequences: who could, for example, produce a

* Sainte-Beuve: Charles Augustin Sainte-Beuve (1804–69): French critic.

piece of Goethe from the world of German politics over the past seventy years! (whereas a piece of Schiller at any rate has been active there, and perhaps even a little piece of Lessing). But the other five! Klopstock became, in a very respectable way, antiquated even during his own lifetime: and so thoroughly that the reflective book of his later years, the *Gelehrten-Republik*, has to the present day been taken seriously by no one. Herder suffered the misfortune that his writings were always either novel or antiquated, to stronger and more refined heads (as to Lichtenberg) even Herder's chief work, his *Ideen zur Geschichte der Menschheit*, was something antiquated as soon as it appeared. Wieland, who lived abundantly and bestowed abundant life, was shrewd enough to realize that his influence would vanish with his death. Lessing is perhaps still alive today – but among young and ever younger scholars! And Schiller has by now fallen out of the hands of youths into those of boys, of all German boys! To descend down to ever more immature readers is, indeed, a familiar way for a book to become antiquated. – And what is it that has repelled these five, so that well-educated and industrious men no longer read them? An improved taste, an improved knowledge, an improved respect for the true and real: thus nothing but virtues which precisely these five (and ten or twenty others with less audible names) first again *implanted* in Germany and which now stand about their graves as a tall forest and spread over them, together with the shadow of reverence, also something of the shadow of oblivion. – But *classics* are not *implanters* of intellectual and literary virtues, they are *perfecters* of them and their highest points of light, which remain standing above the nations after these nations themselves have perished: for they are lighter, freer, purer than they. An exalted condition of mankind is possible in which the Europe of nations will be lost in dark oblivion, but in which Europe will *live on* in thirty very old but never antiquated books: in the classics.

126

Interesting but not beautiful. – This region conceals its meaning; but it has a meaning and one would like to discover what it is: wherever I look I read words and hints of words, but I do not know where the sentence begins that will unravel the riddle contained in all these hints, and I become wrynecked in searching for its starting place.

127

Against innovators in language. – To employ innovations or quaint old terms in language, to favour the rare and strange, to be concerned to augment vocabulary rather than to restrict it, is always a sign of an immature or corrupted taste. A noble poverty, but a masterly freedom within this unpretentiousness, is what distinguishes the Greek artists of speech: they want to have *less* than the people have – for it is they who are richest in old and new terms – but they want to have this less *in better shape*. Their archaisms and uncommon terms are soon added up, but there is no end to our admiration if we have an eye for the light and delicate way they have with the everyday and seemingly long since exhausted in words and phrases.

128

Melancholy and serious authors. – He who reduces to paper what he *is suffering* will be a *melancholy* author. a *serious* author, however, is one who tells us what he *has suffered* and why he is now reposing in joy.

129

Healthy taste. – Why is it that health is not as infectious as sickness – in general but especially in matters of taste? Or are there epidemics of health? –

130

Resolution. – Never again to read a book which was born and baptized (with ink) simultaneously.

131

Improving one's thoughts. – To improve one's style – means to improve one's thoughts and nothing else! – If you do not straightaway agree with this it will be impossible to convince you of it.

132

Classic books. – The weakest side of every classic book is that it is written too much in its author's mother tongue.

133

Bad books. – A book ought to long for pen, ink and writing-desk: but as a rule pen, ink and writing-desk long for a book. That is why books are nowadays of so little account.

134

Presence of interest. – When it reflects on pictures, the public becomes a poet, and when it reflects on poems it becomes a researcher. At the moment the artist calls to it, it never has the *right kind* of interest: presence of interest, not presence of mind, is what it lacks.

135

Choice thoughts. – The choice style of an age of significance chooses not only the words but also the thoughts – and chooses them both out of what is *in current use*: daring and all too fresh-smelling thoughts are no less repugnant to the more mature taste than are rash new expressions and images. Both of them – the choice thought and the choice word – can later easily smell of mediocrity, because the odour of choice things quickly evaporates, and then all that is left to taste in them is the current and everyday.

136

Chief reason for corruption of style. – To desire to *demonstrate* more feeling for a thing than one actually *has* corrupts one's style, in both language and all the arts. All great art has, rather, the opposite tendency: like every man of moral consequence, it likes to arrest the feelings on their course and not allow them to run *quite* to their conclusion. This modesty which keeps the feelings only half-visible can be observed at its fairest in, for example, Sophocles; and it seems to transfigure the features of the feelings when they present themselves as being more sober than they are.

137
In defence of ponderous stylists. – What is said lightly seldom falls as heavily upon the ear as the subject really weighs – the fault, however, lies with the ill-schooled ear, which has to progress from education through what has hitherto been called music on to the school of higher composition, that is to say that of *speech*.

138
Bird's-eye view. – Here torrential streams plunge from many directions into a gorge: their motion is so violent, and draws the eyes so vigorously after it, that the bare and wooded cliffs all around seem, not to sink, but to *flee* down. The prospect arouses in us an anxious fear, as though something inimical lay behind it all from which everything had to take flight and against which the abyss would lend us protection. This region cannot in any way be painted unless one is hovering above it in the air like a bird. Here the so-called bird's-eye view is for once not an artistic caprice but the sole possibility.

139
Daring comparisons. – When daring comparisons are not proof of the writer's wanton mischievousness they are proof of the exhaustion of his imagination. In any case, however, they are proof of his very bad taste.

140
Dancing in chains. – With every Greek artist, poet and writer one has to ask: what is the *new constraint* he has imposed upon himself and through which he charms his contemporaries (so that he finds imitators)? For that which we call 'invention' (in metrics, for example) is always such a self-imposed fetter. 'Dancing in chains', making things difficult for oneself and then spreading over it the illusion of ease and facility – that is the artifice they want to demonstrate to us. Already in Homer we can perceive an abundance of inherited formulae and epic narrative rules *within* which he had to dance: and he himself created additional new conventions for those who came after him. This was the school in which the Greek poets were raised: firstly to allow a multiplicity of constraints to be imposed upon one; then to devise an additional new constraint, impose it upon oneself and conquer it with charm and grace: so that both the constraint and its conquest are noticed and admired.

141
Plentiful authors. – The last thing a good author acquires is plentifulness; he who brings it with him will never be a good author. The noblest race-horses are lean until they have won the right to *rest and recover* from their victories.

142

Panting heroes. – Poets and artists who suffer from asthmatic narrow-chestedness of the feelings are most liable to make their heroes pant: they do not know how to breathe easily.

143

The half-blind. – The half-blind are the mortal foes of authors who let themselves go. They would like to vent on them the wrath they feel when they slam shut a book whose author has taken fifty pages to communicate five ideas: their wrath, that is, at having endangered what is left of their eyesight for so little recompense. – A half-blind man said: *all* authors let themselves go. – 'Even the Holy Ghost?' – Even the Holy Ghost. But with him it was all right; he wrote for the totally blind.

144

The style of immortality. – Thucydides and Tacitus* – both when they composed their works did so with a view to their enduring immortally: if one did not know this from other sources, the fact would already be apparent from their style. One believed he could bestow durability through salting and pickling, the other through boiling and preserving; and neither, it seems, was wrong.

145

Against images and similes. – With images and similes one can persuade and convince but not prove. That is why there is such an aversion to images and similes within science; here the persuasive and convincing, that which makes *credible,* is precisely what is *not* wanted; one challenges, rather, the coldest mistrust, and does so even in the means of expression one employs and the bare walls it presents: because mistrust is the touchstone for the gold of certainty.

146

Caution. – He who lacks thorough knowledge should take care not to publish a book in Germany. For the good German then says, not 'he is ignorant', but 'he is of doubtful character'. – This precipitate conclusion, moreover, does credit to the Germans.

147

Painted skeletons. – Painted skeletons are those authors who would like to compensate with artificial colouring for what they lack in flesh.

148

The grandiloquent style and what is higher. – One learns how to write grandiloquently more quickly than one learns how to write simply and easily. The reasons for this merge into the realm of morality.

149

Sebastian Bach. – Insofar as one does *not* listen to Bach's music as a com-

---

* Tacitus: Gaius Cornelius Tacitus (c. 55 to 120): Roman historian.

plete and experienced expert in counterpoint and every species of the fugal style of composition, and must consequently do without the actual artistic pleasure it affords, it will seem to us when we hear his music as though (to employ a grandiose expression of Goethe's) we were present *as God was creating the world*. That is to say, we feel that here something great is in process of becoming but does not yet *exist*: our *great* modern music. It has already conquered the world because it has conquered the church, national characteristics, and counterpoint. In Bach there is still too much crude Christianity, crude Germanism, crude scholasticism; he stands on the threshold of European (modern) music, but from here looks behind him back towards the Middle Ages.

150
Handel. – Handel, in the invention of his music bold, innovative, true, strong, capable of heroism – often becomes in its working out cold and restrained, indeed weary of himself; he employed certain tested methods of execution, wrote quickly and a great deal, and was glad when he was finished – but not glad in the way God and other creators have been in the evening of their working day.

151
Haydn. – To the extent that genius can be united with an altogether *good* man, Haydn possessed it. He goes precisely as far as the limits morality draws for the intellect; the music he composes is all music with 'no past'.

152
Beethoven and Mozart. – Beethoven's music often seems like a deeply affected *meditation* on unexpectedly hearing again a piece, 'Innocence in Sound', long believed to have been lost: it is music *about* music. In the songs of beggars and children in the streets, in the montonous tunes of travelling Italians, at the dances in the village inn or on carnival nights – that is where he discovers his 'melodies': he collects them together like a bee, by seizing a sound here, a brief resolution there. To him they are *recollections* of a 'better world', in much the same way as Plato conceived of Ideas. – Mozart's relation to his melodies is quite different: he finds his inspirations, not in listening to music, but in looking at life, at the liveliest life of the *south*: he was always dreaming of Italy when he was not there.

153
Recitative. – Formerly recitative was dry; now we live in the age of *wet recitative*: it has melted away and now flows about it knows not where or whither.

154
'Cheerful' music. – If one has gone without music for a long time it afterwards enters the blood all too quickly like a heavy southern wine, and leaves behind a soul narcotically dulled, half-awake and longing for sleep; this is especially the effect of *cheerful* music, which produces bitterness and a sense of hurt, satiety and homesickness all at the same time,

and compels one to gulp down everything again and again as though in a sugared draught of poison. The joyful hall then seems to close in, the light to lose its brightness and become browner: at last it is as though the music were penetrating into a prison cell where a poor wretch lies sleepless from homesickness.

155

Franz Schubert. – Franz Schubert, a lesser artist than the other great composers, nonetheless possessed the greatest *inherited wealth* of music of any of them. He squandered it with liberal generosity: so that composers will have his ideas and inspirations to *feast* on for another couple of centuries. In his works we have a treasury of *unemployed* inventions; others will find their greatness in employing them. – If one may call Beethoven the ideal audience for a music-maker, then Schubert has a right to be called the ideal music-maker himself.

156

The most modern musical execution. – The grand tragic-dramatic mode of musical execution acquires its character through imitating the demeanour of the *great sinner* as Christianity imagines him and desires him to be: the slow pace, the passionate brooding, the agitation through torment of conscience, the terrified praying and pleading, the enraptured grasping and seizing, the halting in despair – and whatever else marks a man as being in a state of great sin. Only the presupposition of Christianity that all men are great sinners and do nothing whatever except sin could justify applying this style of execution to *all* music: insofar, that is, that music is taken to be an image of all human life and action and as such has continually to speak the gesture-language of the great sinner. A listener who was insufficient of a Christian to comprehend this logic might, to be sure, exclaim in horror when witnessing such a performance: 'For Heaven's sake, however did sin get into music!'

157

Felix Mendelssohn. – Felix Mendelssohn's music is the music of the enjoyment of whatever is good and is precedented: it always points back behind itself. How could it have much 'before it', much future!—But then did he *want* a future? He possessed a virtue rare among artists, that of gratitude without mental reservations: and this virtue too always points back behind itself.

158

A mother of the arts. – In our sceptical age actual *devotions* require an almost brutally heroic *ambitiousness*; fanatical eye-closing and knee-bending are no longer enough. Might it not be possible that the ambition to be the last of all the ages in the matter of devotion could become the father of a last Catholic church music, as it has already been the father of the last Catholic style of architecture? (It is called the Jesuit style.)

159

Freedom in fetters – a princely freedom. – The last of the modern composers to behold and worship beauty as Leopardi did, the inimitable Pole, Chopin – no one before or after him has a claim to this epithet – Chopin possessed the same princely nobility in respect of convention as Raphael shows in the employment of simplest, most traditional colours – not with regard to colours, however, but in regard to traditional forms of melody and rhythm. These, as *born to etiquette*, he admits without dispute, but does so playing and dancing in these fetters like the freest and most graceful of spirits – and does so, moreover, without turning them to ridicule.

160

Chopin's Barcarole. – Almost all conditions and ways of life have a *blissful* moment, and good artists know how to fish it out. Such is possessed even by a life spent beside the beach, a life that unwinds tediously, insalubriously, unhealthily in the proximity of the noisiest and greediest rabble – this blissful moment Chopin has, in his Barcarole, expressed in sound in such a way that the gods themselves could on hearing it desire to spend long summer evenings lying in a boat.

161

Robert Schumann. – The 'youth' as the Romantic lyricists of France and Germany dreamed of him in the first third of this century – this youth has been completely translated into sound and song – by Robert Schumann, the eternal youth so long as he felt himself to be in the fullness of his own strength: there are, to be sure, moments when his music recalls the eternal 'old maid'.

162

Dramatic singers. – 'Why is this beggar singing?' – He probably doesn't know how to wail. – 'Then he is doing right: but our dramatic singers who wail because they don't know how to sing – are they too doing the right thing too?'

163

Dramatic music. – To him who does not see what is taking place on the stage, dramatic music is an absurdity, just as a continuous commentary to a lost text is an absurdity. What it is really demanding is that one's ears should be where one's eyes are; that, however, constitutes a rape on Euterpe:* this poor muse wants her eyes and ears left where all the other muses have them.

164

Victory and rationality. – As in the case of other wars, so in that of the aesthetic wars which artists provoke with their works and their apologias for them the outcome is, unhappily, decided in the end by force and not by

---

* Euterpe: muse of music

reason. All the world now accepts it as an historical fact that Gluck* was in the *right* in his struggle with Piccini: in any event, he *won*; force was on his side.

165

On the principles of musical performance. – Do our present-day artists of musical performance really believe, then, that the supreme commandment of their art is to give every piece as much *high relief* as they possibly can, and make it speak in *dramatic* language at all cost? Is this, when applied for instance to Mozart, not simply a sin against the spirit, against the cheerful, sunny, tender, frivolous spirit of Mozart, whose seriousness is a goodnatured and not a dreadful seriousness, whose pictures do not desire to leap out of the wall so as to drive his audience away in terror. Or do you think that Mozartian music means the same thing as 'the music of the stone guest'? And not only Mozartian but all music? – But you retort that the greater *effect* speaks in favour of your principle – and you could be right, provided that no one asked the counter-question *upon whom* the effect was supposed to be produced and upon whom a noble artist *ought to want* to produce an effect at all! Never upon the people! Never upon the immature! Never upon the sentimental! Never upon the sickly! But above all: never upon the dull and stupefied!

166

Music of today. – This latest music, with its strong lungs and weak nerves, is terrified above all of itself.

167

Where music is at home. – Music achieves great power only among people who cannot or are not allowed to discourse. Its principal promoters are therefore princes who want little criticism, indeed little thought at all, to take place in their vicinity; then societies which, under some repression or other (princely or religious), have to accustom themselves to silence but therefore seek all the most powerful charms against emotional boredom (usually everlasting love-affairs and everlasting music); thirdly entire nations in which there exists no 'society' but for that reason all the more individuals with an inclination to solitude, to half-obscure cogitations and to a reverence for everything ineffable: these are the true musical souls. – The Greeks, as a voluble and disputatious people, could therefore endure music only as a *seasoning* for those arts that could actually be talked about and disputed over: whereas it is hardly possible even to *think* clearly about music. The Pythagoreans, those exceptions among the Greeks in many respects, were reportedly also great musicians: they who invented the five-year silence but did *not* invent dialectics.

---

* Gluck ... Piccini: Christopher Willibald von Gluck (1714-87), German operatic composer; Nicola Piccini (1728–1800), Italian operatic composer. The supporters of each clashed in Paris in the 1780's over which of their respective compositions of *Iphigénie en Tauride* was superior, Gluck's 'reform' opera or Piccini's traditional style.

168

Sentimentality in music. – However favourably inclined we may be towards serious and opulent music, there are perhaps, and for that very reason, hours when we are overcome, enchanted and almost melted away by its opposite: I mean by those utterly simple Italian operatic melismas which, in spite of all their rhythmic monotony and harmonic childishness, sometimes seem to sing to us like the soul of music itself. Whether you admit it or not, you pharisees of good taste, it *is* so, and it is now my concern to discuss the riddle presented by the fact that it is so and to offer a few guesses at its solution. – When we were still children we tasted the virgin honey of many things for the first time, and the honey never again tasted so good, it seduced us to life, to living as long as we could, in the shape of our first spring, our first flowers, our first butterflies, our first friendship. At that time – it was perhaps about the ninth year of our life – we heard the first music that we actually *understood*, the simplest and most childish music therefore, not much more than a spinning-out of our nurse's song or the organ-grinder's tune. (For one has first to be *prepared* and *instructed* even for the most trifling 'revelations' of art: there is no such thing as a 'direct' effect of art, however much the philosophers may have fabled of it.) It is to these first musical delights – the strongest of our life – that our sensibilities connect when we hear those Italian melismas: childhood happiness and the loss of childhood, the feeling that what is most irrecoverable is our most precious possession – this too touches the strings of our soul and does so more powerfully than art alone, however serious and opulent, is able to do. – This mixture of aesthetic joy with a moral grief which it is now customary to call 'sentimentality' – somewhat too haughtily, it seems to me (it is the mood of Faust at the end of the first scene) – this 'sentimentality' on the part of the listener, which experienced connoisseurs of art, the pure 'aestheticians', like to ignore, works in favour of Italian music. – Almost all music, moreover, produces a *magical* effect only when we hear the language of our own *past* speaking out of it: and to this extent all *old* music seems to the layman to get better and better and that only just born to be of little worth: for the latter does not yet excite that 'sentimentality' which, as aforesaid, constitutes the essential element of pleasure in music for anyone incapable of taking pleasure in this art purely as an artist.

169

As friends of music. – In the last resort we are and remain well disposed towards music for the same reason we are and remain well disposed towards moonlight. Neither wishes to supplant the sun, after all – both desire only to the best of their ability to illumine our *nights*. And yet – may we not make fun of them and laugh at them nonetheless? Just a little, at least? And from time to time? At the man in the moon! At the woman in music!

170

Art in the age of work. – We possess the conscience of an *industrious* age: and this conscience does not permit us to bestow our best hours and mornings on art, however grand and worthy this art may be. To us art counts as a leisure, a recreational activity: we devote to it the *remnants* of our time and energies. – This is the most general circumstance through which the relationship of art to life has been altered: when it makes its *grand* demands on the time and energy of the recipients of art it has the conscience of the industrious and able *against* it, it is directed to the conscienceless and lazy, who, however, are in accordance with their nature unfavourably inclined precisely towards *grand* art and feel the claims it makes to be presumptuous. It may therefore be that grand art is facing its end from lack of air and the room to breathe it: unless, that is, grand art tries, through a kind of coarsening and disguising, to become at home in (or at least to endure) that other air which is in reality the natural element only of *petty* art, of the art of recreation and distraction. And this is now happening everywhere; artists of grand art too now promise recreation and distraction, they too direct their attentions to the tired and weary, they too entreat of them the evening hours of their working day – just as do the artists of entertainment, who are content to have achieved a victory over the serious brow and the sunken eye. What artifices, then, do their greater comrades employ? They have in their dispensary the mightiest means of excitation capable of terrifying even the half-dead; they have narcotics, intoxicants, convulsives, paroxysms of tears: with these they overpower the tired and weary, arouse them to a fatigued overliveliness and make them beside themselves with rapture and terror. On account of the perilousness of these means it employs, ought one to denounce grand art in the forms in which it now exists – opera, tragedy and music – as the most deceitful of sinners? Not at all: for it would a hundred times prefer to dwell in the pure element of the quietness of morning and address itself to the expectant, wakeful, energetic soul. Let us be grateful to it that it has consented to live as it does rather than flee away: but let us also admit to ourselves that an age which shall one day bring back true festivals of joy and freedom will have no use for *our* art.

171

The employees of science and the others. – The truly efficient and successful scholars could one and all be described as 'employees'. When in their youth they had perfected their skills and crammed their memories, when hand and eye had acquired certainty, they were directed by an older scholar to a place in science where their qualities would be useful; later on, after they themselves had become accomplished enough to detect the gaps and faults in their science, they posted themselves of their own accord to where they were needed. These natures one and all exist for the sake of science: but there are rarer, rarely successful and wholly mature natures 'for the sake of whom science exists' – at least that is what they themselves think – : frequently unpleasant, frequently arrogant, frequently wrong-headed but almost always to a certain extent bewitching men. They are not employees, neither are they employers, they avail themselves of that which these have laboured to ascertain and do so with a certain princely composure and rarely with more than a modicum of praise: as though, indeed, those employees and employers belonged to a lower species of beings. And yet they possess precisely the same qualities as these employers and employees do, and sometimes even in an inferior state of development: they are, moreover, characterized by a *narrow limitedness* foreign to the former, on account of which it is impossible to appoint them to a post or see in them usable instruments – they can live only *in their own atmosphere* and on their own soil. This limitedness proffers them all of a science that 'belongs to them', that is to say all they can bear home with them to their atmosphere and dwelling; they fancy they are collecting together their scattered 'property'. If they are prevented from constructing their own nest they perish like houseless birds; unfreedom is phthisis to them. If they cultivate individual regions of science in the way the others do, it is always only those regions where the fruit and seeds they themselves need will prosper; what is it to them if science as a whole has regions untilled and ill cultivated? They lack all *impersonal* interest in a problem; just as they themselves are personalities through and through, so all their insights and acquirements in the field of knowledge coalesce together into a personality, into a living multiplicity whose individual parts are dependent on one another, cleave to one another, are nourished by the same food, and as a whole possesses its own atmosphere and its own odour. – Natures such as this produce, with their *personality-informed* structures of knowledge, that *illusion* that a science (or even the whole of philosophy) is finished and has reached its goal; it is the *life* in their structure that performs this magic, which has at times been very fateful for science and misleading for those able and efficient workers of the spirit just described, though at other times, when aridity and exhaustion have reigned, it has acted as a balm and like the breath of a cool, refreshing oasis. – The name usually give to such men is *philosophers*.

172
Recognition of talent. – As I was going through the village of S. a boy began cracking a whip with all his might – he had already advanced far in this art, and knew it. I threw him a glance of recognition – in my heart, however, I found it *very painful*. – So it is with the recognition of many talents. We are well disposed towards them when they cause us pain.

173
Laughing and smiling. – The more joyful and secure the spirit becomes, the more man unlearns loud laughter; on the other hand, a spiritual smile is continually welling up in him – a sign of his astonishment at the countless hidden pleasures existence contains.

174
Entertainment for invalids. – Just as grief of soul can lead us to tear at our

351

hair, beat our brows, rend our cheeks or even, as Oedipus did, pluck out our eyes, so when we experience violent physical pain we sometimes call to our aid a violent feeling of rancour by recalling acts of slander and inculpation committed against us, by viewing our future darkly, by acts of malice and stabs-in-the-back we perpetrate in imagination against invisible enemies. And occasionally it is true that one devil drives out another – but one then *has* this other. – Thus what is to be recommended to the invalid is that other form of entertainment that seems to diminish the pain: to reflect on acts of kindness and consideration one might perform for friend and foe.

175
Mediocrity as mask. – Mediocrity is the most successful mask the superior spirit can wear, because to the great majority, that is to say the mediocre, it will not seem a mask – : and yet it is on precisely their account that he puts it on – so as not to provoke *them*, indeed often out of benevolence and pity.

176
The patient. – The pine-tree seems to listen, the fir-tree to wait: and both without impatience: – they give no thought to the little people beneath them devoured by their impatience and their curiosity.

177
The best joke. – The joke I welcome most is that which stands in place of a weighty, not altogether harmless thought, at once a cautionary gesture of the finger and a flashing of the eyes.

178
Accessories of reverence. – Wherever the past is venerated the clean and the cleaners should not be admitted. Piety is uncomfortable without a little dust, dirt and refuse.

179
The great danger for scholars. – It is precisely the ablest and most thorough-going scholars who are in danger of seeing their life set narrower and narrower limits and, in the feeling that this is so, of becoming in the second half of their life more and more disgruntled and intolerant. At first they swim into their science with wide hopes and apportion themselves bolder tasks whose goals they sometimes already anticipate in their imagination: then there are moments such as occur in the life of the great discovering sea-voyagers – knowledge, presentiment and strength raise one another even higher, until a new distant coast dawns upon the eye. Now, however, the rigorous man recognizes more clearly year by year how vital it is that the individual items of research should be as circumscribed as possible so that they can be resolved *without* remainder and that unendurable squandering of energy avoided from which earlier periods of science suffered: every task is done ten times, and then the

eleventh still offers the best result. But the more the scholar gets to know and practise this resolving of riddles without remainder the greater will be his pleasure in it: but the strictness of his demands in regard to that which is here called 'without remainder' will likewise increase. He sets aside everything that must in this sense remain incomplete, he acquires a repugnance and a keen nose for the half-resolvable – for everything that can yield a kind of certainty only in a general and more indefinite sense. The plans of his youth collapse before his eyes: all that remains of them is the merest few knots in the unknotting of which the master now takes pleasure and demonstrates his power. And now, in the midst of all this useful and restless activity, the older man is suddenly and then repeatedly assailed by a profound disgruntlement, by a kind of torment of conscience: he gazes upon himself as upon one transformed, as though he had been diminished, debased, changed into a skilful *dwarf*; he is harassed by the thought of whether his mastery in small things is not a piece of indolence, an evasion of the admonition to greatness in living and working. But he can no longer *attain* it – the time has gone by.

180

The teacher in the age of books. – Now that self-education and fraternal education are becoming more general, the teacher must, in the form he now normally assumes, become almost redundant. Friends anxious to learn who want to acquire knowledge of something together can find in our age of books a shorter and more natural way than 'school' and 'teacher' are.

181

The great utility of vanity. – Originally the strong individual treats not only nature but society and weaker individuals too as objects of plunder: he exploits them as much as he can and then goes on. Because his life is very insecure, alternating between hunger and satiety, he kills more animals than he can eat, and pillages and mistreats men more than is necessary. His demonstrations of power are at the same time demonstrations of revenge against the painful and fear-ridden state of his existence: then again, he wants through his actions to count as being more powerful than he is: when the fear he engenders increases, his power increases. He soon notices that what bears him up or throws him down is not that which he *is* but that which he *counts* as being: here is the origin of *vanity*. The powerful man tries by every means to augment *belief* in his power. – Those he subjects, who tremble before him and serve him, know in turn that they are worth precisely as much as he *counts* them as being worth: so that it is at this estimation that they work, and not at the satisfaction of their own needs as such. We know vanity only in its feeblest forms, in its sublimations and small doses, because we live in a late and very ameliorated state of society: originally it is *the most useful of all things*, the mightiest means of preservation. And the degree of vanity will, moreover, be the greater the more prudent and intelligent the individual is: because it is easier to augment belief in power than to augment power itself, but is so

only for him who possesses spirit – or, as must be the case in these primeval conditions, for him who is *cunning* and *deceitful*.

182

Signs of cultural weather. – There are so few decisive signs of the cultural
weather we must be glad if we find we have at any rate *one* reliable one in
our hands for use in our house and garden. To test whether someone is
one of us or not – I mean whether he is a free spirit or not – one should test
his feelings towards Christianity. If he stands towards it in any way other
than *critically* then we turn our back on him: he is going to bring us
impure air and bad weather. – It is no longer *our* task to teach such people
what a sirocco is; they have Moses and the weather-prophets and the
prophets of the Enlightenment: if they will not pay heed to these, then –

183

Wrath and punishment has had its time. – Wrath and punishment is a present
to us from the animal world. Man will have come of age only when he
returns this birthday gift to the animals. – Here there lies buried one of
the greatest ideas mankind can have, the idea of progress to excel all progress. – Let us go forward a few thousand years together, my friends!
There is a *great deal* of joy still reserved for mankind of which men of the
present day have not had so much as a scent! And we may promise ourselves this joy, indeed testify that it must necessarily come to us, only
provided that the evolution of human reason *does not stand still!* One day
we shall not be able to *find it in our heart* to commit the *logical* sin that lies
concealed in wrath and punishment, whether an individual's or
society's: one day, when heart and head have learned to dwell as close to
one another as now they still stand far apart. That they *no longer* stand as
far apart as they originally did is fairly apparent if we look at the total
course of mankind; and the individual who has behind him a lifetime of
inner labour will have a proud and joyful awareness of distance overcome and closer proximity achieved, and will thus feel entitled to venture
to harbour even greater expectations.

184

Origin of the 'pessismists'. – A little decent food often makes all the difference to whether we look into the future hopefully or hollow-eyed: this
applies even in the highest and most spiritual regions. When the present
generation is dissatisfied with the world and blackens it, these qualities
have been *inherited* from earlier hungry generations. It is often to be
observed in our artists and poets too that, however luxuriously they
themselves may live, their antecedents are not of the best, that much of
their blood and brain that reemerges as the subject and chosen colours of
their works has been acquired from downtrodden and ill nourished forefathers. The culture of the Greeks is a culture of the wealthy, and of the
wealthy from of old moreover: for a couple of centuries they lived *better*
than we (better in every sense, especially on much simpler food and
drink): as a result their brains at length became at once so full and deli-

cate, the blood flowed so rapidly through them like a joyful and sparkling wine, that the good and best things they could do emerged from them no longer gloomy, enraptured and with violence, but fair and bathed in sunlight.

185

Of rational death. – What is more rational, to stop the machine when the work one demands of it has been completed – or to let it run on until it stops of its own accord, that is to say until it is ruined? Is the latter not a squandering of the cost of maintenance, a misuse of the energy and attentiveness of those who service it? Does it not mean throwing away that which is badly needed elsewhere? Will the fact that many of them are maintained and serviced to no productive end not even propagate a kind of contempt for machines in general? – I am speaking of involuntary (natural) and of voluntary (rational) death. Natural death is death independent of all reason, actual *irrational* death, in which the wretched substance of the husk determines how long the kernel shall or shall not continue to exist: in which therefore the stunted, often sick and thickwitted prison warder is the master who decides the moment at which his noble prisoner shall die. Natural death is the suicide of nature, that is to say the annihilation of the rational being by the irrational to which it is tied. Only in the light of religion can the opposite appear to be the case: because then it is the higher reason (God's) which gives the command which the lower reason has, fairly enough, to submit to. Outside the religious mode of thinking natural death is worthy of no glorification. – The wise regulation and disposal of death belongs to that morality of the future, at present quite ungraspable and immoral sounding, into the dawn of which it must be an indescribable joy to gaze.

186

Retrogressive. – All criminals force society back to a stage of culture earlier than the one at which it happens to be standing: they have a retrogressive effect. Consider the instruments society is obliged to create and maintain for itself for the sake of its own defence: the sly police agents, the prison warders, the executioners; do not overlook the public prosecutors and defence lawyers; and ask yourself, finally, whether the judges themselves, and punishment, and the whole process of the courts, are not phenomena much more likely to produce a depressive than an elevating effect on the non-criminal: for no one will ever succeed in covering self-defence and revenge with the cloak of innocence; and whenever man is employed and sacrificed as a means to an end of society's all higher humanity mourns.

187

War as remedy. – To nations growing wretched and feeble war may be recommended as a remedy, assuming they want to continue on living at all: for national consumption is also susceptible to a brutal cure. The desire to live for ever and inability to die is, however, itself already a sign of senility of the faculties: the more fully and ably one lives, the readier one is to relinquish one's life for a single good sensation. A nation that lives and feels in this way has no need of wars.

188

Spiritual and physical transplantation as remedy. – The various *cultures* are various spiritual climates each of which is especially harmful or healthful to this or that organism. *History* as a whole, as knowledge of the various cultures, is *pharmacology* but not the science of medicine itself. The *physician* is still needed who will avail himself of this pharmacology to send each person to the climate favourable precisely to him – for a period of time or for ever. To live in the present, within a single culture, does not suffice as a universal prescription: too many people of the highest utility who cannot breathe properly in it would die out. With the aid of history one can give them *air* and try to preserve them; men of retarded cultures also have their value. – This spiritual regimen is paralleled by a physical one through which, by a medicinal geography, mankind has to discover to what sicknesses and degenerations each region of the earth gives rise, and conversely what curative factors it offers: and then nations, families and individuals must gradually be transplanted for as long and continuously as is needed for our inherited physical infirmities to be conquered. In the end, the whole earth will be a collection of health resorts.

189

Reason and the tree of humanity. – That which in senile short-sightedness you call the overpopulation of the earth is precisely what proffers the more hopeful their greatest task: mankind shall one day become a tree that overshadows the whole earth bearing many milliards of blossoms that shall all become fruit one beside the other, and the earth itself shall be prepared for the nourishment of this tree. That the *still small* beginnings of this shall increase in strength and sap, that the sap shall flow around for the nourishment of the whole and the individual parts through numberless canals – it is from this and similar tasks that the *standard* is to be derived as to whether a man of the present is useful or useless. The task is unspeakably great and bold: let us all see to it that the tree does not *untimely* rot away! Human life and action is no doubt capable of presenting itself to the historical mind in the way in which the life of the ant, with its cunningly raised up hills, stands exposed to all our eyes. Judged superficially, all human existence would, like the existence of the ant, suggest the presence of 'instinct'. A more rigorous examination lets us perceive how whole nations, whole centuries toil to discover and *thoroughly to test* new methods for promoting a great human collective and finally the great collective fruit-tree of humanity; and whatever individuals, nations and ages may suffer in the course of this testing, individuals have always become *wise and prudent* through this suffering, and wisdom and prudence slowly flows out from them to influence the measures adopted by whole nations and whole ages. Even the ants make mistakes; mankind may well be ruined and untimely wither through folly

in its choice of methods; neither for the one nor the other is there an infal-
lible instinct. What we must do, rather, is to *look in the face* our great task
of *preparing* the earth for the production of the greatest and most joyful
fruitfulness – a task for reason on behalf of reason!

190

Commendation of unselfishness and its origin. – For many years two neighbouring petty chieftains had been at strife with one another: they devas-
tated one another's crops, abducted sheep, burned down houses; but
neither obtained a decisive victory over the other, because their power
was roughly equal. A third, who because of the secluded situation of his
domain was able to stand aside from this feud but had reason to fear the
day one of his quarrelsome neighbours should come out decisively on
top, finally stepped between the contestants and solemnly offered his
good offices: and in private he attached to his peace proposal a weighty
condition: he gave each of them to understand that henceforth if one of
them offended against the peace he would make common cause with the
other. They came together before him, hesitantly laid in his hands the
hands that had hitherto been the instruments and all too often the cause
of hatred – and seriously undertook to attempt to keep the peace. They
both saw with astonishment how their prosperity and wellbeing suddenly increased, how each had in his neighbour a willing trading-partner
instead of a crafty or openly mocking illdoer, how each could even assist
and rescue the other in times of need instead of exploiting and augmenting this need of his neighbour as heretofore; it seemed, indeed, as though
in both their domains the race of man had grown fairer since that day: for
their eyes had become brighter, their brows had lost their brooding look,
all had acquired confidence in the future – and nothing is so beneficial to
the soul and body of man than is this confidence. They met together
every year on the day of their treaty, the chieftains together with their followers: and did so in the presence of the mediator whose mode of dealing
they increasingly admired and revered the greater the benefits they owed
to it grew. They called this mode of dealing *unselfish* – their eyes were
fixed far too firmly on the benefits they themselves had harvested from it
to see of their neighbour more than that his condition had changed far
less as a consequence of it than theirs had: it had, rather, remained the
same, and thus it seemed that the latter had had no eye on acquiring
benefits for himself. For the first time one told oneself that unselfishness
was a virtue: such a thing might, of course, have been practised often and
on a small scale in private, but this virtue became truly noticeable only
when for the first time it was painted on the wall in large letters legible to
the whole community. The moral qualities are recognized as virtues, accorded value and an honoured name, and recommended for acquisition
only from the moment when they have *visibly* determined the fate and
fortune of whole societies: for then height of feeling and excitation of the
inner creative energies has become so great in *many* that each brings the
best he has and bestows it upon this quality: the serious man lays his

seriousness at its feet, the dignified man his dignity, the women their gentleness, the young all the hopefulness and future-directedness of their nature; the poet lends it words and names, inserts it in the round-dance of other beings like it, accords it a pedigree and, as is the way with artists, at last worships the creature of his fantasy as a new divinity – he *teaches* worship of it. Thus, because the love and gratitude of everyone has worked on it as on a statue, a virtue at last becomes an *assemblage* of all that is good and worthy of reverence, a kind of temple and at the same time divine personage. Henceforth it stands as an individual virtue, as a distinct entity, which it was not before, and exercises the rights and the power of something sanctified and suprahuman. – In the Greece of later antiquity the cities were full of such abstracts made into human deities (this bizarre expression must be excused for the sake of the bizarre concept it describes); the people had in its own way erected for itself a Platonic 'ideational heaven' in the midst of the earth, and I do not believe that its inhabitants were felt to be less alive than any of the old Homeric divinities.

191
Times of darkness. – 'Times of darkness' is the expression in Norway for those times when the sun remains below the horizon the whole day long: at these times the temperature falls slowly but continuously. – This is a nice simile for all thinkers for whom the sun of humanity's future has for a time disappeared.

192
The philosopher of sensual pleasure. – A little garden, figs, little cheeses and in addition three or four good friends – these were the sensual pleasures of Epicurus.

193
The epochs of life. – The true epochs in life are those brief periods of stand-still between the ascent and decline of a ruling idea or feeling. Here one has attained a state of *satisfaction*: all else is hunger and thirst – or satiety.

194
The dream. – Our dreams are, on the rare occasions when they are for once successful and perfect – usually the dream is a bungled product – chains of symbolic scenes and images in place of the language of poetic narration; they paraphrase our experiences or expectations or circumstances with such poetic boldness and definiteness that in the morning we are always astonished at ourselves when we recall our dreams. In dreaming we use up too much of our artistic capacity – and therefore often have too little of it during the day.

195
Nature and science. – Just as in nature, so in science it is the poorer, less fruitful regions that are first properly cultivated – because it is precisely for this that the means available to *budding* science are approximately

adequate. The cultivation of the most fruitful regions presupposes a care-fully developed and tremendous quality of methods, individual con-clusions already gained, and an organized host of well schooled workers – and all these come together only late in the day. – Impatience and am-bition often make too soon for these most fruitful regions; but the results are then almost nil. In nature the revenge for such losses would be that the colonists starved to death.

196

The simple life. – Nowadays a simple mode of life is difficult: it requires much more reflection and inventive talent than is possessed even by very clever people. The most honest of them will perhaps say moreover: 'I haven't sufficient time to reflect on it. The simple mode of life is too noble a goal for me, I shall wait until wiser men than I have discovered it.'

197

Great peaks and little peaks. – The meagre fruitfulness of the highest and most cultivated spirits and the classes that pertain to them, the circum-stance that they are frequently unmarried and are sexually cool in gen-eral, is essential to the economy of mankind: reason recognizes and makes use of the fact that at the outermost point of spiritual evolution the danger of a *nervously unsound* posterity is very great: such people are the *great peaks* of mankind – they must not taper off into little peaks.

198

Nature never makes a leap. – However vigorously a man may develop and seem to leap over from one thing into its opposite, closer observation will nonetheless discover the *dovetailing* where the new building grows out of the old. This is the task of the biographer: he always has to bear in mind the fundamental principle that nature never makes a leap.

199

Clean, certainly. – He who dresses himself in clean-washed rags is wearing clean clothes, certainly, but looks like a ragamuffin nonetheless.

200

The solitary speaks. – As a recompense for much ennui, ill-humour and boredom, such as a solitude without friends, books, duties or passions must entail, one harvests those quarters of an hour of the deepest immer-sion in oneself and in nature. He who completely entrenches himself against boredom also entrenches himself against himself: he will never get to drink the most potent refreshing draught from the deepest well of his own being.

201

False celebrity. – I hate those supposed beauties of nature which derive their significance fundamentally only from knowledge, especially a knowledge of geography, but in themselves leave the mind thirsting for beauty unsatisfied: for example the view of Mont Blanc from Geneva – a thing without meaning unless knowledge hurry to assist the brain; the mountains closer to us are all more beautiful and impressive – but 'not nearly so high', as that absurd knowledge adds with the aim of diminishing them. The eye here contradicts knowledge: how can it truly rejoice if its rejoicing is grounded in contradiction!

202

Pleasure tourists. – They climb the hill like animals, stupid and perspiring; no one has told them there are beautiful views on the way.

203

Too much and too little. – Everyone nowadays lives through too much and thinks through too little: they are ravenously hungry but at the same time suffer from colic, so that they get thinner and thinner however much they eat. – He who says nowadays 'I have experienced nothing' – is an idiot.

204

End and goal. – Not every end is a goal. The end of a melody is not its goal; but nonetheless, if the melody had not reached its end it would not have reached its goal either. A parable.

205

Neutrality of grand nature. – The neutrality of grand nature (in mountain, sea, forest and desert) pleases us, but only briefly; afterwards we grow impatient. 'Won't these things say anything at all *to us*, then? Don't *we* exist for them?' There arises the feeling of *crimen laesae majestatis humanae.**

206

Forgetting our objectives. – During the journey we commonly forget its goal. Almost every profession is chosen and commenced as a means to an end but continued as an end in itself. Forgetting our objectives is the most frequent of all acts of stupidity.

207

Elliptic of an idea. – When an idea has just risen above the horizon the temperature of the soul is usually very cold. The idea engenders its heat only gradually, and it is at its hottest (that is to say, it is exercising its greatest influence) when belief in the idea is already on the decline.

208

How to have everyone against you. – If anyone nowadays ventured to say: 'he who is not for me is against me', he would at once have everyone against him. – This way of feeling does credit to our age.

209

Being ashamed of wealth. – Our age tolerates only one species of wealthy man, him who is *ashamed* of his wealth. If we hear of anyone 'he is very rich', we at once experience a sensation similar to that which we experience at the sight of a repulsive swelling sickness, of obesity or dropsy: we have forcibly to remind ourselves of our humanity if we are to be able to

* *crimen . . . humanae*: crime of *lèse majesté* against the human race.

associate with such a wealthy man without his noticing the disgust we feel. Should he go so far as to plume himself on his riches, however, our feeling is mingled with an almost pitying amazement at so high a degree of human unreason: so that we feel like raising our hands to heaven and crying: 'poor disfigured, overburdened, hundredfold fettered man, to whom every hour brings *or can bring* something unpleasant, whose limbs are set trembling by *every* event in twenty nations, how can you make us believe you are happy in your state of life! Wherever you appear in public, we know it is a kind of running the gauntlet under eyes that have in them nothing but cold hatred or importunity or silent derision. It may be easier for you to acquire things than it is for others: but your acquisitions are superfluous and give you little pleasure; and *to store up* what you have acquired is *now* in any event a more wearisome thing than any wearisome acquiring could be. You suffer *continually*, for you lose continually. What good is it if you have a constant supply of new artificial blood: the cupping-glasses that sit, constantly sit, on your neck are no less painful! – But, to be fair to you, it is hard, perhaps impossible, for you *not* to be rich: you *have* to store up, *have* to go on acquiring, the tendency of your nature you have inherited is the *yoke* imposed upon you – so therefore do not deceive us, be honestly and visibly *ashamed* of the yoke you bear: since at the bottom of your soul you are in fact weary of it and bear it unwillingly. This shame will not dishonour you.'

210

Intemperance in presumptuousness. – There are men who are so presumptuous that when they publicly commend something great they know no other way of doing so than by representing it as a preliminary stage of and bridge to *themselves*.

211

In the ground of ignominy. – He who wants to rid men of an idea usually does not halt at refuting it and drawing out the worm of illogicality that resides within it: he then, after the worm is dead, goes on to hurl the entire fruit too into the *mud*, so that men will find it indecent and experience disgust at it. He believes that in this way he has found the means of preventing that 'resurrection on the third day' so common among refuted ideas. – He is in error, for it is precisely in the *ground of ignominy*, among the filth, that the kernel of an idea geminates new seeds most speedily. – Therefore: do not deride and befoul that which you want to do away with for good but respectfully *lay it on ice*; and, in as much as ideas are very tenacious of life, do so again and again. Here it is necessary to act in accordance with the maxim: 'One refutation is no refutation.'

212

Free of morality. – Now that minds are becoming freer and less narrow, it is certain that morality (inherited, handed down, instinctual acting *in accordance with moral feelings*) is on the decline: but the individual virtues, moderation, justice, repose of soul, are not – for when the conscious mind has attained its highest degree of freedom it is involuntarily led to them and comes to recognize how *useful* thay are.

213

The fanatic of mistrust and his warranty. – *The old man*: You want to venture on the tremendous task of educating men? Where is your warranty? – *Pyrrho*:* Here it is: I shall warn men against myself, I shall confess publicly all the faults of my nature and expose to every eye my precipitancies, con- tradictions and acts of stupidity. Do not listen to me, I shall say to them, until I have become like unto the least of you, and less even than him; resist and strive against truth as long as ever you can, out of disgust at him who is its advocate. I shall mislead and deceive you so long as you perceive in me the slightest trace of dignity and respectability. – *The old man*: You promise too much, you cannot bear this burden. – *Pyrrho*: Then I shall tell men this too, and say I am too weak and cannot perform what I promise. The greater my unworthiness, the more they will mistrust truth when it proceeds from my mouth. – *The old man*: Do you want to be the teacher of mistrust of truth, then? – *Pyrrho*: Of mistrust such as there has never yet been on earth before, of mistrust of all and everything. It is the only path to truth. The right eye may not trust the left, and light will for a time have to be called darkness: this is the path you must tread. Do not believe it will lead you to fruit-trees and fair meadows. You shall find hard little grains of corn upon it – these are truths: for many decades you will have to consume lies by the handful so as not to die of hunger, even though you know them to be lies. Those grains of corn, however, will be sown and buried, and perhaps, perhaps, there will at some future time be a harvest-day: no one dare *promise* it, unless he be a fanatic. – *The old man*: Friend! Friend! Your words too are those of the fanatic! – *Pyrrho*: You are right! I shall be mistrustful of all words. – *The old man*: Then you will have to stay silent. – *Pyrrho*: I shall tell men that I have to stay silent, and that they should mistrust my silence. – *The old man*: So you are retreating from your undertaking? – *Pyrrho*: On the contrary – you have just shown me the gate through which I must pass. – *The old man*: I do not know – : do we still understand one another completely? – *Pyrrho*: Probably not. – *The old man*: Do you still understand yourself completely? – *Pyrrho* turns around and laughs. – *The old man*: Alas, friend! Laughing and staying silent – is that now your whole philosophy? – *Pyrrho*: It wouldn't be the worst one. –

214

European books. – When reading Montaigne, Larochefoucauld, La Bruy- ère, Fontenelle (especially the *Dialogues des Morts*), Vauvenargues and Chamfort we are closer to antiquity than in the case of any other group of six authors of any other nation.† Through these six the *spirit of the final*

---

* Pyrrho of Elis (c. 365 to c. 270 BC), founder of the school of philosophical Skepticism. The conversation with the old man is modelled on the dialogue *Python* written by Pyrrho's pupil Timon of Phleius (c. 320 to c. 230 BC).

† La Bruyère (1645-96), Fontenelle (1657–1757), Vauvenargues (1715–47), Chamfort (1741– 94): French moralists.

centuries of the *old* era has risen again – together they constitute an important link in the great, still continuing chain of the Renaissance. Their books are above the changes of national taste and philosophical colouring which as a rule every book nowadays radiates and has to radiate if it is to become famous: they contain more *real ideas* than all the books of German philosophers put together: ideas of the kind that produce ideas and which – I am at a loss to finish the definition; it is enough that they seem to me authors who have written neither for children nor for dreamers, neither for young ladies nor for Christians, neither for Germans nor for – I am again at a loss to complete my list. – But to state a clear commendation: if they had been written in Greek the Greeks would have understood them. How much, on the other hand, would even Plato have been *able* to understand at all of the writings of our finest German thinkers, those of Goethe and Schopenhauer, for example, to say nothing of the repugnance their style would have evoked in him, namely its obscurity, exaggeration and occasional thinness and dryness – faults from which the above named suffer least among German thinkers and yet suffer all too much (as a thinker Goethe liked to embrace the clouds more than he should have and it is not with impunity that Schopenhauer almost always wanders among images of things instead of among the things themselves). – On the other hand, what clarity and delicate precision those Frenchmen possess! Even the most acute-eared of the Greeks must have approved of this art, and one thing they would even have admired and adored, the French *wittiness* of expression: they *loved* such things very much without themselves being especially gifted in them.

215
Fashion and modernity. – Wherever ignorance, uncleanliness and superstition are still the order of the day, wherever communications are poor, the landscape is meagre and the priesthood powerful, there we still also discover *national costumes*. Where signs of the opposite of these are to be discovered, on the other hand, *fashion* reigns. Fashion is thus to be discovered next to the *virtues* of present-day Europe: could it actually be their shadow-side? – In the first place, *male* dress that is fashionable and no longer national says of him who wears it that the European wishes to cut a figure neither as an *individual* nor as *a member of a class or nation*, that he has made a deliberate quenching of this species of vanity into a law for himself: then that he is industrious and has little time for dressing and self-adornment, likewise that he finds that everything costly and luxurious in material and design accords ill with the work he has to do; finally, that through his costume he indicates the more learned and intellectual callings as those to which as a European he stands closest or would like to stand closest: whereas it is the brigand, the herdsman or the soldier who shine through the still existent national costumes as being the leading and most desirable situations in life. Within this overall character of male fashion there then exist those little variations produced by the vanity of the young men, the dandies and idlers of the big cities, by those, that is to

say, *who have not yet come to maturity as a European.* – European women have done so *much less*, which is why with them the variations are much greater: they too have no desire for national dress and hate to be recognized as German, French, Russian by their clothing, but they very much like to make an impression as individuals; likewise their clothing is supposed to leave no one in any doubt that they belong to one of the more reputable classes (that they are 'respectable' or in the 'world of society'), and their desire to create this effect is indeed the stronger the more tenuous, or even illusory, their membership of the said classes. Above all, however, the young woman refuses to wear anything the older woman wears, because she believes her value will fall if she is thought to be older than she is: the older woman, conversely, would like to deceive as long as she can through more youthful looking costume – as a result of which contest temporary fashions continually appear in which youthfulness is inescapably and inimitably visible. When the inventive spirit of these youthful artists has revelled for a time in such exposures of youthfulness, or, to tell the whole truth, when the inventive spirit of ancient courtly cultures, of the still extant nations and of the whole world of costume in general has been consulted and the Spanish, the Turkish and the ancient Greek for instance have been coupled together for the presentation of these fair forms, the discovery is invariably made that one has had an ill perception of where one's advantage truly lies; that an effect is more readily produced upon men by playing hide-and-seek with the beautiful body than by naked or semi-naked honesty; and then the wheel of taste and vanity again turns in the opposite direction: the somewhat older young women find they have entered into their kingdom, and the contest between these most charming and absurdest of creatures goes raging on again. *The more* women grow inwardly, however, and cease among themselves to give precedence to the immature as they have done hitherto, the smaller these variations in their costume and the simpler their adornment will become: as to which a correct judgement would take its standards, not from the models of antiquity, *not*, that is to say, from the garments worn by southerly sea-dwellers, but paying regard to the climatic conditions obtaining in northern and central Europe, the regions in which the inventive genius of Europe now has its preferred homeland. – On the whole, therefore, it is *not change* that will characterize *fashion* and the *modern*, for change is a sign of backwardness and that the men and women of Europe are still *immature*: what will characterize it is *repudiation of national, class and individual vanity.* One must, consequently, approve – because it economizes on time and energy—if individual cities and regions of Europe undertake to reflect and devise on behalf of all the rest in the matter of clothing, inasmuch as a sense of form has not been bestowed on everyone; likewise, so long as these variations continue to exist it is really no excessive ambition if Paris, for example, lays claim to being the sole inventor and innovator in this realm. If, out of hatred for this claim by a French city, a German elects to dress differently, as Albrecht Dürer dressed for example, let him consider that the costume he is wearing, though Germans formerly wore it, they invented it just as little as they invented the fashions of Paris – there has *never* been a costume which denoted a German as a German; he should also consider what he *looks like* in this costume and whether the really modern mind, with all the lines and folds the nineteenth century has inscribed in it, might not take exception to someone's wearing clothes like Dürer's. – Here, where the concepts 'modern' and 'European' are almost equivalent, what is understood by Europe comprises much more territory than geographical Europe, the little peninsula of Asia: America, especially, belongs to it, insofar as it is the daughter-land of our culture. On the other hand, the cultural concept 'Europe' does not include all of geographical Europe; it includes only those nations and ethnic minorities who possess a common past in Greece, Rome, Judaism, and Christianity.

216

'German virtue'. – It cannot be denied that from the beginning of the last century on a stream of moral awakening has flowed through Europe. It was only then that virtue again became eloquent; it taught men to discover unforced gestures of exaltation and emotion, it ceased to be ashamed of itself and devised philosophies and poems for its own glorification. If we seek the source of this stream we find first of all Rousseau, but the mythical Rousseau constructed out of the impression produced by his writings – one might almost say, out of his mythically expounded writings – and out of the indications he himself provided (– he and his public worked continually on this ideal figure). Its other origin lies in that resurrection of the Stoicism of the greatest days of Rome through which the French have continued on in the worthiest way the task of the Renaissance. From a gloriously successful imitation of the forms of antiquity they went on to an imitation of its characters: so that they will always have a right to the highest honours as the nation which has up to now given modern mankind its finest books and its finest men. How these two models – the mythical Rousseau and the reawakened spirit of Rome – affected their weaker neighbours can be observed especially in the case of Germany: which, as the result of a novel and wholly unprecedented impetus to seriousness and greatness in willing and self-command, was at last consumed with amazement at its own new virtue and cast into the world the concept 'German virtue' as though nothing more primeval than this had ever been inherited. The first great men who transfused to themselves that French stimulus to greatness and consciousness of moral will were more honest and did not forget where gratitude lay. The moralism of Kant – whence does it come? He gives the answer again and again: from Rousseau and the reawakened Stoicism of Rome. The moralism of Schiller: the same source, the same glorification of the source. The moralism in tones of Beethoven: it is the everlasting hymn of praise of Rousseau, of the French revivers of antiquity, and of Schiller. It was 'German youth' that first forgot gratitude, for in the meantime men had given ear to the preachers of francophobia: that German

youth which for a time stepped into the foreground with more self-confidence than is considered permissible in other youths. When this youth sought after its forefathers it was no doubt right to think of the proximity to Schiller, Fichte* and Schleiermacher: but it ought to have looked for its grandfathers in Paris and Geneva, and it was very short-sighted of it to believe what it in fact believed: that virtue was no more than thirty years old. In those days they accustomed themselves to demanding that the word 'German' should quite casually inspire a mis-understanding of the nature of virtue: and we have not quite disaccustomed ourselves to it even to the present day. – Incidentally, this said moral awakening resulted, it almost goes without saying, only in disadvantages and retrogression for *knowledge* of moral phenomena. What is the whole of German moral philosophy from Kant onwards, with all its French, English and Italian branches and parallels? A semi-theological assault on Helvetius and a rejection of the open views or signposts to the right path which, gained by long and wearisome struggle, he at last assembled and gave adequate expression to. Helvetius is in Germany to the present day the most reviled of all good moralists and good men.

217
Classic and romantic. – Both those spirits of a classical and those of a romantic bent – these two species exist at all times – entertain a vision of the future: but the former do so out of a *strength* of their age, the latter out of its *weakness*.

218
The machine as teacher. – The machine of itself teaches the mutual co-operation of hordes of men in operations where each man has to do only one thing: it provides the model for the party apparatus and the conduct of warfare. On the other hand, it does not teach individual autocracy: it makes of many *one* machine and of every individual an instrument to *one* end. Its most generalized effect is to teach the utility of centralization.

219
Not settled. – We like to live in a small town; but from time to time it is precisely the small town that drives us out into the deepest solitudes of veiled and mysterious nature: it does so when it has again become too transparent to us. Finally, to *recover* from this nature in turn we go to the big city. One or two draughts of the latter – and we taste the dregs of its cup – and the circle that starts with the small town begins over again. – This is the life of modern men: they are in everything somewhat too *thorough* to be *settled*, like the men of other ages.

220
Reaction against machine-culture. – The machine, itself a product of the highest intellectual energies, sets in motion in those who serve it almost nothing but the lower, non-intellectual energies. It thereby releases a vast quantity of energy in general that would otherwise lie dormant, it is true;

* Johann Gottlieb Fichte (1762–1814): German philosopher.

but it provides no instigation to enhancement, to improvement, to becoming an artist. It makes men *active* and *uniform* – but in the long run this engenders a counter-effect, a despairing boredom of soul, which teaches them to long for idleness in all its varieties.

221

The perilousness of the Enlightenment. – All the semi-insanity, histrionicism, bestial cruelty, voluptuousness, and especially sentimentality and self-intoxication, which taken together constitutes the actual *substance of the Revolution* and had, before the Revolution, become flesh and spirit in Rousseau – this creature then went on with perfidious enthusiasm to set *the Enlightenment* too on its fanatical head, which thereby itself began to glow as though in a transfigured light: the Enlightenment, which is fundamentally so alien to the Revolution and, left to itself, would have passed quietly along like a gleam in the clouds and for long been content to address itself only to the individual: so that it would have transformed the customs and institutions of nations only very slowly. Now, however, tied to a violent and impulsive companion, the Enlightenment itself became violent and impulsive. Its perilousness has thereby become almost greater than the liberating illumination it brought to the great revolutionary movement. He who grasps this will also know out of what compound it has to be extracted, of what impurity it has to be cleansed: so as then to *continue* the work of the Enlightenment *in himself,* and to strangle the Revolution at birth, to make it not happen.

222

Passion in the Middle Ages. – The Middle Ages are the era of the greatest passions. Neither antiquity nor our own age possesses this breadth of soul: its *spaciousness* has never been greater and never have men measured on a larger scale. The jungle physique of the barbarian and the over-soulful, over-wakeful, hectically glittering eyes of the disciple of the Christian mysteries, extreme childishness and youthfulness and likewise extreme over-ripeness and weariness of age, the savagery of the beast of prey and the effeminacy and tenuousness of the spirit of late antiquity – at that time all these not infrequently came together in a single person: when he got into a passion, the heart's current had to spread more violently, its eddies whirl more rapidly, its falls be more precipitate than ever before. – We modern men should be happy to have sustained some loss in this domain.

223

Plunder and economy. – All spiritual movements as a consequence of which the great hope to be able to *plunder* and the small to *economize* go forward. That, for example, is why the German Reformation went forward.

224

Rejoicing souls. – Whenever drink, drunkenness and ill-smelling lewdness beckoned, even from afar, the souls of the ancient Germans rejoiced – at other times they were morose; but of these they had, in their own way, a profound appreciation.

225

Debauchery in Athens. – Even when the fishmarket of Athens had acquired its thinkers and poets, Greek debauchery still wore a more refined and idyllic appearance than Roman or German ever did. The voice of Juvenal would there have sounded like a hollow trumpet: a polite and almost childlike laughter would have been the response to it.

226

Greek prudence. – Since the desire for victory and eminence is an inextinguishable trait of nature, older and more primitive than any respect for and joy in equality, the Greek state sanctioned gymnastic and artistic contest between equals, that is to say marked off an arena where that drive could be discharged without imperilling the political order. With the eventual decline of the gymnastic and artistic contest the Greek state disintegrated into inner turmoil.

227

'Eternal Epicurus'. – Epicurus has been alive at all times and is living now, unknown to those who have called and call themselves Epicureans, and enjoying no reputation among philosophers. He has, moreover, himself forgotten his own name: it was the heaviest pack he ever threw off.

228

Style of superiority. – Student-German, the dialect of the German student, has its origin among those students who do not study and who know how to attain a kind of ascendency over their more serious colleagues by exposing everything that is masquerade in education, decency, erudition, orderliness, moderation, and, though employing the terms belonging to these domains just as continually as their better and more learned colleagues, do so with malice in their eyes and an accompanying grimace. It is in this language of superiority – the only one original to Germany – that our statesmen and newspaper critics too now involuntarily speak; it is a continual resort to ironical imitation, a restless, discontented furtive squinting to left and right, a German of quotation-marks and grimaces.

229

The buried. – We withdraw into concealment: but not out of any kind of personal ill-humour, as though the political and social situation of the present day were not good enough for us, but because through our withdrawal we want to economize and assemble forces of which culture will *later* have great need, and more so if this present remains *this* present and as such fulfils *its* task. We are accumulating capital and seeking to make it secure: but, as in times of great peril, to do that we have to *bury* it.

230

Tyrants of the spirit. – In our age anyone who was so completely the expression of a single moral trait as are the characters of Theophrastus* or Molière would be regarded as sick and one would in his case speak of an *'idée fixe'*. The Athens of the third century would, if we could pay it a visit, seem to us populated by fools. Nowadays the democracy of *concepts* rules in every head – *many together* are master: a single concept that *wanted* to be master would now, as aforesaid, be called an *'idée fixe'*. This is *our* way of disposing of tyrants – we direct them to the madhouse.

231
Most dangerous form of emigration. – In Russia there is an emigration of intelligence: one crosses the frontier to read and write good books. In this way, however, one helps to turn the spirit of the deserted fatherland into the extended jaws of Asia that would like to devour little Europe.

232
The state-worshippers. – The almost religious love the Greeks felt for their kings passed over to the polis when kings came to an end. And because a concept can endure more love than a person, and as in particular it gives offence to its lover less often than people who are loved do (– for the more they know they are loved the more inconsiderate they usually become, until in the end they are no longer worthy of love and a rupture occurs), reverence for the polis and state was greater than reverence for princes had ever been. The Greeks are the *state-worshippers* of ancient history – in modern history that role is played by other nations.

233
Against neglecting the eyes. – Could a diminution of eyesight every ten years not perhaps be demonstrated in the educated classes of England who read the *Times*?

234
Great works and great faith. – This man had the great works but his companion had the great faith in these works. They were inseparable: but it was obvious that the former depended wholly on the latter.

235
The socialiser. – 'I am not fond of myself', someone said in explanation of his love of society. 'Society's stomach is stronger than mine, it can digest me.'

236
Closing the eyes of one's mind. – Even if one is accustomed to and practised in reflecting on one's actions, when one is actually acting (though the action be no more than writing a letter or eating and drinking) one must nonetheless close one's inward eye. In conversation with average men, indeed, one must understand how to *think* with the eyes of one's thinking closed – so as to attain and thus comprehend the average man's

* Theophrastus: Greek Peripatetic philosopher (372–288 BC). He began as Plato's pupil, and succeeded Aristotle as President of the School; his *Characters* attempts a typology of human characteristics.

thinking. This closing of the eyes is a perceptible act achievable by an act of will.

237

The most fearful revenge. – If one wants to *revenge* oneself on an opponent as completely as possible one should wait until one has a complete set of truths and justifications in one's hand and can play them out against him with composure: so that exacting revenge and exacting justice coincide. It is the most fearful kind of revenge: for there is no instance above it to which an appeal can be made. That was how Voltaire revenged himself on Piron, with five lines that condemn his entire life and work: as many truths as there are words; that is how he revenged himself on Friedrich the Great (in a letter to him from Ferney).

238

Luxury tax. – People buy their necessities in shops and have to pay dearly for them because they have to assist in paying for what is also on sale there but only rarely finds purchasers: the luxury and amusement goods. So it is that luxury continually imposes a tax on the simple people who have to do without it.

239

Why beggars go on living. – If alms were bestowed only out of pity all the beggars would have starved to death.

240

Why beggars go on living. – The greatest bestower of alms is cowardice.

241

How the thinker uses a conversation. – Without being a listener it is still possible to hear a great deal provided one knows how to see well yet also how to lose sight of oneself for the time being. But people do not know how to make use of a conversation; they pay much too much attention to what they themselves intend to say in response, whereas the true *listener* often contents himself with a brief answer, plus a little for politeness' sake, by way of *speech*, while on the other hand bearing away in his retentive memory all the other has said, together with the tone and gestures *with which* he said it. – In the normal conversation each thinks he is leading the way, as if two ships sailing side by side and now and then gently bumping into one another each faithfully believed the neighbouring ship was following or even being pulled along by it.

242

The art of apologizing. – If anyone apologizes to us he has to do so very well: otherwise we can easily feel that we ourselves are the guilty party and are affected unpleasantly.

243

Impossible company. – The ship of your thoughts moves too deep for you to be able to sail in it on the waters of these decent, friendly, amicable people. There are too many shallows and sandbanks there: you would have to turn and twist and would be in constant embarrassment, and soon they too would be in embarrassment – over your embarrassment, whose cause they cannot divine.

244

Fox of foxes. – A true fox calls sour not only those grapes he is unable to reach but also those he has reached and deprived others of.

245

With our closest acquaintances. – However closely people may belong to one another their common horizon nonetheless still includes all four points of the compass, and there are times when they notice this.

246

The silence of disgust. – Someone undergoes, as thinker and man, a profound transformation and bears public witness to it. And his hearers notice nothing! believe him to be just as he was! – This common experience has already disgusted many writers: they had had too great a respect for the intellectuality of men, and when they perceived their error vowed themselves to silence.

247

Occupied seriously. – The occupations of many rich and noble men are their way of *recuperating* from habitual and too protracted *leisure*: that is why they take them as seriously and intensely as other people take their rare leisure hours and hobbies.

248

Ambiguity of the eyes. – Just as a sudden, scaly trembling passes over the water at your feet, so there are in the human eyes too similar sudden uncertainties and ambiguities which make one ask: is it a shudder of dread? is it a smile? is it both?

249

Positive and negative. – This thinker needs no one to refute him: he does that for himself.

250

Revenge for empty nets. – One should beware of anyone who is filled with the embitterment of the fisherman who after a hard day's work returns home in the evening with empty nets.

251

Not to assert one's rights. – To exercise power costs effort and demands courage. That is why so many fail to assert rights to which they are perfectly entitled – because a right is a kind of *power* but they are too lazy or too cowardly to exercise it. The virtues which cloak these faults are called *patience* and *forbearance*.

252

Light-bearers. – There would be no sunshine in society if the born flatterers and wheedlers, I mean the so-called amiable, did not bring it in with them.

253
At one's most charitable. – When a man has just been greatly honoured and has eaten a little he is at his most charitable.

254
Towards the light. – Men press towards the light, not so as to see better, but so as to shine better. – Him before whom we shine we are glad to regard as light.

255
Hypochondriacs. – The hypochondriac is a man with just enough spirit and pleasure in spirit to take his sufferings, his disadvantages, his faults in earnest: but the region in which he feeds himself is too small; he crops it so fine that in the end he has to look for individual blades of grass. In this way he finally becomes a curmudgeon and miser – and only then is he unendurable.

256
Restitution. – Hesiod advises us that, when a neighbour has helped us out, we should restore to him what he has given us in generous measure, and where possible more abundantly, as soon as we can. For in this way our neighbour is gratified, since his former generosity has proved profitable to him, but we too are also gratified, inasmuch as by giving back a little more than we received we have repurchased the little humiliation we incurred through having to be helped out.

257
More subtle than necessary. – Our capacity for observing whether others perceive our weakness is much more subtle than our capacity for observing the weaknesses of others: from which it therefore follows that it is more subtle than it needs to be.

258
A light kind of shadow. – Close beside dark and gloomy men there is to be found, almost as a rule and as though tied to them, a soul of light. It is as it were the negative shadow they cast.

259
Can we refrain from revenge? – There are so many refined forms of revenge that one who had occasion to revenge himself could at bottom do or refrain from doing whatever he liked: all the world would in time nonetheless come to believe that he *had* revenged himself. Not to revenge himself is thus an option scarcely open to a man: he may not even say that he does not *want* to do so, since contemptuously to refrain from revenge is considered and *felt* to be a sublime, very grievous form of revenge. – From which it follows that one ought not to do anything *superfluous* – –

260

Error in honouring. – Everyone believes he is saying something to the honour of a thinker and pleasant for him to hear if he indicates how he himself has hit upon precisely the same ideas as the thinker's and even upon the same form of expression; and yet the thinker is seldom delighted at such communications: often they make him distrust his ideas and their form of expression, and he secretly resolves to revise both. – If one wishes to honour somebody, one must guard against expressions of agreement: they set both parties on the same level. – In many instances it is a matter of social propriety to listen to an opinion as though it were not our own, as though indeed it belonged outside our horizon: as, for example, when an elderly man of long experience for once opens to us the shrine of his accumulated knowledge.

261

Letter. – A letter is an unannounced visit, the postman the agent of rude surprises. One ought to reserve an hour a week for receiving letters and afterwards take a bath.

262

Prejudiced. – Someone said: I have been *prejudiced* against myself ever since I was a child: that is why I find some truth in all blame and some stupidity in all praise. I usually esteem praise too little and blame too highly.

263

Path to equality. – A few hours' mountain climbing make of a rogue and a saint two fairly equal creatures. Tiredness is the shortest path to *equality* and *fraternity* – and sleep finally adds to them *liberty*.

264

Slander. – If one encounters a truly infamous accusation, one should never seek its origin among one's simple and straightforward *enemies*; for if they were to invent anything of the sort about us they would, as our enemies, inspire no belief. But those to whom we have for a time been of most use but who have for any reason secretly decided there is nothing more they need demand of us – people such as these are in a position to put the infamy into circulation: they inspire belief firstly because it is assumed they would invent nothing that could injure them themselves, then because they have come to know us more intimately. – He who has been thus sorely slandered may console himself with the reflection: slanders are other people's illnesses that have broken out on your body; they demonstrate that society is a (moral) body, so that you can undertake a cure on *yourself* that will be of benefit to others.

265

The child's Kingdom of Heaven. – The happiness of the child is just as mythical as the happiness of the Hyperboreans* of whom the Greeks related. *If*

---

* Hyperboreans: 'the people living beyond the north wind', represented in Greek legend as enjoying a utopian existence; Nietzsche later refers to free spirits as 'we Hyperboreans'.

happiness dwells on earth at all, thought the latter, then it is certainly as far away from us as it can be, perhaps yonder at the edge of the earth. This is likewise the view of older people: *if* man can be happy at all then it is certainly as far away from *our* age as it can be, at the border-line and beginnings of life. For many people the sight of children viewed *through* the veil of this myth is the greatest happiness of which they can partake; they themselves enter the forecourt of the Kingdom of Heaven when they say 'suffer little children to come unto me, for theirs is the Kingdom of Heaven'. – Wherever in the modern world there is some degree of sentimentality the myth of the child's Kingdom of Heaven is somehow active.

266

The impatient. – It is precisely he who is becoming who cannot endure the state of becoming: he is too impatient for it. The youth refuses to wait until, after long study, suffering and deprivation, his picture of men and things is completed: instead he accepts on trust another that stands finished and is offered to him as though it is bound to provide him in advance with the lines and colours of *his* picture; he casts himself on to the bosom of a philosopher or poet and then has for long to deny himself and serve as a vassal. He learns much in the process: but often a youth forgets while doing so what is most worth learning and knowing: himself; he remains a partisan all his life. Alas, much boredom has to be overcome, much sweat expended, before we discover our own colours, our own brush, our own canvas! – And even then we are far from being a master of our own art of living – but at least we are master in our own workshop.

267

There are no educators. – As a thinker one should speak only of self-education. The education of youth by others is either an experiment carried out on an as yet unknown and unknowable subject, or a levelling on principle with the object of *making* the new being, whatever it may be, conform to the customs and habits then prevailing: in both cases therefore something unworthy of the thinker, the work of those elders and teachers whom a man of rash honesty once described as *nos ennemis naturels*. – One day, when one has long since been educated as the world understands it, one *discovers oneself*: here begins the task of the thinker; now the time has come to call on him for assistance – not as an educator but as one who has educated himself and who thus knows how it is done.

268

Pity for youth. – We are greatly distressed if we hear that a youth has already lost his teeth or has become blind. If we knew all that is irreparable and hopeless in his whole being how much greater our distress would be! – Why is it really that we *suffer* over this? Because youth is supposed to continue what *we* have begun, and every diminution of its powers will be harmful to *our* work when it devolves upon it. It is distress that our immortality should be so ill guaranteed: or, if we feel ourselves to be only fulfillers of the mission of mankind, distress that this mission must pass into hands weaker than ours.

269

The ages of life. – The comparison of the four seasons of the year with the four ages of life is a piece of worthy silliness. Neither the first twenty nor the last twenty years of life correspond to a season of the year: assuming, that is, that the said comparison is not supposed to refer merely to white hair and white snow and similar colour effects. The first twenty years are a preparation for life as a whole, for the entire life-year, and are thus a kind of protracted New Year's Day; and the last twenty oversee, absorb, order and codify whatever has been experienced previously: just as, on a small scale, one does with the preceding year every New Year's Eve. Between these, though, there does lie a space of time which can to some extent be compared with the seasons of the year: the time between the twentieth and the fiftieth years (to reckon wholesale in decades – it goes without saying that each individual must refine these crude calculations in accordance with his own experience). These three times ten years correspond to three seasons: summer, spring and autumn – human life does not have a winter, unless one wants to call those cold recurring seasons of solitude, hopelessness and unfruitfulness, our *periods of illness*, the winter seasons of man. The twenties: hot, burdensome, thundery, voluptuous, wearying; years in which we praise the day in the evening when it is over with and mop our brow as we do so; years in which we regard work as hard but necessary – these years of our twenties are the *summer* of life. The thirties, on the other hand, are its *spring*: the air now too warm, now too cold, always disturbing and provoking; sap, abundance of leaves, odour of blossom rising everywhere; many enchanting nights and mornings, the work to which the singing of birds awakens us a true labour of love, a kind of enjoyment of our own vigour, enhanced by present pleasure in future expectations. Finally, the forties: mysterious, like everything stationary; resembling a high, wide mountain plateau wafted by a fresh breeze; above it a clear, cloudless sky which gazes down all day and into the night with the same unchanging gentleness: the time of harvest and the heartiest cheerfulness – it is the *autumn* of life.

270

The female mind in contemporary society. – What women nowadays think of the male mind can be divined from the fact that when they adorn themselves the last thing they have in mind is to emphasize the intellectual qualities of their face: they conceal them, rather, and prefer – for example by a certain arrangement of the hair over the forehead – to give the impression of a lively and lustful sensuality and mindlessness, and this especially when they possess little of these qualities. Their conviction that men are terrified of intellect in a woman is so firm that they are even ready to deny they have any sharpness of mind at all and deliberately impose on themselves a reputation for *shortsightedness*; their objective, no doubt, is to make men more confiding and trusting: it is though a gentle, inviting twilight were spread all around them.

271
Great and transitory. – It moves the observer to tears to see the admiring look of happiness with which a pretty young wife gazes up at her husband. One is filled with autumnal melancholy to think of the greatness as well as the transitoriness of human happiness.

272
Sacrificial disposition. – Many a woman has an *intelletto del sacrifizio** and can no longer enjoy life when her husband refuses to sacrifice her: she then no longer knows where to direct her mind, and changes unawares from the sacrificial beast into the sacrificial priest.

273
The unwomanly. – 'Stupid as a man' say the women: 'cowardly as a woman' say the men. Stupidity is in woman the *unwomanly*.

274
Male and female temperament and mortality. – That the male sex has a worse temperament than the female is also evidenced in the fact that male children are more exposed to mortality than female, plainly because they more easily 'blow their top': their wildness and quarrelsomeness easily exacerbates every ill into something fatal.

275
The age of cyclopean building. – The democratization of Europe is irresistible: for whoever tries to halt it has to employ in that endeavour precisely the means which the democratic idea first placed in everyone's hands and makes these means themselves more wieldy and effective: and those who oppose democracy most on principle (I mean the spirits of revolution) appear to exist merely to impel the various parties ever faster forwards along the democratic path through the fear they inspire. Yet one can in fact feel anxious for those who are working consciously and honestly for this future: there is something desolate and monotonous in their faces, and grey dust seems to have got even into their brain. Nonetheless, it is possible that posterity will one day laugh at this anxiety of ours and regard the democratic work of a succession of generations somewhat as we regard the building of stone dams and protective walls – as an activity that necessarily gets a lot of dust on clothes and faces and no doubt also unavoidably makes the workers a little purblind and stupid; but who would wish such a work undone on that account! The democratization of Europe is, it seems, a link in the chain of those tremendous *prophylactic measures* which are the conception of modern times and through which we separate ourselves from the Middle Ages. Only now is it the age of cyclopean building! We finally secure the foundations, so that the whole

* *intelletto del sacrifizio*: the spirit of sacrifice

future can safely build upon them! We make it henceforth impossible for the fruitful fields of culture again to be destroyed overnight by wild and senseless torrents! We erect stone dams and protective walls against barbarians, against pestilences, against *physical and spiritual enslavement!* And all this coarsely and literally at first, but gradually in a higher and more spiritual sense, so that all the measures here indicated seem to be an inspired collective preparation for the supreme artist of horticulture, who will be able to apply himself to his real task only when these preparations have been fully carried out! – To be sure, given the great length of time which lies between means and end, and given the very great effort of mind and body, an effort spanning the centuries, needed even to create or procure each one of these means, we must not hold it too much against those who are working on the present-day if they loudly decree that the wall and the trellis *are* the end and final goal; since no one, indeed, can yet see the gardener or the fruit-trees *for whose sake* the trellis exists.

276
The right of universal suffrage. – The people did not give themselves universal suffrage; wherever it is now in vogue it has been bestowed upon them and they have provisionally accepted it: in any event, they have the right to hand it back if it does not come up to their expectations. And this seems everywhere now to be the case: for if whenever the occasion for using the vote arises hardly two-thirds of those entitled to vote, perhaps indeed not even a majority of them, come to the ballot-box, this is a vote *against* the entire voting-system as such. – An even sterner judgement is, indeed, justified here. A law which decrees that the majority shall have the decisive voice in determining the wellbeing of all cannot be erected upon a foundation which is first provided by that law itself; an even broader foundation is necessarily required, and this is the *unanimity of all.* Universal suffrage may not be an expression of the will merely of the majority: the whole country must desire it. The objection of even only a very small minority must thus suffice to render it invalid and to abolish it: and *non-participation* in an election constitutes precisely such an objection and thus brings about the downfall of the entire voting-system. The 'absolute veto' of the individual or, not to trivialize the problem, the veto of a few thousand hangs over this system as a requirement of justice: whenever it is employed it must first be demonstrated by the nature of the participation whether or not it is *still valid.*

277
Bad reasoning. – How badly we reason in domains where we are not at home, however well we may be accustomed to reasoning as men of science! It is disgraceful! But it is also clear that in the great world, in affairs of politics, it is precisely this *bad reasoning* that arrives at decisions on all those sudden and pressing questions such as arise almost every day: for no one is completely at home in that which has newly developed overnight; all political thinking, even in the case of the greatest statesmen, is random improvization.

278

Premises of the machine age. – The press, the machine, the railway, the tele-graph are premises whose thousand-year conclusion no one has yet dared to draw.

279

A brake on culture. – Whenever we hear: in that place the men have no time for productive occupations; weapon-practice and parades occupy their days, and the rest of the population have to feed and clothe them; but the costume they wear is striking, often brightly coloured and full of amusing follies; few distinguishing qualities are recognized, individuals resemble one another more than they do elsewhere, or if they do not are treated as though they did; yet they demand and accord obedience without under-standing: they command but take care not to persuade; they have few punishments, but these few are harsh and are quickly carried to their dreadful last extremity; treason is accounted the greatest of crimes, and even criticism of ills and wrongs is ventured on only by the most cour-ageous; human life is cheap there, and ambition often assumes a form that involves putting one's life in danger; – whenever we hear all this we say at once: 'it is a picture of a *barbaric, endangered society*'. Perhaps one of us may add: 'it is a description of Sparta'; another, however, will reflect a little and opine that what has been described is *our modern military machine* existing in the midst of our differently constituted culture and society as a living anachronism, as a picture, as aforesaid, of a barbaric, endangered society, as a posthumous work of the past which for the wheels of the present can have only the value of a brake. – Sometimes, however, a cul-ture is in the greatest need of a brake: namely, when it is going too fast downhill or, as in the present case perhaps, too fast *uphill*.

280

More respect for those who know! – Given the present competitive nature of selling, the *public* is necessarily the judge of the product of work: but the public has no particular specialist knowledge and judges according to the *appearance* of quality. As a consequence, the art of producing an appearance (and perhaps that of developing taste) is bound to be enhanced, and the quality of the product to decline, under the domi-nance of the competitive market. Consequently, if we are to continue to be reasonable we shall at some time have to put an end to this competitive market and replace it with a different principle. Only the skilled producer of the product ought to be the judge of the product, and the public ought to rely on their faith in him and his integrity. Therefore, no anonymous work! At the very least a knowledgeable expert in the product would have to be at hand as guarantor and place *his* name upon it if the name of its originator was unavailable or without significance. The *cheapness* of a product is another way of deceiving the layman, inasmuch as it is only *durability* that can determine whether or not a thing is cheap; but that is hard to assess, and for the layman impossible. – From all of which it follows that what is attractive to the eye and costs little now commands the market – and that can, of course, only be the product of the machine. For its part, again, the machine – that is to say, the means of great rapidity and facility of production – also favours the *most saleable* type of product; otherwise there is no great gain to be made from it; it would be too little used and too often silent. But what is most saleable is, as aforesaid, decided by the public: it will be the most deceptive product, that is to say that which *appears* to be of good quality and also *appears* to be cheap. Thus in this domain of work too our watchword must be: 'More respect for those who know!'

281

The danger facing kings. – Democracy has the capacity, without employing any kind of violence but simply by applying continual constitutional pressure, to render the offices of king and emperor *hollow*: until all that remains is a nought, though a nought perhaps, if that is what one *wants*, possessing the significance of every nought that, in itself nothing, if placed in the right position it multiplies the *effect* of a number by ten. The office of king and emperor would remain a splendid ornament on the simple and practical garment of democracy, the fair superfluity it allows itself, the remnant of all the historically venerable ornaments of its grand-fathers, indeed the symbol of history itself – and in this unique quality something of the highest effectiveness, provided, as aforesaid, it does not stand for itself alone but is correctly *positioned*. – To obviate this danger of being hollowed out, kings now cling with their teeth to their dignity as *warlords*: for this they require wars, that is to say states of emergency in which that slow constitutional pressure of the forces of democracy lets up.

282

The teacher a necessary evil. – As few people as possible between the pro-ductive spirits and the spirits who hunger and receive! For *mediators* almost involuntarily falsify the nourishment they mediate: in addition they want too much *for themselves* as payment for their mediation, and this must be taken from the originating, productive spirits: namely in-terest, admiration, time, money and other things. – Thus we must always regard the *teacher* as a necessary evil, just like the tradesman: as an evil we must make as *small* as possible! – If the principal reason for the distressing condition Germany is now in perhaps lies in the fact that far too many want to live, and live well, by trade (that is to say, to try to buy as cheaply as possible from the producers and to sell as dearly as possible to the con-sumers, and thus to profit at the greatest possible expense of both), then a principal reason for its distressing spiritual condition is certainly to be found in the over-abundance of teachers: it is on their account that so little is learned and that little so badly.

283

The respect-tax. – When someone we know and honour, whether he be a physician, artist or artisan, does or makes something for us, we are happy to pay him as much as we can, often indeed beyond our real capacities: on the other hand, we will pay someone unknown to us as little as we can get away with; this is a struggle in which everyone fights for every foot of land and for which he makes everyone fight him. In the case of work done *for us* by someone we know there is something *beyond price*, the feeling and invention he has put into his work *on our account*: we believe we can express our sensibility of this in no other way than through a kind of *sacrifice* on our part. – The highest tax is the *respect-tax*. The more the competitive market dominates and we buy from strangers and work for strangers, the lower this tax will be: whereas it is in fact the standard of measurement of the degree of *commerce* between human souls.

284

The means to real peace. – No government nowadays admits that it maintains an army so as to satisfy occasional thirsts for conquest; the army is supposed to be for defence. That morality which sanctions self-protection is called upon to be its advocate. But that means to reserve morality to oneself and to accuse one's neighbour of immorality, since he has to be thought of as ready for aggression and conquest if our own state is obliged to take thought of means of self-defence; moreover, when our neighbour denies any thirst for aggression just as heatedly as our state does, and protests that he too maintains an army only for reasons of legitimate self-defence, our declaration of why we require an army declares our neighbour a hypocrite and cunning criminal who would be only too happy to *pounce upon* a harmless and unprepared victim and subdue him without a struggle. This is how all states now confront one another: they presuppose an evil disposition in their neighbour and a benevolent disposition in themselves. This presupposition, however, is a piece of *inhumanity* as bad as, if not worse than, a war would be; indeed, fundamentally it already constitutes an invitation to and cause of wars, because, as aforesaid, it imputes immorality to one's neighbour and thereby seems to provoke hostility and hostile acts on his part. The doctrine of the army as a means of self-defence must be renounced just as completely as the thirst for conquest. And perhaps there will come a great day on which a nation distinguished for wars and victories and for the highest development of military discipline and thinking, and accustomed to making the heaviest sacrifices on behalf of these things, will cry of its own free will: *'we shall shatter the sword'* – and demolish its entire military machine down to its last foundations. *To disarm while being the best armed,* out of an *elevation* of sensibility – that is the means to *real* peace, which must always rest on a disposition for peace: whereas the so-called armed peace such as now parades about in every country is a disposition to fractiousness which trusts neither itself nor its neighbour and fails to lay down its arms half out of hatred, half out of fear. Better to perish than to

hate and fear, and *twofold better to perish than to make oneself hated and feared* –
this must one day become the supreme maxim of every individual state! –
As is well known, our liberal representatives of the people lack the time
to reflect on the nature of man: otherwise they would know that they
labour in vain when they work for a 'gradual reduction of the military
burden'. On the contrary, it is only when this kind of distress is at its
greatest that the only kind of god that can help here will be closest at
hand. The tree of the glory of war can be destroyed only at a single stroke,
by a lightning-bolt: lightning, however, as you well know, comes out of a
cloud and from on high. –

285

Can property be reconciled with justice? – If there is a strong feeling that the
possession of property is unjust – and the hand of the great clock has
again come round to this point – two ways of remedying the situation are
proposed: firstly an equal distribution, then the abolition of property and
its reversion to the community. The latter remedy is especially beloved of
our socialists, who bear a grudge against that Jew of antiquity for saying:
thou shalt not steal. In their view the seventh commandment should read
rather: thou shalt not possess. – Attempts to act in accordance with the
first recipe were often made in antiquity, always only on a small scale, to
be sure, yet with a lack of success from which we too can still gain instruction. 'Equal allotment of land' is easily said, yet how much acrimony is
produced by the divisions and separations this necessitates, by the loss of
ancient valued property, how much reverence is injured and sacrificed!
One digs up morality when one digs up boundary-stones. And how
much more acrimony among the new owners, how much jealousy and
enviousness, since two allotments of land have never been truly equal,
and even if such a thing were possible human envy of one's neighbour
would still not believe in their equality. And for how long would this
equality, unhealthy and poisoned at the roots as it is, endure! Within a
few generations inheritance would here have divided one allotment
among five people, there given one person five allotments: and if stern
laws of inheritance obviated such improper arrangements there would
still be equal allotment of land, to be sure, but at the same time an abundance of the unprovided-for and discontested who possessed nothing
except feelings of envy towards their neighbours and relations and a
desire that all things should be overturned. – If, however, one wishes to
follow the *second* recipe and restore property to the *community*, with the
individual as no more than a temporary tenant, then one will destroy the
land. For upon that which he possesses only in passing man bestows no
care or self-sacrifice, he merely exploits it like a robber or a dissolute
squanderer. When Plato opines that with the abolition of property
egoism too will be abolished the reply to him is that, in the case of man at
any rate, the departure of egoism would also mean the departure of the
four cardinal virtues – for it has to be said that the foulest pestilence could
not do so much harm to mankind as would be done him if his vanity

disappeared. Without vanity and egoism – what are the human virtues? Which is not intended remotely to imply that these are merely names and masks of such virtues. Plato's utopian basic tune, continued on in our own day by the socialists, rests upon a defective knowledge of man: he lacked a history of the moral sensations, an insight into the origin of the good and useful qualities of the human soul. Like the whole of antiquity he believed in good and evil as in white and black: thus in a radical difference between good and evil men, good and bad qualities. – If property is henceforth to inspire more confidence and become more moral, we must keep open all the paths to the accumulation of *moderate* wealth through work, but prevent the sudden or unearned acquisition of riches; we must remove from the hands of private individuals and companies all those branches of trade and transportation favourable to the accumulation of *great* wealth, thus especially the trade in money – and regard those who possess too much as being as great a danger to society as those who possess nothing.

286

The value of work. – If we wanted to determine the value of work by how much time, effort, good or ill will, compulsion, inventiveness or laziness, honesty or deception has been expended on it, then the valuation can never be *just*; for we would have to be able to place the entire person on the scales, and that is impossible. Here the rule must be 'judge not!' But it is precisely to justice that they appeal who nowadays are dissatisfied with the evaluation of work. If we reflect further we find that no personality can be held accountable for what it produces, that is to say its work: so that no *merit* can be derived from it; all work is as good or bad as it must be given this or that constellation of strengths and weaknesses, knowledge and desires. The worker is not free to choose *whether* he works, nor *how* he works. It is only from the standpoint of *utility*, narrower and wider, that work can be evaluated. That which we now call justice is in this field very much in place as a highly refined instrument of utility which does not pay regard only to the moment or exploit opportunities as they occur but reflects on the enduring advantage of all conditions and classes and therefore also keeps in mind the wellbeing of the worker, his contentment of body and soul – *so that* he and his posterity shall work well for our posterity too and be relied on for a longer span of time than a single human life. The *exploitation* of the worker was, it has now been realized, a piece of stupidity, an exhausting of the soil at the expense of the future, an imperilling of society. Now we already have almost a state of war: and the cost of keeping the peace, of concluding treaties and acquiring trust, will henceforth in any event be very great, because the folly of the exploiters was very great and of long duration.

287

On the study of the body politic. – The worst ill-fortune for him who nowadays wants to study economics and politics in Europe, and especially in Germany, lies in the fact that, instead of exemplifying the *rule*, conditions actually obtaining exemplify the *exception* or *transitional* and *terminal states*. For this reason one has first to learn to see past the immediate factual data and to direct one's eyes, for example, to North America – where one can still *see* and seek out the inaugural and normal motions of the body politic, if only one *wants* to – whereas in Germany this can be done only through arduous historical study or, as aforesaid, with a telescope.

288

To what extent the machine abases us. – The machine is impersonal, it deprives the piece of work of its pride, of the individual *goodness* and *faultiness* that adheres to all work not done by a machine – that is to say, of its little bit of humanity. In earlier times all purchasing from artisans was a *bestowing of a distinction on individuals*, and the things with which we surrounded ourselves were the insignia of these distinctions: household furniture and clothing thus became symbols of mutual esteem and personal solidarity, whereas we now seem to live in the midst of nothing but an anonymous and impersonal slavery. – We must not purchase the alleviation of work at too high a price.

289

Hundred-year quarantine. – Democratic institutions are quarantine arrangements to combat that ancient pestilence, lust for tyranny: as such they are very useful and very boring.

290

The most dangerous follower. – The most dangerous follower is he whose defection would destroy the whole party: that is to say, the best follower.

291

Destiny and the stomach. – One slice of bread and butter more or fewer in the stomach of a jockey can occasionally decide the outcome of the race and the betting and thus affect the fortunes and misfortunes of thousands. – So long as the destiny of nations continues to depend on the diplomats, the diplomats' stomachs will continue to be the object of patriotic anxiety. *Quousque tandem** –

292

Victory of democracy. – All political powers nowadays try to exploit the fear of socialism in order to strengthen themselves. But in the long run it is democracy alone that derives the advantage: for *all* parties are nowadays obliged to flatter the 'people' and to bestow on it alleviations and liberties of every kind through which it will in the end become omnipotent. As socialism is a doctrine that the acquisition of property ought to be abolished, the people are as alienated from it as they could be: and once they have got the power of taxation into their hands through their great parliamentary majorities they will assail the capitalists, the merchants and the princes of the stock exchange with a progressive tax and

---

* *Quousque tandem*: How much longer...? (the beginning of Cicero's outburst in the Senate against the conspirator Catiline).

slowly create in fact a middle class which will be in a position to *forget* socialism like an illness it has recovered from. – The practical outcome of this spreading democratization will first of all be a European league of nations within which each individual nation, delimited according to geographical fitness, will possess the status and rights of a canton: in this process the historical recollections of the former nations will be of little account, since the sense of reverence for such things will gradually be totally uprooted by the domination of the democratic principle, which thirsts for innovations and is greedy for experiments. The corrections of frontiers which prove necessary will be so executed as to serve the *interests* of the large cantons and at the same time those of the whole union, but not to honour the memory of some grizzled past. The task of discovering the principles upon which these frontier corrections should be made will devolve upon future *diplomats*, who will have to be at once cultural scholars, agriculturalists and communications experts, and who will have behind them, not armies, but arguments and questions of utility. Only then will *foreign* policy be inseparably tied to *domestic* policy: whereas now the latter still has to run after its proud master and gather up in a pitiful little basket the stubble left behind after the former has reaped its harvest.

293

End and means of democracy. – Democracy wants to create and guarantee as much *independence* as possible: independence of opinion, of mode of life and of employment. To that end it needs to deprive of the right to vote both those who possess no property and the genuinely rich: for these are the two impermissible classes of men at whose abolition it must work continually, since they continually call its task into question. It must likewise prevent everything that seems to have for its objective the organization of parties. For the three great enemies of independence in the above-named threefold sense are the indigent, the rich and the parties. – I am speaking of democracy as of something yet to come. That which now calls itself democracy differs from older forms of government solely in that it drives with *new horses*: the streets are still the same old streets, and the wheels are likewise the same old wheels. – Have things really got less perilous because the wellbeing of the nations now rides in *this* vehicle?

294

Circumspection and success. – That great quality of circumspection which is at bottom the virtue of virtues, their great-grandmother and queen, is by no means always crowned with success in everyday life: and he who had wooed this virtue merely for the sake of achieving success would end up disappointed. For *practical* people hold it in suspicion and confuse it with cunning deceitfulness and hypocritical slyness: he, on the other hand, who obviously lacks circumspection – the man who acts precipitately and therefore sometimes acts wrongly – has in his favour the prejudice that he is a worthy, reliable fellow. Practical people do not like the circumspect man and think he is a danger to them. On the other hand, the circumspect man can easily be taken for timid, narrow-minded, pedantic – impractical and easy-living people especially find him uncomfortable *because* he does not live superficially as they do, heedless of duty and practical affairs: he appears among them as their embodied conscience and the sight of him makes the daylight grow pale. If he thus lacks success and popularity, however, he can always console himself with the reflection: 'this is the high *tax* you have to pay for possessing something of great value – it is worth it!'

295

*Et in Arcadia ego.** – I looked down, over waves of hills, through fir-trees and spruce trees grave with age, towards a milky green lake: rocky crags of every kind around me, the ground bright with flowers and grasses. A herd of cattle moved and spread itself out before me; solitary cows and groups of cows farther off, in vivid evening light close to the pinewood; others nearer, darker; everything at peace in the contentment of evening. The clock indicated nearly half-past five. The bull of the herd had waded into the white, foaming brook and was slowly following its precipitate course, now resisting it, now yielding: no doubt this was its kind of fierce enjoyment. The herders were two dark-brown creatures Bergamask in origin: the girl clad almost as a boy. To the left mountain slopes and snowfields beyond broad girdles of woodland, to the right, high above me, two gigantic ice-covered peaks floating in a veil of sunlit vapour – everything big, still and bright. The beauty of the whole scene induced in me a sense of awe and of adoration of the moment of its revelation; involuntarily, as if nothing were more natural, I inserted into this pure, clear world of light (in which there was nothing of desire or expectation, no looking before and behind) Hellenic heroes; my feeling must have been like that of Poussin and his pupil:† at one and the same time heroic and idyllic. – And that is how individual men have actually *lived*, that is how they have enduringly *felt* they existed in the world and the world existed in them; and among them was one of the greatest of men, the inventor of an heroic-idyllic mode of philosophizing: Epicurus.

296

Calculation and measuring. – To see many things, to weigh them one against the other, to add and subtract among them and to arrive rapidly at a fairly accurate sum – that produces the great politician, general, merchant: it is speed in a kind of mental calculation. To see *one* thing, to find in it the sole motive for action and the judge over all other actions, produces the hero, also the fanatic – it is facility in measuring according to a standard.

297

Do not want to see prematurely. -- For as long as one is experiencing

* *Et in Arcadia ego*: And I, too, in Arcadia; employed by Goethe as the motto of his *Italian Journey*.
† *Poussin and his pupil*: probably Claude Lorraine (1600–82), who lived in Rome after 1620 where he was a contemporary of Poussin's (1593–1665). The poetic lighting of Claude's Mannerist landscapes forms an obvious contrast with the heroic drama of Poussin's.

something one must give oneself up to the experience and close one's eyes: that is to say, not be an observer of it while still *in the midst* of it. For that would disturb the absorption of the experience: instead of a piece of wisdom one would aquire from it indigestion.

298

From the practice of the sage. – To become wise one must *want* to experience certain experiences, that is to say run into their open jaws. This is very dangerous, to be sure; many a 'sage' has been gobbled up in the process.

299

Fatigue of spirit. – Our occasional indifference and coldness towards men, which is interpreted as harshness and deficiency of character in us, is often only a weariness of spirit: when we are afflicted with this other people are burdensome or a matter of indifference to us, as we are to ourselves.

300

'One thing is needful'. – If we are sensible the only thing that need concern us is that we should have joy in our hearts. – Alas, someone added, if we are sensible the best thing we can do is to be wise.

301

A testimony to love. – Someone said: 'There are two people upon whom I have never thoroughly reflected: it is the testimony to my love for them.'

302

How we try to improve bad arguments. – Many people throw a piece of their personality after their bad arguments, as though this will make them run a straighter course and transform them into good arguments; just as even after he has thrown the ball the skittle-player continues to try to direct its course with gestures and wavings of the hands.

303

Integrity. – It is still very little if one is an exemplary person with regard to rights and property; if, for example, one never steals fruit from other people's gardens as a boy, never walks across unmown fields as a man – to cite small things which, as is well known, offer a better demonstration of this kind of exemplariness than do big ones. It is still very little: one is still only a 'juridical person' with that degree of morality of which even a 'society', a cluster of men, is capable.

304

Man! – What is the vanity of the vainest man compared with the vanity which the most modest possesses when, in the midst of nature and the world, he feels himself to be 'man'!

305

The most needful gymnastic. – A lack of self-mastery in small things brings about a crumbling of the capacity for it in great ones. Every day is ill employed, and a danger for the next day, in which one has not denied oneself some small thing at least once: this gymnastic is indispensable if one wants to preserve in oneself the joy of being one's own master.

306

Losing oneself. – Once one has found oneself one must understand how from time to time to *lose* oneself – and then how to find oneself again: supposing, that is, that one is a thinker. For to the thinker it is disadvantageous to be tied to one person all the time.

307

When it is necessary to depart. – From that which you want to know and assess you must depart, at least for a time. Only when you have left the town can you see how high its towers rise above the houses.

308

At noon. – He who has been granted an active and storm-filled morning of life is overcome at the noontide of life by a strange longing for repose that can last for months or years. It grows still around him, voices recede into the distance; the sun shines down on him from high overhead. Upon a concealed woodland meadow he sees great Pan sleeping; all things of nature have fallen asleep with him, an expression of eternity on their face – that is how it seems to him. He wants nothing, he is troubled by nothing, his heart stands still, only his eyes are alive – it is a death with open eyes. Then the man sees many things he never saw before, and for as far as he can see everything is enmeshed in a net of light and as it were buried in it. He feels happy as he gazes, but it is a heavy, heavy happiness. – Then at length the wind rises in the trees, noon has gone by, *life* again draws him to it, life with unseeing eyes, its train of followers sweeping along behind it: desire, deception, forgetfulness, destruction, transience. And thus evening rises up, more active and more storm-filled even than the morning. – To truly active men the more long enduring states of knowledge seem almost uncanny and morbid, but not unpleasant.

309

Beware of your portraitist. – A great painter who has unveiled and set down in a portrait the completest expression of the moment of which a man is capable will, if he afterwards meets him again in real life, almost always believe he is seeing only a caricature of him.

310

The two principles of the new life. – *First principle*: life should be ordered on the basis of what is most certain and most demonstrable, not as hitherto on that of what is most remote, indefinite and no more than a cloud on the horizon. *Second principle*: the *order of succession* of what is closest and most immediate, less close and less immediate, certain and less certain, should be firmly established before one orders one's life and gives it a definitive direction.

311

Dangerous susceptibility. – Talented people who are indolent will always appear somewhat irritated when one of their friends completes a sound piece of work. Their jealousy is aroused, they are ashamed of their laziness – or rather, they fear that the active man will now despise them even *more* than before. It is in this mood that they criticize the new work – and their criticism becomes an act of revenge through which they completely alienate its author.

312

Destruction of illusions. – Illusions are certainly expensive amusements: but the destruction of illusions is even more expensive – regarded as a source of amusement, which is what it undeniably is for many people.

313

The monotony of the sage. – Cows sometimes wear an expression of wonderment halted on the way to a *question*. In the eye of the higher intelligence, on the other hand, the *nil admirari** lies extended like the monotony of a cloudless sky.

314

Do not be ill too long. – One should take care not to be ill too long: for the conventional obligation to manifest signs of sympathy will soon make the witnesses of one's illness impatient, since it costs them too much effort to maintain this condition in themselves for long – and then they will pass directly over to doubting your character and will arrive at the conclusion 'he *deserves* to be ill, and we no longer need to exert ourselves to feel sympathetic'.

315

Hint for enthusiasts. – He who likes to be carried away and wants to be borne along easily on top should see to it that he does not become too *heavy*: which means, for example, that he does not learn a great deal and in particular does not let himself be *filled* with science. For this makes one ponderous! – take care, enthusiasts!

316

Knowing how to surprise oneself. – He who wants to see himself as he is must understand how to *surprise* himself, torch in hand. For it is with the spiritual as it is with the bodily: he who is accustomed to looking at himself in a mirror always forgets how ugly he is: it is only through the painter that he recovers an impression of it. But he then grows accustomed to the painting and forgets how ugly he is a second time. – This happens in accordance with the universal law that man *cannot endure* the unchangeingly ugly; or if he can, it is only for a moment: in every case he forgets it or denies that it is ugly. – It is upon this moment that moralists have to count if they are to display their truths.

317

Opinions and fish. – One possesses one's opinions in the way one pos-

* * *

* *nil admirari*: admire nothing

388

sesses fish – insofar, that is, that one posseses a fishpond. One has to go fishing and be lucky – then one has *one's own* fish, *one's own* opinions. I am speaking here of living opinions, of living fish. Others are content to possess a cabinet of fossils – and, in their heads, 'convictions'. –

318
Tokens of freedom and unfreedom. – To satisfy one's necessary requirements as completely as possible oneself, even if imperfectly, is the road to *freedom of spirit and person*. To let others satisfy many of one's requirements, even superfluous ones, and as perfectly as possible – is a training in *unfreedom*. The sophist Hippias, who had himself acquired, himself produced, everything he wore, within and without, represents in precisely this the road to the highest freedom of spirit and person. It does not matter if everything is not equally well made, pride will patch up the tattered spots.

319
Belief in oneself. – In our age we distrust everyone who believes in himself; in former ages it sufficed to make others believe in us. The recipe for obtaining belief *now* is: 'Do not spare yourself! If you want to place your opinions in a believable light first set fire to your own house!'

320
At once richer and poorer. – I know a man who had already as a child accustomed himself to think well of the intellectuality of men – that is to say, of their genuine devotion to things of the spirit, their unselfish preference for what is known to be true, and the like – but on the other hand to have a modest, indeed a poor idea of his own brain (his judgement, memory, presence of mind, imagination). When he compared himself with others he always came out badly. In the course of years, however, he was compelled, at first once then a hundred times, to learn otherwise on this point – a fact which would, one might think, have given him great joy and satisfaction. And he did indeed experience something of this; but 'nonetheless', as he once said, 'there is in it also a bitterness of the bitterest kind which I did not know in earlier life: for since I have come to assess men and myself more justly my mind seems to me to be of less use; I seem to be unable to do any good with it, because the minds of others do not know how to accept it: I now see always before me the terrible gulf between those who can offer help and those who need it. And thus I am tormented by having to enjoy the fruits of my mind all by myself, so far as they are enjoyable at all. But *to give* is more blessed than *to have*: and what is the richest of men in the solitude of a *desert*!'

321
Modes of attack. – The grounds upon which we believe or do not believe in something are with very few people indeed nearly as strong *as they could be*. To shatter belief in something it is as a rule in no way necessary at once to bring out one's heaviest cannon; with many people it is enough simply to launch an attack with a certain amount of noise: so that often a popgun

will do. Against very vain people all that is required is the *appearance* of a heavy attack: they see themselves being taken very seriously – and are glad to give in.

322

Death. – The certain prospect of death could introduce into every life a precious, sweet-smelling drop of levity – and yet you marvellous apothecary souls have made of it an ill-tasting drop of poison through which all life is made repulsive!

323

Remorse. – Never yield to remorse, but at once tell yourself: remorse would simply mean adding to the first act of stupidity a second. – If we have done harm we should give thought to how we can do good. – If we are punished for our actions, let us endure our punishment with the feeling that we are thereby already doing good: we are deterring others from falling victim to the same folly. Every ill-doer who has been punished is entitled to feel he is a benefactor of mankind.

324

To become a thinker. – How can anyone become a thinker if he does not spend at least a third of the day without passions, people and books?

325

The best remedy. – A little health now and again is the invalid's best remedy.

326

Don't touch! – There are dreadful people who, instead of solving a problem, tie it in knots and make it harder for others to solve. He who does not know how to hit the nail on the head ought to be asked not to hit it at all.

327

Forgotten nature. – We speak of nature and forget to include ourselves: we ourselves are nature, *quand même** – . It follows that nature is something quite different from what we think of when we speak its name.

328

Profundity and tedium. – With profound men, as with deep wells, it takes a long time for anything that has fallen into them to reach the bottom. The spectators, who usually fail to wait long enough, can easily come to regard such men as harsh and immovable – or as tedious.

329

When it is time to vow loyalty to oneself. – Sometimes we stray on to a spiritual course that contradicts our talents; for a time we struggle heroically against wind and tide, at bottom against ourself: we grow weary, gasping; what we achieve brings us no real joy, we feel we have paid too highly for it. Indeed, we *despair* of our fruitfulness and of our future, per-

---

* *quand même*: nonetheless

haps in the midst of victory. At long last we *turn round* – and now the wind is blowing *into* our sails and driving us into *our own* channel. What happiness! How *sure of victory* we feel! Only now do we know what we are and what we want, now we vow to be loyal to ourselves and *have a right* to do so – because we know what it means.

330
Weather prophets. – Just as the clouds tell us the direction of the wind high above our heads, so the lightest and freest spirits are in their tendencies foretellers of the weather that is coming. The wind in the valley and the opinions of the market-place of today indicate nothing of that which is coming but only of that which has been.

331
Steady acceleration. – People who start slowly and find it hard to feel at home in a thing sometimes possess afterwards the quality of steady acceleration – so that in the end no one knows whither the current will yet carry them.

332
The three good things. – Greatness, repose, sunlight – these three things embrace everything a thinker desires and demands of himself: his hopes and duties, his claims in the intellectual and moral spheres, even in the way he lives day by day and the quality of the landscape where he dwells. They answer firstly to *elevating* thoughts, then to *quietening*, thirdly to *enlightening* – fourthly, however, to thoughts which participate in all three qualities, in which everything earthly comes to transfiguration: it is the kingdom where there reigns the great *trinity of joy.*

333
Dying for 'truth'. – We would not let ourselves be burned to death for our opinions: we are not sure enough of them for that. But perhaps for the right to possess our opinions and to change them.

334
Having one's fixed price. – If one wants to *count* for precisely what one *is*, one has to be something that has *its fixed price.* But only the commonplace has its fixed price. Thus this desire is either the result of an intelligent modesty – or an unintelligent immodesty.

335
Moral for house-builders. – One must remove the scaffolding once the house has been built.

336
Sophoclism. – Who has ever put more water into their wine than the Greeks! Sobriety and gracefulness combined – that was the privilege of the nobility of Athens at the time of Sophocles and after him. Imitate them who can! In life and in works!

337
The heroic. – The heroic consists in doing a great thing (or in *not* doing a

thing in a great fashion) without feeling oneself to be in competition *with* others *before* others. The hero always bears the wilderness and the sacred, inviolable borderline within him wherever he may go.

338
Nature as Doppelgänger. – There is many a spot in nature where, with a pleasurable shudder, we rediscover ourself; it is nature as the fairest kind of *Doppelgänger*. – What happiness awaits him who experiences such a sensation in just this spot, in this continual sunny October air, in this roguish play of the breeze from morn till night, in this purest brightness and temperate coolness, in the whole charm and gravity of the hills, lakes and forests of this high plateau that has fearlessly stretched itself out beside the terrors of the eternal snow, here where Italy and Finland have entered into a union and all the silvery tones of nature seem to have made their home: – how happy he who can say: 'there are certainly greater and fairer things in nature, but *this* is mine and known to me, a blood relation, and more indeed than that'.

339
Geniality of the sage. – The sage will involuntarily mingle with other people as genially as a prince and, all differences of talent, rank and morality notwithstanding, easily be inclined to treat them as equals: which, as soon as it is noticed, causes great offence.

340
Gold. – All that is gold does not glisten. A gentle radiance pertains to the noblest metal.

341
Wheel and brake. – The wheel and the brake have differing duties, but also one in common: to hurt one another.

342
Disturbances while thinking. – The thinker must regard everything that interrupts his thoughts (disturbs them, as we say) with equanimity, as though it were a new model coming in to offer herself to the artist. Interruptions are the ravens which bring food to the solitary.

343
Possessing much spirit. – To possess much spirit keeps one *young*: but in exchange one must endure being thought *older* than one is. For men read the characters inscribed by the spirit as signs of *experience of life*, that is to say of having experienced many, and many bad things, of suffering, error and remorse. Thus, one is thought not only older but *worse* than one is when one possesses much spirit and shows it.

344
The proper way to win. – One ought not to want to win if one has the prospect of overtaking one's opponent by only a *hair's breadth*. The good

victory must put the conquered into a joyful mood, it must possess something divine that does not *put to shame*.

345

Illusion of superior spirits. – Superior spirits have difficulty in freeing themselves from an illusion: they imagine they excite envy among the mediocre and are felt to be exceptions. In fact they are felt to be something quite superfluous which if it did not exist no one would miss.

346

Demand of cleanliness. – Changing one's opinions is to one nature just as much a demand of cleanliness as changing one's clothes: for another, however, it is only a demand of vanity.

347

This, too, is worthy of a hero. – Here is a hero who has done nothing but shake the tree as soon as the fruit was ripe. Do you think this too little? Then take a look at the tree he shook.

348

Measure of wisdom. – Growth in wisdom can be measured precisely by decline in bile.

349

Calling error unpleasant. – It is not to everyone's taste that truth should be called pleasant. But at least let no one believe that error becomes truth when it is called *unpleasant*.

350

The golden watchword. – Many chains have been laid upon man so that he should no longer behave like an animal: and he has in truth become gentler, more spiritual, more joyful, more reflective than any animal is. Now, however, he suffers from having worn his chains for so long, from being deprived for so long of clear air and free movement: – these chains, however, I shall never cease from repeating, are those heavy and pregnant errors contained in the conceptions of morality, religion and metaphysics. Only when this *sickness from one's chains* has also been overcome will the first great goal have truly been attained: the separation of man from the animals. – We stand now in the midst of our work of removing these chains, and we need to proceed with the greatest caution. Only the *ennobled man may be given freedom of spirit*; to him alone does *alleviation of life* draw near and salve his wounds; only he may say that he lives for the sake of *joy* and for the sake of no further goal; and in any other mouth his motto would be perilous: *Peace all around me and goodwill to all things closest to me*. – With this motto for individuals he recalls an ancient great and moving saying intended for *all* which has remained hanging over all mankind as a sign and motto by which anyone shall perish who inscribes it on his banner too soon – by which Christianity perished. The time has, it seems, still *not yet come* when *all* men are to share the experience of those shepherds who saw the heavens brighten above them and heard the words: 'On earth peace, good will toward men'. – It is still *the age of the individual.*

The Shadow: Of all you have said nothing has pleased me *more* than a promise you have made: you want again to become a good neighbour to the things closest to you. This will benefit us poor shadows, too. For – admit it – you have hitherto been only too happy to slander us.

The Wanderer: Slander? But why have you never defended yourselves? You were close enough to our ear, after all.

The Shadow: It seemed to us we were much too close to venture to speak of ourselves.

The Wanderer: How very tactful! You shadows are 'better men' than we are, that I can see.

The Shadow: And yet you called us 'importunate' – us, who understand at any rate one thing well: to stay silent and wait – no Englishman understands it better. It is true we are to be found very, very often following behind man, yet we are not his slaves. When man shuns the light, we shun man: our freedom extends that far.

The Wanderer: Alas, the light shuns man much more often, and then you too desert him.

The Shadow: It is often with sorrow that I have deserted you: it seems to me, who am greedy for knowledge, that much that is dark still adheres to man because I cannot always be with him. If the reward were a perfect knowledge of man I might even agree to be your slave.

The Wanderer: But do you know, do I know, whether you would not then change unawares from slave to master? Or, though still a slave, come to despise your master and live a life of abasement and disgust? Let us both be content with such freedom as you have – you *and* me! For the sight of one unfree would embitter for me all my joy; I would find even the best things repulsive if someone *had* to share them with me – I want no slaves around me. That is why I will not have even a dog, that lazy, tail-wagging parasite who has become 'doglike' only through being the slave of man and who is even commended for loyalty to his master and willingness to follow him like his –

The Shadow: Like his shadow, that is how they put it. Perhaps today too I have already been following you too long? It has been the longest day, but we have reached its end, be patient a little while longer! The grass is damp, I am getting cold.

The Wanderer: Oh, is it already time for us to part? And I had to end by hurting you; I saw it, you grew darker as I did it.

The Shadow: I blushed, in the colour in which I am able to blush. It occurred to me that I have often lain at your feet like a dog, and that you then –

The Wanderer: And could I not, in all haste, do something to please you? Is there nothing you want?

The Shadow: Nothing, except perhaps that which the philosophical 'dog' desired of the great Alexander: that you should move a little out of the sunlight, I am feeling too cold.

The Wanderer: What shall I do?

The Shadow: Step under these trees and look out at the mountains; the sun is sinking.

The Wanderer: – Where are you? Where are you?

INDEX

In this index Nietzsche's section/aphorism numbers are used, rather than page numbers. Because he published the various parts of *Human, All Too Human* on three different occasions, restarting his numbering each time, it is necessary to indicate in the parts: 'I' indicates what is now the first volume, 'II' indicates what is now the first part of the second volume (published separately but as a continuation of the work under the title *Assorted Opinions and Maxims*) and 'WS' indicates what is now the second part of the second volume (published separately under the title *The Wanderer and His Shadow*). 'P' indicates Nietzsche's 1886 preface to the specified volume of the two-volume edition.   R.S.

CAMBRIDGE TEXTS IN THE HISTORY OF PHILOSOPHY

Titles published in the series thus far

Arnauld and Nicole *Logic or the Art of Thinking* (edited by Jill Vance Buroker)

Boyle *A Free Enquiry into the Vulgarly Received Notion of Nature* (edited by Edward B. Davis and Michael Hunter)

Conway *The Principles of the Most Ancient and Modern Philosophy* (edited by Allison P. Coudert and Taylor Corse)

Cudworth *A Treatise Concerning Eternal and Immutable Morality* (edited by Sarah Hutton)

Descartes *Meditations on First Philosophy*, with selections from the *Objections and Replies* (edited with an introduction by John Cottingham)

Kant *The Metaphysics of Morals* (edited by Mary Gregor with an introduction by Roger Sullivan)

La Mettrie *Machine Man and Other Writings* (edited by Ann Thomson)

Leibniz *New Essays on Human Understanding* (edited by Peter Remnant and Jonathan Bennett)

Nietzsche *Human, All Too Human* (translated by R.J. Hollingdale with an introduction by Richard Schacht)

Schleiermacher *On Religion: Speeches to its Cultured Despisers* (edited by Richard Crouter)